Scientists, Engineers, and Organizations

Scientists, Engineers, and Organizations

Terry Connolly
Georgia Institute of Technology

 **BROOKS/COLE ENGINEERING DIVISION**
Monterey, California

Brooks/Cole Engineering Division
A Division of Wadsworth, Inc.

Printed in the United States of America

10   9   8   7   6   5   4   3   2   1

Library of Congress Cataloging in Publication Data

Connolly, Terry
  Scientists, engineers, and organizations.

  Bibliography: p.
  Includes index.
    1. Science—Vocational guidance.   2. Engineering—
Vocational guidance.   3. Organizational behavior.
I. Title.
Q147.C57   1983   650.1'0245   82-22703
ISBN 0-534-01409-7

Sponsoring Editor: Ray Kingman
Book Production: Michael Bass & Associates
Manuscript Editor: Linda Rageh
Interior Design: Lorena Laforest Bass
Cover Design: David Aguero
Illustrations and Typesetting: TechGraphics
Production Services Manager: Stacey C. Sawyer

The author is grateful to the copyright holders for granting permission to reprint the following materials.

Pages 329 and 337. From Janos, L. Timekeepers of the solar system. Reprinted by permission of Science 80 magazine, © American Association for the Advancement of Science.

Page 342. From Roe, A. Changes in scientific activities with age. Science, 1965, 150(3694), 313–318. Reprinted by permission of the author and Science, © 1965 by the American Association for the Advancement of Science.

Excerpts from James (page 329) and Williams (pages 332 and 337), Weick (page 335), Peters (page 337), and Sayles (page 340) are from Executive magazine and reprinted by permission of the publisher, © 1980, Cornell University, all rights reserved.

Pages 336 and 338. From Preston, C. (Ed.). The Wall Street Journal Cartoon Portfolio. Dow Jones Books, 1979. Reprinted by permission of Dow Jones, Inc., © 1979, all rights reserved.

Page 340. Cartoon by David Hills, used by permission of the Center for Creative Leadership, © 1980, all rights reserved.

Contributors

DANIEL J. BRASS
Pennsylvania State University

DARYL E. CHUBIN
Georgia Institute of Technology

EDWARD J. CONLON
University of Iowa

M. LYNNE MARKUS
Massachusetts Institute of Technology

MORGAN W. McCALL
Center for Creative Leadership

ALAN L. PORTER
Georgia Institute of Technology

FREDERICK A. ROSSINI
Georgia Institute of Technology

GERRIT WOLF
University of Arizona

Preface

With very few exceptions, scientists and engineers practice their professions as employees of organizations. Doctors, dentists, and lawyers frequently practice alone or in small partnerships, but scientists and engineers are commonly employed by large corporations, business firms, universities, research laboratories, or consulting groups. In such large and complex organizations, professional success turns as much on expertise in coping with organizational life as on mastery of technical matters. Learning something of how organizations function is an important part of the professional training of a scientist or engineer.

This book offers an introduction to the organizational realities likely to face a young scientist or engineer, and to some of the issues arising in organizations that he or she will encounter in the course of a professional career. It is planned as the core of a one-quarter or one-semester course at the advanced undergraduate or early graduate level. The topics covered correspond generally to those found in introductory texts on organizations: motivation, communication, leadership, decision making, and so on. However, the emphasis and approach within each topic have been selected with a particular, rather specialized audience in mind: the scientist or engineer about to enter his or her first professional job.

The book is in two parts. Part I contains ten chapters that provide an integrated treatment of organizational phenomena at an introductory level. Part II consists of eight readings prepared for this volume, which examine particular issues in greater depth. The design is intended to provide the advantages both of a single-authored overview

(Part I) and of in-depth treatments of particular topics, written by specialists (Part II).

In preparing a book, every author incurs personal and intellectual debts too numerous to acknowledge, let alone repay. The present volume is no exception. Rather than list those that I remember and insult those I forget, I hope my friends and colleagues will be gracious enough to accept my heartfelt thanks for the ideas and encouragement that have made this book possible. The researchers on whose work the book is primarily based are acknowledged, if inadequately, in the references. I owe special thanks to the students at the Georgia Institute of Technology who, over the past decade, have tolerated my struggles to bring these materials to life in the classroom.

The writing of this book would not have been possible without the steady support of my wife, Penelope. Despite the pressures of her own busy professional career, she has invariably found the time and energy both for probing review and criticism of the book and for patient encouragement of its author. It is to her that the work is dedicated.

—Terry Connolly

Contents

Part II. Contributed Papers

Part I
An Introduction to Organizational Behavior

Chapter 1

Purpose and Organization of the Book

I have spent most of my professional life learning, doing, and teaching two very different crafts: electrical engineering and organizational behavior. The two seem very dissimilar. Engineering design is highly mathematical, closely tied to a physical science base, well developed, and practiced only by highly trained professionals. Organizational behavior is rarely mathematical, is loosely tied to various behavioral sciences, is poorly developed, and is practiced by almost everyone, amateur and professional alike. What possible connection could there be between the two crafts? And, more pointedly, why should someone preparing for a career as a professional scientist or engineer bother to learn about how organizations work?

The most obvious answer, of course, is that nearly all of us spend nearly all our lives in organizations of one kind or another. We learn in organizations, we earn our livings in them, we join organizations for sport, for company, for politics, for worship. We draw our first (and probably our last) breaths inside the walls of organizations. Outside of our families (also organizations), it is rare for us to do anything that does not involve us in some fairly direct way with an organization. Since organizations are so pervasive in our lives, common sense requires us to learn a little about how they behave, and how we behave in them.

For scientists and engineers, the case is even sharper. In school we learn mainly facts, concepts, laws, procedures, and skills involved in solving disciplinary problems. In professional work, however, we quickly find that these are not the only, or even the most important,

3

skills we need to function effectively. In addition to our specialist technical skills, we need to be able to work effectively with our colleagues, our superiors, and our subordinates. We need to be able to work with clients, so that our designs meet their needs. Skills in planning, communication, motivation, coordination, leadership—all of these and more are needed, along with our "hard science" training, if we are to function as mature professionals, as people who can really "get the job done."

This book is intended to provide an introduction to some of the central things that happen in organizations, and how they relate to the work of engineers and scientists. Its design has been strongly influenced by my attempts to teach engineering and physical science students, mainly juniors, seniors, and graduate students at the Georgia Institute of Technology, about the elements of organizational life. Much of the material has also been used in teaching business students and in training programs for more senior personnel—scientists, engineers, and managers—employed in various organizations. Although others may (and, I hope, will) get something useful from this book, it is primarily aimed at the advanced undergraduate and graduate student, reaching the end of his or her training and looking around for additional professional skills in preparation for a working career.

This book, then, is my attempt to answer the question: "What do we know about organizations that would be relevant to the young scientist or engineer about to enter professional life?" Any attempt to answer that question within the confines of a single book is bound to be incomplete. There is now an enormous body of research on various aspects of organizations. The selection presented here is obviously shaped by my own interests and biases, as well as by my judgment of relevance to an audience of engineers and scientists.

Before turning to an outline of what this book is, let me say a final word about what it is not. It is not a book on scientific or engineering management. Such books exist, and they serve a useful function in training managers how to use various techniques commonly found in scientific and engineering contexts: PERT charts, shop scheduling, research planning, job evaluation, and a host of others. Most successful managers would agree, however, that people skills are the most important part of effective management. Organizational behavior aims to sharpen these skills by focusing on how people, individually and in groups, behave in organizations. Organizational behavior is the applied science of human behavior in work settings. It is not the same thing as management, any more than knowledge about design of internal combustion engines is the same as knowing how to drive a car. In both cases, however, knowing how the machine works is a great help to operate it effectively. Organizational behavior studies how the human aspects of the organizational machine operate. I find the study of these matters interesting and useful. This book is my attempt to convey both the interest in and the use of organizational behavior.

ORGANIZATION OF THE BOOK

Imagine that we have just finished spending a day looking around a medium-sized manufacturing operation—say, a plant with a couple of hundred employees manufacturing steel office furniture. We have been asked to write a short essay describing what is going on at the plant. Where do we start?

The basic problem with this assignment is that it has to be short, and we have seen a great deal. We have seen *people:* on the phone, in meetings, operating machines, driving fork-lift trucks, eating lunch, talking in the halls. We have seen *materials:* steel sheets in stacks, rolls of vinyl, cans of paint. We have seen *machines:* benders and punches and cutters. In short, we have seen a great deal. And, most likely, since this is our first visit to the organization, it all seems a bit chaotic and confusing. How can we summarize it so that it makes sense?

What we need, clearly, is a perspective, some method of organizing our perceptions so that they fit together and make sense. There are dozens of alternative perspectives to choose from. If we are thinking of investing in the company, we might be interested in a financial perspective: How much money is being spent on materials, labor, rent, utilities? How many of each sort of product are being produced, and what do they sell for? Or we might be interested in the technology of production: How do the various activities fit together? What are the operations that transform the raw materials into the final products? Or we might be interested in the people who work there: Who are they? Are they mainly men or women? Black or white? Young or old? How much do they earn? Do they enjoy their jobs?

Any one of these approaches, or others, would give us a way of organizing our description. Each would also steer us away from including large portions of what we saw. If we stress the financial side, we probably will not have much to say about the people side. If we focus on the individuals and their work, we will probably leave out the way their jobs fit together and affect one another. There does not seem to be any single perspective that lets us describe everything we see going on in an organization. We have to make a choice, bearing in mind that whatever perspective we take will give us something and cost us something. It will guide both what we tend to leave in, and what we tend to leave out.

The perspective emphasized in this book is what is called a "cognitive" approach to organizations. It focuses on people's thinking activities: the information they have available, how they use it, what decisions they make, how these decisions are communicated to others. When I go into an unfamiliar organization I tend to ask questions like: "What is this person thinking about?" "Who decides about that?" "How does information about this activity get developed, and where does it go?" "How does a problem like X get handled?" In the back of my mind, then, is what might be called a "model" of what an organization is and how it works. In simple terms, the "model" looks something like a wiring diagram, where the "components" are individual people, and the "wires" are channels of information flow between them.

For example: Here is Jim, a skilled lathe operator, who turns out the steel pivot shafts that connect the seat to the legs of a swivel desk chair. How does he know the dimensions of the piece he is working on now? Well, on top of his lathe is an engineering blueprint with the dimensions marked. So my first link shows an information link from the design office to Jim. How many of this particular shaft should he make? Jim has a work order, signed by his supervisor, ordering 120 shafts for this particular chair. So I draw in a second link from Jim to his supervisor. Every so often, Jim goes over to his young apprentice at the next lathe and gives him a few hints on how to do the job he is working on. In goes another link on my diagram, connecting Jim to his apprentice. If I continue with this observation, I end up with a pretty detailed picture of what information flows to Jim, how he processes it, and what information flows out.

I now follow one of the links—say, the one that connects Jim to his supervisor—and start the same process again. What are the supervisor's linkages? What decisions does he make? Whom does he get orders, advice, opinions from? Whom does he give them to? Bit by bit, as I follow the flow of information from one person to another, I build up a picture of how the organization works. It is not a complete picture, obviously, but I find it a very useful one. It is the skeleton around which Part I of this book is organized.

In Chapter 2, we will look at what individuals do when they solve problems and make decisions. Chapter 3 examines the processes by which people acquire and make sense of the information they use in these activities. Chapter 4 looks at motivation, treating it basically as a decision-making process in which people choose what to work on and how hard to work. These three chapters, then, focus primarily on the individual.

Subsequent chapters consider the individual's work interactions with others. Chapter 5 looks at how information is transferred from one person to another. Chapter 6 looks at the general processes by which people influence one another's behavior, and Chapter 7 focuses on the specific influence process called leadership. Chapter 8 considers conflict processes in organizations. Chapter 9 is concerned with people working with others in groups, and the last chapter, Chapter 10, looks at the organization as a whole, its structure, and its goals. The early chapters are thus mainly concerned with individuals, the middle chapters with pairs and small groups of individuals, and the last chapter with the large clusters we call organizations. The topics covered are, clearly, very diverse. The thread that binds them together is the twin focus on information processing and decision making.

Part II offers eight papers written by specialists in their fields. They offer more depth on each topic than is possible in the body of an introductory text. In my own teaching, I like to use a few "guest lecturers," both to bring some fresh perspectives to the class, and to give the class the benefit of in-depth expertise on topics that I feel are especially important. It would be a fortunate class indeed that was exposed, in a single course, to eight guest lecturers as varied and as expert as the eight included here. The topics they have chosen vary widely: career patterns of scientists and engineers; job design; organizational design; sociotechnical systems; leadership and the professional; technology assessment; interdisciplinary groups; and organizational change. In many cases their papers discuss, in more depth, issues mentioned in the text, and these connections are pointed out at numerous places.

In summary, this book attempts both breadth and depth of coverage of topics in organizational behavior of particular relevance to scientists and engineers. Part I treats a wide range of topics, tying them together around the twin themes of information processing and decision making. Part II aims for more depth, treating a selection of relevant topics in greater detail. I hope the book manages to convey to you, the reader, what I and my collaborators feel about studying organizational behavior: that this is a field that is exciting and interesting, and also useful. You will probably have trouble remembering all the details of what you will read here; but if we can leave you with some of our sense of the fascination of organizational life, as well as with some of its content, we will be well satisfied with our efforts.

Chapter 2

Problem Solving and Decision Making

ACTIVITIES INCLUDED IN SOLVING PROBLEMS

In everyday usage, "problem," "decision," and "choice" tend to be used more or less interchangeably. As you approach graduation, you become increasingly aware that you must "decide" on your future activities—whether or not to apply to graduate school, look for a job, or take some time off. You have to "choose" among various alternatives. You may feel the whole business becoming a "problem" that you feel you have to "solve." Perhaps "problem" has some negative overtones, and "choice" seems more pleasant, but, for most of us, the three terms mean pretty much the same thing.

Decision theorists can also be careless in using these three words. If pressed, however, most would admit to the value of keeping the three somewhat distinct, with "problem solving" as the broadest term, and "choice making" the narrowest. In the broadest sense, a "problem" is said to exist when an individual becomes aware of a significant difference between what *actually is* and what is *desired.* I examine my checking account and find myself almost out of money; I want a new stereo, which costs $800: I have a problem. Or, you have been getting Cs in a course, and want an A: you have a problem. Or, the air is getting more and more polluted and we would like it clean: we all have a problem.

If a "problem" is "a significant difference between actual and desired," then a "solution" is clearly something that reduces this difference to the point at which it loses significance. A problem is "solved" when the difference becomes too small for us to care about, not necessarily when it reduces to zero. Most of us can live with reality being short of perfection without being aware of a problem! The various activities we call "problem solving," then, are the things we do to reduce the difference between actual and desired states to an acceptable level.

Problem solving embraces a number of component activities, all tightly interwoven with one another. Idealizing the process, we can distinguish the following five components: problem identification, alternative generation, choice, implementation, and monitoring.

Problem Identification

In life, problems do not come to us prepackaged, the way they do on final examinations. Generally we start with a feeling that something is wrong and have to devote a good deal of effort to get a clear understanding of the problem. Think, for example, of how much time and effort a medical doctor devotes to diagnosis—that is, to turning our hazy complaint about not feeling well into a precise statement of what the real problem is. Similarly, an engineer might invest weeks or months of effort refining a client's vague problem ("excessive energy costs") into a precise understanding of exactly what energy sources are currently being used, for what purposes, at what costs, and so on. In many cases, once the problem has been correctly identified the solution is trivially easy.

Most of us are strongly oriented to solving problems and tend to spend too little time formulating them carefully. Some authors have suggested that, in addition to weighing the familiar Type 1 and Type 2 errors, we should beware of "Type 3 errors"—solving the wrong problem. Changing the problem formulation just a little often has dramatic effects on how we go about solving it. For example, if we formulate the problem of air pollution as "I'm coughing too much," a bottle of cough suppressant is a plausible solution. If, however, we formulate the problem in terms of air quality, we are more likely to think of solutions such as moving away or campaigning for reduced auto and smokestack emissions. An even more suggestive formulation sees the pollution problem as "valuable chemicals in the wrong places," which starts us thinking about possible profits to be made, not just costs to be borne, in keeping the materials in their proper places (and out of people's lungs).

A key part of the problem identification or formulation phase is clarifying exactly what will count as a satisfactory solution. What criteria will it have to meet? What constraints do we want to apply? Take the pollution problem again. The air currently carries a burden of various concentrations of several gases and particles, a state we find unacceptable. But what levels *are* acceptable? Do they all have to reach zero before we will regard the problem as solved? And are we prepared to pay *any* price for getting our solution? Closing every factory? Taking every car off the road? Probably few of us want to go this far. But getting the problem properly formulated requires us to say just how far we do want to go, what our goals or objectives or criteria are for an acceptable solution. The first cluster of problem-solving activities, then, are those concerned with moving from our initial, generally vague sense of what the problem is to a clear specification of it: in what ways, exactly, does the actual situation differ from what we wish it to be? And what criteria must a possible solution meet before we will regard it as acceptable?

Alternative Generation

A second cluster of problem-solving activities involves efforts to think up one or more actions that might help the situation. This may require considerable creativity or merely routine searching around. It may turn up hundreds of likely-looking candidates in five minutes, or it may take months of hard work to find even one. We may be able to come up with several broad alternatives in an instant—for example, "ferry," "bridge," or "diversion" as alternatives to a valley-crossing problem— but still have a lot of work to do before we can really start to evaluate each. Which are feasible? What will each cost? What environmental impact will each have?

As with the identification phase, we often short-circuit the alternative generation phase in our eagerness to get to the solution. Once we see a problem in a certain way, we tend to think of only one class of possible solutions, and often pass up much neater, cheaper, or better solutions. We have all had the infuriating experience of pounding away on one method of solution to a mathematical problem, only to find later that a different approach cracks it in three lines. Many of what we think of as "elegant" problem solutions share this trick of seeing a way of solving it quite different from the candidates we were considering. Sifting through a list of alternative solutions often blinds us to the fact that there exists a clear winner that never made it to the list. We carefully examine every mousetrap and poison on the market, and never examine the possibility of simply getting a cat.

Choice

Once the problem is clearly identified and the alternative possible solutions are clearly laid out, we are ready to make our choice. The problem formulation tells us what we are looking for: for example, an amplifier with the following frequency response, at the following power output, with not more than this percentage of distortion, and at less than this price. Our alternative generation has provided us with information about the characteristics of the amplifiers available in the shops. We now sift through the list, weighing each against our criteria, until we find the one that meets our needs most closely. Then we choose that one.

Anyone who has managed to reduce any important problem to such a trivial choice procedure deserves a medal. In reality, choice is vastly more complex than this simplified sketch suggests—and, for most of us, generates a lot more anxiety and difficulty than the simple, mechanical checklist approach would imply. In our amplifier purchase decision, for example, we are likely to encounter difficulties, such as:

- What if more than one alternative meets the criteria? Both the Yagimoto X (at $720) and the Boomer (at $750) exceed my performance specifications, and both are under $800. The Boomer looks nicer, but the X has more power. What is my tradeoff between price, power, and appearance?

• What if none of the alternatives meets the criteria? All the amplifiers meeting my specifications cost over $800. Should I spend more? Or should I relax my criteria? Again, the tradeoff problem.

• What if I cannot be sure? Other things being equal, an amplifier that performs well for ten years is more attractive to me than one that needs fixing in five years. But even well-made instruments sometimes break within a week, and even poor ones sometimes last for years. How can I estimate the chances of a breakdown? And how do I crank this information into my calculations?

Choice theorists tend to approach these questions by building a formal model, in this case, a model of the purchaser's objectives. For example, the theorist might suggest that the purchaser evaluates different amplifiers by a simple weighted average of price, power, appearance, and reliability:

$$\text{Value} = a_1 (\text{Power}) - a_2 (\text{Price}) + a_3 (\text{Appearance}) + a_4 (\text{Reliability})$$

The purchaser indicates how important each of the features is by setting the four weights $a_1 - a_4$. Each possible amplifier is then simply "scored" on each of the four dimensions, and a value calculated for each. The assumption is that the purchaser will be best pleased with the amplifier that achieves the highest "value" by this method.

Such an approach to making complex choices can often be useful, but it needs to be examined carefully. The model is so clear and straightforward that it is easy to forget that it is merely a model, an attempt to represent our desires in mathematical form. The equation above, for example, implies that the purchaser is prepared to make tradeoffs between each of the features of an amplifier; a little more of one feature will make up for a little less of another. This might be true up to a point, but would any purchaser really want an amplifier that was handsome, powerful, and cheap, but totally unreliable?

These objections can, of course, be taken care of by making the model more complex, for example, by setting lower bounds on each feature. The point here is simply that choice is a complex process, and one should look carefully at any procedure that offers to make it easy. It is all too easy to be misled by elegant formal devices like the model presented above and forget to ask the crucial question: "Is this what I really want?"

Implementation

We have defined problem solving as closing the gap between real and desired. A problem is not solved by analysis, creativity, or choice: we need to *do* something to bring about the change. Solutions need to be implementable, and they need to be implemented. Will Rogers once proposed that the way to eliminate U-boats in the North Atlantic was to boil the entire ocean, so that they would turn pink and pop to the surface like shrimp. When asked how he planned to do this, he protested that he was the grand strategist, and left all the details to his subordinates. Many of us take a similar, if less extreme, position in our first work assignments after graduating. We are trained in the analytical skills of problem solving, and tend to stop after we have chosen our recommended solution and written a report showing why the solution is so good. Few real problems actually get solved this way. We need to build in the implementation phase of the work, to find the money, time, effort, and resources needed, to make sure that the other people involved understand what is happening, and that they are motivated to play their parts.

All this is perfectly obvious, but still worth saying. One of the biggest gaps between academic training and actual practice is that the former deals only with the analytic phases of problem solving, while the latter depends on getting action. Operations research (OR) analysts, for example, are notorious for their fascination with the quantitative, modeling parts of their work and neglect of actual implementation of their solutions. Too few have the real-world skills, interest, and just plain savvy to realize that there is more to problem solving than merely finding the optimal solution. A truck-routing schedule that involves scrapping the current fleet of trucks, having drivers work two-hour shifts with three-hour breaks, or that requires the dispatcher to start work at 3 A.M. is not likely to be implemented, no matter how elegantly it solves the abstract problem of routing.

Monitoring

An astute problem solver retains a little humility. No matter how thorough he or she has been in moving through the problem formulation, alternative generation, choice, and implementation phases, there is still a chance that things will go wrong. Perhaps the problem was formulated with an important criterion left out (for example, the dispatcher's working hours). Perhaps the "best" solution was not implemented properly, or the assumptions about how it would work are not borne out in practice. Or, most critically, perhaps the problem situation has changed, and the problem we were trying to solve is not the problem we are currently facing.

For all these reasons, good problem solvers monitor the results of the implementation carefully, to check whether or not it is working as anticipated. This critical feedback loop may provide nothing more than the warm glow of seeing that one's plans worked out as expected. Much more often, however, there will be smaller or larger deviations from these expectations and further problem-solving efforts will be required. Indeed, as we shall see later, there are plenty of situations where attempting solutions amounts to little more than trial and error. In these cases, good monitoring and feedback become especially critical. Trial and error only works if you can see where you have made an error!

PROBLEM-SOLVING SEQUENCES

It is wrong to suppose that these five activities fit neatly together into a sequence over time:

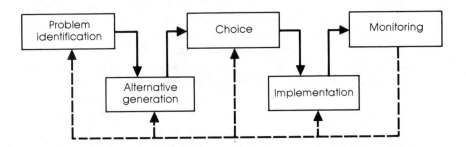

The primary virtue of such a diagram is that it identifies the different activities that go into problem solving. It is, however, downright misleading to expect that these activities flow (or should flow) from left to right in a fixed sequence. As we have noted, people jump to and fro between activities in anything but an orderly way; and work at one phase is extensively influenced, or even distorted, by the others. The illustration may be a useful way of reconstructing what one has done, in a report to one's teacher or one's boss, but it is not likely that you will ever see any real problem get solved this way.

Solutions often chase problems.   Most of us carry around ideas that might be politely called "solutions looking for problems." Perhaps we have always wanted to get a Wizzo ten-channel high-precision solid-state digitizer for our lab. Or, more sinister, we would love to find a way to get rid of Joe, that obnoxious senior technician who is the only person who knows how to fix the old centrifuge. When a well-funded new research project comes along, our thoughts naturally run to a design that absolutely requires a Wizzo; and, when a budget cutback threatens, the centrifuge (and thus Joe) seems like the only sensible place to make economies. This sounds cynical, and may be, but it may be entirely unconscious. Our pet "solution" just shapes the way we see the problem.

Criteria often chase solutions.   Suppose we got our Wizzo digitizer. Looking back a year later, it turns out that it did not work especially well on the project we bought it for. But we find ourselves justifying it on other grounds. It is important for laboratory morale that we have the most modern equipment; it kept us in touch with the Wizzo Company, so we get first news of other advanced equipment. Neither of these aims occurred to us at the time we made the purchase, but, looking back, they seem entirely sensible objectives. We are endlessly inventive in discovering ways of making our past decisions look sensible, not just to our bosses and our colleagues, but to ourselves. Read any autobiography to see how rarely people made mistakes—in retrospect! (See also "Rationality versus Rationalizing," later in this chapter.)

Problems often get clear only after they have been solved.   Although the Wizzo device was of only marginal use for the project, we have had a lot less trouble with Joe, the senior technician, since it was installed. After some discreet inquiries, we find out why. A major source of his habitual bad temper before the Wizzo arrived was that Joe felt that his skills were being wasted in endless boring hours of entering data from laboratory records onto a keypunch machine. The new digitizer does all this automatically, and he is now able to do much more of the interesting, skilled work on which he prides himself. His mood is, understandably, much improved. The Wizzo solved a problem—Joe's dissatisfaction with his work assignments—that you didn't even realize existed. Once again, the orderly problem-solving sequence seems to have run backward.

Summary

We have defined the general process of problem solving as a series of activities aimed at reducing or eliminating a perceived difference between the way a situation actually is and the way we want it to be. Within this general process, we have discussed five kinds of activities or "phases." The first three—problem identification, alternative generation, and choice—are included in what is normally referred to as "decision making." Two further phases—implementation and monitoring of the chosen solution—emphasize the action-taking side of problem solving, the requirement that we do not simply solve the problem on paper, but put our thoughts into action and watch how they turn out.

Logically, we can think of these five phases as running in an orderly way from problem identification to solution monitoring. However, in practical settings, we often find the phases much less clear: we move to and fro through the different activities in all sorts of orders, rarely completing one phase before we move on to another, and with our activities at one phase shaping what we do at another.

SOME SIMPLE CHOICE MODELS

As we noted earlier, decision theorists have tended to focus on the "choice" part of the problem-solving process, ignoring the other parts. That is, they generally assume that the problem is well formulated, that all the alternatives are known, that the consequences of each alternative are understood, and that whichever alternative is chosen will be implemented. This focus obviously leaves out a great many interesting processes! It does, however, allow choices to be represented clearly, and it will help later discussion if we look briefly at how this is done.

Choice, to a decision theorist, concerns the evaluation of present alternatives in light of the future consequences of each. Do you want to toss a coin to see who will pay for both our lunches, or shall we each pay for our own? You are offered two alternatives. In one, you certainly pay for just one lunch; in the other, you may pay for two, or you may get lucky and not pay at all. Which alternative do you prefer? There are two useful ways to represent such choices: decision trees and payoff matrices. A decision tree is simply an orderly network linking alternatives to consequences, as shown in Figure 2.1. It is usual to use small squares to show decision points (here, "Toss" or "Don't toss"), and small circles to show chance events (here, the result of the toss).

An alternative way of representing the same problem is shown in Figure 2.2. Here the alternatives are represented by rows, the result of the coin-toss by columns, and the cell entries show the outcomes.

Clearly, neither of these representations is much help for a problem as simple as this. Their real value is in helping to clarify more complex situations. Decision trees are particularly useful when there are several chains of choices all linked together. For example, in trying to estimate the risk of a major accident at a nuclear power plant, one needs

Figure 2.1.   A Simple Decision Tree for the Lunch Problem

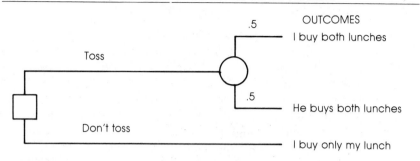

Figure 2.2.   A Simple Payoff Matrix for the Lunch Problem

ALTERNATIVE	COIN COMES UP	
	Heads	Tails
Agree to toss	Buy both lunches	Buy neither lunch
Don't agree to toss	Buy my lunch only	Buy my lunch only

to consider many complex sequences of events: IF the main coolant pump fails AND the backup system is out for maintenance AND the operator opens the wrong valve accidentally OR this instrument malfunctions . . . A decision tree is of great value in tracing out the thousands of such strings of events, and estimating the chances of each occurring.

Payoff matrices are especially useful for representing situations in which the consequences of your decisions are influenced by the decisions of others. For example, your company's decision whether or not to market a particular product needs to consider whether or not your competitors introduce a similar product. As the number of possible alternatives open to each side grows, it is useful to construct a payoff matrix for each pair of alternatives, to be sure that all the possibilities are properly considered.

DECISION RULES AND UNCERTAIN CONSEQUENCES: THE EXPECTANCY MODEL

Decision trees and payoff matrices both focus our attention on selecting an action now in light of its likely future consequences. Looked at in this way, a decision involves two sorts of guesses about the future:

1. What will happen if I choose a particular action?
2. Will I like that set of consequences or not?

Decision theorists have generally considered the second guess as being relatively straightforward. They assume that decision makers know what they want, or have "stable preference orderings" over different outcomes. (There are, however, situations in which this assumption seems clearly wrong. March [1978] discusses several situations, such as eating unfamiliar foods or listening to unfamiliar music, in which one's actions are intended to *change* one's tastes.) Generally, though, tastes or preferences for outcomes are treated as "given."

On the first guess—what consequences will flow from different actions—decision theorists distinguish three situations:

1. **Certainty:** The consequences of each action alternative are known for sure. Action 1 will lead to Outcomes A and B; Action 2 will lead to Outcomes C and D. In this situation, choice reduces to simply evaluating each package of consequences against one's known preferences, and selecting the one which, on balance, offers the most of what one wants.

2. **Risk:** One does not know for sure the consequences of each alternative, but can assess a probability of each consequence resulting from each alternative. Action 1 will lead to Outcome A with probability 0.5, and to Outcome B with probability 0.1. Action 2 will lead to Outcome C with probability 0.7, and to Outcome D with probability 0.3. In this situation, it is often reasonable to apply the decision rule: "Discount the value of each outcome by the probability of its occurrence"—the so-called "expected value rule." For example, one might evaluate a simple gamble such as a coin toss with a one-dollar stake as being worth 50 cents. Over a long series of such bets, one would collect the dollar about half the time, so a 50 percent discount would be reasonable. (Again, there are interesting exceptions to this rule. For example, would you rather have $1 million for sure, or toss a coin for $5 million? The latter has a higher "expected value" ($2.5 million), but most people would hesitate to gamble the opportunity to be rich for life, and would choose the certain $1 million. However, the payoff-discounted-by-probability rule seems generally sensible for small stakes and repeated plays.)

3. **Uncertainty:** In this situation, one knows what consequences might follow from each alternative, but cannot assess the relevant probabilities. Action 1 might lead to Outcomes A and B, Action 2 might lead to Outcomes C and D, but the relevant probabilities cannot be estimated. A variety of interesting decision rules have been suggested for this situation (see, e.g., Raiffa [1968] for an excellent introduction). A cautious decision maker might select a "minimax"

strategy, choosing the alternative that offers the best set of outcomes if everything goes as badly as it could. A bold optimist might go with a "maximax" strategy, choosing the alternative that will yield the highest value if everything goes as well as it could. (Note, by the way, that it is easy to think of situations in which one is much more uncertain than this formal treatment of "uncertainty" allows. For example, one might have no idea of what alternatives are available, what the consequences of each might be, or how desirable each is. Decision theorists have had little to say about such extremely uncertain situations, though they are clearly common in the real world.)

Organizational researchers have made great use of decision models derived from the "expected-value" decision rule. In its simplest form, this "expectancy model" suggests that people's actual choices are, in fact, guided by the "payoff-discounted-by-probability" rule, though the outcomes considered, their desirability, and the probabilities of each flowing from a given alternative are all assessed subjectively. (Note that there is a long step here from the decision theorist's suggestion that people *should* choose in this way to the researcher's interest in describing how people *actually* choose.) The basic form of the expectancy model can be shown as a decision tree:

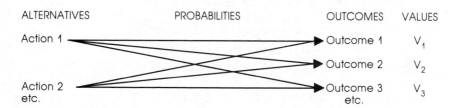

ALTERNATIVES	PROBABILITIES	OUTCOMES	VALUES
Action 1		Outcome 1	V_1
		Outcome 2	V_2
Action 2 etc.		Outcome 3 etc.	V_3

Decision rule: Select action alternative with highest net value, where

$$\text{Net value of action}_i = \sum_{\substack{\text{All } j \\ \text{Outcomes}}} P_{ij} V_j$$

In this form, the model is merely a generalization to several outcomes of the decision rule discussed earlier under "Risk." Each action is linked probabilistically to several outcomes; the action's "net value" is simply the sum of the value (positive or negative) associated with each outcome, discounted by the probability of the action leading to that outcome.

For descriptive purposes, researchers relabel the "probability" terms in the above model with "expectancies"—subjective beliefs about what consequences will follow from each alternative. The assumption here is that, if we wish to understand people's choices, we need to know what *they think* the probability is that a particular action will lead to a particular consequence, not what the *objective* probability of that consequence might be. A descriptive model of this sort forms the heart of what is called the "expectancy theory" of work motivation, a theory we will examine in more detail in Chapter 4.

GOOD DECISIONS AND GOOD DECISION PROCESSES

In the "game" called Russian Roulette, the "player" puts a bullet in one of the six chambers of a revolver, spins the magazine, puts the gun to his head and pulls the trigger. If he is lucky, the hammer hits an empty chamber, and he collects the bet. If not, he is dead.

As it happens, the odds are said to be much better than one in six. The weight of the single bullet tends to make the cylinder stop with an empty chamber at the top, or firing position, improving the player's odds considerably. So, in most cases, the player will win the bet. But, even so, most of us would regard "playing" this game as an act of insanity or extreme desperation. Even if one wins, the decision to "play" is not a sensible one.

There is an important general point to be made here: one cannot judge how good a decision was by its outcomes. Even very good decisions can have disappointing outcomes, and very bad decisions can have good outcomes. Of course, if you bet against the odds repeatedly you will lose in the long run. But in any particular decision, you may decide badly and still get lucky (or vice versa).

If we cannot judge the quality of a decision from its outcomes, is there any way to distinguish good and bad decision making? Most decision theorists would argue that there is: examining the *process* by which the decision was arrived at. We look for what is called "procedural rationality," for a decision-making procedure that seems to offer the best chance of making a sound decision. Janis and Mann (1977), drawing on a large body of previous analysis, have identified seven criteria by which such "procedural rationality" may be judged. The decision maker:

1. Reviews a wide range of possible alternatives
2. Reviews the full range of objectives and values

3. Weighs both costs and risks, positive and negative consequences, that could flow from each alternative
4. Searches intensively for relevant new information on each alternative
5. Assimilates this new information carefully
6. Reexamines all alternatives before making a final decision
7. Makes detailed implementation and contingency plans, covering both expected consequences and anticipated risks. (Janis and Mann, 1967: p. 11)

These two authors describe such a process as "vigilant decision making." It is worth noting that they do not expect "vigilance" as the normal pattern. In fact, much of their work is concerned with the circumstances under which people will depart from "vigilance," and thus adopt less successful decision processes. (We shall have more to say about this in Chapter 9, on group processes.) We should emphasize, again, that no procedure guarantees satisfactory outcomes. The claim is only that a rational procedure, such as that sketched above, gives us the best chance of making good decisions and thus, on the average, enjoying satisfactory outcomes. We still need good luck and a benevolent environment to make any given decision a winner!

RATIONALITY

Most of us pride ourselves on being rational, especially in matters to do with our work. It is, however, often difficult to pin down exactly what we mean when we claim to have acted "rationally." Is it rational for you to be reading this book? Was it rational for me to write it? I hope neither decision is obviously crazy, but there is a long gap between "clearly rational" and "obviously crazy." What is changing as we move from one to the other?

"Rational" is generally used to describe decisions or actions based on thinking and reasoning. It is perfectly sensible to snatch your hand away from a hot stove, but we generally think of that as a reflex action rather than a rational one. It is perfectly sensible to eat plums (if you happen to like them), but we generally see that as a matter of taste, not a matter of rationality.

We can define rational behavior in terms of the general problem-solving model discussed earlier. Strictly, we would be choosing rationally only if:

1. We could specify exactly what we were aiming for
2. We examined every possible alternative action open to us
3. We could predict all the consequences of each alternative
4. We chose the alternative that generated most of what we wanted (and least of what we did not want).

This set of requirements will be familiar to anyone who has studied economics. Economists build much of their theory on the assumption that people, at least in the aggregate, act rationally in this sense.

Practically, of course, we cannot hope to be fully rational by these standards. Our values and aims are at least somewhat unclear and conflicting. We can never be sure that we have examined every possible alternative. Even for the ones we do examine, we can only anticipate some of the more immediate consequences, and have great difficulty judging how likely each is. And, as we try to do more and more of each of these things, we get more and more overwhelmed with information, and it becomes harder and harder to find the time, energy, and sheer mental ability to digest it all and pick the best alternative.

(If you find yourself agreeing that this is a fair description of other people, but not of yourself, think for a moment about some trivial purchase you have made recently—say, a toothbrush. What would it take to make this a strictly rational purchase decision? How worn was your old one? How serious is using an old toothbrush, in terms of later dental decay? How good was the new one? Did you check other shops for a better price? Within what area? What does it cost, in time, gasoline, and wear on the car to drive to another store? And so on, with no limit in sight. Obviously, it is crazy to devote a full-scale effort at being rational to trivial decisions like buying toothbrushes; but it should be just as obvious that we could not achieve complete rationality, even if we were to try.)

SATISFICING

We should not assume that, because people are not completely rational in the strict sense, they are irrational. It is clear that people often, especially in matters connected with their jobs, intend to be as rational as possible. Herbert Simon, who won a Nobel prize for his studies of organizational decision making, suggests that we should think in terms of "bounded" rather than strict rationality. These "bounds" are imposed both by our weaknesses as decision makers and by the difficulties of the situations we have to cope with. We get by reasonably well in most cases by simplifying the decision process. That is:

1. We consider only a few major value dimensions
2. We examine only a few possible alternatives
3. We consider only some of the main consequences of each alternative
4. We choose the first alternative that reaches some level we think of as "good enough."

To emphasize the distinction between this model and the strictly rational process, Simon uses the term "satisficing" for the boundedly rational process, in contrast to "optimizing" for the strictly rational process. He suggests that people are better described as "satisficers" than as "optimizers." Satisficing certainly fits better with the psychological evidence we shall look at in Chapter 3 than does optimizing.

The idea of satisficing as a decision process has several important implications for understanding how decisions get made in organizations. One is that, while there is only one optimal solution to most decisions, there may be many equally good satisficing solutions. For example, I may review alternatives in a different order than you do. If we each stop when we find an alternative that is "good enough," we can easily find ourselves disagreeing about what should be done. This will often mean that the final choice has to be made on some ground other than the logic of the problem itself, for example, which of us is senior, which of us is more persuasive, which of us gets in first. Such factors do, in fact, make a great deal of difference in most organizational decisions—as they could not if decisions were made on strictly rational grounds.

A second interesting implication of "satisficing" is that, if we couple it to a mechanism for resetting our ideas of what is "good enough," we will often edge in on an optimal solution. Researchers use the term "level of aspiration" for the standard that an individual currently regards as "good enough." For most of us, if we do better than our "level of aspiration" on one try, we tend to set it higher the next time. Conversely, if we fall short of our "level of aspiration," we tend to revise it downwards. This resetting can get us quite close to optimality, without having to go through all the difficult steps noted earlier. For example:

Suppose you are in charge of a small manufacturing plant, and have to make a decision as to how much the plant will produce. If you set production targets too low, the plant will have idle capacity, sales will be lost, and profitability will suffer. On the other hand, if you try to produce too much, machine maintenance may be neglected, people will work too hard (and perhaps get sick or injured), and so on. Finding the optimal balance is, clearly, a very tricky decision. As a satisficer, however, suppose you set a target at 105 percent of last month's production. If you achieve this level without too much strain for a few months, you may reset your aim to 110 percent. Perhaps this level shows a number of danger signals, and cannot be reached without stress. You reset your aim down a little, perhaps to 108 percent, and find that this works satisfactorily on a regular basis. You have found an acceptable balance between overproduction and underproduction —without ever having to solve the highly complex problem of finding the analytic optimum.

There are, of course, traps to trying to solve problems in this way. As an analogy, consider the problem of getting to the top of a mountain (where the top represents the true "optimal solution"). If you have an accurate map of the entire mountain, you can locate the top and plan the best route to get there—that is, you can use the "analytic" approach. Suppose, however, that you do not have a map. You may do quite well by merely checking which way is uphill from where you are at any moment, and climbing that way. This will work fine if the mountain is a single peak, like a cone. However, if the mountain has several minor peaks, as well as the real one, you may need to go *downhill* at some point on your way to the top. The satisficing-and-search method will trap you near one of the minor peaks. In other words, it is a potentially "conservative" approach. It will help you make minor improvements from where you are now, and with luck these improvements may add up to a very large gain. But it may trap you in dead ends, while the really large payoffs are somewhere else.

LIMITATIONS ON RATIONALITY

As we have seen in several of the examples discussed thus far, rationality is very difficult to achieve. Indeed, it is probably no exaggeration to say that it is impossible to achieve, in any strict sense, once one gets beyond highly simplified situations such as gambling games. Even when we try our best to be rational, we cannot achieve it fully. It will be convenient to list here the major constraints that limit our approximations to rational choice.

Human Information-Processing Limits

We are able to think of only a few—a very few—bits of information at a time. Without trying to specify exactly how many, a reasonable estimate is somewhere in the region of seven distinct, meaningful "chunks" of information (Miller, 1956), a humblingly small number. These "chunks" can vary in information content from single digits to complex symbols or images, but we seem to be able to process only about seven of them in our short-term memories. Clearly, we are better off using rich "chunks" than otherwise, hence the critical role of powerful notational systems such as matrices: they allow us to think about a complex set of relationships as a single symbol. Several fascinating studies of chess players suggest the same point. Grand masters are no better than novices at remembering random arrangements of chess pieces on a board. They are, however, hugely superior at remembering positions from real games. It appears that they have the ability to store board positions as powerful "chunks," where a large region of the board is stored as a single "chunk": a "Sicilian corner," for example. Thus, learning dense, informationally rich chunks is a powerful way of using what little short-term memory we have, but about seven bits remains the upper limit. This is clearly a critical constraint on our ability to weigh up mentally the many factors that enter into any complex decision.

Situational Pressures

The organizational world is often a busy, even a hectic place, especially as one moves into the ranks of management. Studies of how typical managers spend their time (for example, Mintzberg, 1973) have found what experienced managers already know: the day is broken up into many small activities, one thing is constantly interrupted by another, and attention must be rapidly redirected from one matter to another. In fact, Mintzberg found that a typical managerial activity took less than ten minutes! Obviously, it is sometimes possible to allocate longer chunks of time to an important issue, to break up the problem into smaller pieces that can be dealt with singly, or to work on it outside of normal business hours. But, equally obviously, such long blocks of uninterrupted time are the exception, not the rule. Time and attention are scarce managerial resources. Most decisions are made with a minimum of either, suggesting a very different way of deciding than the cool, reflective, careful analysis implied in our earlier discussion of rational decision processes.

Informational Limits

Managers appear to live in an informationally rich environment. Their world is full of memos, reports, computer printouts, production figures, personnel reports, journals, laboratory reports, and so on. But does this make them well informed in terms of the decisions they have to make? In many cases, it does not. As Ackoff (1967) suggests, it may be more accurate to think of managers as suffering from an overabundance of irrelevant information. True, the particular number you are looking for may be right on your desk. But if it is buried in the middle of a 200-page printout, it might as well not be there at all.

An English organizational researcher, Anthony Downs, suggests three important features of a manager's information supply. (1) When a manager starts to think about a problem, available relevant information is likely to be scarce. (2) Additional information can frequently be found, but at a significant cost in money, effort, and delay. (3) Some of the most critical information is never available at decision time, that is, information about the future. This last, of course, is inherent in any decision process, and the risk or uncertainty of future events must be considered in making the decision. In the next chapter, we shall look at some of the errors that we are all prone to make in predicting events.

As a practical matter, we should not expect decisions made by real people in real organizations to meet the criteria for strict rationality. Put bluntly, in any reasonably complex problem we are generally not smart enough, and we do not have (and cannot get) enough information to choose rationally. Thus such simplifying decision processes as satisficing are not simply a matter of taking a lazy, second-rate approach. In most settings they are all we are capable of.

RATIONALITY VERSUS RATIONALIZING

As we have seen, choosing rationally is a very difficult business, especially when the decision is an important one. However, we have strong cultural values in favor of rational choice, and these values are reinforced in the context of organizational life. We are insulted if a friend says of a decision we have made, "That's irrational!" If the comment comes from our boss, it is worse than an insult: it is a threat to our job.

The central difficulty about choosing rationally is that it turns on our guesses about the future. *What if* we choose Alternative A? *What if* the stock market falls twenty points? *What if* I ask that person for a date and he/she turns me down? Questions like this are immensely easier if we are looking back in time, rather than forward. (See the next chapter for a discussion of prediction errors.) Once we know what has happened, it is usually easy to reconstruct our choices so that we look rational in retrospect—this is the process we call "rationalizing." The sorts of remarks that tip you off that someone (yourself, maybe?) is rationalizing include:

"I realized it was risky at the time." (Something has gone wrong.)

"I had a hunch that it would work out." (Something has gone right.)

"It got messed up down the line." (I made a good decision but someone else implemented it badly.)

"Looking back, what I was really trying to do . . ." (The choice did not meet the original objectives, but here is another set of objectives it *did* meet.)

As usual, it is a lot easier to spot these tricks when someone else is playing them, but it is worth bearing in mind that we all spend a lot of time rationalizing—making sense of the past, rather than of the future. This has costs. For one thing, it takes up time and energy we could be better using for something else. Rationalizing also prevents us learning from our mistakes: if we see no mistake, there is nothing to learn from! And it sets false expectations, for us and for others. If everyone else is making all these superrational decisions, how come I find them so difficult? Maybe I should be cautious and not confess my confusions. This leads to defensive decision making. It becomes less important to make the right choices than it is to have a defensible way of making them.

Rationalizing is both common and dangerous. As we shall see later in this book, we all do it, very often without being aware that we are. We are taught from an early age to "act sensibly," so that rationalizing becomes second nature to us. Organizations reemphasize this value. As a result, much time and energy are absorbed in making sense of the past instead of making sense of the future. And choices are often made so as to be defensible, instead of being right.

Still more worrying, some recent studies (e.g., Staw, 1980; Staw and Fox, 1979) suggest that our tendency to rationalize the past may even shape our future decisions. For example, if we have been responsible for funding a research project that seems to be failing, we are prone to pouring more money into it, in hopes of bailing it out and thus making our original decision look good, instead of cutting our losses and going on to something else. As well as wasting time and effort "reinventing" the past, rationalizing may distort our future decisions, too.

PROGRAMMED VERSUS UNPROGRAMMED DECISIONS

Given the time and energy that are used to solve a problem, even if we are not especially rational about it, we all develop ways to economize on this effort. Some of these ways seem to be "wired in" as physical reflexes. We do not *decide* to snatch our hands from a hot flame, or to blink when an object comes close to our eyes. At a second level, most of us develop habitual ways of doing things, so that they take virtually no mental effort or attention. For example, I have a fairly automatic sequence of activities for getting up in the morning. From the time the alarm rings to the time I get into my car, I have gone through 45 minutes of tooth-brushing, showering, coffee-drinking, and so on, without thinking about it or even being aware I am doing it. In fact, not being a morning person, I am rather upset if I am forced to think, for example, by a telephone call in the middle of my routine.

Between elaborate problem solving and such habitual routines is a large category of "programmed decisions." These are not really habits, in the sense of unfolding in the same way every time. But nor are they full-scale decisions. They are more like packaged subroutines in computer programming. They may have a variety of "IF" statements calling up different branches, but, once a particular branch is activated, a predictable sequence unfolds within it.

For example, once I am in my car, I do not always drive to school the same way. If a certain traffic light is red, I turn earlier. If the traffic seems to be heavy on the freeway, I get off onto a side street. I have a regular search routine for finding a parking place on the campus. If you recorded my route from home to office for a year, you might find dozens of different alternatives, all of which I used at least once. But this is not to say that I review them all each morning and choose which one will work best that day. My complex pattern of switching routes is really generated by a few choices, with large chunks of routine evoked by each.

Organizations develop hundreds of decision "programs" of this sort, many of them highly elaborate. Just as with packaged subroutines in computer programming, these decision programs let the organization get a lot done without thinking very much about each case. A university, for example, has "programs" for admitting students, for getting the buildings cleaned, and so on. Once they are set up, they run almost without anyone thinking about them. A newly created university department has to solve a large number of difficult problems in an "unprogrammed" way before the first student arrives: what materials the student should learn, how he or she is to be examined, where he or she will live, and so on. But once you have the "program" established, it is almost effortless. A few quick decisions—regular or advanced placement? specialty? financial aid?—and the whole complex sequence unfolds automatically.

This marvel of efficiency has its costs, of course, One is that it may make the work very boring for the employees. Designing an electric motor is complex and fun, but not if it is reduced to plugging the performance specifications into a design package. A second, and familiar, problem is that programs require standardized rules to evoke them, so they have to treat people and problems in preset categories. Human beings experience this as depersonalizing. If we happen not to fit the categories, we are forced into one that does not quite fit, or we are dealt with as a special case—often painfully, since the efficiency of the program turns on having as few special cases as possible. Anyone who has tried to take a nonstandard mix of courses will know the problems one can encounter.

An important aspect of understanding how organizations work is to be able to trace out these decision programs. What matters do they cover? How elaborate are they? How are exceptions dealt with? Organizations differ a great deal in these areas. We tend to think of government agencies as having very elaborate decision programs: for example, what welfare benefits is a particular client entitled to? (These rules and procedures, as well as being relatively efficient, help to offset personal biases on the part of the welfare caseworker.) On the other hand, a small research-based company might be highly unprogrammed, with very few standard procedures and most issues decided on an *ad hoc* basis. These two organizations will operate very differently—and they will be very different as places to work in!

DECISION EVENTS AND DIFFUSE DECISIONS

Thus far most of the discussion has considered a decision as essentially an event. A single individual, at some point in time, weighs up a set of alternatives against a set of criteria and choses one alternative to implement. In short, decisions are identifiable events; decision makers are identifiable individuals.

However, the stress on the single decision maker, and the single decision event, is misleading as a description of what actually happens in organizations.

Some years ago, when I was working on my dissertation research, I became interested in NASA, the American space agency. At that time NASA was spending hundreds of millions of dollars annually on research projects. The decisions as to what got funded and what did not seemed interesting, and my dissertation was intended to look into how these decisions got made. Obviously, the first thing to do was to find the decision maker and go talk to him or her.

Finding the decision maker turned out to be a frustrating business. No one would admit to making such an important decision. The research scientists on the bench denied making it: they merely submitted outlines of projects they thought would be useful or interesting and waited to see what got funded. The branch chiefs in the laboratories denied making it: they simply reviewed the proposals they received, and sent the most promising ones up the line. Senior laboratory managers denied making it: they merely reviewed projects on the basis of promise, balance across different laboratory areas, and so on. And so it went. At every level of management, everyone I talked to felt that the "real" decision was made somewhere else. Of course, each gave advice, made recommendations, proposed, reviewed, coordinated, evaluated, and so on—everything except actually making a decision! Even the most senior people in the agency's management denied making the decision. As one of them told me, "By the time suggestions reach me, there's very little actual choice left—it's already been made by the people further down the line."

It took me a long time to realize that the reason I was getting all these confusing answers was that I was asking a stupid question. I was doing the equivalent of walking into an automobile plant and asking, "Who makes the cars around here?" The answer is, of course, that a *process* is what makes cars—and a *process* is what makes important organizational decisions. Decision processes extend over long periods of time, and involve many people at various organizational levels and at different geographical locations. I christened them "diffuse decision processes," to emphasize their dispersion over time, people, organizational level, and geography (Connolly, 1977).

It is useful to think in terms of a spectrum of decision phenomena:

	Focused decision events	Diffuse decision processes
Time-frame	Short	Long
Number of participants	One	Many
Organizational locations	One	Many
Geographical dispersion	None	Large

I have found this idea of a spectrum of decision types to be a very helpful framework in organizing my thinking—and, indeed, for organizing this book. Most of the present chapter, for example, has been concerned with focused decision events: single individuals making choices at a single point in time. The next chapter continues this emphasis, looking in more depth at how we gather and make sense of information in making our decisions. Chapter 4 treats motivation mainly in terms of how people make decisions on such matters as how hard to work—again, a relatively focused, individual-level decision.

Later chapters move into more multiperson, diffuse kinds of decision processes. For example, matters of power, influence, and leadership can be seen in terms of one individual affecting the decisions of another. Chapter 8, on conflict and conflict resolution, clearly has this same interest, since we look at choices shaped not only by one's own interests and desires but by those of others. Communication (Chapter 5) is the process by which information is transmitted and thus the process by which individual decisions are coupled together. The multiperson emphasis emerges still more strongly when we look at decision making in groups (Chapter 9). Finally, in Chapter 10, organizational structures are treated as procedures (both formal and informal) by which diffuse decision processes are made more orderly and structured.

SUMMARY

We have defined a "problem" as a perception that a significant difference exists between actual and desired situations, and a "solution" as an action taken to close this gap. The process between includes several components: problem identification, alternative generation, choice, implementation, and monitoring. These five components do not generally follow this neat sequence, but tend to be interwoven with one another, often in complex ways. No matter what sequence is followed, good outcomes cannot be guaranteed, because the future is always uncertain. However, we did propose several criteria for decision processes that seem to raise the probability that good decisions can, on the average, be made.

It is clear that human beings are not capable of "strict rationality" in the optimizing sense. Our efforts at rationality are constrained by our limited ability to process information, and by scarcity of information, time, and attention in real organizational settings. We should think of behavior in terms of "intended rationality," where we "satisfice" by searching for the first alternative that is "good enough" in terms of some current "level of aspiration." Revising levels of aspiration after successful and unsuccessful search can allow us to make continual incremental improvements, but may trap us into local, rather than global, maxima.

Although rationality is hard to achieve (or even to approximate), we are often expected to pretend that our actions are, in fact, rational. This leads to "rationalizing," attempts to reconstruct the past so as to make decisions that were made appear to have been rational. Rationalizing is dangerous: it makes it difficult to learn from our mistakes, it can lead us to make defensible (rather than good) decisions, and it can trap us into throwing good money after bad, trying to justify the original bad decision.

Most organizational decisions are made in a "programmed" way, with a series of predictable steps unfolding one after the other rather like a computer program subroutine. These "programs" are important to the organization's decision-making efficiency, and free up time and resources for the rare, "unprogrammed" problem. They do, however, standardize procedures, making decisions less flexible, and the work less interesting.

The last section of the chapter suggested a spectrum of decision types, running from the focused decision event (one individual choosing at one point in time) to the diffuse decision process (many individuals involved over a long period of time). Much of the remainder of this book can be seen in terms of this range of decision activities. Individual processes of perception, inference, judgement, and motivation emphasize the decision-event end of the scale. Authority, influence, leadership, and conflict fall in the middle of the scale. Communication, groups, and organizational structure raise issues toward the highly diffuse, decision-process end of the scale.

The processes of problem solving, decision making, and choice clearly rely on the people involved having access to relevant information. In the next chapter, we discuss how people acquire and make sense of information, how the processes can go wrong, and some of the things we can do to avoid these traps.

DISCUSSION QUESTIONS: CHAPTER 2

1. Select a problem that you feel is important, either in a broad social sense (e.g., energy, the environment) or in a personal sense (e.g., how to make more money, what job to choose). For the problem you have chosen:

   a. Write a brief, concise problem formulation, including the criteria for a good solution.

   b. Suggest three alternatives that might solve the problem.

   c. Describe how you would choose among the alternatives. (You may have to invent numbers for costs, probabilities, etc., but try to use reasonable numbers.)

   d. Describe how you would go about implementing your chosen solution.

   e. Suggest how you might monitor the situation so as to be sure that your chosen solution was actually working.

2. After completing the above assignment, reconsider your problem formulation. Do you wish to change or clarify it? Do any new alternatives occur to you? Might your choice now be different?

3. Suppose you are considering two different ways of spending your next day off: going to a concert or going to a picnic. The picnic will be more fun if it's sunny, but the concert will be more fun if it rains.

   a. Draw a decision tree to represent your choice situation.

   b. Draw a payoff matrix to represent your choice situation.

   c. Suppose you value the four possible outcomes as follows:
   Picnic and sunny: + 10
   Picnic and rainy: – 10
   Concert and sunny: + 6
   Concert and rainy: + 8

   Which activity would you choose if you were sure it would be sunny? If you thought the probability of rain were 50 percent? If you had no idea what the probability of rain was?

4. Why can't we evaluate how well a decision was made by just looking at its consequences? How can we rate how well a decision is made?

5. What do we mean when we say a decision maker is "satisficing"? How is this different from "optimizing," and when might the two amount to the same thing? What factors make it likely that satisficing is more common than optimizing in real decisions?

6. What is the difference between "rational" and "rationalizing" activities? Why might the latter be dangerous in organizations?

7. What is the difference between "programmed" and "unprogrammed" decisions? Which is more common in organizations? Why?

Chapter 3

Perception and Inference

THE NATURE OF PERCEPTION AND INFERENCE

Since human information processing is so central to our approach to organizations, we must look carefully at where the information being processed comes from in the first place. At first glance, this may seem like a pretty trivial question. Surely we collect our information straight-forwardly through our senses—we see, hear, feel, smell, or taste things for ourselves. Our senses are merely *sensors,* instruments that record what is happening outside us and relay the facts directly to us.

If we think about it a bit more, however, at least two things are wrong with this view. One is that only a tiny part of what we know about the world comes to us first-hand. Most of what we know comes to us from others, often over long, complex communication channels. This makes distortion a serious possibility, as we shall see in Chapter 5. The major problem with the "senses are sensors" view, however, is that it simply is not true. We do not merely register "what is out there." What happens is an amalgam of the interaction between ourselves and the object or person we are in relation to, and the context in which it all takes place. Our knowledge and understanding of the outside world is thus much more fallible than we would like to think, a fact that has important implications for organizational life.

In this chapter, we shall be concerned with two processes, perception and inference, by which we learn about the outside world. "Perception" generally refers to the direct experience of an object, person, or situation. "Inference," in contrast, has a stronger element of thinking about, of understanding, of going beyond, the raw data. The distinction between the two processes is not always a sharp one, but can be seen roughly in a few examples:

- A medical doctor *perceives* certain symptoms in the patient, and draws some *inferences* as to what diseases might be causing them.
- We *perceive* a sequence of events involving two cars; we *infer* that the driver of one committed a driving error.
- We *perceive* the instrument readings at which two samples of steel fracture; we *infer* that one has a greater tensile strength than the other.

That is, we generally think of *perception* as being immediate, direct, and primitive grasping of the outside world. *Inference* has a greater flavor of thinking about, chewing over, drawing conclusions about, or understanding that same reality. Errors in either process lead us to mistaken views of reality, and contribute to misguided actions. We shall thus be concerned not only with how the processes work, but also with evidence for when and how they go wrong.

PERCEPTION: AN ACTIVE PROCESS

Read aloud, slowly, the proverb shown below:

```
AN APPLE A
DAY KEEPS THE
THE DOCTOR AWAY
```

Do you notice anything odd about it (other than the fact that it probably is not true)? Now that you have been alerted, you will probably notice that the word "THE" appears twice. Most people do not notice this the first time.

Now look at another boring truism and count the number of times the letter "F" appears in it. (Just look; do not put your finger or pencil on the page.)

```
FINISHED FILES ARE THE
RESULT OF CAREFUL WORK
AND THE EFFORTS OF YEARS
OF PRACTICE
```

How many did you count? I have used a chart like this in classrooms for years, and it is rare for anyone to count correctly the first time. The correct count is eight. If you get a lower count, check to see which letters you missed. We shall have more to say about this in a moment.

What can we learn from party tricks like this? Though the examples are trivial, they remind us to be a little careful in trusting the evidence of our eyes. In both examples, we are quite likely to "see" what is not there, even when the stimulus is a clear black-on-white set of words, and we are asked to look at it carefully. It should not surprise us, then, when we hear witnesses in a courtroom giving different accounts of events they say briefly, perhaps while emotionally aroused, and some time ago. Just because their stories differ does not necessarily mean that someone is deliberately lying; quite probably they perceived, and now recall, different things.

It is a mistake to think of perception as a simple, passive, emotionally neutral data-gathering process. Despite our strong conviction that what we see is what is really there, we need to be constantly aware that our perceptual processes are, in fact, quite easily fooled—and the consequences can be important. We need to think of perception as an active process, involving some complex interactions between: (1) ourselves, the *perceivers*; (2) the object or person or situation we are perceiving, the *stimulus*; and (3) the surrounding setting and situation, the *context*, in which all this is taking place.

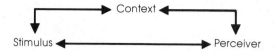

Perceiving Objects

Perceiving objects is generally a less complex process than perceiving other people, so we shall consider object perception first. The process is affected by characteristics of each of the three elements listed above.

Stimulus Factors

A number of factors make some stimuli more readily perceived than others. Most of these factors are familiar from our everyday lives, since designers of everything from advertisements to safety equipment to cockpit instruments spend considerable effort to get us to pay attention to some objects rather than others. For example:

1. **Size.** We are more likely to perceive large objects than small ones. Advertisers seem always to want larger billboards, larger magazine pages, larger product packages, to get our attention. A small tube of glue comes packaged on a 4 × 6-inch sheet of cardboard. Companies seem to vie with one another for the largest high-rise building for their corporate headquarters. The huge ex-football player probably gets the attention of his subordinates (and of his superiors) more easily than does his more average-sized colleague.

2. **Intensity.** Loud noises are more noticeable than quiet ones, bright colors more than dull, well-lit objects more than dimly lit ones. Television commercials are a little louder than the programs they interrupt; a cunningly placed spotlight on one actor leaves the rest of the stage almost invisible.

3. **Repetition.** A stimulus is more likely to be perceived if it is repeated several times than if it is presented only once. Again, advertisers are only too aware of this rule, as the constant repetition of the TV, radio, and print commercials attests. The practice of repeating orders or instructions several times increases the chance that subordinates will grasp what is being said.

4. **Contrast, novelty, and motion.** We are more likely to notice differences than sameness. (This rule probably saves us from an unending diet of large, loud, and endlessly repeated commercials, which is what the first three rules would produce.) In a room of shouting people, a quiet voice can be dramatically effective, just because of its novelty and contrast with the rest. The one soldier who faints on a hot parade day is dramatically more visible (contrast and motion) than the hundreds of others who stay at unmoving attention. A

flashing light is a far more effective warning signal than one that shines steadily.

These factors make sense if we think of our perceptual mechanisms as filtering out just one or two elements from the hundreds that compete for our attention at any moment. Even in a quiet classroom, there are dozens of things we could look at, hear, smell, or touch at any moment. Why pay attention to the teacher? Teachers cannot do much about their physical size (though they often stand on a stage), but they can raise their voices (intensity), drop to a quiet murmur (contrast and novelty), walk across the stage (motion), and repeat the key points of their lectures, both speaking and writing (repetition). With all these devices, some of the students will notice some of the lecture some of the time.

Context and Perceiver Factors

As well as being affected by characteristics of the object perceived (the stimulus), our perceptions are also shaped by the context in which it is placed and by the person doing the perceiving. A number of familiar visual illusions turn on this. For example, in the Muller–Lyer illusion shown in Figure 3.1a, most people see the line with the in-turned fins as shorter than the line with the out-turned fins, though both are actually the same length. Similarly, the upper shaded block in Figure 3.1b seems longer than the lower one (the Ponzo illusion). In Figure 3.1c, the straight line looks slightly bent when seen against the background of the concentric circles. And in Figure 3.1d the central character appears either as a number 13 or as a capital letter B, depending on whether we read across (the letters context) or down (the number context).

It appears that these perceptual distortions turn on what we have learned to see, and on what we expect to see. In Figure 3.1d, for example, it is only because we have learned the alphabet and the number sequence that reading across or down leads us to expect (and thus to see) a number or a letter. In Figure 3.1b, our eyes have learned to see the converging lines as evidence of perspective (as in railway lines converging in the distance), so that the upper bar is seen as further away, and thus bigger, than the lower bar.

Visual jokes operate on a similar principle: a visual pattern appears meaningless until we are told a verbal context. For example, does either of the patterns in Figure 3.2 mean anything to you? They did not to me, until I was told that one was a giraffe walking past a window, and the other was a man playing a trombone in a telephone booth. With the added context, both become pictures!

Sometimes our skills trip us up. In the "Apple a Day" example we saw earlier, it is precisely our skill as readers that makes it hard for us

Figure 3.1.   Context and Visual Perception

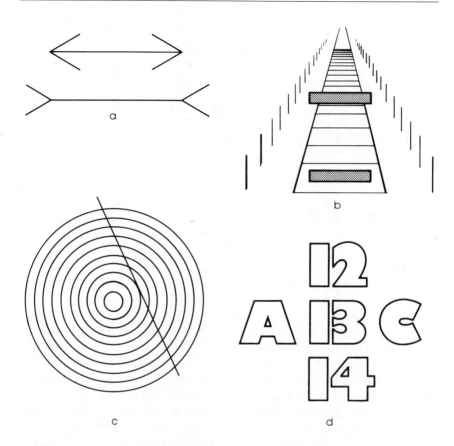

to notice the repeated word. We read not by pondering every word, but by sampling and filling in. We see "apple," "day," and "doctor," and the whole sentence clicks into place—which makes us efficient readers, but inefficient error-spotters. Similarly, in the "Count the Fs" example, we are particularly liable to miss the F in the word "OF." As skilled readers, we treat "OF" as a single symbol, not as two letters—and make mistakes in our letter-counting as a result.

Selective Perception and Professional Training

It should be emphasized that these effects are not confined to visual tricks and illusions. Our professional skills and interests lead us to see things in a certain way, highlighting some features and playing down others. A study by Dearborn and Simon (1953) demonstrates this process. They gave a group of twenty-three executives a long case study to

Figure 3.2.   Meaningless Patterns?

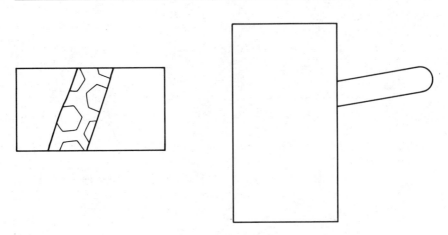

read as part of a training program. The case provides a great deal of factual material about a moderate-size steel company, but little evaluation or interpretation. When the executives were asked to describe what they saw as the steel company's major problem, their answers strongly reflected the departments each represented. Sales managers tended to see sales problems, production managers saw problems with "clarifying the organization," and so on. What we see is influenced both by what we expect to see and by what we are skilled at seeing.

Such "selective perception" is much more likely as we move away from the simple world of black-and-white pictures we have been using as illustrations. As the Dearborn and Simon study suggests, complex situations can be looked at from various perspectives, and the perspective one chooses has a strong influence on the problem formulation processes discussed in Chapter 2. Suppose, for example, that a group of engineering professionals were asked to come up with solutions to the problem of automobile fatalities—the fact that over 50,000 people die on American roads every year. We might expect each engineer to formulate this problem in a different way. For example, a mechanical engineer might think in terms of designing a more crash-resistant car; an electrical engineer might think in terms of proximity sensors or automatic control systems; a civil engineer might consider alternative highway designs with better vehicle separation or cushioned bridge abutments; a chemical engineer might think of devices to detect alcohol on the driver's breath. Each specialist would likely formulate the problem in terms of his or her particular expertise. The group would clearly have a lot of work to do before they could come up with a single definition of the problem they could all share. The selective perception of each individual would get in the way of a shared formulation.

What makes the problem worse is that, in addition to seeing things a certain way, we tend to get "locked in" to our way of seeing. For another visual example, look at Figure 3.3*a* (known as a Necker cube). Most people have no trouble organizing this set of lines into a sketch of a cube. But which cube do you see? Is the shaded face the one nearest you, or is it away from you? With a bit of effort, you can switch from one to the other, but it is almost impossible to see both at once. Once you have seen it one way, it takes a real effort to see it another. Similarly, in Figure 3.3*b*, you may see a rather ugly black vase against a white background, or two profiled faces in white against a black background. You may even be able to switch from one to the other, but you tend to "lock on" to what you see.

This active organizing of the incoming information is perhaps the most important, and the most complex, aspect of perception. As pointed out at the beginning of this chapter, it is wrong to think of perception as a neutral, objective gathering of data. Instead, we need to be aware of how actively we are involved and how much "sense-making" we do. We are all so "good" at this, and do it so automatically, that it is hard to notice unless we are confronted with something unusual—such as a colleague who sees something different from us, but just as clearly. But what we see, and the way we make sense of it, depends heavily on us, our skills, motivations, personalities, experiences, and interests. Jerome Bruner did a beautiful little study in which he simply asked children to draw a picture of a dime. He found that, on the average, rich children drew the coin smaller than did poor children—it was, quite simply, "less money" to them. The children's needs and motivations affected what they perceived.

There are many well-known stories in which problems that appear insoluble when the situation is perceived in one way are readily solved when the perspective is shifted. In one such story, the manager of a

Figure 3.3. Two Ambiguous Drawings

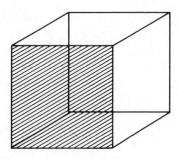 

large hotel hired a group of consulting engineers to try to solve a problem. The hotel guests were complaining about excessive delays in waiting for elevators. The engineers tried various approaches. Could the elevators be made to run faster? They could not. Could they be scheduled to stop only at floors where the queues of guests were longest? After much complicated computer modeling, this approach helped a little, but the complaints kept coming. Finally, one of the group, stepping outside the professional way of looking at the situation, suggested that the manager simply install large mirrors next to each elevator door. Amazingly, the complaints stopped almost immediately! Apparently the mirrors provided the waiting guests with enough distraction that they didn't notice how long they had to wait. Stories such as this have a useful function in reminding us that there may be more than one productive way to look at a situation!

Perceiving Other People

If perceiving a fixed object turns out to be a complex, active process, it is not surprising that the process becomes still more complex when the focus of our perception is another person. People are complicated, and so are our perceptions of them. We perceive a wide range of traits quickly: how friendly the person is, how rich, how well educated, how honest, how attractive. Secondly, people (deliberately or not) distort our perceptions of them. They may try to appear as friendly or honest, when they are not. Furthermore, we process a range of information about others which they are not aware of sending us. Tone of voice, body posture, amount of eye contact, and so on, all affect our perceptions, though they are generally not within the awareness of either person. Finally, we are generally forming our impressions at the same time that we are interacting, and thus changing what the other is sending to us. If we perceive someone as friendly, and are friendly toward them, they are likely to be friendly back, confirming our original impression. If we perceive someone as unfriendly, we are cool and unfriendly toward them, or may stop interacting altogether. Again, this tends to confirm our original impressions.

Since person perception is both complex and important, a great deal of research has been aimed at understanding the process (see Zalkind and Costello [1962] for a useful review). Here we cannot do more than sample a few of the highlights of what this research has shown. One common theme in much of this research is our tendency to go far beyond the data we have in creating an impression of another person. From a single photograph, or a single brief meeting, we form quite strong and often stable impressions of a person's characteristics, personality, work habits, and a host of other features. These cannot possibly be solidly based in the data we are given. We build sky-scrapers of understanding from tiny scraps of raw data. It is clear that much of the building material comes from ourselves, and from the situation, not from the person we are perceiving.

Stereotypes.   Suppose I am about to introduce you to someone you have never met before, and I tell you just one single descriptive word about the stranger: that (s)he is, say, a professor, a Pole, a black person, a jock, a blonde, a union steward, a stamp collector, a psychologist. Chances are that just this one word will trigger a whole set of expectations for you about what the person is going to be like—and these expectations may well overwhelm your impressions of the person when you actually meet him or her. These ready-made packages of expectations and attributions, typically triggered by a single descriptor, are "stereotypes." They are an important part of what we, the perceivers, bring to the perception of someone else.

It should be noted that stereotypes are not necessarily hostile to the group we label with them. The word originated in printing, as a method of making metal printing plates. Pictures printed by this process are not favorable or unfavorable: they are simply *all the same.* In perception, then, our stereotypes of "engineer" or "professor" do not necessarily imply that we like or dislike all engineers or professors. They simply imply that we tend to see them as all the same. Bigoted people may think that all members of particular racial or ethnic groups are much the same, and be prejudiced against all equally. On the other hand, we may hold stereotypes of groups toward which we have favorable feelings. The problem with stereotypes is not that they reflect hostility, but that they lead us far beyond the data we actually have about a particular person into assuming all sorts of other things we cannot possibly know. Instead of a unique human being, we see an example of a preformed, prepackaged category.

An example may suggest the difficulties stereotyping leads to in organizational life. Haire (1955) showed an identical photograph to groups of managers and union people, telling them only that the photograph was of either a manager or a union representative. Changing labels made a sharp difference in the impressions each group formed of the individual. For example, far more of the managers described the person as "honest" when he was labeled as a manager than when he was labeled as a union leader. Similarly, each group felt the person in the photograph was more trustworthy, reasonable, and able to see the other's point of view when labeled as a member of their group than as a member of the other. It seems clear that this "good guys/bad guys" stereotyping would make union–management negotiation more difficult. The assumption that "they're all the same" does not help one to form an honest, one-to-one working relationship.

Halo Effect.   A second simplifying, and distorting, trap we often fall into in forming impressions of others is called "halo effect." If we like someone, we tend to see them as more intelligent, more attractive, more honest, and so on. If we dislike them, we tend to see them as less intelligent, attractive, honest, and so on. That is, where stereotyping leads us to think that "all X's are alike," halo effect leads us to think that "good characteristics all go together." Again, the detail of a particular individual is blurred into a hazy (and unjustified) simplified image.

Halo effect is an important source of error in situations where we rate other people on a range of traits and abilities. For example, in job interviews, the interviewer who finds the applicant attractive may overrate job-related skills, intelligence, or experience. Friendly students may get higher grades in class than their work deserves, if the teacher allows the halo effect to carry over into appraisals of in-class performance. On a job satisfaction questionnaire, employees who basically like their jobs tend to give high ratings to all aspects of it, even those aspects that are not especially good. Conversely, employees who do not like their jobs tend to be negative even on the few positive aspects of their work.

This is not to suggest that we are unable to distinguish one trait from another, and assess each separately. The halo effect is a common tendency, not an iron law. It seems to operate most sharply (1) when the trait is one for which the corresponding behavior is least obvious (how do you expect someone who is "warm" to behave?); (2) when we are judging traits that we know little about; and (3) when the trait has some sort of moral overtone (for example, "honest" or "generous") (Bruner and Taguiri, 1954). A study by Grove and Kerr (1951) found that employees of a financially troubled company were so worried that their insecurity haloed over into their assessments of the company's pay and working conditions, which were objectively quite good. Thus, once we have formed an impression on some central characteristic, our assessments of less central matters are likely to be influenced by the halo effect.

Perceptual Defense.   From what we have said thus far, it is clear that our perceptual processes are heavily biased toward consistency. We tend to see what we expect to see, and to make different things fit together into a consistent overall image. There is evidence that we actively tune out inconsistent or threatening information to defend ourselves against disturbing events. This process of creating blinders to filter out disturbing data is known as "perceptual defense." For example:

For most college students, the characteristic *intelligent* is inconsistent with their stereotype of a factory worker. Haire and Grunes (1950) studied the reactions of a group of students told that a particular factory worker was, in fact, intelligent. They found four common reactions. A very few of the students admitted that they found the description inconsistent or conflicting. They recognized the conflict, but did not change their stereotype. A second group denied the characterization and clung onto their belief that factory workers are not intelligent. But the two commonest reactions were either (1) to wall off the new information, with only a slight change in the remainder of the image; or, (2) to invent other characteristics to make intelligence consistent with a largely unchanged stereotype. For example, "lack of initiative" was added to the image, so that the imaginary worker could be "intelligent" (as described), but somehow having an offsetting handicap to keep the stereotype consistent.

Characteristics of Perceiver and Perceived

In the review mentioned earlier, Zalkind and Costello noted a number of characteristics of the two people involved—the perceiver and the person being perceived—that tend to influence perceptions. First, knowing and accepting oneself makes it easier to perceive others accurately. Also, person perception is not a single skill: we may be very good at judging one set of traits, such as work skills and habits, and very bad at judging others, such as honesty or generosity. Our perceptions of others are also often shaped by our own characteristics. In extreme form, this is known as "projection," a defense mechanism in which we attribute to someone else undesirable feelings in ourselves. For example, an old study by Murray (1933) showed that people who had just finished playing a dramatic game called "Murder" were much more likely to attribute maliciousness to people in a set of photographs than were other people seeing the photographs without having played the game. We are quick to see our own faults in others, and to allow our own emotional state to influence our judgments of other people.

In organizational settings, our perceptions are also influenced by the other person's status and role. For example, Thibaut and Riecken (1955) have shown that two people acting in the same way are perceived differently depending on whether their status is high or low. A senior person acting cooperatively is seen as *wanting* to cooperate, a junior person doing exactly the same is seen as *having* to cooperate. There also seem to be differences from one role to another. If the director of research argues for increased R&D spending, (s)he might be seen as self-interested. If the director of marketing does the same, a quite different impression results—the argument may, in fact, be much more persuasive (Walster, Aronson, and Abrahams, 1966).

SUMMARY

We have tried to show that perception, the process of registering the outside world, is not as straightforward as it seems. Far from a simple collection of raw data, perception is an active process involving the stimulus, the perceiver, and the context. We are affected by the size, intensity, repetition, contrast, novelty, and motion of inanimate stimuli. The context in which the stimulus appears also shapes our perception, as in the visual illusions where objects appear different when placed against different backgrounds. Finally, characteristics of ourselves, the perceivers, affect what we perceive. Our skills, expectations, training, needs, and motivations can all lead us to perceive things in different ways. Once we have seen something in one way, it is very difficult to reorganize our perceptions: we tend to become locked in.

The process of perception is still more complex when the stimulus is another person. First, since our perceptions shape our behavior, and our behavior in turn affects the other person's behavior, we can get into self-fulfilling prophecies. If I expect you to be friendly, it is more likely that you will, in fact, act in a friendly way. Second, we all have stereotypes of other groups of people, and these lead us to expect all members of a group to be similar. Third, the halo effect colors our perceptions so that we tend to expect another person's characteristics to hang together consistently. We expect attractive people to also be intelligent, friendly, and generous, and unattractive people to show less of these desirable characteristics—quite wrongly, of course.

As in object perception, we tend to hang on to our perceptions of people, even when we receive information that does not fit. This process is called perceptual defense.

Characteristics of the two people involved, and of the context in which they interact, also affect person perception. Self-knowledge and acceptance seem to make us more accurate perceivers of others, though person perception is not a single skill—we may be good at judging some traits, bad at judging others. "Projection" is the label for our tendency to see in someone else our own characteristics or emotional states. Finally, and of particular interest in organizational settings, our perceptions are influenced by the other person's role and status.

What all this suggests is that perception, far from being the simple matter of gathering facts about the outside world, is a complex, active, and error-prone process. The data we collect is anything but "raw," in fact, it is thoroughly "cooked," in many cases. In the second section of this chapter, on "inference," we will look at another group of processes that can leave us with mistaken understandings of what is going on.

INFERENCE: COMMON SENSE AND FORMAL INFERENCE

Once we have gathered some information by perception, we typically want to reach a conclusion from it. Given these symptoms, what disease is present? Given these meter readings, what can we infer about the test sample? Given this sequence of events, which driver was at fault? Obviously, we make inferences of this sort every day. How good are we at doing so?

A useful way to approach this question is to compare our performance as "common-sense scientists" with that of more formal scientists. By "common-sense science" is meant our everyday efforts to find out what is true in the world, so that we can make sensible decisions. Does drinking orange juice reduce the number of colds we get? Does the Speedo Super-Graphite racket improve our racket-ball game? Does attending the lectures help us to learn differential equations, or is spending the time working the problems just as good? In each case one could easily think of a formal science experiment that would leave us with pretty confident answers. But in everyday life we arrive at beliefs about these and a host of other matters without doing such formal science. We just weight up the evidence that comes to hand and draw our inferences. We act, in other words, as "common-sense scientists" or, what amounts to much the same, as "intuitive statisticians." (Note that each of the problems above involves a probabilistic rather than a deterministic answer; no one expects orange juice, new rackets, or changed study habits to work all the time for everyone.) How well do we do?

Up till about ten years ago, the research evidence mainly suggested that we do pretty well. Recently, however, a number of studies have shown that we are prone to important errors and biases in estimating uncertain quantities and predicting uncertain futures. As with our earlier discussion of perception, it seems that the processes that allow us to do well in most circumstances also routinely trip us up in particular areas. We shall here review what is known about these processes, and sketch how they may lead us astray.

Heuristics

Several researchers, notably Amos Tversky and Daniel Kahneman, have explored the ways in which we go about probabilistic inference tasks. They have identified three common rules of thumb, or "heuristic principles," that people commonly follow: representativeness, availability, and anchor-and-adjustment.

Representativeness.   Suppose you see me walking across the campus accompanied by a man who is in his thirties, suntanned, dressed in tennis gear, carries a tennis racket, and is not smoking. Is my companion a tennis professional or a fellow engineering professor? You cannot be sure, of course, but what is your guess?

Most people would guess "tennis pro." But, when you think about it, that is a pretty poor guess. There tend to be fairly few tennis pros walking around a university campus, but there are many engineering professors. Further, since you know that I am an engineering professor, it is even more likely that my friends will be too. And plenty of people play tennis (or at least walk around looking as if they do), even engineers.

What seems to mislead us in judgments of this sort is what is called the "representativeness" heuristic. We expect small samples of a process or class to be "representative of," or to resemble, the process or class they come from. We have stereotypes of what engineering professors and tennis pros look like. When we see someone who is *similar to* our stereotype, we judge it *likely* that the person is one of the stereotyped class. In doing so, we ignore other relevant information that is far more useful—in this case, the information that I am an engineering professor, and on a university campus, so that it is entirely likely that the person I am walking with is a colleague, not an outsider.

There seem to be two things going on here. One is that we expect small samples to be more representative of their underlying process than they actually are. The second is that the appearance of similarity overwhelms the other relevant information we have available. If, in the above example, I tell you nothing about my friend, most people will bet with the "base rate" and guess that he is a professor. Now, how much *extra* information have you got when you learn he is dressed for tennis? Not all that much, surely? It is, of course, a bit more likely that you will find a tennis pro in tennis clothes than an engineering professor; but hardly enough to outweigh the strong probability you formed before you had any information on appearance.

It is, of course, perfectly valid to expect samples to reflect the populations they come from. But, as sampling theory tells us, the resemblance need not be very close, especially for small samples. Our intuition here seems to be poor: we expect small samples to mirror population characteristics more closely than they actually do. For example:

Male and female babies are about equally likely to be born. Even with 50:50 odds, you would not be surprised that, on a given day, a particular hospital delivered 60 percent male and 40 percent female babies. Are 60:40 days commoner at large or at small hospitals?

Most people who have not studied sampling theory guess 60:40 days about equally likely at large or small hospitals; they both seem equally far from the population mean of 50:50. In fact, they are much more likely at small hospitals, since the sample size there is smaller, and wide variations from the mean are more likely.

We seem generally to have poor intuitions about what we should expect from random processes. A familiar example is the "gambler's fallacy," the belief that, after a long run of black numbers on a roulette wheel, a red is to be expected, so that the totals of reds and blacks will become more "representative" of the underlying fairness of the wheel. In fact, of course, chance is not "self-correcting" in this way. The unusual run of blacks will not be *corrected* by a subsequent run of reds, it will merely be *diluted* by subsequent turns.

In addition to our misconceptions about chance mechanisms and about the effects of sample sizes, other common biases appear to turn on the representativeness heuristic. We routinely ignore the limits on predictability. For example, we tend to predict that people who do very well in class (say, in the top 5 percent) will do equally well (that is, in the top 5 percent) in their jobs ten years later, despite everything we know about how poorly school performance can predict on-the-job performance. Again, we seem to expect one sample of behavior (excellent job performance) to be highly representative of another (excellent school performance). Similarly, almost all employers persist in using selection interviews despite the enormous evidence that they have essentially no predictive value. Again, they seem to expect one sample of behavior (how we act in a one-hour interview, under abnormal conditions) to be highly representative of another (how we will perform on the job).

A final, and rather subtle, example of the biases that can be caused by overuse or misuse of the representative heuristic is in what is called the "regression fallacy." One form of this fallacy is reflected in the (actually sound) advice that you should, whenever possible, take over an operation that has recently done particularly poorly. Chances are that, even if you are not a brilliant manager, performance will improve. Similarly, if you want to sell a certain brand of toothpaste, try it out on patients who have an unusually high number of cavities. Chances are that any extreme point on a time series will be followed by lower values next time. Regression toward the mean will generally imply that any extremely high, or extremely low, value will tend to be followed by one nearer the mean. Poor performance figures tend to turn up, high cavity counts tend to turn down, and, in each case, the statistical cheat can claim not just success, but success with the toughest cases!

Tversky and Kahneman (1974) note a particularly worrying implication of this widespread failure to develop correct intuitions about regression effects. Suppose you are in charge of training novices at some difficult task, and you believe (contrary to most scientific evidence) that people learn best when they are punished for their failures, not when they are praised for their successes. Regression effects will tend to give you data "confirming" your theory. After a failure, you punish the individual, and he or she will, on the average, perform better next time, but because of regression to the mean, not because of your punishment. Conversely, after an exceptionally good performance, people will tend to do worse the next time (again, regressing to their mean performance). If you praised them for the exceptional performance, you may infer (again, falsely) that praise leads to poorer performance.

Availability.   Are there more cats or dogs in your neighborhood? Are there more people in your town over six feet tall than under five feet? Are most of the cars on the road today U.S. made or imported? The way we usually try to answer such questions without doing serious research is to think about those examples we can bring to mind. Take cars. You mentally go down the list of people you know who own cars, and estimate a rough percentage of U.S. and imported. This is, in general, a perfectly sensible procedure. Classes in which you can readily think of lots of examples are generally larger than classes of which you can think of few. How readily you can think of examples—how "available" examples are to you—is a good rough-and-ready guide to how frequent or likely the class is.

Availability is, of course, not a perfect guide, and it can get us into serious trouble. For example, I was sure George McGovern was going to win the 1972 election. Virtually all my friends were enthusiastic McGovern supporters and, though I knew they were not exactly a random sample of the population, it was easy to think of examples of "McGovern supporter," and hard to think of an example "Nixon supporter" whom I knew. As you may recall, Nixon won the election by a large margin.

This suggests one of the more obvious biases on availability as a guide to frequency: the sample of examples we can bring to mind is biased. Sometimes we realize this and make allowances (though, as we shall see in the next section, we generally do not make enough allowances). If the first question above were "Are there more cats or moles in your neighborhood?" you would realize right away that examples would be a poor guide. Even if the place is teeming with moles, you do not expect to see many. But sometimes the bias is less obvious. For example, in English, are there more words that start with the letter r or that have an r in the third position? Since we can readily cluster words by their first letter, we have no trouble thinking of dozens of words that start with an r. However, it is rather more difficult to bring to mind words with an r in third place, since our mental dictionaries do not work that way. So we conclude that there are more first-place r words—wrongly, as it turns out.

Another factor that influences the availability of examples is, of course, how likely we are to remember the examples in the first place. We remember the dramatic, vivid, salient single incident while we forget the dozens of routine, dull pallid counterexamples. The careful detailed statistics on how reliable a particular car is get overwhelmed by the single dramatic story from a friend of all the troubles he had with that car. People drive more carefully just after seeing a wreck, although they ignore the daily dangers of driving. People tend to over-estimate the risk of death from dramatic causes and those heavily reported in the newspapers (such as homicide), and underestimate causes that seem less dramatic, or are less often emphasized in the news media. In each case, the ease with which we can think of exam-ples biases our assessment of the probability, even when ease is a product of something other than frequency of occurrence.

Anchoring and Adjustment.   A third useful rule of thumb that can sometimes trip us up is to make a first rough estimate and then adjust it in light of the evidence. Suppose, for example, I were to ask you to esti-mate what percentage of current engineering undergraduates are women. You might start by guessing, e.g., 2 percent, and then revising. Perhaps you recall seeing one engineering class with maybe half a dozen women out of forty or fifty. This suggests that you should revise your first guess upward. Alternatively, if you first guessed 50 percent, recalling the same class would suggest that you should revise your estimate down. (The correct figure, by the way, is currently around 18 percent.)

The trouble with this anchor-and-adjust procedure is that we may tend to weight the anchor too heavily and adjust too little. For example, Tversky and Kahneman (1974) showed that, even when the starting point is generated by an obviously random mechanism such as a wheel of fortune, final estimates are strongly influenced by it. We typically revise our judgments in the right direction from the starting point, but not enough.

As an example, suppose you are in charge of two machines, each of which produces one-third defective parts in normal operations. One machine has developed a problem and is producing two-thirds defec-tives. A silly record-keeping slip has confused the records and you can-not tell which machine is which—that is, if I pick either machine, you would bet me 50:50 that it is the high-defect machine. What odds would you give me if we now looked at a sample of five parts from the machine, and found four defectives? This sample certainly suggests that I have picked the high-defects machine, but how sure can we be? Would you bet me 2:1? 3:1? 5:1?

Most people shift their initial 50:50 estimates too little in light of this sample. The true odds are 8:1 for the sample described; we can be pretty confident that we are sampling from the high-defects machine, but we learn less from the sample than we should, and bet only 3 or 4 to 1.

To check your intuition again, how would you bet if the sample was of twenty parts, and twelve turned out defective? Again, most people shift their odds in favor of the high-defects hypothesis, but not enough. (The correct odds here are 16:1—the sample is even more informative than the first one.)

The phenomenon of revising our estimates in the appropriate direction, but not by a large enough amount, is called "conservatism" (a technical word, not the same as political conservatism!). The discovery of this phenomenon (Edwards, 1965) was one of the first serious attacks on our abilities as "intuitive statisticians." In the present context it serves to underline the basic trap of using the anchor-and-adjust method of making estimates. The procedure is a sensible one, but we tend to give the anchor too much weight, and adjust too little.

Other Inferential Errors

In addition to the three "judgmental heuristics" we have looked at so far—representativeness, availability, and anchor-and-adjust—recent research has identified a number of other weaknesses in our intuitive inferences. We cannot examine these in detail (Hogarth [1980] is a good introductory source for a survey), but three areas seem to have important organizational implications, and should be noted briefly:

Overconfidence.   Oskamp (1965) reports a simple little experiment with a suggestive result. He gave psychiatrists four-page descriptions of psychiatric patients and asked them, after reading each page, to make a diagnosis and also to rate their confidence in it. He found that the diagnoses after reading only one page were as good as those reached after all four pages. Confidence, however, went on increasing with each page of information, finally becoming much too high—the doctors were guessing they would be right far more often than they actually were. In short, Oskamp's experiment (and several others) suggests that getting more and more information may not improve the accuracy of our inferences, but seems to increase our confidence in them.

Einhorn (1980) suggests that overconfidence in our judgments is common. He notes, for example, that we are often not in a good position to learn how accurate our predictions actually are, and that it would be costly to find out. For example, if we hire people into our company and the people we select usually do well, we tend to feel that our selection procedure is a sound one. However, that inference is suspect: if all the applicants are good, any procedure will produce the same results. We never find out how good the people we do not hire actually are.

They may be even better than the ones we hire. In short, we are not in a good position to learn about how good our judgment is in this case.

Einhorn also suggests an example of how we might contribute to fooling ourselves. Suppose you are a waiter at a busy restaurant, and work for tips. You probably have a hunch about who the good tippers are and make sure to give them good service. If so, you never find out if your hunch is any good. The people you thought were heavy tippers get good service, and tip well. The ones you thought were cheap get bad service, and tip badly. Your actions, as well as your judgments, influence the results. If you do not realize this, you will tend to be overconfident in how good your judgment is.

Mechanisms of this sort are everywhere in organizations. The boss rarely finds out that (s)he has made a bad decision, since most of us are reluctant to tell him or her. It is often hard to trace consequences to their causes, so we tend to pay attention to the positive results of our actions and play down the failures. We encourage subordinates whom we expect to do well and discourage those we expect to do badly. Just like the waiter in Einhorn's example, we take the later results as confirmation of our wisdom, forgetting that the results might just as plausibly be the result of our encouragement.

Assessing Correlation. We are surprisingly bad at assessing whether or not two variables are correlated. For example, suppose I were interested in whether engineering or nonengineering undergraduates do better in engineering graduate school. I look back through the school records, and come up with the following table:

| | | GRADUATE SCHOOL | |
		Success	Failure
UNDERGRADUATE MAJOR	Engineering	87	40
	Other	23	11

Do you see any relationship in these numbers between undergraduate major and graduate school success? Actually, there is none, but it is easy to be fooled. I could point out, for example, that almost 80 percent of our successes were engineering undergraduates—which sounds persuasive, until you realize that so were the same percentage of our failures.

Research (e.g., Ward and Jenkins, 1965) has shown that most of us do poorly in assessing associations between measures, even when they are presented in simple 2 × 2 tables such as that above. We seem to focus on the "positive hits" cell (the eighty-seven engineering undergraduate/graduate successes in the example), and forget that we need all four cells to infer association.

If we have trouble assessing covariation from a 2×2 table, think how much harder it is to do this in everyday life. Suppose you are curious to find if there is a relationship between people's clothes and their behavior—are well-dressed people less friendly than casually dressed people? First, the variables are not sharply defined: what, exactly, counts as "well-dressed" or "friendly"? Second, we do not get the relevant data all at once, as in the 2×2 table; it accumulates over time (or we dig it out of our memories, probably very selectively). Finally, our sampling is likely to be heavily biased. We are more likely to recall a vivid example (a particular aloof clotheshorse, or a very friendly slob) than the great mass of reasonably neat, reasonably friendly people we meet.

The evidence (e.g., Jennings, Amabile, and Ross, 1980) suggests that we are poor at assessing covariation in real-world settings. On the one hand, we are unlikely to notice even strong correlations unless we are specifically looking for them. On the other hand, if we believe two variables are correlated, we find "confirming" evidence even when there is none. For example, there is evidence that exercising just before going to bed delays getting to sleep. I believe exactly the opposite, and make a point of exercising before going to bed, to avoid insomnia. We all have dozens of these ill-founded beliefs. Most are probably harmless enough, but some may mislead us seriously. At the same time, we are probably missing many relationships that could help us significantly in our work and personal lives.

Attribution Errors.   Over the past decade or so, social psychologists have studied extensively one inferential process: how we attribute causes to what we observe people doing. This research has produced a mass of interesting findings and arguments, but it is too extensive to be reviewed here (see Jones [1979] for a useful introduction). We should, however, note one recurring theme in this work, a finding so basic that Ross (1977) refers to it as the "fundamental attribution error."

You observe an incident of behavior: a student racing through an exam, a car driver involved in a minor accident, a friend putting money in the Salvation Army collection box. How do you explain the behavior? In particular, do you tend to explain it in terms of something about the person (for example, their cleverness, their clumsiness, their generosity) or the situation (how easy the exam was, how small the parking space, how persuasive the request for money)? That is, do you tend to explain the behavior in terms of the person's disposition to behave that way, or in terms of the situation?

Obviously, reasonable explanations will involve both the people and the situations. Ross's argument, however, is that we frequently overemphasize the person's disposition and underemphasize the situational demands. This bias towards dispositional rather than situational explanations is the "fundamental attribution error." Where individual and situation interact to shape behavior, we are biased toward seeing aspects of the person as the key cause, not aspects of the situation.

Interestingly, this bias does not extend to our explanations of our own behavior. If I see you doing well on an exam, I am likely to explain your performance in terms of your ability, energy, or hard work. However, if I am doing well on the same exam, I tend to explain this in terms of how easy the exam is. When you give money I explain it by your generosity; when I give money, I explain it by the skill of the collector. Your car wreck is caused by your clumsiness; mine is caused by unfortunate circumstances.

The key here seems to be not just a self-serving tendency, but where we are placed as observers. Observing your behavior, I focus on you, and am led to explanations couched in terms of your character or disposition. Observing my own behavior, I focus on the situation around me, and construct my explanations from what I see. I observe my own behavior from the inside, but I observe yours from the outside. This shift in perspective yields different observations, and different explanations. We tend to judge others by their actions and ourselves by our intentions.

These attributional phenomena have broad and important implications for our organizational and personal lives. At the least, they suggest that we should be careful in assuming that other people do what they do because they are what they are—that is, in using exclusively dispositional sorts of explanations. If a subordinate performs poorly, we should not be too hasty to assume that (s)he is lazy or incompetent. We should train ourselves, instead, to look carefully at the situation. Are the tools and equipment working properly? Is the pay scheme reasonable? Are necessary raw materials flowing properly? We probably cannot do much to change people, but as managers we can do a lot to change situations. The findings from attribution theory strongly suggest that this is a powerful position to be in. The situation is probably more powerful than we think in changing behavior. If we can change it, we can probably get the behavior we want.

SUMMARY

In the second section of this chapter we have examined the possible failures of our inferences, paralleling the earlier examination of perceptual processes. We discussed three rules of thumb, or "judgmental heuristics," that we seem to use commonly in dealing with probabilistic situations. Using the "representativeness" heuristic, we draw conclusions from samples by the extent to which they resemble (or "represent") the properties of an assumed underlying population. The procedure is reasonable enough, except that we have poor intuitions about how close a resemblance to expect: small samples are poor guides to population characteristics.

The "availability" of examples is another reasonable rule of thumb for dealing with probabilistic inferences, but it can mislead us. Examples come to mind easily when we have good search procedures, or when they are dramatic or recent, as well as when they are objectively common. The third rule of thumb, "anchor-and-adjust," is another sensible procedure, but we tend to overweight the anchor and adjust too little in light of more specific evidence.

We also looked briefly at evidence for other biases and errors in our inference making. We tend to be overconfident in our inferences, we are poor at assessing covariation, and we tend to attribute other people's behavior too much to them and too little to the situation.

As a final comment, we should not be too hasty in taking the evidence on both perception and inference to suggest that "people are pretty dumb." Obviously, the studies we have looked at tend to report interesting failures of our information-gathering and sense-making abilities. It is not interesting to do studies that show that people most often do pretty well, though such cases are certainly much more common. What we have seen is that our abilities to learn about the world are not infallible, not that they are routinely terrible. The evidence should not lead us to throw up our hands. It should, in my view, make us a little more humble about our abilities, and a little more ready to use what help is available. After all, we can overcome many visual defects with the aid of a ruler, and we can overcome many inferential errors by using proper statistical procedures to supplement intuitive judgments. Our brains are remarkable instruments. They are capable even of inventing methods to overcome their deficiencies. We need to know what these methods are, and when to use them.

This chapter and the one immediately preceding have tried to lay out some of the basic ideas involved in a "cognitive" approach to studying organizations. Chapter 2 focused on how we process information once we have acquired it, in solving problems, choosing, and making decisions. Chapter 3 looked at the two basic processes, perception and inference, by which we gather information from the outside world and try to make sense of it. In the next chapter we will look at one of the most central decisions people make in their work lives: what they will work on, and how hard they will work—that is, motivation.

DISCUSSION QUESTIONS: CHAPTER 3

1. Highway engineers have developed various methods to get drivers to pay attention to warning signs. How do they use the six stimulus factors (size, intensity, repetition, contrast, novelty, and motion) to achieve this?

2. How do our professional training and skills affect our perceptions of a problem? For example, how might a mechanical engineer, an electrical engineer, and a civil engineer approach the problem of improving access to a building for handicapped people? What difficulties might these different approaches lead to if the three had to work together on the problem?

3. If you were asked to evaluate the job performance of a subordinate, how might your evaluation be distorted by: (a) stereotyping; (b) halo effect; (c) perceptual defense? What steps might you take to overcome these distortions?

4. What is meant by an "inferential heuristic"? Give a brief definition of: (a) the representativeness heuristic; (b) the availability heuristic; (c) the anchor-and-adjust heuristic. Give an example of a situation in which each heuristic might be used, and how it might affect our inferences. What might be done to overcome the resulting biases?

5. Why might our known tendencies toward: (a) overconfidence in our judgments; (b) poor ability to assess covariation; and (c) attributional errors lead to significant practical problems? Give an example for each.

Chapter 4

Motivation

PAST, PRESENT, AND FUTURE IN EXPLAINING MOTIVATION

If you spend more than a few minutes in any regular work setting, it quickly becomes obvious that some people get a lot more work done than others. One designer finishes a project in half a day, another takes all week. One programmer can write and debug a program in a quarter the time another takes. The observation is common enough that we might rarely stop to think about why this is so. But the differences are large, and they are important to the organization. If we can find a way to turn a high proportion of our employees into high performers, we are obviously on the road to being successful as an organization. The question of why some individuals perform better than others is the central question of the present chapter.

If we were to ask a high-performing employee why he or she was working so hard, we would probably get one of three kinds of answers: those relating to the past, those relating to the present, and those relating to the future.

Past-oriented explanations. "It's just a habit, I guess." "It was drilled into me as a child." Such answers direct our attention to things that have happened before we asked the question—perhaps a long time before. They remind us that people bring different histories to the job. The difficulty with such explanations, from a practical point of view, is that they do not suggest what we might do to change other employees' behavior.

Present-oriented explanations. "I find this job interesting and fun." "It's challenging to me to try to find a good way of solving this problem." These explanations focus on the here-and-now of the work, and they may give us some useful ideas as to how to change the work so that people will find it more interesting. For all too many jobs, however, it is hard to see how they could be changed to be made really interesting.

Future-oriented explanations. "I work hard because that's the way to make more money [or get ahead, or take care of my family]." Explanations of this sort direct attention to the employee's expectations about what the future consequences of working hard will be, what satisfactions working well will lead to.

All three kinds of explanations offer a partial understanding of why it is people do or do not work hard. In this chapter, we shall try to build at least the outlines of a theory of work motivation that includes all three sorts of explanations. As promised in Chapter 2, the core of this theory will be the expectancy model of individual choice. That is, we shall start by assuming that people choose some level of work effort, and that they do so in light of their evaluation of the consequences of that level of effort compared to others, and of their assessment of the likelihood that their effort will lead to those consequences.

THE EXPECTANCY MODEL

As a starting point, we shall first consider two examples of how the general ideas of the expectancy model might be applied to work-related choices. We shall then present a simple motivational model based on expectancy ideas. The rest of the chapter will be spent refining and extending that simple model to take account of some of the subtler aspects of work motivation. The full model is summarized at the end of the chapter.

Example 1: An Expectancy Model of Job Choice

Suppose you are coming to the end of a degree program, and have received two job offers. For simplicity, let's suppose they pay the same and are both in your area of interest. One is in New York, a large, well-established company offering lots of security and good travel opportunities around the country. The other is in Los Angeles, a small but promising company that is hoping to expand nationwide, but has not yet. Which job will you choose?

Applying the basic expectancy model idea of discounting consequences by their probability, we might structure the decision as follows. First, what are the relevant outcomes? We might specify four outcomes relevant to our job choice:

- 0_1: Live in a desirable location
- 0_2: Enjoy job security
- 0_3: Enjoy good travel opportunities
- 0_4: Prospect of rapid promotions.

Second, how desirable do you find each of these outcomes? Using a scale from $+5$ (highly desirable) to -5 (highly undesirable), with 0 as neutral or "Don't care," we can try to rate each of these four outcomes. This is, of course, a personal rating; there is no "right answer." For me, all four outcomes are desirable, but I would rate 0_1 and 0_3 (location and travel) as highly desirable ($+5$), 0_4 (promotions) rather less ($+3$), and 0_2 (job security) not very high ($+1$).

The third step, as usual, is to rate each of the jobs in terms of how likely each is to lead to each outcome. For example, I think I could find a desirable place to live in either Los Angeles or New York, but it would be more likely in New York: rate LA a 0.4 probability, New York a 0.8. From the description, job security seems more likely in the New York than the LA job: 0.9 for New York, 0.5 for LA. Working through the list of outcomes in this way, I might end up with a summary table:

EXPECTANCY JOB_i — $OUTCOME_j$

Job_1 (New York)	Job_2 (LA)	Outcome	Desirability
0.8	0.4	O_1: Live in desirable location	+5
0.9	0.5	O_2: Enjoy job security	+1
0.8	0.5	O_3: Good travel opportunities	+5
0.1	0.6	O_4: Good promotion prospects	+3

My net rating for the two jobs, then, is:

Job_1: $(5 \times .8) + (1 \times .9) + (5 \times .8) + (3 \times .1) = 9.2$

Job_2: $(5 \times .4) + (1 \times .5) + (5 \times .5) + (3 \times .6) = 6.8$

Clearly, Job_1, the New York offer, is more attractive to me. From the information summarized above, you would predict that I will be more strongly motivated to take Job_1 than Job_2.

There is evidence that such models do a reasonable job of predicting which jobs people choose. Vroom (1966), for example, used a model of this sort to predict the job choices of a group of business-administration students after graduation. Connolly and Vines (1976) found that a model of this sort correctly predicted about three-quarters of the choices made by a group of high-school students selecting an undergraduate college. (Note, incidentally, that building such models is directly useful to the organization. If we know what factors shape the decisions of people we try to hire, we can start to reshape our recruiting efforts to attract more of the candidates we want.)

The underlying model here is the simplest form of the expectancy model. It simply relates action choices to outcomes in a single step:

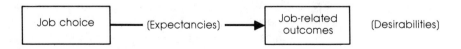

The model must be refined and extended to cover actual performance on a job, since it is rare to have a clear, direct choice between working well and working poorly. The next example suggests some of the refinements needed.

Example 2: An Expectancy Model of Job Performance

Once a person has chosen a job, we are interested in how well he or she will perform in it. However, the person cannot choose this directly. Rather, we should think of the person as choosing a level of effort to devote to the job (since this is largely under the person's control), and then think through how that level of effort gets translated into level of performance. This requires three extensions of our simple model:

1. We cannot assume that achieving a particular level of performance is the work-related outcome the person evaluates directly. At least part of the value we might place on performing well (or poorly) reflects our anticipation that such performance will lead to other rewards that we value: pay raises, promotions, praise from the boss, etc.

2. We cannot assume that increasing our level of effort will lead directly to increasing our performance. To work effectively, one needs both the ability to do the job and the motivation to do it well. There is nothing more frustrating than having a strong desire to improve one's performance, but not having the ability. For example, if I simply do not have the skills for a task, no amount of motivation will help. If the raw materials are not available when I need them, or if I work at a machine that runs on a fixed cycle-time, no amount of extra effort on my part will increase production. Organizational theorists often express this fact as

$$\text{Performance} = f(\text{Ability} \times \text{Motivation})$$

This is not to pretend that we know exactly what the function looks like, or can measure the variables accurately enough to estimate it. It is merely to remind ourselves that both motivation and ability are needed for performance. If either is zero, the product will be zero.

3. We cannot assume that performance increases linearly with motivation. If we try harder in a task, we will generally improve our performance—but only up to a point. I have reasonable driving skills, and would probably turn in fair lap-times driving a racing car on a proper circuit. If a moderate amount of money were at stake, I could push a little harder, and probably improve my lap-time. But if the amount of money were very large, I would probably push too hard for my skills, and either crash or drive less skillfully. We have probably all had the experience of "clutching" on important exams—getting so

highly motivated that we make silly mistakes or forget things we know well. We need to be sure that someone is undermotivated before we try to increase their motivation. For everyone on every task, there is some level at which they become overmotivated and performance starts to suffer.

To accommodate these additional factors, we need to extend our basic expectancy model into a two-step model. The first step looks at the individual's beliefs about how his or her level of work effort is related to level of work performance. The second step considers the person's beliefs about the relationship between each level of performance and subsequent work-related outcomes. Diagrammatically:

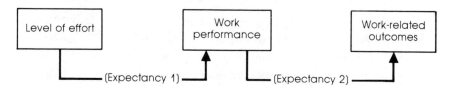

Note that there are two distinct expectancy terms in this model:

1. Expectancy 1 is the individual's belief that a given level of effort will lead to a given level of performance. This relationship is affected by factors such as the individual's ability, the resources and equipment available, and the point at which overmotivation occurs—although, as always, the model is primarily concerned with the individual's beliefs about this relationship, not about some "objective truth."

2. Expectancy 2 is the individual's belief that a given level of performance will lead to given levels of work-related outcomes. The central question here is what the individual believes about how the organization's reward system operates (which, again, may or may not accurately reflect what actually happens). A question such as "How likely is it that a very good job performance will earn you a 20 percent pay increase next year?" would tap Expectancy 2. In contrast, Expectancy 1 questions would be of the form "How likely is it that working very hard will lead to very good job performance?"

We can extend the earlier job choice example to illustrate this two-step expectancy model. Instead of already having job offers in hand, we are just starting to look for jobs, How much effort will we devote to the search? We might consider two alternatives: an "all-out effort" (trying to improve our grades, getting our resumés nicely printed, buying new clothes, practicing our interview skills, and so on), or a "moderate effort" (doing nothing special other than applying and doing a little background research on the companies we applied to). Given the same two companies as before, and the same expectancies (now labeled as Expectancy 2 terms), we saw that the New York job was more attractive than the LA job. But to measure Expectancy 1 we need to ask more questions:

How likely is it that an all-out effort will lead to an offer from the New York firm? From the LA firm?

How likely is it that a moderate effort will lead to an offer from the New York firm? From the LA firm?

Suppose I thought it quite likely that the LA firm would offer me a job regardless of my level of effort, so I score:

E1 (High effort → LA offer) = E1 (Moderate effort → LA offer) = 0.8

The New York firm, however, has a reputation for being rather snobbish, and may frown on applicants who appear too eager. Believing this, I might rate:

E1 (High effort → New York offer) = 0.2

and

E1 (Moderate effort → New York offer) = 0.6

Given the attractiveness ratings for the two jobs we developed earlier (9.2 for the New York job, 6.8 for the LA job), we can now compute the attractiveness of the two levels of search effort:

Value of high effort = (0.2 × 9.2) + (0.8 × 6.8) = 7.28

Value of moderate effort = (0.6 × 9.2) + (0.8 × 6.8) = 10.96

On these numbers, our prediction is that a moderate level of search effort will be chosen.

Summary: The Expectancy Model View of Motivation

At this point, it might be useful to pull together the ideas on motivation we have been discussing and state them a little more carefully. Essentially, the expectancy model considers motivation in terms of the net attractiveness to the individual of each of some action alternatives available. The options commonly considered are a range of levels of effort, so that an individual who finds high effort the most attractive option is said to be motivated toward high effort, and an individual who finds a lower level of effort more attractive is said to be motivated toward low effort. The same formulation can, as in our examples, be applied to other choices, such as those between alternative jobs or organizations.

The expectancy model treats the relative attractiveness of the various options as resulting from the individual's beliefs about the consequences to which each option will lead, and his or her evaluation of these consequences. In the work motivation context, it is often useful to distinguish two sorts of consequences: first-level outcomes, e.g., job performance; and second-level outcomes, that is, the rewards the individual receives as a result of particular levels of job performance.

The individual's beliefs are captured in the model by two expectancy terms. The first, Expectancy 1, taps the individual's beliefs that particular actions (such as choosing a level of work effort) will lead to particular first-level outcomes (such as a particular level of job performance). The second term, Expectancy 2, taps the individual's beliefs that first-level outcomes will lead to second-level outcomes (such as valued rewards). At each of the two stages, the model applies the "payoff-discounted-by-probability" rule to predict the effect on the individual of later, but uncertain, consequences.

We have been a little casual thus far in using terms such as "attractive" or "desirable" to refer to the person's valuing of outcomes. The technically correct term is "valence," the satisfaction the individual anticipates from receiving or avoiding an outcome. It is useful to have a technical term, to remind ourselves that anticipated satisfaction is not the same as the actual satisfaction we experience when we get the outcome—and it is anticipation, not experience, that matters in the expectancy model. In the next section, we shall look at how "valence" attaches to particular outcomes, as we look at the thinking of several authors on work-related needs.

THE VALUE OF OUTCOMES: NEEDS AND VALENCES

The expectancy model, as we have developed it thus far, considers only the *process* by which people choose where and how hard they will work. In this section we will look more closely at the *content* of these choices, asking specifically why it is that particular outcomes become attractive or unattractive to individuals. That is, we will go beyond simply asking people what consequences of their work-related behavior they find desirable or undesirable, and consider where these expressed values come from.

In expanding the expectancy model from Example 1 (the job choice) to Example 2 (the level of effort choice), we started to consider a chain of consequences flowing from a choice. We suggested that people find a particular outcome desirable because they think it will lead to other desirable outcomes, and so on. Jim reads the course assignments because he thinks it will help his grades, which will improve his chances of getting into graduate school, which will increase his later earnings, which will . . . The sequence has no obvious endpoint. The analyst makes an essentially arbitrary cut in the stream of consequences that follows from some action, defines consequences at that point as "outcomes," and tries to rate the attractiveness of these outcomes to the individual making the choice.

As we move farther and farther down the stream of consequences, we tend to formulate outcomes in terms of rather general, basic needs— broad categories of satisfactions that seem to drive very different behaviors. For example, we see a man spending his money on fashionable clothes, on a new sports car, and on a widely advertised after-shave lotion. We might well speculate that each behavior is motivated by sexual desire: these very different activities are all oriented toward the same goal of attracting female companions. Such broad, general categories of goals are labeled "needs."

Maslow: The Hierarchy of Needs

One of the most familiar theories of human needs is that suggested by Maslow (1943). Maslow suggests that human needs can be grouped into five broad categories; and that only one group is likely to be operating at a given time, with one group becoming active when a previously active one starts to become satisfied. The specific order of activation or "prepotency" is:

1. **Physiological needs:** food, water, sex, shelter
2. **Safety needs:** stockade, moat, castle, life insurance
3. **Social needs:** friendship, affection, love, belonging, acceptance
4. **Ego/esteem needs:** achievement, freedom, independence, status, recognition, prestige
5. **Self-actualization needs:** literally, making the "self" into something "actual"; achieving one's own unique humanity in some real way.

Maslow suggests that these groups of needs operate as a hierarchy, with the higher needs dormant until all the lower-level needs are satisfied. It would thus be odd (as, indeed, we tend to think of it) for a painter to be working on his or her masterpiece while all the lower needs like hunger were unsatisfied. As a general rule, people do not pay much attention to the higher-order needs unless their bellies are full, and likely to remain so.

Maslow's theory is a little difficult to weigh up empirically. Although we can think of exceptions, it does fit our experience pretty well: in the main, really hungry people do not get turned on to Mozart. As one need becomes satisfied, we do seem to move on to others: there is something crazy about people who habitually go on eating after they are well fed, or who spend all their time worrying about their safety when all obvious threats are taken care of. And it is hard to think of any specific need that cannot be mapped onto one of these five categories.

On the other hand, it's hard to think of any way to test the theory rigorously, since we cannot tell ahead of time, for any particular person, where (s)he will be on the hierarchy. We may guess that a certain person seems to be well taken care of at Levels 1 and 2 (physiological and safety), and thus predict that (s)he will be motivated by Level 3 (social) needs. If, however, we find a person mainly oriented to Level 5 (self-actualization) needs, then we have to assume either that the sequence is not working for them, or that they are easily satisfied at Levels 3 and 4. In strict form, the theory will withstand almost any particular set of data. Hall and Nougaim (1968) attempted to test the theory for a group of managers entering a large company, and found little support for the hierarchy notion. Their discussion of the problems in testing the theory is especially interesting. A more recent review of studies testing Maslow's theory, and also reaching generally negative conclusions, is given by Wahba and Bridwell (1976).

Without pretending that Maslow's theory is rigorously proved, we can draw two very important ideas from it. One is that many particular needs are powerful because of their links to several groupings in the hierarchy. Think, for example, of how effective money is in satisfying each class of needs. It seems very effective at Levels 1 and 2, somewhat effective at Levels 3 and 4, and only rarely effective (or even necessary) at Level 5. Money, then, is generally a strong need-satisfier (or has large positive valence), but less so as one moves up the hierarchy More generally, behavior is likely to be motivated by several different needs, not just one.

A second important implication is that satisfied needs do not motivate. For a professor operating at Level 4, an honorary degree might be a powerful motivator; after one has several, another such degree is likely to draw a "ho-hum" reaction. When one has no friends, acquiring a few is likely to be very important; when one has many friends, most of us find gaining a few more less important. When one is poor, money is a powerful motivator; when rich, it is generally less so. This tendency of active needs to shift with the degree to which they are satisfied has important implications for designers of organizational reward systems.

McClelland: Need for Achievement

A second theory of human needs important to organizational behavior is that developed by David McClelland and his collaborators (McClelland, 1961; McClelland and Burnham, 1976). This is a data-based theory, and the methodology is of some interest. You are shown a black-and-white picture of some situation. For example, one shows a man in shirt-sleeves, seated at a drawing board on which is a hazy photograph of a family group. The man is looking at this board thoughtfully. You are asked to write a five-minute story describing what is going on. The full test consists of six such pictures.

From the stories people write, McClelland has developed a fairly complex scoring scheme that measures which one of three basic motives shows up most often in an individual's stories. People whose stories tend to emphasize themes like getting things done, taking responsibility, solving problems, and getting results are scored high in "need for achievement," abbreviated as nAch. Stories that stress relationships with other people, social activities, and being in company, are scored high on "need for affiliation" or nAffil. Finally, people whose stories emphasize controlling other people, persuading, influencing others, and getting one's way, are scored high on "need for power" or nPower. Thus, by scoring all six stories, McClelland generates a set of three scores reflecting the relative strength of a person's needs in three important motivational areas: achievement, affiliation, and power.

A great deal of McClelland's research has explored what sorts of behavior are associated with high and low scores on each of these dimensions. For example, high nAch seems to be associated with people who:

1. Like situations where they take responsibility for solving problems
2. Prefer moderate risks to very high or low ones, and set moderate achievement goals
3. Like concrete feedback on how well they are doing.

As illustrations, McClelland (1961) shows that people scoring high on nAch prefer a problem involving their skills to a straight gambling game offering the same probability of success. That is, they prefer tasks involving their skills, where they take responsibility for results, to those involving just chance. Children with high nAch tend, in a ring-toss game, to stand far enough from the peg that they score about 50:50 hits. Low nAch children distribute themselves widely, some standing very close and getting all ringers, others standing a long way away, and rarely scoring.

A particularly interesting finding in McClelland's work is that high nAch seems to be characteristic of successful business people and entrepreneurs. Successful managers often score high on this need, while successful scientists, for example, are generally nearer to average on it. McClelland suggests that scientists often work in areas where significant results take many years to achieve, while managers live in a world where there is a great deal of quick, concrete feedback:

monthly sales figures, profit reports, etc. Thus, nAch seems to be a need for achievement of a particular kind. A Nobel prize is a major achievement—yet prize winners do not seem especially high in nAch, compared to successful managers. It is the combination of personal responsibility, moderate risks, and clear feedback that seems to turn on the high nAch person—precisely the characteristics of managerial work.

(This also provides an interesting view of money in the managerial world. The emphasis on financial results may be less a matter of simple greed than a way of getting clear feedback on how well one is doing. Interestingly, McClelland reports that successful government executives score as high on nAch as do private-sector executives. Providing concrete performance feedback in nonprofit organizations is clearly an important problem, if one is to keep these high nAchievers motivated.)

Herzberg: Motivators and Hygienes

A third theory of work-related needs is implicit in the work of Fredrick Herzberg (1968). Herzberg's research approach is simplicity itself. He and his co-workers simply asked a large number of people to describe incidents that had led them to feel especially satisfied, or especially dissatisfied, about their jobs. They then tabulated the responses to learn what sorts of factors were associated with each sort of incident.

One might expect that one set of factors would be a mirror image of the other. If getting a promotion led people to feel more satisfied with their jobs, then not getting a promotion would lead to dissatisfaction. Interestingly, this is not what Herzberg found. Instead, his data tend to show fairly little overlap between the two sets. Some factors, e.g., achievement, were frequently mentioned as causing satisfaction, but their absence was rarely mentioned as causing dissatisfaction. Conversely, matters to do with company policy and administration were often mentioned as causes of dissatisfaction, but rarely as causes of satisfaction.

These findings led Herzberg to propose what he calls a "two-factor theory" of work motivation. He argues that satisfaction and dissatisfaction are not really two ends of the same continuum, but two separate dimensions. The opposite of satisfaction is *no* satisfaction; the opposite of dissatisfaction is *no* dissatisfaction. (This appears to mean that one could be both highly satisfied and highly dissatisfied, at the same time, a problem Herzberg never resolves adequately.) Herzberg's terminology suggests what he has in mind. In personal health, attention to hygiene helps one to be free of disease—not positively healthy, just disease-free. By analogy, Herzberg calls the factors leading to dissatisfaction "hygienes." He refers to the other factors, those associated with satisfaction, as "motivators," suggesting that these are the things that really lead people to be turned on to their jobs. The major factors he lists under each group are:

Satisfiers or "Motivators"	Dissatisfiers or "Hygienes"
Achievement	Company policy and administration
Recognition	Supervision
The work itself	Relationships with super-
Responsibility	visors, peers, and
Advancement	subordinates
Growth	Working conditions
	Salary
	Personal life
	Status
	Security

As Herzberg points out, the satisfiers tend to be associated with the *content* of the job, while the dissatisfiers tend to be associated with its *context*.

Herzberg suggests that a two-level need hierarchy can be seen as underlying these groupings. The "hygienes" are associated with basic physiological needs (such as food, here represented by salary). The "motivators" are associated with achievement and psychological growth. Job characteristics that relate to one set of needs are largely irrelevant to the other. As Herzberg sees it, the design of jobs should first provide adequate levels of the hygiene factors, then focus on the motivators. Adding further hygienes to a job that is already adequate on these features will have no useful effect.

There are a number of problems with Herzberg's work. First, the theory is not stated very carefully. We noted earlier that people can be highly satisfied and highly dissatisfied at the same time. There is a slide from calling the positive factors "satisfiers" (i.e., leading to satisfaction) to calling them "motivators" (i.e., leading to high performance). We have plenty of evidence that performance and satisfaction do not necessarily go together, but the shift of terminology suggests that they do. A second problem is with Herzberg's reading of his own data. Salary, for example, is mentioned about equally often as a "turn-on" and as a "turn-off"; but Herzberg places salary firmly in the "hygiene" group, arguing that it is not central to good job design. Finally, although some other researchers have supported Herzberg's results, they have all used his technique of asking people to recall critical incidents. Other researchers who have tried other approaches have generally failed to replicate his results. (Several of these nonsupporting studies are reviewed by Dunnette, Campbell and Hakel [1967].) In short, although two-factor theory is frequently cited in management texts, it should be treated with considerable caution, in my view.

Summary: Outcomes, Needs, and Valances

Do these three theories, singly or together, leave us with a complete understanding of human needs and how they are satisfied at work? Clearly, the answer is "No." We need to learn a lot more before we can reliably predict what outcomes will affect the behavior of a particular individual in a particular setting. We need to know:

1. Whether needs are relatively stable characteristics of an individual (as McClelland suggests), whether they change slowly with normal growth and maturing (Maslow), or whether they are liable to change quite quickly as a function of the situation (as Herzberg seems to imply).

2. How to predict what specific outcomes will help to satisfy general categories of needs in specific settings. For this purpose, Herzberg is helpful, since his theory is derived from the specifics of real jobs. McClelland and Maslow are both more general; it is difficult to know what behaviors will satisfy a particular individual's "growth" needs, let alone his or her "self-actualization" needs.

On the other hand, we can learn useful lessons from these theories. First, they remind us that human behavior is likely to be determined by multiple needs. Anyone who declares, "The only thing that makes people work is . . ." is oversimplifying, regardless of what ends the sentence. Second, we are alerted to the fact that a person's active needs are likely to change from time to time, and from situation to situation. Finally, we should bear in mind that a theory of needs is not the same thing as a theory of motivation. The former may well give us an idea of what people will strive for. However, for a useful theory of motivation, we need a theory of how behavior is associated with these strivings. It is precisely this feature that makes the expectancy model so attractive. An individual's needs are included by means of his or her rating of the desirability or "valence" of the various outcomes. Actual behavior is included by means of the actions from which the individual chooses. And beliefs about the situational consequences of each action in satisfying each need (or attaining each outcome) are included by means of the expectancies linking actions to outcomes. The expectancy model thus provides a framework in which desires, beliefs, and actions can be accommodated. It emphasizes that any action is likely to have multiple consequences; and that any particular need can be satisfied in a variety of different ways. For all its imperfections, expectancy theory is a complete theory of motivation, in a way that theories of needs are not.

MODIFYING THE VALUE OF OUTCOMES

In the last section, we looked at the linkages between an individual's work-related outcomes and the more general needs that give these outcomes their motivational power. We will now consider some of the subtler aspects of how particular outcomes acquire value for an individual. First, we will look at the question of whether a particular outcome is built into the work (an "intrinsic" reward) or coupled to it externally by the organization's reward structure (an "extrinsic" reward). Second, we shall look at how the person's perception of the fairness or "equity" of a reward affects it value. Finally, we will look at some research on a simple but powerful procedure, the setting of explicit work goals, which seems to provide a motivational bonus for many people.

Intrinsic and Extrinsic Rewards

In the simple view of expectancy theory we have used so far, behavior is influenced by the expectation of future payoff. We study hard because we think that this action will later lead to some valued outcome, such as better grades or higher pay. There are, of course, other reasons for doing something, the most obvious of which is that it is fun, interesting, or enjoyable at the time. That is, some activities are "intrinsically" rewarding, as well as (or instead of) being "extrinsically" rewarding. For most engineers, for example, it is "intrinsically" rewarding to find out how some device works, or how to make it work better. They need no "extrinsic" reward to induce them to engage in such activity—indeed, it is often difficult to get them to stop endlessly refining adequate designs and turn them over for production. (Florman [1976] gives a delightful analysis of just what is so fascinating about engineering work.) In many skilled and professional jobs, such intrinsic rewards are an important part of what motivates people in their work.

The expectancy model can be readily extended to include these intrinsic rewards, and also helps explain why they are so powerful.

The basic logic of the model argues that people discount future outcomes by the probability of attaining them. Receiving a million-dollar bonus for some activity is highly desirable; but it will not affect your actions unless you think there is some probability greater than zero of your actions leading to the reward. With intrinsic rewards, however, there is no such discount. If you perform the activity, then you receive its intrinsic rewards (and punishments) for sure—that is what is meant by "intrinsic." If you enjoy running a computer, playing football, or managing a grocery store, the reward of enjoyment itself makes the activity more attractive to you, regardless of the extrinsic rewards and punishments that may also result. The expectancy model thus deals with intrinsic rewards by assigning them an expectancy of 1.0 for attaining the outcome by engaging in the relevant activity.

There is some evidence questioning this simple view. Suppose, for example, that you have loved playing baseball all your life and have unusual talent at the game—that is, that you find playing baseball intrinsically rewarding. Expectancy theory would predict that, if you are now also paid for playing, you will be even more motivated to play. The intrinsic reward (enjoyment) and the extrinsic reward (money) act additively. But does this prediction hold up in fact? There are certainly examples in the sports press of players who lose their intrinsic pleasure in playing the game when they start to get paid for it: when the paycheck stops, they stop playing.

Some studies by Deci in the early 1970s (Deci, 1971, 1972) tried to examine this question more carefully. Deci asked college students to solve a series of puzzles that he had proved earlier were intrinsically interesting. After a practice session, one group of students was told that they would be paid for solving the next group of puzzles, while the other half were not. Deci timed how long each group played with the puzzles during a rest session following this group of puzzles, arguing that interest would be reflected in this voluntary playing. He found that students who had been paid for solving the puzzles played less with them during their free time than did those who were not paid. It appeared that paying had the effect of reducing or eliminating the intrinsic interest of the puzzles.

For obvious reasons, these studies caused some flurry among motivation theorists. They raise the possibility that paying people for intrinsically interesting work tends to take all the fun out of the work, merely replacing the "free" motivation of intrinsic interest with the "expensive" motivation of payment. We need not review all the subsequent studies here (see Staw [1977] for a careful review). The central results are:

1. The effect found by Deci seems to be real, despite several criticisms of his original study.

2. The effect is found only when three conditions are satisfied: the task must be inherently interesting; the extrinsic rewards offered (e.g., pay) must be salient to the subjects; and the subjects should not expect to be paid ahead of time.

The three preconditions seem to limit the situations in which Deci's effect will be found in normal industrial work, which is often dull, and for which people expect to be paid. It may, however, be significant in voluntary organizations, such as social clubs, or in voluntary tasks (such as training apprentices) within industrial organizations. In such limited situations, the sad possibility exists that, by paying people to do certain activities, we may be destroying part of the intrinsic reward of the activities.

Equity Theory

Suppose your professor turns back to you a homework assignment with a grade of B. You felt you had done a pretty good job on it, and a B seems perfectly fair. Now, after class, you find that everyone else in the class made As, several for work that doesn't seem as good as yours. How do you feel about your B now? Would you feel differently if you found that everyone else had got Cs?

In fact, most people do feel rather differently about the rewards they receive for their work when they compare them to what others receive. A 10 percent salary increase seems flattering if everyone else in your group got zero, but most unflattering if everyone else got 20 percent. Thus, we have to introduce yet another refinement into our simple expectancy model. The "valence" of an outcome is not just a matter of one individual anticipating getting it. We need to include the different valences the same outcome might take on when compared to someone else's outcomes.

The underlying notion here is equity, the sense that something is fair. Note that it is not just a matter of some people getting more and others less. Most of us feel it is fair for someone else to make more money if they are doing more or better work than we are, or if they are better qualified, or perhaps if they have been on the job longer. Our sense of unfairness, or inequity, comes about when we feel that someone else is getting a better "deal"—getting more out for what they put in—than we are. Of course, inequity also exists when we are getting a better deal than is the person we compare with, but we may feel less upset when the inequity is on our side!

Several researchers have tried to clarify equity and inequity. The work of Adams (1965) in particular has been most influential in organizational behavior. Adams formulates the problem in terms of "inputs" and "outcomes," both defined rather broadly. One's "inputs" include such things as one's skills, qualifications, seniority, job effort, and personal characteristics; "outcomes" include both intrinsic and extrinsic job-related rewards. Given these broad definitions, Adams defines "equity" as a person's perception that his or her ratio of outcomes to inputs is the same as the ratio enjoyed by another person who is chosen as a basis for comparison. That is, one experiences equity when, in comparison with another person,

$$\frac{\text{Own outcomes}}{\text{Own inputs}} = \frac{\text{Comparison person's outcomes}}{\text{Comparison person's inputs}}$$

I may know that my division chief makes three times the salary I do, but still feel it to be fair if I judge him or her to be working harder, bearing more responsibility, or using greater skills, qualifications, or experience on the job than I do. I feel the comparison person's ratio of inputs and outcomes to be much the same as mine.

What happens when we feel inequitably treated? The basic prediction of equity theory is that the experience of inequity is unpleasant, and we try to do something about it. One obvious strategy is to shift the person we are comparing ourselves to. If I feel inequitably paid compared to my division chief, I can probably convince myself that (s)he is not really a fair comparison, since that is a very different job from mine. Perhaps I can find a more acceptable comparison in a colleague at my level, a comparison that reduces my feelings of inequity. This shifting of comparison people does seem to go on, but equity theory has had a difficult time predicting just how.

The theory has been much more successful (and much more interesting) in predicting how people react to inequities when the comparison level is not easily shifted. A number of experiments have been conducted in roughly the following format. Subjects are recruited (generally students) on the understanding that they will be paid a certain rate, either per hour or per piece. When they show up for the experiment, they are told that they will be paid more or less than this amount, generally with some cover story such as the experimenter having run out of money, or having excess money from the budget. The performance of subjects who have had their feeling of equity manipulated in this way is then compared with that of subjects paid the advertised rates.

The theory makes different predictions for over- and underpayment, depending on whether the pay is per hour or per piece. For example, if you are over-equitably paid by the hour, you can restore your feelings of equity by working harder, thus increasing your inputs to match your outcomes. This extra effort might increase either the quality or the quantity of your work, or both. Conversely, under-equitable hourly pay would lead to reduced job effort to restore equity. In piecework, however, the prediction is different. If you feel overpaid, you can restore equity only by improving quality; if you produce more, your earnings go up proportionally, and your ratio of outcomes to inputs remains the same. Conversely, in piecework underpayment, equity theory predicts that you will reduce quality while pushing up quantity.

There is a good deal of experimental evidence that people do, in fact, react to feelings of inequity in just these ways. (For a review, see Goodman and Friedman [1971].) Within the limits of laboratory experiments with student subjects, people who have been led to feel that they are being paid inequitably (either too much or too little) tend to adjust their inputs so as to restore equity. There is also some evidence (Penner, 1967) that people who feel inequitably paid tend to leave organizations much more than those who feel equitably paid. Though real-world studies are few in this area, there seems to be quite strong support for equity theory as summarized here.

The general idea of fairness follows what we would expect by common sense. We are all trained to have some idea of "what's fair," and to feel uncomfortable when we are dealt with unfairly. However, some of the findings of equity theory are not obvious, and could easily be useful. For example, suppose that you are put in charge of a manufacturing operation where the workers are paid on a piecework basis, and you find that quality is a nagging problem. Without equity theory, most of us would not think to connect the pay rate and the quality problem. Indeed, we might react the other way, reducing the rate per piece since most pieces were of marginal quality anyway. Equity theory would suggest getting at the quality problem by *raising* the rate per piece. Workers could then restore their feelings of equity by keeping quantity the same, but improving quality. I know of no real organization where this has been consciously tried as a proper experiment, but it certainly seems to be worth a try. One would, of course, want to monitor the effects of such a change over time. Most of us are pretty good at reevaluating our inputs so as to match any feelings of overpayment we may experience! Overall, equity theory is an appealing body of development in motivational theory. It picks up some commonsense notions, makes them a little more precise, demonstrates that, at least in the laboratory, unexpected effects can be reliably produced, and, finally, gives us some ideas to try out in the real world.

Goal Setting

In one of the oldest bad-news/good-news jokes, the pilot tells the passengers, "We're hopelessly lost—but we're making excellent time." Most of us can still raise a smile at that line; we know the feeling well. We find ourselves working hard, but not entirely clear as to what we are trying to accomplish. We have piles of data from our experiment, but find that we are not too clear on what the experiment was designed to discover. We spend an evening catching up on our technical reading, but the material slips away, since we had no clear purpose in our reading.

For most of us, the sense that we are unsure what we are trying to accomplish soon leads to a slackening of effort. Conversely, if we have a clear goal—solving a certain number of problems, testing a well-specified hypothesis in an experiment, producing a certain number of items—we find ourselves putting more energy into the task. In fact, this simple step of formulating clear goals has been shown, in a wide variety of situations, to have an important motivational effect. As we shall show in a moment, goal setting may be the critical ingredient in a number of the popular motivational techniques.

The laboratory experiments demonstrating the effectiveness of goal-setting are quite simple. Groups of subjects are put to work on a task: generating ideas by brainstorming, assembling Tinker Toys, doing arithmetic problems, or whatever. One group is given a vague goal ("Work hard," or "Do your best"), while the other is given a specific, numerical goal, such as how many toys they should aim to make, or how many ideas they should try to generate. The results are remarkably consistent: people assigned goals do better than those not assigned goals; and difficult goals are more effective than are easy ones. (A number of such studies are reviewed in Latham and Yukl [1975].)

If goal setting is so straightforward and effective, why has it not been tried before? Well, of course it has. Taylor's work on "scientific management" in the early 1900s emphasized setting very specific production goals (mainly for blue-collar workers). The goals were set with the aid of work measurement ("time and motion studies") and backed up with cash incentives. "Scientific management" seems to have been quite effective, if a little inhumane. More recently, the technique known as "management by objectives" (MBO) has emphasized the setting of clear goals and objectives, with careful monitoring of performance and planning for attainment. The core of both techniques may well be the fact that clear goals were set.

A strong body of evidence suggests that goal setting is a useful, and practicable, technique. A recent review by Latham and Locke (1979) includes ten studies, in field settings, of the effects of goal setting compared to nonspecific instructions like "Do your best." Substantial and sustained performance improvements were found in each case, with the goal-set group averaging about 17 percent better performance than nongoal-set groups. The technique seems to be both simple and effective.

Goal setting seems to be most effective when certain conditions are met. First, the goal must be (1) specific and (2) challenging. Second, the individual must accept the goal and believe that it is attainable. Acceptance is in part a function of how the goal is selected: records of previous performance, work study, company goals, and joint discussion may all have a place here. Acceptance also requires that the employee trust the supervisor, that the supervisor be helpful and supportive, and that the employee does not see goal setting as an attempt at exploitation. (Suitable financial incentives or other rewards may be helpful here.) Finally, the individual must have the skills and resources necessary to achieve the goal, and must get feedback on attainment. If these three conditions are met, evidence suggests that performance will be high, and that employees will feel pride and confidence in their level of achievement.

George Odiorne, a long-time promoter of MBO (Odiorne, 1965), tells a revealing anecdote on goal-setting. By unofficially letting a manager see a written copy of the specific goals his boss wanted him to achieve, Odiorne brought about a dramatic improvement in the manager's performance. The boss was very impressed, since he had always rated the manager as a poor performer, and wanted to know what Odiorne had done to bring about this improvement. When Odiorne confessed that he had let the manager see the (secret) list of the boss's goals, the boss exploded: "I knew it, the ***** cheated!" One wonders why the boss's goals should be a secret, since it seems clear that knowing what the goals are is a considerable help and incentive to achieving them.

OPERANT CONDITIONING: A CONTRASTING VIEW

We have thus far not mentioned one of the most famous names in motivation theory, B. F. Skinner, nor the "operant conditioning" techniques with which he is associated. These ideas are a little hard to integrate with the expectancy model, but not impossible. We shall first review the basic ideas of Skinner's approach, and then see how they might be fitted in with our other approaches.

Skinner rejects the idea that behavior can be explained in terms of such concepts as intentions, expectancies, and attitudes. Such things are not observable, he argues, and thus not useful for science. Instead, Skinner stresses the role of the environment in shaping behavior. Behavior is shaped by its consequences, not by our expectations about its consequences. Specifically, he is concerned with three classes of observables:

1. **Stimulus:** an observable event that leads to a response

2. **Response:** an observable unit of behavior following a stimulus

3. **Reinforcer:** a consequence of a response that changes the probability of the same response following the same stimulus in the future.

Note that none of these key terms involves thinking. They are simply observable events.

The basic result of the operant conditioning research, backed up by thousands of laboratory studies with animals and a growing body of evidence from humans, is this: if a particular stimulus-response pair is followed by a positive consequence, it is more likely that that stimulus will evoke the same response in the future. If the consequence is negative, that response to that stimulus becomes less likely. Reward increases the probability of getting the rewarded behavior, punishment reduces the probability.

The core of the operant conditioning technology is the use of consequences (rewards and punishments) to alter the strength of the linkage between stimuli and responses. *Operant learning* strengthens this linkage, either by *positive reinforcement* (giving something pleasant for the desired behavior) or *negative reinforcement* (removing something unpleasant for the desired behavior). *Extinction* is the process of weakening a particular stimulus-response link, and may occur in two different ways: by *removal of the reinforcers* for the response, or by the use of *punishment* for the response. Punishment tends to produce faster extinction than does mere nonreinforcement, but has undesirable side effects, as we shall see. Unfortunately, punishment seems to be the most widely used technique for shaping behavior.

So far, there is no real clash between Skinner and an expectancy theorist, except in the emphasis on thinking. Skinner stays away from hypothetical mental processes; an expectancy theorist sees them as essential. Both would agree that behavior is shaped by the "environmental contingencies" of behavior, with desirable consequences making a certain behavior more likely to occur and undesirable consequences making it less likely. However, there is an impressive body of data in the work of Skinner and others on what are called "reinforcement schedules" that does suggest some real, practical differences between the two approaches.

A "reinforcement schedule" refers to the relationship between responses and reinforcers. If you receive the reinforcer each and every time you perform the desired behavior, you are on what is called a "continuous" reinforcement schedule. If only some of the responses are reinforced, an "intermittent" reinforcement schedule is being used. Four such intermittent schedules are commonly used; they have different consequences in terms of learning and persistence.

1. **Fixed ratio:** Reinforcement is given every n^{th} response. For example, a fixed ratio of 3:1 would involve a reinforcer every third response. A money bonus paid for every tenth item produced would be such a schedule. This schedule produces strong response rates.

2. **Variable ratio:** Reinforcement is given *on the average* after every n responses. Many gambling machines provide a reinforcement schedule of this sort: a slot machines pays off, on the average, every n plays—but sometimes more, sometimes less often than n. Responses learned under such a schedule are regular and frequent, and also more resistant to extinction than when learned under fixed ratio schedules. This resistance to extinction surely helps enrich casino owners.

3. **Fixed interval:** Reinforcement is given for the first response after a fixed period of time. Response rates tend to be high immediately after the reinforcement, low otherwise. A regularly scheduled inspection, such as one encouraging visit per hour, might produce a fixed-interval response: high activity right after the boss's visit, low the rest of the time.

4. **Variable interval:** Like the fixed interval, but irregularly spaced to average out to a fixed period between reinforcements. Response rates here tend to be more regular than under fixed interval reinforcement. The boss still averages one visit an hour, but the visits are irregularly scheduled.

The evidence on the different effects of different reinforcement schedules indicates a limitation of expectancy theory. The latter clearly suggests that people act to maximize their gains, so that continuous reinforcement with large rewards would be most effective. However, excellent data show that intermittent reinforcement is more effective in maintaining a behavior once it has been learned (e.g., Yukl, Wexley, and Seymour, 1972). Obviously, we need to be cautious in applying the "payoff-discounted-by-probability" rule of expectancy theory.

The implications of operant conditioning theory for organizational reward systems have only recently been explored at all widely. (For examples, see Nord, 1969; Hamner and Hamner, 1976.) Without attempting any complete review, two such implications should be noted here:

1. **Use of punishment:** The use of punishment to reduce undesired behavior is probably more widespread than it is effective. It is, of course, effective in inducing someone to stop a specific behavior. Thus it is reinforcing for the user. For example, if a student starts reading a newspaper in one of my classes, a single sharp reprimand is usually enough to make him or her to stop—and I am reinforced by getting compliance, and am thus more likely to use the same approach the next time. However, punishment has several drawbacks. One is that there are generally lots of behaviors I do not want, but only one or a few that I do want. Getting the behavior I

want by extinguishing all the others one at a time is not efficient. Second, the student punished is likely to be angry and uncooperative, and may take some other opportunity to get back at me—forcing me into further responses, or even getting us into a fight. Finally, the other students are also punished, since few of us enjoy seeing another reprimanded, so I am likely to have an uncalculated impact on their behavior, too. In short, punishment as a way of shaping behavior is often ineffective. Better results are generally obtained by using a careful mixture of positive reinforcement and extinction by nonreinforcement.

2. **Design of pay systems:** The Skinnerians' close attention to the effects of different reinforcement schedules has numerous implications for how effective pay schemes should be designed. For example, the standard monthly salary with annual raises (often across-the-board, or close to it) is a poor scheme in reinforcement terms. The reinforcement is given on a fixed interval schedule, with long delay and often no connection between the desired behavior and the reinforcer. We would predict much stronger impact on behavior for a variable ratio scheme, administered on a much shorter time frame, and with pay increases contingent on desired performance.

In short, techniques based on operant conditioning are starting to have a real impact in the organizational world. Like expectancy theory, the techniques demand careful analysis both of the situation in which behavior occurs and of the consequences of behavior. The Skinnerians consider only observable events outside the individual; expectancy theory emphasizes the individual's desires, expectations, and choices. Despite this apparent difference, the two are very close in many practical respects (see Petrock and Gamboa [1976] for a careful analysis of the differences and similarities). The Skinnerians' data on the effects of different reinforcement schedules suggest that expectancy theory's simple treatment of probabilities needs refining. Overall, however, the two approaches seem more complementary than opposed.

A CAUTIONARY NOTE ON DESIGNING REWARD SYSTEMS

Both expectancy theory and operant conditioning theory remind us that people's behavior is shaped by its consequences. An organization's reward system is, essentially, a specification of what consequences will follow from particular behaviors: "If you work hard, you'll make a bonus"; "If you work here for twenty-five years, you'll get a gold watch"; "If you work too hard, you'll be rejected by your work group." (Note that both formal and informal reward systems are operating here.) Much evidence exists indicating that these reward systems do, in fact, greatly affect our behavior. We thus need to be very careful in deciding just what consequences will flow from particular behaviors. The old motto "You get what you pay for" might also serve as a warning: you tend to get *exactly* what you "pay" for (or reward), and it may not be *exactly* what you hoped for. For example, if an instructor likes active student participation in class discussions, (s)he may make participation count toward the grade. The reward, then, is for speaking up—not for saying intelligent things, but for talking. This tends to produce a lot of chatter but doesn't ensure that the discussion will be worthwhile. Similarly, professors often complain that students only study what is on the exams, not the broader issues they would like the students to understand.

The problem here is general. As Steven Kerr (1975) has pointed out, it is foolish to reward one behavior while hoping for another. However, when what we hope for is hard to measure precisely, we have to base rewards on some related measure—and what gets rewarded is the behavior that gets measured, not the one we hope for. If the reward is for talking, students talk. If the grade is based on exam content, students study exam content. Kerr points out several important examples where this slippage between what we want and what we can measure has serious effects. For example, we would like doctors to keep us healthy, but they really earn their living by treating us when we are sick. They thus tend to do a lot of "treating"—prescribing drugs, operating—even if it is not good for our health. (The ancient Chinese are said to have had a much neater system; you paid the doctor when you were healthy and stopped when you got sick. The doctor had a strong incentive to help you get well as soon as possible, which is, of course, what you want!)

The reward system for professors has similar problems. They are expected to do both teaching and research. However, research output is much easier to measure (by looking at publications, for example). Research therefore makes more difference to salary and promotion chances than does teaching. As students know, the system often biases professors toward taking research more seriously than teaching. Even within research, it is easier to count one's publications than to evaluate how good they are. Researchers thus tend to publish many small papers instead of a few really good ones. Similarly, students may start out to get a sound education, but find that performance on exams is what gets measured. They drift into being "grade oriented" and forget that getting an education was the point of the exercise.

The central problem is that rewards need to be based on something we can measure, and what we can measure is rarely exactly the behavior we want. The reward system steers people to perform well on what is measurable and to neglect what is really the objective. In business, this is known as "managing the books, not the business," that is, operating so that the accounting reports look good, even if the actual business suffers. This is a serious problem in setting up practical, effective reward systems.

A GENERAL MODEL OF WORK MOTIVATION

In this chapter we have reviewed a number of theories that bear on the work motivation process. Figure 4.1 outlines an attempt to tie these ideas together into a single overall framework.

The logic of the figure can be summarized as follows:

1. The focus of the model is on an individual's choice (conscious or unconscious) of how hard (s)he intends to work in the next time period—the level-of-effort choice.

Figure 4.1. Summary Model of Individual Work Motivation

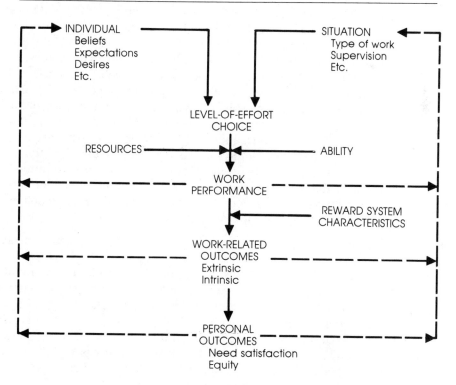

2. This choice is a function of the individual's beliefs, perceptions and desires, and aspects of the situation, such as type of work, supervision, etc.

3. Over time, the chosen level of effort leads to a level of work performance, with the individual's ability and the available resources acting as moderators. For example, even very high effort will lead to poor performance if the individual does not have the necessary skills, or the necessary materials to do the work.

4. A given level of work performance leads to work-related outcomes: extrinsic rewards such as pay, promotion, or bonuses; and intrinsic rewards such as a sense of achievement, the exercise of craft skills, etc. Goal achievement may also be treated as a work-related outcome.

5. These work-related outcomes lead, directly or indirectly, to personal outcomes: need satisfactions, such as those described by Maslow, Herzberg, and McClelland. These satisfactions are moderated by considerations of equity, with a particular level of need satisfaction being experienced as more or less positive depending on whether or not it is seen as fair in comparison with others.

6. Finally, levels of work performance and work-related and personal outcomes feed back both on the situation and on the individual to set up the initial conditions for the next level-of-effort choice. For example, the level of work performance achieved may show that a given job is complete, and that a new task must be started (feedback to situation). Similarly, the individual's experience with effort, performance, and outcomes may change the individual's expectancies that future effort will lead to future performance (Expectancy 1) and that future performance will lead to desired outcomes (Expectancy 2). The person's active needs may change as a function of the needs satisfied by the previous outcomes (feedback to individual). (This model includes the individual's inner state in the form of expectations, desires, etc. A Skinnerian would simply focus on the observables: effort, performance, and outcomes.)

The model is, of course, merely a sketch of a highly complex process. Its primary purpose is to show how the several partial theories we have reviewed can be fitted together into an overall understanding of the motivational process. If you are able to go through the model and review what each theory contributes to our understanding of each part of the model, you have a very good grasp of this chapter's materials. More important, if you can go through the model and answer the question: "What could a manager do to change the process at X point?" you have grasped an important core of practically useful implications. (You might also want to read Daniel Brass's paper on job design, Reading #3.

in light of this model.) After all, motivation—our own and that of our subordinates—is crucial to organizational success. By understanding the complexity of the process, we can hope to change these motivations in positive ways: higher accomplishments and higher satisfactions.

Up to this point in this book, we have focused mainly on the single individual, gathering information, solving problems, choosing how hard to work, and so on. But an organization is more than a number of individuals who happen to work in the same place: they work *together*, influencing each other's work in a wide variety of ways. The ways in which people influence one another is the focus of the rest of the book. In the next chapter we will look at the process of communication by which people share information with one another. More complex influence processes will be taken up in later chapters.

DISCUSSION QUESTIONS: CHAPTER 4

1. Suppose you wanted to test expectancy theory as a model of how hard an individual will work in a particular course. What questions would you need to ask? Start by listing three or four specific outcomes that might be affected by the choice of how hard one works: e.g., gain a good grade, learn some interesting material, enjoy a full social life, feel overworked. For each outcome, you will need to provide a scale to rate how desirable or undesirable the outcome is for the individual (i.e., its "valence"). (The scale should run from negative to positive to accommodate undesirable outcomes.)

   You now need to specify what alternatives the individual is choosing between, e.g., "Work hard" versus "Work normally." Write these alternatives as column headings next to your list of outcomes. Provide a scale for the individual to assess his or her "expectancy" that choosing each alternative will lead to receiving each outcome. For example, for two alternatives and four outcomes, you will need eight expectancy measures. Be careful about the question you use to measure these.

   Now go through the questionnaire you have constructed and answer as you think some real student (perhaps yourself) would. Use these numbers to calculate a net desirability score for each alternative (i.e., the sum of the expectancy × valence terms for each alternative). These net desirability scores will obviously be in arbitrary units, but by comparing them you should be able to make a prediction as to how hard this student will work in this course. Can you think of a way to test your prediction?

2. The expectancy model is, basically, a straightforward application of the rational choice model to motivational matters. How must the model be modified to accommodate the following ideas:

   a. Maslow's hierarchy of needs

   b. McClelland's work on need for achievement

   c. Herzberg's ideas on motivators and hygienes

   d. The distinction between intrinsic and extrinsic motivation

   e. Adams's work on equity theory

   f. The motivational effects of goal setting

   g. Skinner's findings in operant conditioning

3. Under what circumstances might a highly motivated employee still perform poorly? How would you react in such a situation?

4. The behavior that organizational reward systems can measure is never exactly the same as the behavior that the organization wants. What undesirable behaviors might be seen in a reward system that:

   a. Pays fruit pickers by the number of baskets of fruit they picked?

   b. Pays a bonus to workers in a nail-manufacturing plant by the tonnage of nails shipped?

   c. Never promotes design engineers whose designs failed in testing?

Chapter 5
Communication

"It is remarkable that human communication works at all, for so much seems to be against it; yet it does." (Colin Cherry, On Human Communication. MIT Press, 1965, p. 12.)

THE UNEXPECTED COMPLEXITY OF COMMUNICATION

Given the orientation of this book toward organizations as information-processing and decision-making machines, it is clear that communication is one of the central processes of interest. As with the earlier discussion of perception and inference, we need first to take a step backward, in order to take two steps forward. That is, we generally think of ourselves as good at communication. It is relatively rare that we experience a serious breakdown in communications, to find ourselves having difficulty making ourselves understood. While most of us would agree that we could sharpen our communication skills, we feel that we have plenty of skills to sharpen. Communication is one of those things that most of us regard as a pretty straightforward business.

The quotation from Colin Cherry above suggests that our notions about this "straightforwardness" are not entirely justified. It is not that communication is a simple business, but that we are extremely skilled at it. Think, for a moment, about a wink—the act of closing one eye for an instant. First, most of us have little trouble telling when this is, in fact, a "communicative act" and when it is merely a blink. Second, think of all the possible messages this wink might convey. It might tell us that the person winking is playing a joke on someone else, and is letting us in on the joke. It might be a signal that some sort of mischief is starting—or it might be the signal that starts the mischief. It might even be a parody of the whole business, with the speaker demonstrating to us how someone else, perhaps a clumsy plotter, gave some game away with a clumsy, obvious wink. This single wink, then, is most ambiguous; it might easily mean all sorts of different things. What is truly remarkable is that most of us would have no trouble figuring out which of these meanings was intended. As Colin Cherry's remark suggests, human communication is astonishing in that it generally works so well, when there are so many things that can go wrong with it.

In this chapter, we shall be looking in some detail at how this success is accomplished, and how failures arise. In the first section, we shall focus on the basic elements of a communication process, involving one person sending, and the other receiving, messages. In the second section, we shall examine the consequences of stringing many of these individual links together in an organizational context. Before we take up these issues, however, it will be useful to look briefly at just why communication is so important to working professionals.

COMMUNICATION SKILLS AND TECHNICAL SKILLS

You have just graduated from engineering school with a degree in electrical engineering and a specialty in heavy electrical machines. You have taken a job as a designer of large electric motors. What skills do you bring to the job? What skills do you need to do it effectively?

Your academic training has given you considerable expertise in the technical aspects of the work. You will know a good deal about the relative advantages of AC and DC machines, about series and parallel connection, about start-up torque and full-load losses, about cooling arrangements and lubrication systems, about overload protection and noise reduction—in short, you will have mastered the basic technical skills of designing electric motors. But will this mastery guarantee your success on the job?

The answer is, emphatically, "No!" The skills we have just described cover only one part of what an effective engineer needs to know—the part that extends from having a well-formulated set of design specifications (the technical problem) to coming up with a satisfactory design (the technical solution). Learning such skills is the core of academic training in engineering. On the job, however, we need a variety of other skills, especially skills in communication. We need to be able to communicate effectively with:

Clients. The motor we are trying to design is not just an abstract solution to an abstract problem; it is intended to solve a real problem for a real client. A 1,000 horsepower motor intended to drive a rock-crushing machine, for example, is very different from one intended to haul coal out of a deep mine. Working with the client to develop a realistic set of design specifications requires excellent communication skills.

Colleagues. It is rare for any individual, however competent, to solve a significant technical problem entirely alone. Much more commonly, one calls on one's colleagues for advice, suggestions, second opinions, and specialized expertise. Being able to ask for, and to give, such informal consulting help demands skill at communication.

Other co-workers. There is a long step from specifying and solving the technical problems of a given design to having a workable piece of hardware ready to ship to the client. The technical solution one has chosen has to be communicated to a draughtsperson to prepare detailed manufacturing drawings. The production department must be consulted to work out how and when the machine is to be built. The test department must be consulted to work out the tests the machine will have to pass before being certified as meeting the design specifications.

The list of those with whom the designer must deal could easily be extended, but these three examples are sufficient to establish the central point: technical skills are needed to solve technical problems, but communication skills are needed to bring the technical solution into being as an actual working device. Working in an organization is, crucially, working with other people. The first requirement of doing this effectively is to be able to communicate with them. The remainder of this chapter looks at how the communication process works, and offers some suggestions as to how it can be made to work better.

COMMUNICATION BETWEEN INDIVIDUALS

The basic elements of a communication link are two individuals, a *sender* and a *receiver*, connected by some *channel* over which a *message* can be transmitted. For example, if I want to invite you to a party, I might send you a written invitation (message) through the mail (channel); or, if we worked in the same office, I might ask you orally (message), using the air between my vocal chords and your eardrum as the channel; or I might call you on the telephone, using the electrical impulses transmitted along the wire (plus our two telephone instruments) as a channel. These basic elements are sketched in Figure 5.1.

In Figure 5.1 we have labeled three additional features of considerable importance in showing how communication works. First, there is an *encoding* step between the sender and the channel. Encoding represents the complex process by which the sender's meaning is transformed into a signal on the channel—for example, my writing and mailing your invitation. At the receiver's end, there is a *decoding* process, by which the receiver transforms the signal back into a meaningful message. (My handwriting is terrible, so "decoding" is a good description of what the receiver must do to figure out my message!) Finally, as the figure shows, there is *noise* at each point in the communication

Figure 5.1.   The Basic Elements of a Communication Link

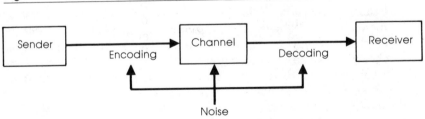

process—unwanted or irrelevant signals that can get confused with the intended signal. With the spoken message, noise can be taken literally to include other conversations going on in the room, or the sounds of construction work outside the window. Similarly, noise on a telephone link includes the crackling and hissing sounds we hear when the connection is bad, or other conversations that might break in. We also use noise to include irrelevant signals that creep into a written message, such as writing that shows through the page from the other side. "Noise," in short, is used to describe any unwanted or irrelevant signals. If I wrote my party invitation on a sheet of newspaper, the printed news would be "noise" in relation to my invitation; you might read the news instead of my invitation, making the news an unwanted or irrelevant signal from my point of view.

Communication Breakdowns

We can use the simple diagram of the communication link to develop a list of what is necessary for a link to work effectively (or, looked at the other way, what elements can lead to communication breakdown). Some of the requirements are obvious. If the sender's meaning is to be encoded, transmitted, and decoded accurately by the receiver, the two must be plugged into the same channel. This includes both "physically in contact" with the channel and "paying attention to" it. We are all skilled at tuning out most of the signals to which we are exposed, enabling us to pay attention to the few in which we are interested. As teachers find, merely saying something in class is no guarantee that students will receive the message. In any class, it is probably safe to assume that some significant fraction of the students are "tuned in" to something other than the teacher, such as the attractive person in the next seat, the newspaper folded under the desk, the view from the window, or a mental replay of last night's party. The receiver, then, must be both physically in contact with, and paying attention to, the sender's channel before accurate communication is possible.

A second obvious requirement for effective communication is that sender and receiver share a common "codebook." If you are "coding" your messages in Spanish and your listener does not know the language, you will not communicate effectively. In such simple cases, of course, the problem becomes obvious at once, and the two individuals either switch to a language that both understand or find an interpreter who shares both "codebooks" and can thus bridge the gap. Special-purpose codebooks are often devised for specific communication problems: for example, the sign-language codebooks used by ground crews directing the taxying of an aircraft; those used to communicate with crane operators when shouted instructions might be misunderstood;

and the sign languages used by the deaf to converse. In most of these cases, it is clear that a special language is being used, and a potential receiver is aware almost immediately whether or not the "code" is a familiar one.

The danger arises when two people think they are using the same codebook when in fact they are not. North Americans, for example, learn a language that is only roughly the same as the language one learns growing up in England. The small but important differences have provided Hollywood with hundreds of easy jokes, and sometimes lead to annoying confusions. A friend of mine, for example, spent a frustrating couple of weeks trying to straighten out travel arrangements with an English university that had promised him a "return ticket" to attend a conference. He was about to purchase a one-way ticket himself, before I pointed out to him that, in England, a "return ticket" means what Americans call a "round-trip" ticket!

In technical settings, "unshared codebook" problems often occur when we use jargon or technical terms that also have an everyday, nontechnical meaning. Jargon terms are often useful within a group of technical specialists, as a convenient shorthand for referring to some concept or procedure. When a term gets outside the group, however, it can cause confusion. For example, computer users communicate with one another swiftly and accurately with terms such as "booting" a system, "crashing" a program, or attempting to make a procedure "friendly." These terms also have meanings in nontechnical English, and it is easy to imagine the misunderstandings that nonspecialists can get into if they interpret such terms in their nontechnical sense.

A third source of communication error is noise. We may break this down further into channel noise, encoding noise, and decoding noise, focusing on the step in the overall process at which the undesired signal enters. The notion of a "signal-to-noise ratio" (SNR) is useful here. When the signal is strong and noise is weak, the SNR is high, and signals are easily distinguished from the noisy background. As the SNR drops, we finally get to the point at which the signal cannot be distinguished from the background, and communication breaks down. If, for example, a teacher writes on a chalkboard lightly (weak signal) and is careless about cleaning off what was written on the board earlier (high noise), the SNR may be too low for the students to be able to decode the message being written on the board.

In summary, as suggested by Figure 4:1, there are three requirements for a particular communication link to work effectively:

1. **Intact channel:** The physical connection between the sender and the receiver must be intact, and both must be paying attention to it.
2. **Shared codebook:** The code used by the sender in transforming his or her meaning into a message must be known to, and used by, the receiver.

3. **Adequate signal-to-noise ratio (SNR):** The signal on the channel must be powerful enough, or the noise on the channel weak enough, for the receiver to be able to tell one from the other.

Overcoming Communication Breakdowns

If communication is really so vulnerable to breakdowns and errors, how is it that we normally manage to communicate effectively? Several general error-reducing strategies are available:

1. **Improving SNR:** We can often find a way to improve the signal-to-noise ratio of a noisy channel. We can move a conversation to a quieter location, clean the chalkboard more carefully, or redial a telephone number in hopes of getting a better connection.

2. **Channel switching:** We may be able to switch from an unsatisfactory channel to a more satisfactory one. If we are having trouble describing a technical drawing over the telephone, we may switch to a visual channel by sending the receiver a copy of the revised drawing. If we are having trouble conveying our ideas in a letter, we can try the telephone, or arrange a face-to-face visit.

3. **Serial redundancy:** In speaking, we routinely repeat what we have said several times, perhaps in slightly different words. This can compensate both for channel noise (because the probability of getting the same noise signal interfering each time is reduced) and for coding noise (because the rewording of the message is not likely to be as confusing as is any single choice of words).

4. **Parallel redundancy:** We often try to send the same message on several channels simultaneously. In speaking, for example, we convey much of our meaning by tone of voice, facial expression, gestures, perhaps body posture, and physical distance from the listener. We might sketch our ideas on a piece of paper while we talk, using visual and oral channels simultaneously. Gestures can communicate a great deal. Think, for example, of how effectively a good mime can convey a story, using no spoken words at all. An effective teacher or other public speaker often uses all these channels simultaneously in getting a message across to his or her audience.

5. **Feedback:** An especially important mechanism for error-reduction involves the receiver sending messages indicating understanding or nonunderstanding back to the sender. In conversation, we nod and smile to indicate that we are getting the message, or raise our eyebrows and look puzzled to indicate otherwise. Good speakers pause often for questions and responses. Important letters may ask the receiver to acknowledge receipt. Radio users have several phrases —"roger," "over," and so on—to indicate that a message is complete, and to check whether the receiver actually received it.

It should be noted that these error-correcting strategies have a cost. Assuming that the sender has chosen the best available channel (Strategy 1) and has improved the SNR as far as is practicable (Strategy 2), either form of redundancy (Strategies 3 and 4) or feedback (Strategy 5) requires more message-sending than would a single message sent once. These strategies use up communication resources—they tie up the sender and receiver and the channel(s) in use. Further, they may introduce additional confusion. Imagine a teacher introducing a course with a statement that it will be interesting and exciting, but speaking in a flat, bored tone of voice. Which message is the class to believe? Probably, we will respond (consciously or not) more to the nonverbal signals than to the spoken message. In such cases, we are getting conflicting messages, and must do some work to decide which one is the real one.

Multiple Messages and Defensive Communication

So far we have been discussing communication in terms of transferring a message—a little bundle of meaning—from one person to another. Everyday communication is, of course, much richer than this. Part of what makes communication so wonderfully complex is that, within a single episode, we are often sending and receiving a variety of messages simultaneously. Listen, for example, to two students, a man and a woman, talking as they leave a class. The words they are using seem to be about the quiz they just had. But if you pay attention, you may see other things going on at the same time: a little flirtation; some boasting about how easy one of them found the quiz; a lead-up to asking to borrow notes from an earlier missed class; perhaps a gentle dig at the other for working too hard; or perhaps an indirect check to see if the other views the professor the same way. The whole conversation may not last a minute but it could still leave the careful analyst with plenty to think about. As we commented earlier, humans are extremely skilled communicators!

At least three levels of communication can be found in most real communications. First, there is the *overt content*, the topic of the conversation, the subject of the essay, or whatever. A second level is what we might call the *self-presentation* of the people involved, the signals by which I try to convey to you what kind of person I want you to think I am. Subtly, and generally unconsciously, we present ourselves as intelligent, witty, lively, conventional or otherwise, spontaneous or reflective, emotional or cool, and a score of other characteristics—all within the confines of a brief chat about the weather or some similar mundane topic! It is often unclear just how, or just how well, we manage this presentation of ourselves, but it is clear that we all do it much of the time, and that we pick up an impression of others just as swiftly.

A third level of communication is what might be called the *tactical* level, the tricks by which we try to influence the other person to do something we want, to impress them, or to establish our status relative to theirs. This overlaps partially with self-presentation, of course. You present yourself to your professor as a serious hardworking student to back up your tactical interest in getting a grade changed. You present yourself to your boss as an energetic go-getter to back up your tactical interest in getting a pay raise. Again, a good deal of this may be done unconsciously, but it is still a familiar and important part of normal communication.

An important implication of this multiple-level aspect of communication is that the three levels often interfere with one another, both in the sender and the receiver. The professor may have trouble hearing why you deserve a better grade because he is involved in presenting himself as a friendly and reasonable, but firm, teacher. He may also be trying to keep from being outmaneuvered by you into doing the extra work the grade change requires. There is so much going on at the self-presentation and tactical levels that another person literally may not hear much of the overt content of what you have to say.

Jack Gibb (1961) coined the phrase "defensive communication" for this interference between the various communication levels, and the distortions and breakdowns in communication to which they can lead. He lists six types of behaviors that tend to set up defensive, distorting climates, and suggests for each the sort of behaviors that lead to supportive, open climates:

1. **Evaluative versus descriptive:** "Your report is late" is descriptive; "You are irresponsible" is evaluative, and makes the hearer defensive.

2. **Controlling versus problem-oriented:** If the speaker seems to be trying to control our reactions or behavior, we resist (defensive). Focusing on our joint problem allows both of us to contribute to solving it.

3. **Strategic versus spontaneous:** We react defensively to someone we see as trying to manipulate us, or as having a hidden agenda. Straightforward, honest reaction to the shared situation is more supportive.

4. **Neutral versus empathetic:** "Mr. Cool," the calm, unemotional, unflustered individual, makes most of us defensive, since the speaker seems detached from us as real people. We respond more positively to someone who conveys warmth and concern for us as individuals.

5. **Superior versus equal:** If the other person comes across as feeling smarter, more attractive, more powerful, or whatever, we tend to defend ourselves by trying to get back at him or her. We are less threatened when we are treated as individuals just as worthy as the speaker.

6. **Certain versus provisional:** We are put off by people who seem to know all the answers. They make us feel as though we must pretend to know them, too, which gets in the way of exploring the difficulties we actually see. Sharing one's own doubts makes it easier for others to do the same.

Most of these characteristics are reasonably obvious. If you think about someone you find "easy to talk to," you will probably find that they have many of these supportive characteristics. Conversely, people we find difficult to talk to tend to have more of the characteristics that arouse our defensiveness. However, just knowing these characteristics does not make it easy to change our behavior. The ways we communicate are often deeply rooted—in habit and in our personalities—and it takes a lot of effort and practice to change them. Even if we are not about to change ourselves or others, it is worth bearing in mind that we send and receive messages at these three levels—overt, self-presentation, and tactical—every time we communicate, and that the different levels may interfere with one another. If we experience difficulty at the overt content level, it may be worth asking ourselves whether something is going on at the other levels to arouse our (or our listener's) defensiveness. In communication, there is an entire symphony going on, and it is easy to lose the melody line altogether.

So far, we have been looking at communication in its normal, everyday sense. We now turn to communication processes in a particular context: the organization.

THE ORGANIZATIONAL CONTEXT

More May Not Be Better

Communication is so interwoven with almost every organizational process that it is difficult to discuss it separately from the other processes. When we discuss power and influence (Chapter 6), we will see that control of communication channels is a crucial element in exercising power (as every competent revolutionary knows: TV stations and newspapers are always among the first things seized in a revolution). When we talk about conflict (Chapter 8), we will emphasize the danger of escalation distorting or severing communication between the conflicting parties. When we look at group processes (Chapter 9), we will focus on the patterns of communication between the group members. In short, whatever we look at in organizations, we seem to end up looking at communication processes as well.

This leads a lot of people who should know better to see "communications problems" as the underlying cause of almost everything that goes wrong in an organization. If a fire destroys half the plant, someone is sure to diagnose a "communications problem" between, say, the security staff and the supervisor of the department where the fire started. If a new product fails to sell, someone will see "communications problems" between, say, market research and product development. Even interpersonal difficulties, disagreements and arguments get glibly diagnosed as "communications problems." We should be suspicious of any insight that yields the same diagnosis for a wide range of diseases.

Clearly, communications are woven into so many aspects of organizational life that anything that happens is likely to have a communications aspect. The trap is that once we have diagnosed a problem as being centrally due to communications failures, we tend to try to cure it by improving communication, and that will generally be taken to mean *increasing* communication. After the fire, we set up elaborate new information channels and joint planning committees between security and plant supervisors, when installing an effective sprinkler system might be more useful. Market research and product development work on refining their communications with one another, drawing attention away from the need for good new product ideas and good research on them. The two argument-prone individuals spend months refining the open communication between them, and discover that they do, in fact, dislike one another and might do well to keep apart as much as possible!

The assumption that *better* communication is the same as *more* communication underlies the failures of many of the first generations of computer-based management information systems (MISs). Designers of the early MISs assumed, reasonably enough, that managers would manage better if they were better informed. With the advent of powerful computers (and fast printers!) in the early 1960s, this assumption was quickly translated into what seemed to be an effort to bury every manager in printouts. Daily, literally hundreds of pages of fan-fold started to appear on managers' desks. The printouts were, of course, largely ignored; most managers are much too busy to read hundred-page reports on a daily basis. Learning from these lessons, current information-system designers pay much more attention to tailoring the information supply to the manager's real needs, not to providing the largest printout possible.

To guard against the "more is better" trap, it is worth keeping in mind that organizations are, to an important degree, devices for *minimizing*, not for maximizing, communication between individuals. Consider the number of two-person communication links possible at a party of 100 people: 4950 (= 100 × 99/2), with each person participating in 99 conversations. It would take over eight hours to have a five-minute conversation with everyone at the party. In contrast, an organization of about the same size might be arranged by assigning one person as boss, ten as supervisors, each supervisor having ten subordinates (111 people in all). There are now only 110 two-person communication links, a mere 2.2 percent of the 4950 links at the party. One important function of organization structure, then, is to *eliminate* a vast number of the possible communication links among its members. (We will discuss this notion further in Chapter 10.)

Content and Direction of Communications

Managers spend most of their time communicating, perhaps as much as 75 percent, according to studies by Mintzberg (1973). By far the largest proportion of this communication is verbal, either face-to-face or by telephone. What do they talk about? The content varies with organizational direction, with whether they are talking to their subordinates, their peers, or their superiors. Katz and Kahn (1978) suggest the following major categories for the primary content of communication in each of these directions:

1. **Downward communication** is likely to involve instruction, both on the subordinate's specific job and on the practices and procedures to be followed in doing it. Second, bosses give their subordinates feedback on how they are doing. Finally, though this aspect is often neglected, they provide the subordinate with a rationale for the job, why it is important, how it fits into the larger picture of the organization's activities and what these larger purposes are.

2. **Upward communication** is largely the mirror image of these content categories. Subordinates report on what they are doing and what problems they are encountering, how existing policies and procedures are working, and their ideas as to what needs to be done and how it should be done. They may also pass on similar information about the activities of their peers, though this is inhibited by the informal taboo on "ratting to the boss."

3. **Lateral communication**—communication between two people at the same organizational level—includes both information concerned with coordinating their interlocked work activities and information communication for social and emotional support. People at the same

organizational level may share many interests other than work coordination: they are often of similar ages and backgrounds, or are at similar stages of their careers. They may also share an interest in diluting the boss's power over them by comparing notes, sharing secrets, and pooling their information.

These categories may be reasonably obvious to anyone who knows how organizations operate. It is worth noting, however, not only the wide variety of things that are communicated, but also the potential for them to conflict with one another. As was discussed earlier, we are more likely to tune out or distort messages from senders we see as evaluative, controlling, or superior—precisely the characteristics we would expect of a boss trying to tell us how to do our jobs. Of course, we make allowances for our superiors acting in a superior manner. Nonetheless, the basic point remains that communication channels in organizations are used for many different sorts of messages. A channel that works for one sort of message (e.g., giving orders) is not likely to be as effective for another (e.g., giving personal advice or getting accurate feedback). This conflict between different types of messages is a primary cause for communication distortion, the topic to which we now turn our attention.

Distortion of Communications

Communication distortion is the "slippage" between what a sender thinks (s)he has sent and the message as interpreted by the receiver. For example, a study by Burns (1954) traced what happened to 237 messages sent by a group of managers. The managers reported 165 (about 70 percent) as being instructions or decisions for their subordinates—a surprisingly high proportion. Of the same 165, the subordinates classified only 84 (a little over half) as instructions or decisions. We can speculate as to how this difference in perceptions arose. Perhaps the managers tried to reduce their subordinates' resistance to being ordered to do something by carefully phrasing the instructions: "Perhaps you could . . ." or, "I'd like to suggest that you . . . " However it happened, the subordinates tended to report many of the "orders" as information or advice, not as instructions. There was significant slippage between what the sender thought (s)he was sending and what the receiver thought (s)he was receiving. In half these messages, the two parties did not agree on what the message was. Distortion had crept in.

Organizational Context and Distortion

Going back to our sketch of the communication process (Figure 5.1), we can add several other sources of possible distortion specifically resulting from the process occurring in an organization. For example:

1. **Sender motivation:** My boss is not just the person I "report to." (S)he
is also the person who evaluates my performance and decides my
pay raises. I am thus likely to underreport job difficulties and over-
report job successes, to overstress positive evaluations of the boss's
ideas and underemphasize negative ones. Read (1962) found these
biases to be common, particularly for ambitious, upwardly mobile
managers, who seem to be more sensitive to their bosses' influence
over their future career prospects.

2. **Receiver characteristics:** Organizational messages arrive with the
sender clearly labeled. Military officers' uniforms clearly indicate
their rank, so that receivers know how to treat orders. Written communications are signed by the sender (generally with name *and
title*), memoranda come "from the desk of" the sender, and so on.
Labeling sets up expectations in receivers as to what sorts of messages they will receive. As we saw earlier, expectations are often
useful, but in some situations they can obscure message content. As
a teacher, I assume that a student who comes to see me during my
office hours wants to talk about course content. It often takes me a
while to realize that a particular student wants to talk about a personal problem.

3. **Channel characteristics:** In organizations, communication channels
are not just connections between people. They are also labeled with
organizational meanings such as status or in-group/out-group identity. We tend to pay closer attention to messages from people who
have power in our lives, or who are organizationally close to us (e.g.,
our immediate work group) than to messages from people less significant to us. Gross (1968), for example, suggests that the United
States military's failure to anticipate the Pearl Harbor attack was
the result of ignoring information provided by low-ranking officers
at a unit with a bad reputation. This channel, in other words, had
been labeled as having low value, so the information it provided was
heavily discounted—with disastrous results, in this case.

4. **Message characteristics:** We have already discussed the multilevel
nature of many organizational messages, and the possibilities of
interference among the various levels. It is worth reemphasizing
that such between-level interference happens everywhere, but it
may be particularly severe in organizations, where single channels
serve for such a range of important message content.

Organizational Geometry and Distortion

One part of communication distortion, then, arises because the communication channel is placed in an organizational context. A second

group of distortion factors flows from what we might call the "geometry" of the organization. Two specific aspects of this "geometry" concern us here: (1) serial repetition and (2) convergence/divergence.

Serial repetition.   There is an old party game called "Whispers" (in England; "Gossip" in the United States), in which a message is whispered to one person, who then whispers it to another, and so on until the last person announces what (s)he has heard and the message is compared to the original. The results are often hilarious. A message that started out as "There's something wrong with my car" might come out as "It's time to head for the bar."

What makes the game interesting is not simply that messages are distorted when they are repeated inaccurately. If the message gets 50 percent garbled at each repetition, we would expect to retrieve only 1/64, or about 1.6 percent, of the original context after six repetitions. What is interesting is that what comes out generally makes some sense —not the original sense, but not just random words or noises, either. As we saw with perception, humans tend to "make sense" of what they see or hear. If the message is unclear, we reconstruct it into something meaningful. In serial repetition, it is not just repeated garbling, but repeated sense-making, that shapes the final version.

The same processes can occur in organizations. A statement is issued from the top of the company: "We need to improve our product reliability." The director of manufacturing passes this on to his subordinates, embellishing and clarifying its implications for the division: "We need tighter quality control." The production manager calls in the production supervisors and lectures them on sloppy quality control, adding a few warnings about the need for keeping to official inspection procedures generally. The quality control supervisor, feeling defensive, starts a program of 100-percent inspection, instead of the old sampling method, and production comes to a virtual standstill while every prescribed test is done on every item produced. It makes no difference that the reliability problem (if one existed) might have been traceable to a single underdesigned component. The net result of apparently minor rephrasings and embellishments at each stage of the communication process is that a very different message was received at the end from that intended at the beginning. Serial repetition can lead to large communication distortions.

Convergence/divergence and overload.   A second obvious point about the "geometry" of hierarchical organizations is that channels from below any position in the center converge; managers have many subordinates, but only one boss. If I have a five-minute chat with each of my twelve subordinates every morning, that is only a brief interruption for them, but the first hour of my work day is gone. If each subordinate summarizes for me what (s)he plans to do today, I receive an enormous amount of information very quickly. If I now repeat the process with my own boss, who is also gathering information from many subordinates, the compression effect is multiplied. Our capacity for absorbing and using information is very limited, and information channels converge from below. What flows up the organization must be highly summarized, and even then much of it will not be effectively processed.

One direct implication of channel convergence is that contact between a subordinate and a superior is likely to be seen very differently by the two participants. For the subordinate, direct conversation with the boss is likely to be relatively rare, and thus highly significant. From the boss's point of view, conversations with subordinates are relatively common, and thus much less significant. Even if the subordinate picks a single issue to discuss with the boss, and it is the only thing they talk about, the issue is only one of many the boss discusses that day.

The significance of this difference in the configuration of channels above and below a position is borne out in various research findings. Webber (1970) found that superiors believe that they communicate with their subordinates more freely than the subordinates see them as doing. Similarly, Lawler, Porter, and Tannenbaum (1968) found that managers felt better about their contacts with their superiors (the unusual events) than they did about contacts with their subordinates (the commonplace events). Part of this can be explained simply by the superior-subordinate relationship, but part of it seems to be due to the relative frequencies of upward and downward communication imposed by the shape of the organization.

A second implication of the upward convergence of communication channels in organizations is simply that a lot of information flows upward into each position, and that overload is a perpetual threat. There is plenty of research evidence to show that managers spend an enormous percentage of their time communicating—not thinking, or planning, or reading, or deciding, but simply processing information (see McCall, Morrison, and Hannan [1978] for a useful review of these studies). What happens when the torrent of information exceeds what the individual is capable of processing?

Miller (1960) suggests seven broad categories of reaction to information overload. Some are clearly dysfunctional for the organization as a whole (though they may save the individual from going crazy); others can go either way, depending on how they are done. Miller's seven categories are:

1. **Omission:** Some or all of the incoming information is simply ignored and not processed. For example, a letter is not answered.

2. **Error:** Some or all of the incoming information is processed wrongly. For example, you dash off a quick answer to a letter, but fail to provide the information requested.

3. **Filtering:** Some information is omitted, but on a systematic basis. For example, calls are screened for importance, and the less important ones are ignored.

4. **Queueing:** Incoming information is processed to the extent possible, with the excess stored to be dealt with later when the pace eases. For example, phone callers are put on hold, memos are kept for later attention.

5. **Approximation:** The details of the incoming messages are ignored, and the content summarized into simpler, broad categories. For example, instead of keeping track of the nature and causes of particular breakdowns, a hard-pressed manager might simply keep count of how many such incidents were reported.

6. **Multichanneling:** If one channel is becoming overloaded, one could switch some messages to another channel. For example, some people seem to be able to do this internally: read their mail, carry on a conversation, and monitor the TV news all at the same time. Alternatively, an overloaded manager might switch one stream of messages to a different organizational channel. When such a switch assigns one area of the manager's activity to a subordinate, decentralization results.

7. **Escape:** The individual who is getting overloaded can simply leave the situation, either by physically leaving or mentally tuning out.

If we suppose that all the information coming in has some value to start with, we can assess the organizational cost of these various reactions. Omission and error are costly: the information simply is not properly processed. Filtering and queueing are at least selective as to what will and what will not be processed. If effectively done, the information omitted or delayed is less important or urgent than that processed. Similarly, approximation tries to retain the crucial features of the messages while dropping out the details, though it would probably make more sense for the sender to produce the summary than for the receiver to have to do so. Multichanneling, at least in the organizational decentralization sense, is somewhat similar to sender-based approximation, in that the subordinate to whom the responsibility is delegated will presumably now report only the results, not the details, of the information (s)he receives. The manager who escapes the torrent of information is probably saving his or her sanity, but may well be damaging the organization.

The listing serves to reemphasize two earlier comments. First, our ability to process information is severely limited; the ability to process information is one of the crucial limits on how organizations function. Second, it is useful to think of organizations from the communication-limiting, not the communication-enhancing, perspective. Much of what happens is the result of efforts to restrict flow of information, not to increase it. Experienced managers develop strategies for limiting their information intake. They tend to read only "executive summaries" of reports, not the reports themselves (a point worth bearing in mind when writing reports). Winston Churchill, heading the British war effort in the early 1940s, fired off requests for information with the words, "Pray let me have this day, on one side of a sheet of paper, your views on. . . ." He wanted his information fast, and he wanted it boiled down to the basics.

COMMUNICATION IN RESEARCH AND DEVELOPMENT

Many of the processes we have discussed so far can be illustrated in one particularly interesting organizational context, the research and development (R&D) laboratory. Communication is crucial in R&D. Many scientists and engineers spend at least some portion of their professional lives in such settings, so findings from such environments are of direct interest. The central business of the R&D lab is the production of new knowledge and ideas, and communication is central to such work. In this final section of the chapter, we will look briefly at some of the findings from research studies of communication in R&D settings. We will focus on a study by Allen and Cohen (1969), embellishing a few of the points they make.

Allen and Cohen's study examined the communication patterns they found in industrial R&D labs. They traced, for example, the sources of scientific and technical ideas being worked on in the labs. They found that only about 15 percent came directly from the scientific and technical literature. In fact, one of their basic observations was that the bulk of communication was internal. People within the lab talked mainly to one another, not to outsiders. (These were industrial laboratories, and the patterns of communication may be different from academic laboratories. Industrial scientists are more likely to be "locals," in that their primary interests and contacts are within the organizations for which they work. Academic scientists tend to be more "cosmopolitan," less involved with their employing organization, and having broader contacts with people working on related problems in other organizations.)

Communication between lab members and the outside world is commonly a two-step process, passing through a small number of researchers referred to as "gatekeepers." These individuals tend to maintain a broad network of outside contacts, both with other individuals and with the scientific literature, and serve as middlemen for contact between the other members of the lab and the outside world. This two-step process is intriguingly parallel to one found earlier in mass communication. Researchers in that area (e.g., Katz and Lazersfeld, 1955; Rogers, 1962) found that, for example, people rarely form their political opinions directly from the mass media. Instead, they are more influenced by "opinion leaders," people they already know and respect, who act as a link between the mass media and the individual. Similar two-step processes have been found in such areas as medical doctors learning about new drugs and farmers adopting new types of corn. In each case, communication seems to flow from the literature to the individual through relatively few "gatekeepers" or "opinion leaders." In the R&D lab, such individuals are of great value to the individual researcher, and need to be carefully nurtured by the organization.

Several of our earlier comments on how communication patterns are shaped are well illustrated in Allen and Cohen's work. For example, they found that friendship nets and technical discussion nets tend to overlap one another; a channel that is used for one is more likely to be used for the other. They also found that status had a sharp effect on who talked to whom. Researchers with Ph.D.s, the high-status people in a lab, tended to be cliquey, talking mainly to each other both socially and technically. The lower-status (non-Ph.D.) employees tended to initiate communications with the high-status group more often than with their own peers. Allen and Cohen suggest that the lower-status individuals wanted to share in the reflected glory of the work of the higher-status doctorate holders. Whatever the reason, it is clear that status was a powerful influence on communication processes.

Finally, Allen and Cohen found that the information communication patterns were heavily influenced by the formal organizational structure, the hierarchy and the work group. This is somewhat surprising, in light of the strong scientific norms about open exchange of information, but is perhaps explicable if one recalls that these were industrial R&D labs. In one of my own studies (Connolly, 1975), I found that communication nets tended to follow the organizational hierarchy only for researchers dealing with development or project work. For those involved in more basic research, the pattern tended to be both less centralized and less hierarchical, with people sharing ideas and discussion with whomever seemed relevant to their current problems, regardless of rank or department.

In short, Allen and Cohen's study is well worth reading for a glimpse of how the flow of ideas and discussions in an R&D lab is shaped. Individuals take on different roles in these processes, with some deeply involved, others almost isolated. The nets that emerge are shaped by status, friendship, scientific and technical interests, organizational level, and work group affiliations. It is from such subtle, complex communication processes that one of the organization's truly vital assets, the novel idea, sometimes emerges.

SUMMARY

We have examined the basic elements of the communication process: sender, receiver, channel; message, encoding, decoding. We discussed the requirements for such a process to work effectively, and suggested the various ways in which it could go wrong. The basic requirements include an intact channel, a shared codebook, and an adequate signal-to-noise ratio. Strategies for reducing error include improving signal-to-noise ratios, channel switching, serial or parallel redundancy, and feedback. We also noted that communication channels typically convey multiple messages simultaneously, including overt content, self-presentation, and tactical or manipulative messages. These multiple messages may interfere with one another as in the distortion associated with defensive communication.

Placing these processes in the organizational context, we noted first that communication is interwoven with every other organizational process. This can lead to an overdiagnosis of "communication problems," and to an overprescribing of "improved communication." It is a common error to assume that more communication is always better. In fact, it is useful to think of organizations as communication-minimizing, rather than communication-maximizing, arrangements.

Within organizations, the content of communications is shaped by direction, with different messages going to superiors, subordinates, and peers. Again, conflict among the various messages is possible and can lead to communication distortion. The degree of distortion is influenced by characteristics of the sender and receiver, those of the channel, and those of the message itself. Further, the geometry of the organization's structure contributes to distortion, both by requiring serial repetition of messages and by inducing overload in upward flows. People react in various ways to overload, and some reactions are more harmful to the organization than others. A fundamental problem for organizations, we suggested, is in balancing the huge quantities of information handled with the very limited ability of individuals to process information.

The final section of the chapter illustrated several of the communication processes discussed in the special context of R&D laboratories, where the communication of ideas is crucial.

DISCUSSION QUESTIONS: CHAPTER 5

1. You are employed in the development laboratory of a major aerospace company. You have developed a chemical that, if added to aircraft fuel, promises to reduce significantly the risk of fire if the aircraft crashes. You have completed a detailed technical report on your work.

   Identify at least six other individuals or groups with whom you would have to communicate your discovery in order to get it adopted. Would your technical report be equally suitable for all these audiences? Describe the features that would be especially relevant and especially irrelevant for each audience. Outline a communication plan for reaching these six audiences, including: (a) the order in which you would approach them; (b) the content you would emphasize for each; and (c) the format (e.g., written report, formal presentation, informal discussion) you would choose for each audience.

2. Communication distortion or breakdown can result from noise at the encoding, transmission, or decoding stages. Give an example of each form of breakdown for the following communication processes:

   a. Transmitting a design specification by means of an engineering drawing from the design office to a machine operator on the shop floor

   b. Presenting a new technical idea from a researcher to the New Products Review Committee

   c. Informing a subordinate of yours that his or her work over the past year has been unsatisfactory

   Which of these three processes do you think would be most liable to distortion? Why? What might you do to overcome this distortion?

3. What is meant by "defensive communication"? What can be done to overcome it?

4. Is more communication generally the same as better communication? Why or why not? Give examples.

5. Organizations frequently arrange for employees to go together on retreats at a place remote from the plant or laboratory to discuss important issues. Suggest three reasons why communication might be expected to be better in such a setting than it is in normal day-to-day work.

6. Senior managers often complain that they are the last to know about serious problems within the organization. Why is this so, and what can the organization do about it?

Chapter 6

Power, Authority, and Influence

We see people exercising power every day. A policeman puts up a hand and traffic stops. A professor assigns a homework exercise and the students complete it. The baseball manager tells the pitcher to leave the game and the pitcher leaves. It is often difficult to know exactly *why* a particular person has power, or exactly *what* it is (s)he has. But there is no problem recognizing its consequences; things are done the way the power-holder wants them to be done, even when others would like them done differently. The drivers would rather not waste time, the students would rather not do the homework, the pitcher would rather stay in the game, but, in each case, they do as they are told. The power-holder is the one who does the telling.

Many people are somewhat uneasy talking about power in this straight-forward way. After all, our society is based on ideas about the equality of individuals, and there seems something wrong with some people being "more equal" than others. We think that in organizations deci-sions should be made by cool, rational analysis. When they are not, we complain about "office politics," by which we generally mean that power, rather than reason, was used in making the decision. Because engineers and scientists hold strong professional values toward rational analysis, they tend to be particularly upset at decisions they see as "political." We shall see in this chapter that viewing power as the dirty side of organizations is a mistake. Without power differentials, organi-zations could scarcely operate at all; and the way power is allocated has a rationality all its own. Power is necessary and useful. Our aim here is to understand something of where power comes from, who gets it and how, and how it is used.

SOURCES OF POWER

The first thing to notice about power is that it is not a property of an individual, but of a relationship. You can give all the orders you like but, if no one obeys them, you have no power. The power of your signa-ture on a check is limited to what you have in your bank account. One useful way to look at power is to ask why the person on the receiving end does what the power-holder wishes. A useful set of categories is suggested by French and Raven (1959), who suggest five different resources that give power to those who hold them.

Reward Power

The most obvious reason for us to obey someone else is that (s)he can give us something we want if we obey, or withhold it if we disobey. This involves a fairly explicit "if-then" promise: "*If* you're quiet, *then* I'll buy you an ice cream"; "*If* you answer all the problems, *then* I'll give you an A"; "*If* you exceed last month's production, *then* I'll give you a bonus." In each case, the use of reward power involves a promise about the future, and the promise has to be believed for the process to work. The reward must also be conditional on obedience. We have to believe both "if, then" and "if not, then not." A bonus for high production works only if average or low production produces no bonus.

Coercive Power

The mirror-image of reward power is coercive or punishment power. We obey someone because (s)he can punish us if we do not. The promise here is "unless, then." "*Unless* you exceed last month's production, I'll fire you." Rewards and punishments are often lumped together under the term "sanctions," which can be either positive (reward) or negative (punishments). There are, however, important differences between rewards and punishments. Being rewarded for doing something will generally make us like both the person doing the rewarding and the activity being rewarded. Being punished for not doing something will tend to have the opposite effects; we end up hating both the job *and the* boss. Consequently, we think about quitting (if we can find another job). Hence coercive power can only be effective if there are side constraints to prevent the person punished from leaving the scene. A professor may be able to use coercive power in required courses, but if (s)he tries it in elective courses, half the class may drop the course. (See also the earlier comments on punishment in Chapter 4.)

It is worth noting that many, perhaps most, of the rewards and punishments we see used in everyday life are more symbolic (praise, disapproval) than primary (food, money). Most of us respond as quickly to the professor's approving nod, or a boss's disapproving frown, as we do to tangible consequences like getting an "A" or being fired. This is valuable for the power-holder, because these sanctions are less prone to being used up than are the primary sanctions. Few supervisors can afford to give bonuses to, or to fire, their entire work groups. They can, however, praise or reprimand their subordinates without fear of running out of words. Power-holders thus tend to prefer symbolic to primary sanctions. Whether or not these nonprimary sanctions will work depends on the context in which they are used, the relationship between boss and subordinate. Aspects of this relationship and context form the basis for French and Raven's other three classes of power base.

Legitimate Power

One of the commonest, but also most complex, power bases is implied when we explain our obedience in terms such as "ought to" or "has a right to." We obey a police officer directing traffic because we feel that (s)he "has a right to" direct traffic. We obey our boss because we feel that we "ought to." Indeed, we may not even explain it that far: we just explain our obedience by saying, "Well, (s)he *is* the boss," leaving implicit the argument that one ought to obey bosses (or parents or police officers or professors). We do not calculate the chance of rewards or punishments, we just obey because it seems like the right thing to do. Legitimate power of this sort is what is specifically meant by "authority"—the person is "authorized" to give orders, and we accept that authority.

Where does this feeling of acceptance come from? It seems to be deeply rooted in our upbringing and our experiences of our culture, in what is referred to as our "socialization." We are not taught these values explicitly. We just absorb them, in the same way that we absorb all sorts of other cultural values, from acceptable ways of using a knife and fork to "proper" ways of behaving toward our elders, peers, and juniors. No one has to explain to most of us that we should be quiet at a symphony concert, although being loud at a rock concert is perfectly all right. Similarly, we just seem to absorb the idea, from a lifetime's experience, that it is legitimate to obey people in certain positions, at least in particular matters. We accept their authority as "legitimate."

Three points are particularly worth keeping in mind about legitimate power. One is that it attaches to the role or position, not just to the person. It is not necessary that our boss be outstandingly pleasant or clever, or use rewards and punishments skillfully. We obey because (s)he is the boss, and obeying the boss is legitimate. (Of course, there are exceptions. If our boss got the job by nepotism—by being the owner's relative—we may feel that the appointment itself was illegitimate, and accept the boss's orders less willingly. That is, accepting the boss's legitimacy is a part of accepting the legitimacy of the whole system.)

A second interesting feature of legitimate power is the range of subtle cues that are used to establish it. When signing an official order, the holder of legitimate power will tend to use the job title: Joe Blow, *President;* Mary Rowe, *Chief Engineer.* Indeed, the person's name is often dropped altogether, and the order carries only the person's title or position. Memos come "from the desk of," as if we were to obey a piece of furniture! Uniforms seem to work in the same way. If the person holding up a hand in front of my car wears a police uniform, I obey the command; if not, I may ignore the command. Only *uniformed* mail carriers are allowed to put things into your mailbox. Note also how carefully the legitimacy of uniforms is guarded. It is an offense to dress as a police officer if you are not one. In time of war, someone captured behind enemy lines is treated either as a spy or as a prisoner of war, depending on whether or not (s)he is wearing the appropriate uniform.

Finally, it is worth noting how subtly most of us have learned the rules about just what the limits on legitimate authority are. For example, most students will obey a professor who tells them to do certain embarrassing things (such as standing in front of the class) but not others (taking off their clothes). It is all right for the boss to instruct us on work-related matters, and even on matters only loosely related to work such as style of clothing, but it would be wrong for the boss to attempt to influence whom we marry or where we live. There were recently a number of lawsuits about whether or not it was legitimate for a boss to ask his or her secretary to make and serve coffee. Such things are rarely covered by the job description, but we all have strong feelings about where the line between legitimate and illegitimate orders falls.

Legitimate power is both the commonest and the subtlest of everyday power types. It turns on a common internalized sense that certain people, in certain positions, have a right to give orders about certain matters. We grant authority to position-holders, without questioning their right to give orders of certain kinds, as long as they are behaving in their roles (in uniform, etc.). The limits on these roles are rarely spelled out, but we still have clear understandings of where the limits fall.

Referent Power

The technical term "referent" is here used in the same sense as in "reference group," a group with which one feels a sense of identity, a feeling of being one with its members. Referent power is based on one's attraction to, or identification with, another individual. It might loosely be called the "my hero" effect: I like or admire this person, so I try to behave or believe as (s)he does. I do not need any explicit order or instruction. The merest suggestion, or even just my guess, as to what this person wants is enough for me to start behaving in that way.

Referent power is close to what is often referred to as "charisma," a special personal gift for inspiring others. The word is probably over-used; we see everyone from successful football coaches to successful car salespeople described as charismatic. There are, however, many historical examples of people of great influence who seem to have had this inspirational quality: religious leaders such as Christ or Muhammad; political leaders such as Winston Churchill or John Kennedy (or in an evil way, Adolf Hitler). These people seem to have possessed referent power on a vast scale, inspiring nations in extraordinary ways. We can also see referent power at work, on a much smaller scale, in our everyday lives.

Note that while legitimate power is attached specifically to the person's role or position, referent power is specific to the person. It is this particular person, not as chief engineer or research director, whom I find myself trying to emulate. I read the same journals, dress like, and try to see problems as (s)he would. If that person leaves, and is replaced by someone I feel less identified with, the whole basis of my compliance changes.

Referent power is thus difficult for an organization to use. On the one hand, it produces very powerful effects around the person who has it, and uses none of the organization's resources of bonus payments and other rewards or punishments. On the other hand, it is hard to predict and control. You cannot *require* an employee to be charismatic, or fire someone for not being so! Because the power is lodged in the person, it may be used to ends the organization does not want. After all, successful revolutionaries often seem to have the personal qualities needed for great referent power. A revolutionary may inspire a research group toward a brilliant scientific breakthrough; but could just as easily lead the group off to a competitor's laboratory! From the organization's perspective, people with strong referent power can be a double-edged sword.

Expert power

The last of the five power bases we shall examine is that of expertise. When a doctor tells you, "Take two of these pills every morning," you obey because you trust the doctor's expertise, not because (s)he is your boss, or your hero, or can reward or punish you. When the lab assistant explains how to connect a particular instrument, you obey for similar reasons. One takes instructions from lawyers in legal matters, from cooks about cooking, and from local residents about street directions, all for the same reason: they are experts who have knowledge you do not.

Like referent power, expertise power can pose problems for organizations. Your boss (whose power is legitimate) tells you to solve a particular design problem one way, but a subordinate (a leading expert in the matter) tells you that way will not work, and the problem should be approached quite differently. Whom shall you listen to? In simpler times the confict was perhaps less likely to arise. The boss would also be a master craftsman, combining legitimacy and expertise. In advanced science and technology fields, however, the conflict is common. Junior people are very often experts in particular specialties. This has important implications for the way organizations can be designed and run, as we shall see later in chapter 10.

AN EXAMPLE: HOW JUNIOR EMPLOYEES GET POWER

Understanding the differences between these five power bases—reward, coercive, legitimate, referent, and expert—and their implications can help us to understand what power we have over others, and vice versa. In most cases power comes from some mixture of the five bases, and the effectiveness of particular mixtures may not be obvious. We have all come across people who, although officially "the boss," have little or no real power. More interestingly, one can often find people who are actually quite powerful, although from their official position in the organization one would not expect them to be. The boss's secretary, the custodian, or the clerk who checks travel expenses often turn out to be powerful, despite their low job titles and pay rates. How can this be?

An interesting analysis of this question is given by David Mechanic (1962). He shows that low-ranking employees can acquire considerable power by such means as:

1. **Expertise:** If the lab assistant is the only person who knows how to fix a balky piece of equipment, even senior researchers have to deal carefully with him or her. For example, they have to fit their work around the assistant's schedule, rather than vice versa. This power is still more important if the expertise is critical and the expert is hard to replace.

2. **Effort:** In a university, most professors cannot be bothered with the work of ordering supplies or scheduling classes. One of the secretaries may take on the job, and thereby acquire considerable power over the professors, because they either go along with the secretary's wishes or do the work themselves.

3. **Attractiveness:** Attractiveness, or charisma, is a power resource. There is no reason to expect that it follows organizational level, so it is available to both junior and senior employees.

4. **Position:** Mail-room employees and switchboard operators are at the center of important communication networks, and thus acquire a power base. By deciding which calls go through, which are asked to hold, the switchboard operator can make the senior person's job much easier—or harder. Because they know what is going on, mail-room clerks are valuable people to know in the organization. Not all important information flows through official channels, and it can be very useful to know in advance when a particular meeting is to be scheduled or a particular decision made.

5. **Coalitions:** I tend to be somewhat absent-minded about the administrative details of professoring, and am, as a result, often caught with overdue grade sheets, lost travel receipts, etc. One of the women in my department knows how such things can be fixed—*and* she knows who can fix them, since she has a network of friends around the campus, and they do small favors for one another. Not surprisingly, she is a powerful person in my life!

6. **Rules:** Like most large organizations, my university has a huge rule book. I am totally ignorant of many of the rules. The people who can tell me about the rules, and how to get around them, are important to me.

Hence, Mechanic shows how a careful exploration of who really commands the various power bases can improve our understanding of where the power lies in organizations. A lab assistant, although he or she has little legitimate power, may be quite powerful as a result of another power base, such as expertise, effective control over important resources, effective ways of getting something done, or ways around the official system. The analysis reminds us that it is always a good idea to make sure you get on well with the support staff. It also suggests several ways in which you can use your own opportunities to acquire some power, even as a junior employee.

POWER IN THE ORGANIZATION

How Departments Get Power

So far we have discussed power mainly in the context of two individuals, the power-holder and the power-target. We now expand the discussion to consider how power is distributed within the organization. In most organizations, some departments are clearly more powerful than others, even though they may be shown as equals on the organization chart. How do such power inequalities come about? Are they a result of "mere politics" or is there something more interesting about them? We shall look at both these questions in this section.

An example will help the discussion. Consider the case of an imaginary firm manufacturing domestic appliances such as clothes washers and driers, refrigerators, and ranges. Its basic organizational structure is shown in Figure 6.1. Five vice presidents report to the president: VP Manufacturing, who supervises the metal forming, electrical, and assembly and test divisions; VP Sales and Marketing, in charge of a domestic and an overseas division; VP Development, who supervises an R&D laboratory and a product development division; VP Employee Relations, who supervises the industrial relations and personnel divisions; and VP Finance and Accounting, who supervises these two divisions. Other corporate staff functions reporting to the president include the office of corporate counsel (legal matters) and the office of computing services.

Let us drop in on an important meeting of the corporate planning group—the president and the five vice presidents. VP Development has

Figure 6.1.   Organization Chart for a Domestic Appliance Company

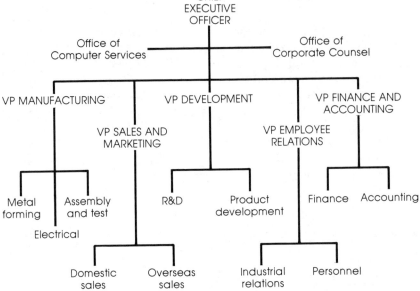

just reported the results of tests of a new product his group has been working on for some time, a microwave oven, which he is arguing should be added to the present product line. The other VPs have strong views on the matter. VP Sales and Marketing is strongly in favor: the company needs a glamorous new product to liven up their range and give them a "high technology" image. VP Manufacturing is strongly opposed: he already has enough trouble meeting current production schedules. His difficulties will multiply if he adds a new product that he sees as not ready yet for full-scale production, and that involves novel technologies with which his division is not familiar. VP Finance and Accounting is uneasy about raising the money for the new capital equipment the new oven will require. Finally, VP Employee Relations is worried that hiring workers with the right skills for the new product will be difficult and costly, and may distort the new wage and salary structure her group has been working on for the past two years. It is going to be a long meeting!

Note, first, that there is nothing underhand or malicious about the characters in the situation we have sketched. The five VPs are all highly competent at their jobs, and all are interested in the company's success. The disagreement arises because each of them emphasizes, quite properly, the effects of the decision on his or her division. The decision is important, complex, and highly uncertain as to results. There is no obviously rational, analytical way of making it. We do not need to invent any self-seeking or empire-building motivations for the VPs to know that serious disagreement will occur. It is highly likely that when all the arguing and number-crunching is done, the decision on the microwave oven will be importantly influenced by the relative power of the planning group participants.

According to the organization chart, all five are at the same level, and thus equally powerful. However, this is most unlikely to be true in practice: some will be more powerful than others. Can we predict which VPs will be more powerful, which less? Perhaps we can, but only if we know a little more about the company's history. For example, consider these three alternative scenarios:

1. Suppose the company has a history of costly strikes. Two years ago, a key group of skilled workers struck, stopping production for four months. They finally accepted a 30 percent wage increase, making them the highest-paid hourly employees in the company. The other hourly workers bitterly resented this, and have been on the verge of striking since. The new wage and salary structure the VP Employee Relations has been working on is intended to resolve some of these problems. With this history, we would predict that the vote of VP Employee Relations would be weighed heavily in deciding on the new microwave oven. She, in short, would acquire significant additional power.

2. Suppose the company, because of the excellent quality of its products, has always enjoyed a good reputation with consumers. Despite a number of plant expansions it has always had trouble meeting demand, and the sales department has had to impose a quota on its dealers. The products virtually sell themselves, and sales is always pressing manufacturing to increase production. VP Manufacturing, who rose through the ranks of production engineering, has always insisted on careful inspection and quality control, often putting these ahead of production quantity. With this history, we would predict that VP Manufacturing would carry considerable power in influencing the microwave oven decision.

3. A few years ago the company marketed a new refrigerator with poorly placed cooling coils. Sometimes a joint in the coils leaked when the refrigerator was pushed back against a wall, releasing a poisonous coolant. Two customers died, a dozen were seriously injured, and the company is facing multimillion dollar lawsuits for damages. Given this history, we would expect the planning group might well be expanded to include the senior attorney from the office of corporate counsel, and

that (s)he would have a very influential voice in the microwave oven decision.

Strategic Contingencies Theory

What these three examples suggest is a version of what is known as the "strategic contingencies" theory of organizational power (Hickson et al., 1971; Pfeffer and Salancik, 1974). This theory argues that all organizations face a fairly small number of problems that are both (a) important (i.e., strategic, not tactical) and (2) highly uncertain (i.e., not only complex, but difficult to predict and solve). The functions in the organizations that deal with these problems acquire power, and are able to mobilize the organization's resources to deal with them. Thus, in the first example, *labor problems* were the major "strategic contingency," and the employee relations function, which dealt with those problems, gained power. In the second example, *production* was the critical problem, giving power to VP Manufacturing. When the central problem is legal, as in the third example above, lawyers gain influence.

All this sounds perfectly simple and sensible, as it is. What is worth noting is that this theory gives a less self-serving perspective on the whole issue of organizational power. If power distributions actually work this way (and there is evidence that they often do), power becomes a key mechanism in lining up the organization with the world it actually lives in. If relative power in the planning group were distributed by some other rule—for example, the seniority of the respective VPs, or the size of their budgets—then influence over key decisions would not necessarily reflect anything about how important the various considerations are. What strategic contingencies theory offers is a way of allocating, and shifting over time, the power of different organizational functions. It shifts power so as to give more to those functions that deal with the organization's most pressing problems. What could be more sensible?

There are two closely related reasons why things do not always work this smoothly. First, power is not a precision instrument, with individuals and departments gaining only the power that allows them to deal with the specific critical problem. Power acquired by having critical-problem skills can also be used to influence other matters. Second, since most people would rather have more power than less, they will tend to use the power they have (a flexible tool) to preserve and expand their power. These two factors tend to "freeze" power distributions that might fit one set of problems, even after the critical problems have changed and a new power distribution is required.

Consider again the third example discussed above, where the critical problem was a huge product liability suit, and the legal department gained in power. The head of the legal department gained an influential voice in the corporate planning group, because (s)he was able to deal with the company's critical problem. With this new power, (s)he is likely to ask for full membership in the planning group, implying promotion to full vice president status. This, in turn, would plausibly lead to expansion of the legal department into a full-blown division, with an increased budget. Given the importance of legal matters to the company, lawyers from this division would be appointed to other important committees, such as the new products group or the employee relations committee. Little by little, lawyers start to appear at all the key points in the company and become a force to be reckoned with. From their original base (ability to deal with the product liability suit), they are now influential in many other decisions—including, critically, decisions as to who becomes influential! The power of the legal function has become "institutionalized."

Again, this is not necessarily just a cynical power-grab. As we saw earlier, lawyers tend to see problems in legal terms, just as engineers tend to see them in engineering terms, and accountants in accounting terms. Problems do not generally announce themselves as "critical." Someone has to see them that way, and convince others about it. With lawyers on the key committees, legal aspects of problems tend to become more widely recognized as critical. Because they are problems only lawyers can solve, the lawyers' power increases again. Even without self-interested empire building, power tends to be self-amplifying and self-perpetuating. Power distributions thus have a tendency to reflect yesterday's "critical contingencies" for the organization, not necessarily today's or tomorrow's.

USING POWER: TARGETS, STRENGTHS, AND LIMITS

Thus far we have been mainly concerned with how people and groups in organizations come to have power. McCall (1979) has pointed out that power is largely a matter of being in the right place, at the right time, with the right resources, and doing the right thing. What we have tried to do so far is to enrich this summary statement and to show in concrete terms some of the main ways in which power arises. We now turn briefly to some of the issues that arise in using power.

First, who and what is the target? Very different power tactics are needed to influence a specific behavior of one specific individual on one specific occasion than to influence a broad class of behaviors, for a group of people, over a long period of time. For the first, a single verbal instruction may suffice. For the second, some more economical way of

using power, for example, standing orders or standard operating procedures, is needed. Similarly, an effort to change on particular decision of a committee will need different tactics than if the aim is to
change the *kinds* of decisions the committee makes. For the first purpose, I might try to persuade a majority of the current members to
accept my point of view; for the second, changing the membership of
the committee to include more of my allies might be more effective.

An interesting range of such power tactics was found by George
Strauss (1962) in his study of how purchasing agents acquire and use
power in a company. These tactics are particularly interesting because
the purchasing agents he studied dealt primarily with other departments in the organization at the same hierarchical level—production
scheduling, quality control, engineering, etc. The agents thus had to
deal with the conflicts that came up by means of lateral relationships
with these other departments. They had no hierarchical authority to
call on. Their primary tasks were to negotiate with suppliers outside
the firm and to keep on top of deliveries. Because the specifications,
quality, and delivery times of the materials they bought were important
to other departments, a variety of conflicts commonly came up. For
example, production scheduling might submit a requisition with an
unusually short delivery date, requiring the purchasing agent either to
harass suppliers with whom he needs to maintain good relationships or
to resist the demand in some way. Strauss found five common tactics
the agents used in resisting demands:

1. **Using rules.** If there is a standing rule about minimum lead times,
   the agent might invoke this. If not, he might ask for justification in
   writing, or ask the ordering department to pay for extra costs (such
   as air-freight charges).

2. **Evading rules.** The agent might "go through the motions" of trying to
   get speedy delivery, but not really try; or might even just ignore the
   requisition (a breach of the rules, but often hard for the ordering
   department to do anything about).

3. **Personal/political.** The agent might use friendships, or promises of
   future favors, either directly with the ordering department or
   indirectly through other departments, to get the request modified.

4. **Educational/persuasive.** The agent might try direct persuasion to
   convince the ordering department that the request was unreasonable. Less directly, he might try to get the same effect by, for
   example, getting the ordering department boss to sit in on discussions with the supplier, to see what difficulties were being made.

5. **Organizational.** The agent might try to get the requisition procedure
   changed (e.g., to require prior approval of purchasing for all requi-
   sitions) or even attempt to change the organization's structure (e.g.,

integrating both purchasing and scheduling into a "materials" department).

As we have noted, these tactics are often very effective. We do not need to assume that the purchasing agents were selfish, malicious, or power hungry. What most of them seemed to be doing was using the power resources available to keep their departments working smoothly by buffering them from excessive outside influences. Certainly, some empire building and status climbing was going on, but there was also a good bit of give and take, covering of genuine emergencies, and effort to make the department run well. The agents used their power both for good and otherwise, but they certainly found ways to acquire it, and were subtle about how they used it.

One of the things we can learn from such studies is that any single form of power has strengths and weaknesses when we come to use it. French and Raven's five bases of personal power—reward, coercive, legitimate, referent, and expert—provide numerous examples. Reward and coercive power, for example, tend to get used up if we use them often, while the other three do not. They also require that the power holder can monitor a subordinate's behavior quickly and accurately, which may not always be possible. For example, if I threaten to fire an employee unless (s)he stops a particularly dangerous work behavior, I need to be able to determine whether or not (s)he has stopped to be able to carry out my threat. In contrast, if the employee shifts to safer working methods because of identification with an admired senior craftsperson, no monitoring from outside is needed. In legitimate, referent, and expert power, the motivation to obey comes from within the person obeying. In reward and coercive power, it comes from outside.

Using power effectively is a delicate matter. Most effective power users seem to mix and match, varying the resources and tactics they use to match particular situations. Kotter (1977) suggests that power is used most effectively by using first the subtlest, least abrasive methods available, and resorting to the harsher methods only as a last resort. Threats of firing, for example, should probably be used only after encouragement, persuasion, and other alternatives have been thoroughly tried.

One reason for this strategy is that harsh methods tend to produce power-limiting responses. If a plant's management is heavily punitive and authoritarian, the employees are more likely to form a union, strike, leave, or use sabotage to get back at the management, thereby reducing management's power. If Strauss's purchasing agents were able to gain complete power over the other departments, it seems likely that the other departments would retaliate in some way, perhaps forming a coalition to persuade higher management to rein in the agents, perhaps setting up purchasing departments of their own. In general, unsubtle or abusive use of power is likely to provoke one or more power-limiting responses, such as:

1. **Retaliation.** As we saw earlier, even low-ranked members of the organization can hold significant power. If they feel badly used by a power-holder, they are likely to use their own power to hit back. The boss who abuses a secretary is likely to find messages going astray, letters mailed late, and embarrassing (if untraceable) leaks of confidential information.

2. **Regulation.** The robber barons of the later nineteenth century acquired vast fortunes by oppressing their workers, employing children, and allowing horrible working conditions. They also inadvertently brought about the extensive governmental regulation of hours of work, minimum pay rates, and safety of working conditions.

3. **Escape.** If those who hold power use their power excessively, those over whom they wield it may simply move, perhaps to another job, another organization, another area of work, or even to another country.

4. **Opposing coalitions.** A group of people all aggrieved over the same power holder can form a coalition to depose him or her, or to limit the oppressive power. Unions are one example of a formal coalition opposing company management; workers achieve power by pooling their control of the labor supply. A mutiny aboard ship and an informal slow-down on the assembly line are examples of the same kind.

5. **Resource depletion.** The power holder may be forced into using up the resource(s) underlying his or her power. Instead of reacting to threats, the subordinates can force the supervisor to take disciplinary action and then appeal the actions. The supervisor is then forced to justify each and every decision, taking up time and making it more likely that higher management will intervene.

6. **Substitutes.** If the power base centers on control of a particular resource, it may be undermined or eliminated by development of alternative means of acquiring that same resource. The power of the bank to dictate spending decisions is limited by the availability of other sources of money. The power of the internal computer expert is limited by the availability of outside consultants. In each case, the alternative may cost more, but may be worth it, to limit the power of the original person or group.

These and other tactics generally set limits on how far a particular power holder can go in exploiting his or her resources. But perhaps the most familiar limit is that the experienced power holder knows where the limits of power are, and stays within them. If everyone uses every power resource to its fullest extent, the organization is likely to fall apart, hurting everyone in it. It is common enough that yesterday's subordinate becomes tomorrow's boss, so self-interest dictates that one be prudent about not abusing one's present power. There are good practical reasons why most of us share a "norm of reciprocity" about the use of power. We stick to what is seen as fair, in a sense that is hard to define but that is generally well understood. It is only when someone plays outside these rules of fair play that limiting tactics such as those listed above come to be used.

POWER AS CONTROL OF DECISION PROCESSES

A useful way to think about power is to consider how the power holder shapes the decision making of the person over whom (s)he has power. Even the mugger's power can be seen in this way. The threat, "Give me your wallet or I'll kill you," still leaves me with a decision to obey or not, though I would be very stupid to disobey. More generally, one could consider each of the variables in the expectancy model and think about how each could be operated by a power holder.

For example, some of the structural tactics may allow the power holder to influence who gets to make a particular decision, by influencing appointments to key jobs or membership on key committees. It may also be possible to influence the information available to these decision makers, by changing flows of information or assembling evidence. The power holder may be able to influence which alternative actions are considered, what consequences flow from each, and what values are attached to these consequences. Reward and coercive power both operate directly on the consequences that follow from the person doing one thing rather than another. Referent power might be seen as controlling the value of one particular outcome: being like the person identified with. Expert power turns on the expert being able to provide sound information on the consequences of particular actions.

At the strategic level, control of the decision process is again key. Strategic contingencies theory argues that precisely those who are able to deal with the most pressing and uncertain decisions will gain in power. They acquire control over the key decisions because they are seen as able to make them well. This in turn allows them to influence other aspects of the organization's decision-making process to produce the outcomes they value. They are able to shape ill-defined problems into ones that need their expertise, as in emphasizing the legal aspects rather than the engineering aspects of new-product decisions, in our earlier example. Thus, at both the individual and the organizational level, the acquisition and use of power can be mapped directly into control over one or another aspect of the decision process.

SUMMARY

We defined "power" as the ability of one person to get things done as (s)he wishes, even when others disagree. This ability is a characteristic of the relationship between two or more people, not of any one person. We identified several sources of power: reward, coercive, legitimate, referent, and expert. Some combinations of all five can be used effectively, but some interfere with the use of others.

Analysis of who holds which power bases in particular situations helps us to understand how power is acquired. Low-ranking members of the organization can acquire power by various means: expertise, effort, attractiveness, position, forming coalitions, or adroit use of rules. The actual distribution of power in an organization is thus considerably more complex than is implied by one's position in the hierarchy.

The distribution of power in the organization is considered by strategic contingencies theory, which holds that individuals and units acquire power to the extent that they are able to deal successfully with important, high-uncertainty problems facing the organization. In an example, we saw how different departments acquired power and were later able to consolidate and extend this power, by their ability to cope with the key problem facing the organization. Power shifts are an important way in which organizations respond to their changing environments, though probably not in any precise or speedy way.

The use of power needs to be tailored to the person or group—the target—it is aimed at, and to the situation. Various tactics of power use were discussed in an example of how one department head, the purchasing agent, exercised power over others nominally at the same level. These tactics include using and evading rules, personal/political tactics, educational/persuasive approaches, and organizational tactics. The choice of tactic is a delicate matter: power is not a precision instrument; it can affect the user as well as the target. In particular, the target can respond to abuse of power in various ways: by retaliation, by getting the power holder regulated, by escape, by forming opposing coalitions, by forcing the holder to use up his or her power base, or by developing substitutes for the resource controlled by the power holder.

In the final section, we considered power in terms of ability to shape another's decision. At the individual level, we saw that power holders can operate in a variety of ways, such as influencing who gets to make the decision, what alternatives are considered, what information is available, the consequences that flow from each decision, and the value attached to these consequences. At the organizational level, strategic contingencies theory describes exactly this shift of influence over decision making as the basis of power allocation.

CLOSING COMMENT

A final point needs to be reiterated in closing this chapter. We suggested earlier that, particularly for scientists and engineers, the use of power is seen as somehow unsavory, underhand, not fair, or otherwise irrational—as a "bad thing." I hope this bias has now been dispelled. Power is inherently neither good nor bad, and it seems to be essential for organizations to run at all. It is found at every level, from the lowest employee to the highest. Each can use the power (s)he has for good or bad purposes. Used carefully, power provides the engine for effective organizational functioning, for getting something accomplished. To the extent that strategic contingencies theory is true, the shifting of power distributions is an important way of keeping the organization in touch with the reality of its world. Obviously, abuse of power can have serious consequences, although the limitations on abuse may stop it from continuing indefinitely. In any event, power exists, and must be reckoned with. It must be understood, grasped, and used carefully. Merely to deplore it, to complain about self-seekers and office politics, is to ignore an important lever for influencing the organization's activities.

DISCUSSION QUESTIONS: CHAPTER 6

1. Junior employees often complain that they have trouble getting their ideas put into practice—that is, that they have insufficient power. How might a junior employee go about acquiring significant power in the form of:

   a. Reward power

   b. Coercive power

   c. Legitimate power

   d. Referent power

   e. Expert power

   Rate each of these power bases in terms of how easily a junior employee might acquire them.

2. Strategic contingencies theory suggests that departments acquire power in proportion to their ability to deal with the organization's critical problems. Why might the actual distribution of power in an organization differ from this apparently desirable form?

3. Suppose you are a member of a service department such as maintenance or computer programming. How might you use the five tactics described by Strauss (1962) to gain some autonomy and resist the demands placed on you by the departments you serve? Would this be in the organization's interests or not?

4. Because you were highly successful in using the five tactics in Question 3, your service department became very powerful. How might the client departments react to this development?

5. A colleague complains to you that an excellent technical idea of his for how the manufacturing department could increase its output has been rejected because of "office politics"—that is, because the manufacturing department has the power to reject proposals from outsiders. How might you argue that it is a good thing for manufacturing to be in a position to do this, even if it means they reject some good technical ideas?

Chapter 7

Leadership

Of all the subjects covered by organizational behavior, leadership is perhaps the most frustrating. We see examples of what we believe to be good or bad leadership around us every day. Sports teams play well or badly, and it seems obvious that it has something to do with the coach or manager. Project groups come up with good or bad designs, and it seems obvious that it has something to do with the project leader. Orchestras play well or badly, apparently as a result of the conductor. Whole corporations raise their profits, or head towards bankruptcy, as chief executives come and go. Leadership, in short, seems to affect every area of life, and in a rather clear-cut way.

Yet, when we sit down to digest what is known about this interesting phenomenon, we come up with a complex and unsatisfactory picture. There is a mountain of research—literally thousands of studies—looking at leadership in all sorts of contexts, from leaders of nations to leaders of small discussion groups, from sports teams to juries. Despite this enormous effort, we still lack satisfactory answers to most of the key questions: What exactly is effective leadership? Can we select, or train, people who will be effective as leaders? How much of a difference does leadership actually make? Can we learn to become more effective as leaders?

For each of these questions we have intriguing, if partial, answers. The available research suggests that leaders do, in fact, make some difference, though not as much as we might expect. We may be able to raise our own effectiveness as leaders, but, again, not as much as we might hope. We are a long way short of an understanding of effective leadership that would allow us to be effective in every situation, every time. At best, we can hope to raise our batting averages a few points, certainly not to hit home runs off every pitch.

In this chapter, we will summarize some of the major themes in current leadership research, and try to identify those areas that offer some hope of improving our own leadership skills.

APPOINTED AND EMERGENT LEADERS

People become leaders in one of two ways. The most obvious way is by appointment: if you are the *head* of the applied physics branch, the *chair* of the grievance committee, or the *captain* of the lacrosse team, your title indicates that you hold the job of leadership. It is in your job description that you will act as the leader. However, there is a second way by which people become leaders: they emerge as the group operates. In any classroom discussion, someone commonly takes on the role of discussion leader—making notes on the blackboard, directing the traffic of who speaks when, proposing action plans, and making summaries. No one has to appoint such a person. He or she just emerges, generally with at least the tacit consent of the group, to handle these necessary functions. There is no guarantee that the appointed leader and the emergent leader will be the same person, although that is clearly a happy situation when it happens. (In fact, one basic idea of simple democracy is to achieve this end: people choose as official, or appointed, leader someone who has already demonstrated informal, or emergent, leadership skills.)

Which of the "power bases" discussed in Chapter 6 does each of these leaders have available? Appointed leaders have formal, legitimate power; emergent leaders may not. Appointed leaders also have, at least in theory, a wide range of reward and coercive resources on which to draw—pay, promotion, work assignments, firing, etc.—although these may be severely limited by formal procedures or union rules. Emergent leaders also have some reward and coercive powers; their opinions and judgments are valued. A pat on the back from such a person may be a powerful reward and a harsh word a powerful punishment. However, their most important power resource is their referent and expert power, resources that may not be available to the appointed leader at all. Thus, emergent leaders may, in fact, be in fairly powerful positions, while the official, appointed leader may be relatively powerless.

Who becomes an emergent leader? Studies comparing emergent and appointed leaders suggest that:

1. **Overall intelligence is not a large factor.** Both sorts of leaders seem generally to be at or a little above the average intelligence of the group (Stogdill, 1948).

2. **Social skills matter.** Emergent leaders have good social skills much more often than appointed leaders do (Stogdill, 1948).

3. **Situational factors make a difference in the emergence of a leader.** Having strong skills in the specific task facing the group makes emergent leadership more likely (Hollander, 1964; Stogdill, 1974). Good athletes tend to emerge as leaders on the sports field; good scholars tend to emerge as leaders in class discussion.

4. **Some apparently trivial aspects of the situation can affect leadership emergence.** Seating arrangements can make a difference, with those sitting at the ends of a table more likely to emerge as leaders than those sitting on the sides (Strodtbeck and Hook, 1961). Similarly, being at the hub of a communication net makes leadership emergence more likely (Leavitt, 1951).

No single type of person regularly emerges as a leader. Rather, it is a matter of being in the right place, at the right time, with the right skills (both task related and social). This conclusion will recur in the remainder of this chapter, as we turn from the question of who becomes a leader to who becomes an *effective* leader.

EFFECTIVE AND INEFFECTIVE LEADERS

Given that a group has a leader, appointed or emergent, what determines whether or not that leader will be effective? By "effective," we mean here that the group has a task to do or a problem to solve. If the task is performed well under Leader A, and poorly under Leader B, we shall rate Leader A as more effective than Leader B. However, we shall add the stipulation that effective task performance is not achieved at the expense of the long-term viability of the group. A leader who achieves good task results at the cost of low member satisfaction, high internal levels of conflict, or other signs of "wearing out" of the group will not be rated as effective.

A great deal of early leadership research was aimed at identifying personal characteristics, "leadership traits," that distinguished effective leaders from ineffective ones. Are effective leaders more intelligent than ineffective ones? Superior orators? Taller? Of a higher-class upbringing? Each of these, and dozens of others, have been investigated, but the overall results have been meager and confusing. Stogdill (1948), reviewing well over a hundred studies available at the time, summarized his results as follows:

The findings suggest that leadership is not a matter of passive status, or of the mere possession of some combination of traits. It appears rather to be a working relationship among members of a group, in which the leader acquires status through active participation and demonstration of his capacity for carrying cooperative tasks through to completion. Significant aspects of this capacity for organizing and expediting cooperative effort appear to be intelligence, alertness to the needs and motives of others, and insight into situations, further reinforced by such habits as responsibility, initiative, persistence, and self-confidence. (Stogdill, 1948: p. 69)

In short, it is not just a matter of who you are, but of what you do, and what the situation demands.

Frustration with the "leader trait" approach led to greater research interest in analysis of leader behavior, of situations, and of how these fit together to affect effectiveness. One aspect of leader behavior that has been extensively studied is the extent to which the leader allows participation of the subordinates in making decisions. For example, Tannenbaum and Schmidt (1958) suggested a scale of participation from boss centered to subordinate centered:

Boss-centered
leadership

Subordinate-centered
leadership

| 0 | 1 | 2 | 3 | 4 | 5 | 6 | 7 | 8 | 9 | 10 |

On this scale, an entirely boss-centered approach (scale value 0) is when the boss makes a decision alone, and merely announces it to the group. In the middle range are such approaches as presenting a tentative decision to the group for suggestions or approval. Scale value 10 indicates an approach where the leader essentially turns the problem over to the group, for them to decide within limits set by the boss. Tannenbaum and Schmidt discuss the factors that might lead one to choose a particular point on this scale to operate. Forces in the leader, forces in the subordinates, and forces in the situation are all considered. However, this discussion is largely paralleled by a more refined model we shall consider in a moment, so we need not review the details here.

An interesting sidelight: Tannenbaum and Schmidt titled their paper "How to Choose a Leadership Pattern." The implication is that there is a choice to be made; moving away from the idea of a fixed set of traits, leaders are thought of as able to act in a variety of different ways. This is at least a questionable assumption. Probably most of us have some region of the spectrum at which we operate most comfortably. In many organizations, subordinates similarly have strong expectations about how leaders should behave. In military organizations, for example, officers' behavior is expected to be at the low end of the scale. In universities, in contrast, deans are expected to create at least an appearance of strong group involvement in such major decisions as hiring and promoting faculty. In both settings, leaders who violate expectations may face difficulties. Thus, both the setting and our personal limitations restrict the leadership styles we may use.

A somewhat more complex way of describing leader behavior emerged from extensive research conducted by a group at Ohio State University (Fleishman and Peters, 1962). From a very large number of measures of particular leader activities, the Ohio State group identified and labelled two important dimensions of how leaders actually behave:

1. **Consideration:** The extent to which the leader is considerate of the subordinates' feelings, respects their ideas, and develops mutually trusting working relationships with them.

2. **Initiating structure:** The extent to which the leader clarifies and defines the subordinates' work roles, relationships, channels of communication, and ways of getting the job done.

Descriptions of leader behavior in terms of "consideration" and "initiating structure" have come to be the hallmark of Ohio State leadership studies.

Two comments are needed here. First, the two dimensions are considered independent of one another, so that a particular leader may be high on both, low on both, or high on one and low on the other. Second, as has become clear from later research, the two dimensions do not capture all of what leaders do. The dimensions focus on the way the leader sets up the internal workings of the group, in terms of task-oriented ways of operating (initiating structure) and interpersonal ways of operating (consideration). They do not consider important external matters such as the leader's dealings with superiors, with other work groups, or with suppliers of raw materials or necessary information. In short, they describe some important features of the internal operations of the group, as they are affected by the leader.

MODELS OF EFFECTIVE LEADERSHIP

Numerous models of how to be an effective leader have been proposed by different researchers. It is probably fair to say that, at this point, no one of them has emerged as the clear winner in terms of producing the most reliable high-quality leaders. (This, of course, produces heated partisan conflict at meetings of leadership researchers!) Several of the models have been developed into elaborate and expensive training programs, which further complicates dispassionate appraisal of relative strengths and weaknesses.

Virtually all models that are still receiving serious research attention and development are what might be called "situational," "diagnostic," or "contingency" models. That is, they all argue that an effective leader must first undertake a diagnosis of the situation in which (s)he is to operate, and only then select a course of action. Included in the diagnostic phase are different aspects of the situation: characteristics of the task, of the subordinates, and of the leader. Different models suggest different lists of alternatives from which the leader is to choose. Some emphasize degree of participation, others emphasize behaviors in terms of the Ohio State dimensions, and others suggest alternatives of a quite different sort. We shall review a sampling of several of the currently more popular models.

Fiedler's Contingency Model

Fiedler (1967, 1976) has developed a leadership model that has some of the aspects of the old "leadership traits" ideas. In his model, effectiveness is determined by an interaction between a personal characteristic of the leader and a rating of the overall favorableness of the situation in which (s)he is to lead. The personal characteristic is considered to be relatively fixed, so the leader's key diagnostic task is to weigh up the situation and decide whether or not it fits with his or her personality. If it does not, the leader should change the situation or possibly get a replacement who fits the situation better.

The specifics of this model may be summarized as follows:

Diagnostic phase.

Assessing situational favorability. Three factors affect how favorable the situation is for the leader: leader-member relations, task structure, and leader position power. Generally, it is easiest to be a leader when: (1) the group respects, accepts, and trusts the leader; (2) the task is clear and well structured, so everyone knows what to do and how to do it; and (3) the leader has real power (to hire and fire, give raises, or promote). If all three factors are positive, the leader is in a most favorable situation; if all are negative, the situation is most unfavorable. In mixed situations leader-member relations are most important, and position power least important, in determining situational favorability. Figure 7.1 illustrates this idea.

Assessing the leader's personality. Fiedler's model also assesses the characteristic of the leader known as his or her "Least Preferred Coworker" (LPC) score. The LPC score is derived from asking the leader to rate the person with whom (s)he has been least able to work well. The questionnaire simply lists sixteen pairs of adjectives, such as:

Uncooperative	1	2	3	4	5	6	7	8	Cooperative
Inefficient	1	2	3	4	5	6	7	8	Efficient
Boring	1	2	3	4	5	6	7	8	Interesting

Figure 7.1. Determinants of Situational Favorability in Fiedler's Model

	Highly favorable						Highly unfavorable
	SITUATIONAL FAVORABILITY						
	1	2	3	4	5	6	7	8
Leader-member relations	Good				Poor			
Task structure	High		Low		High		Low	
Position power	Strong	Weak	Strong	Weak	Strong	Weak	Strong	Weak

People who tend to rate their least preferred co-worker low on these dimensions, called "low LPC" people, seem to be showing a pretty harsh, judgmental feeling about the co-worker they are imagining, while those who score high seem to be more forgiving and people oriented. There is some dispute about just what the LPC measures and whether it really is a stable personality characteristic. Fiedler suggests that it is a measure of whether one is primarily task motivated or relationship motivated. He allows that an individual can be both, but that one or the other characteristic is primary and will emerge in pressure situations. Roughly, then, low LPC scores suggest that the leader is primarily task oriented, while high LPC scores suggest that (s)he is more person oriented.

Effective Choices.   The core of Fiedler's model is the evidence he has accumulated that there is a relationship among situational favorability, the leader's LPC, and group performance. This evidence indicates that:

1. Low LPC leaders do well in the more favorable situations (sectors 1, 2, and 3 in the diagram) and in the least favorable situation (sector 8).
2. High LPC leaders do well in the moderately favorable situations (sectors 4 and 5).
3. There is no relationship between LPC and effectiveness in the remaining two sectors (6 and 7).

Just why these relationships seem to hold is a matter for speculation, but the practical implications are reasonably clear. First, you need to find out what your LPC score is. In Fiedler's view, there is not much you can do to change this, at least in the short run, so to be effective you either have to take on only those leadership situations where your LPC fits, or to try to change the situation into one that fits. This focus on manipulating the situation to fit the leader is unique to Fiedler's approach. Most of the other currently popular models tend to emphasize the relative flexibility of the leader's behavior, treating the situation as basically fixed. Fiedler reminds us that selecting, or changing, the situation to fit our styles is an option that should not be neglected.

Fiedler's model has been criticized on various grounds, including questions as to what exactly the LPC measures, whether or not LPC is stable over time, just *how* it is that LPC and situation interact, and how precisely situations can be diagnosed (see, e.g., Ashour, 1973). In response, Fiedler continues to turn out studies supporting his model and to train managers how to achieve a good match between their LPCs and their situations. He has achieved a measure of practical success, while leaving important questions unresolved. His major contributions have been to force us to look seriously at the situation and whether it can be manipulated. He has also reminded us that the easy assumption that we can change our behaviors readily to fit leadership requirements may not be true.

The Vroom-Yetton Model

The Vroom-Yetton model of leadership (Vroom and Yetton, 1973) focuses on a single aspect of the leader's behavior: the extent to which the leader shares decision-making power with his or her subordinates. "Power sharing" is similar to "degree of participation" in the Tannenbaum and Schmidt scale, discussed earlier. Vroom and Yetton consider the leader as choosing from five possible alternatives along this scale:

Autocratic:

AI: Leader solves the problem alone, using available information.

AII: Leader solves the problem alone, after collecting necessary information from subordinates.

Collaborative:

CI: Leader consults with subordinates individually, gets their ideas and suggestions, then decides alone.

CII: As CI, but consultation takes place in a group meeting.

Group:

GII: Leader chairs group meeting aimed at reaching a consensus decision.

The model suggests that effective leadership results when a suitable style is chosen from this list in light of the requirements of the situation. The diagnostic phase consists of a series of questions aimed at discovering what these requirements are.

Diagnostic phase.   In somewhat simplified form, the five key diagnostic questions in the Vroom-Yetton model are:

1. **Is decision quality important?** A decision may be unimportant either because the stakes are small, or because all the alternatives are of equal value. For example, I may not care much where the company picnic is held or who is to represent us at some social function. On the other hand, the choice of the new research director may be very important; but, if the choice is between three excellent candidates, I may still not care which one is chosen.

2. **Do I have adequate information?** Care is needed in making this assessment. We all tend to overestimate our own expertise com-

pared to our subordinates'. A realistic judgment is needed as to whether or not the leader has adequate information.

3. **Is the problem structured?** If information gathering is needed, do I, the leader, know what the necessary information is, and where it can be found?

4. **Is there a problem with acceptance of a solution?** This question covers two issues. First, is it essential that the subordinates accept the decision? Second, if it is essential, will they accept a decision made autocratically by me? The leader has an acceptance problem only if acceptance is essential, and autocratic decisions will be resisted. In these circumstances, involving the group may be necessary for effective implementation of the solution.

5. **Do my subordinates share my goals?** If I delegate the decision to my subordinates, will they use the same choice criteria as I would? If my subordinates share my goals, I will be more prepared to share my power with them than I would otherwise be.

The leader's answers to these five questions provide a diagnosis of the situation. The remainder of the Vroom-Yetton model links this diagnosis to a choice of one of the five styles listed earlier (AI, AII, CI, CII, and GII). In many situations, the diagnostic questions eliminate some style choices but leave more than one in the "feasible set." A choice can be made from the "feasible set" on other grounds, which we will discuss later.

Effective choices. It will be convenient to consider three different types of problem, defined by the answers to the first two diagnostic questions listed above. If decision quality does not matter, we shall refer to the problem as a "Type 1." If quality matters and the leader has the relevant information, the problem is "Type 2." If quality matters and the leader does not have the relevant information, the problem is "Type 3."

Type 1 (quality not a problem): If I, as a leader, do not care which solution is picked, other issues such as availability of information and problem structure do not matter. My only question concerns decision acceptance. If acceptance is not a problem, all five decision styles are still open to me. If, however, acceptance is important, and the group will resist an autocratic decision, then a fully participative style (Style GII) would be the best approach. In summary, for these problems, the leader's decision tree is simple:

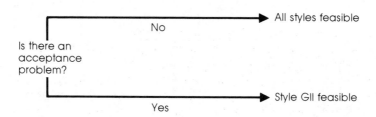

Type 2 (quality matters; leader has relevant information): Since I have the information, I *can* make the decision if I wish to. On the other hand, some degree of delegation might help acceptance. However, I care about solution quality, so I have to consider whether or not the subordinates share my goals before I turn the problem over to them. This gives four options for these types of problem:

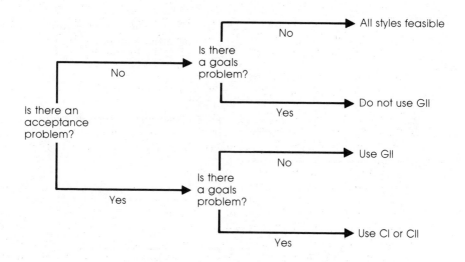

Type 3 (quality matters; leader does not have relevant information):

a. Structured problem: Type 3 problems are the trickiest. Decision quality matters, and the leader has to involve the group somehow, because (s)he does not have the necessary information to make a good decision alone. AI is precluded: I have to consult with the group. But the options leaving me a good deal of control (AII or CI) are still open, since I know where to go for information. My choice, then, turns on the acceptance and goals questions as before:

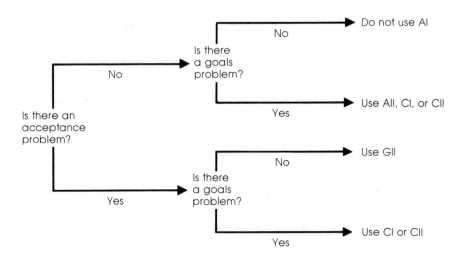

b. *Unstructured problem:* Here we have the same difficulties as above with the extra wrinkle that I do not know where to go for the information. This cuts further my list of options, eliminating both of the modestly participative approaches AII and CI. Striking these, we are left with:

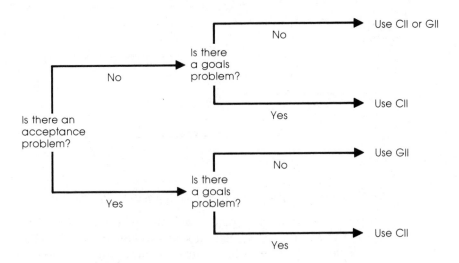

Laying out all possibilities in this way may seem complicated, but the underlying logic is simple. We start with all five possible decision styles and eliminate options as we work through the list of diagnostic questions. If I cannot make the decision on my own, AI is out. If I do not care about what is decided, then I only have to worry about possible problems with acceptance by the subordinates; and this is generally helped by involving them in making the decision. If I need the group's input to make a good decision, I can still be fairly nonparticipative if I know where to go for information. If not, I am forced to fairly high participation (CII or GII). Finally, turning the problem over to the group is risky if I suspect they will apply criteria counter to mine (or the organization's) in making the decision. If our goals clash, GII is out.

Note that a range of approaches is feasible for several problem types. How do we make this choice? Here Vroom (1976) suggests a final strategy consideration: the tradeoff between time and people development. In general, the more participative the decision process, the longer it takes. On the other hand, decision participation allows subordinates to develop their problem-solving skills, to become informed, and to feel more involved in the organization's affairs. When several decision styles are feasible, one can choose on the basis of a tradeoff between time (both speed and work hours) and people development. Thus, the same decision that, in an emergency, has to be handled by style AI might, in more leisurely times, be handled by style GII. Again, the situation shapes the preferred decision approach.

Does the Vroom-Yetton method work? Do leaders following its recommendations really lead more effectively? There is not yet any convincing evidence that they do, though there are some encouraging signs. Vroom (1976) asked managers to describe decisions they felt they had made particularly well—or particularly badly. The decisions reported as successful tended to have been made by procedures that the model would have recommended; the unsuccessful decisions more often were made by methods the model would advise against. In general, managers seemed to vary their styles less from one situation to another than the model would recommend. For example, a manager might use only AII and CI, never using the other styles at all. Vroom also found that managers tend to get subordinate input more often, and delegate authority less often, than the model calls for.

In summary, the Vroom-Yetton model is a complex version of a "contingency theory" of leadership behavior, focusing particularly on the situational factors that should influence the leader's choice of a level of subordinate participation. The logic it uses has some solid support in the research literature, and the model as a whole seems to identify high-percentage approaches, as reported by working managers. There is not, however, any solid body of evidence at this point that leaders trained in these procedures actually end up with better decision processes. The model continues to be developed and may provide more reliable evidence of its soundness in the future.

Consideration/Structuring Models

The Ohio State dimensions of leader behavior—consideration and task structuring—have formed the basis for a number of models of effective leadership. Perhaps the simplest is that popularized by Blake and Mouton (1964), the managerial grid. The basis of the managerial grid is simply the replacement of the two dimensions of *behavior* with measures of a leader's *orientation*; that is, tendencies to act in certain ways, rather than reports of actual behaviors. This allows one to describe a range of management styles:

	High	3	2
PEOPLE ORIENTATION			
	Low	4	1
		Low	High

TASK ORIENTATION

A manager whose style falls in Quadrant 1 is strongly task oriented and not at all people oriented: the tough, cool, all-business taskmaster. A manager who falls in Quadrant 3, in contrast (strong people orientation, low task orientation), would be more the warm, friendly "nice-guy" type. (Blake and Mouton scale each dimension from 1 to 9 so that, for example, the two styles just mentioned would be referred to as "1,9" and "9,1" managers, respectively.)

The basis of managerial grid training is not really a contingency model at all. It simply aims to train all managers, regardless of task and situation, to operate in Quadrant 2, the "high-high" or "9,9" style. This may, in fact, be the most generally useful of the four styles. However, there is serious question whether it is universally appropriate. For example, in simple, routine, high-speed tasks such as those commonly found in manufacturing, Quadrant 1 (task-only) might be more effective. Conversely, a leader of a highly productive group of R&D professionals might be most effective in Quadrant 4, doing little on either task or people dimensions. In short, there is no difficulty finding studies in which "high-high" leaders are effective, nor is there any trouble finding counterexamples.

A review by Kerr and his colleagues (1974) attempted to bring some order into this mixed evidence. In general, leaders who are high on structure tend to have more productive groups, with lower satisfaction. This fits the stereotype of the taskmaster: the work gets done, but grudgingly. Highly considerate leaders tend to have happier groups, but often at the expense of production. (These findings seem to underlie the "myth of the high-high manager"; leaders high on both dimensions could be expected to have the best of both worlds, a group that is both productive and satisfied.) However, these general tendencies are moderated by a number of situational factors:

1. High structuring by the leader seems to have an effect only when such structuring is not already provided by the work. For example, if the task is highly ambiguous or the group members are intolerant of ambiguity, structuring by the leader helps both task performance and satisfaction. If these features are not present, leader structuring does not help performance, and reduces satisfaction.

2. Considerate behavior by the leader improves satisfaction only if the organization is a generally considerate place. Considerate behavior is ineffective in cold, hostile, or inconsiderate organizations.

3. Workers on inherently interesting jobs react less to either dimension of leader activity than do those on boring jobs.

There are, then, fairly clear exceptions to the rule that high-high is the universal best style. Structuring behavior helps performance only if the task is unstructured. Consideration helps satisfaction only if there is no adequate alternative source of satisfaction (such as interesting work). Providing either structure or consideration when not needed is unhelpful and may actively hinder. Studies suggesting that high-high leaders are often effective may thus tell us more about the work people do than about good leadership: if most people are working in ill-structured, uninteresting jobs, high-high leaders may be effective; structuring helps productivity and consideration introduces at least some payoffs interpersonally, which increases satisfaction.

An interesting model, also based on the Ohio State dimensions of leader behavior, has been advanced by Hersey and Blanchard (1969) under the title of "life cycle" or "maturity" theory. Although research support for this approach is not strong, the model provides a clear example of the diagnostic approach we have been exploring, and we therefore review it briefly here. In this approach, the central diagnostic task the leader must face is assessing the "maturity" of the group to the specific task. By "maturity" they mean a rather precise assessment of three things:

1. The extent to which the group has the skills necessary for the task

2. The extent to which the group is ready to take responsibility for accomplishing the task

3. The extent to which the group finds the task inherently satisfying.

A group low on all three characteristics is scored as "immature" while a high score on the three dimensions reflects "maturity."

Life-cycle theory asserts that effective leadership consists of moving successively through the four quadrants of the structure/consideration grid in response to the growing maturity of the group to the task. As an illustration, Hersey and Blanchard suggest an approach to teaching a small child a new skill, e.g., tying shoelaces. Suppose that the initial assessment is that the child is completely "immature" to this task, low on skills, taking responsibility, and inherent interest. What is required, they argue, is an "all task" approach (Quadrant 1 in the earlier diagram). The parent demonstrates, allows the child to practice the skill, and instructs. As the child starts to get the hang of it, the leader (parent) rewards the child with praise and encouragement, maintaining task focus as well (Quadrant 2, or "high-high" behavior). As the child progresses, the parent phases out task instruction, maintaining encouragement (Quadrant 3), and, finally, with the child fully "mature" to this particular task, the parent turns it over to the child entirely (Quadrant 4). Thus the term "life-cycle": the leader's overall task is to move the group or subordinate to full maturity, at which point the leader's task is complete (see Figure 7.2).

This model is less well developed than several of those we have examined and solid research support is scanty, but it is a useful reminder that the situational assessment demanded by all the models is not a one-time thing. Over time the situation is likely to change, so that new leadership styles are demanded for effectiveness. Leadership style used at one time influences the situation at a later time. Achieving a match between situation and style is a dynamic, continuous task.

The Ohio State dimensions of initiating structure and consideration are two of the best-researched areas of leadership. One or the other, or both, of these dimensions have been found to be associated with leadership effectiveness in many studies, though not always in the same way. The popular managerial grid training approach has emphasized a universal practice of "high-high" leadership; the evidence suggests that such a style is often, but not always, effective. Other readings of the evidence have led to subtler, more complex situational models, taking into account the nature of the task, the organizational climate, and the changes over time in the maturity of the group to the task.

Figure 7.2. Life-Cycle Theory

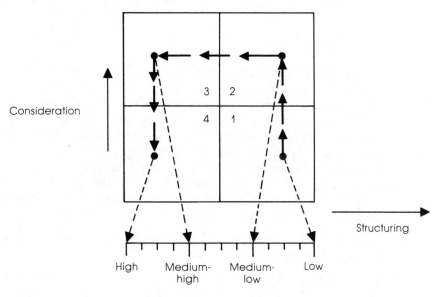

SUBORDINATE MATURITY TO TASK

Path-Goal Theory

The last and in many ways the most satisfactory of the theories of effective leadership we shall consider here is known as path-goal theory (Evans, 1970; House and Mitchell, 1974). This theory draws on much of the earlier research work. It is arranged so that it may be continuously refined and extended as new evidence comes in; and it is firmly based on a well-studied motivation theory, the expectancy theory we examined in an earlier chapter.

The core idea of path-goal theory is that effective leadership consists in increasing the subordinates' motivation toward, and satisfaction in, the performance of their tasks. The leader's task is twofold: "increasing the number and kinds of personal payoffs to subordinates for work-goal attainment" (i.e., the "goals" element), and "making paths to these payoffs easier to travel by clarifying the paths, reducing road blocks and pitfalls, and increasing the opportunities for personal satisfaction en route" (i.e., the "path" element) (House and Mitchell, 1974).

The underlying motivational theory is a version of expectancy theory. It can be sketched as follows:

As before, we assume that people do things they believe to be in their interests. That is, people are more likely to engage in a particular work activity if it is intrinsically interesting or they expect it to lead to other valued payoffs. Similarly, they will be more likely to exert effort in the activity if (1) doing so is likely to lead to good performance and (2) good performance is likely to lead to valued payoffs for them. Path-goal theory argues that the leader has a role to play at each stage in making it more likely that subordinates will choose the paths the leader desires. Let us examine the process step-by-step, and see what the leader might be able to do, and when it is likely to work.

How can the leader make it more likely that the follower will engage in the desired activity?

The leader's prime goal here is to achieve a good match between the individual and the job, either by good initial selection of recruits, or by improved job design or job training.

How can the leader make it more likely that the follower will exert effort in the desired activity?

First, the leader must make it clear just what the desired activity is (i.e., path clarification). Clarity may be achieved by instruction and monitoring. Participation in decision making may also help. By participating, the subordinate learns more about the reasons underlying particular path choices, how the activities fit together, and how the achievement of others is dependent on his or her performance. Second, the leader must help the subordinate see the connection between the activities to be performed and the goals to be achieved. Helping the subordinate set clear personal achievement goals, and expressing confidence that (s)he will attain them, both help motivation. The leader can also help by setting priorities and resolving role conflicts. Again, personal support and consideration may help in reducing any tensions and anxieties the subordinate may experience.

All this is aimed at (1) clarifying the subordinate's "path" (i.e., the activities toward which effort is to be directed), and (2) making that path more attractive than others (such as exerting lower levels of effort, or effort directed elsewhere). However, the critical question remains: does the subordinate see effort directed along this path as leading to important personal rewards?

*How can the leader make it more likely that the subordinate's efforts
will lead to valued rewards?*

The focus here is on the subordinate's belief in the connection between
effort, successful performance and valued rewards. The leader has
various options in trying to enhance this belief. First, the subordinate
must feel that successful performance is properly measured. (S)he
must receive feedback on how well (s)he is doing, and must agree that
the performance measures are reasonable. Second, the subordinate
must believe (and it must, in the long run, be true) that achieving good
performance is the best-rewarded outcome.

Again, the leader has several options. Training, coaching, and skills
development make it more likely that effort will, in fact, lead to
improved performance. For most of us there is nothing more frustrating
than trying hard at a task and persistently failing because we do not
have the necessary skills. Second, good performance feedback
requires both that the leader is sufficiently well informed for the
assessment to be accurate, and that the leader has the skills to give
feedback effectively. The leader must be clear about what exactly the
subordinate needs to do to improve performance, and must be non-
threatening and supportive in communicating this to the subordinate.
Being told that one is performing poorly is threatening, and we tend to
close our ears and act defensively. The skilled leader must be able to
give feedback without hitting this stone wall.

Finally, the leader has to deliver. Rewards valued by the subordinate
must actually result from good performance. This sounds obvious but it
is frequently forgotten. For example, across-the-board pay raises violate this requirement, since good and bad performance get rewarded
equally. Offering promotions or extra responsibility is not likely to be
an effective incentive for a subordinate who does not want them.
Indeed, it may be a real disincentive to good performance. To be effective, the rewards offered must be (1) contingent on good performance,
and (2) valued by the subordinate.

As we saw in our earlier discussion of motivation (Chapter 4), the
leader is not limited to formal organizational rewards such as pay or
promotion. (S)he can also provide interpersonal rewards, such as
praise and approval; social rewards, such as group recognition and
esteem; and outsider feedback (e.g., by establishing client relationships,
so that the final impact of good performance is more clearly visible to
the subordinate). To the extent that goals are set participatively, good
performance may be *self*-rewarding, since the subordinate then feels
the goals are personal ones. Leaders who monopolize the limelight may
cut off members of their group from receiving rewards in the form of
credit or recognition for good work. Allowing credit where it is due is

likely both to increase the subordinate's satisfaction in good performance and enhance the leader's reputation for fair and considerate behavior. And a leader who exerts upward influence in the organization is more likely to be able to secure for the group and its members both the resources they need for performing well, and the rewards that such achievement merits.

Note, again, how the various pieces fit together. The basic diagnostic question, coming directly from the expectancy model, is: "What is needed here before this individual will perform well, and feel good about it?" To answer that question, the leader must be sensitive to the differences in interests, abilities, and goals of the group members. Offering large pay bonuses to an individual who lacks the necessary skill to perform, or offering a promotion to a person who would rather have time off, or presenting a weekly "best worker" award that the group regards as insulting, trivial, or not given on merit—all these suggest a leader who either is not clear what (s)he is doing, or who is out of touch with the individuals in the group. The requirement that leaders provide valued, contingent rewards is simply stated, but highly complex to bring about in practice.

OTHER ISSUES

None of the models we have reviewed gives a completely satisfactory account of all the evidence. However, in addition to the debates about which model best fits the data, there are three other, perhaps more fundamental, matters we should mention briefly.

What Causes What?

Each of the approaches we have discussed implies that what the leader does (or is) affects the way the group operates. We should bear in mind that influence can, and probably does, work the other way: the way the group operates influences what the leader does. For example, if your group works well, you may well adopt a looser, friendlier style of supervision than you would if you saw them working poorly. Lowin and Craig (1968) demonstrated exactly this, by having people believe that they were supervising another individual (actually a stooge) who sometimes performed well, sometimes badly. When the stooge performed badly, the supervisors became less considerate, initiated structure more, and supervised more closely. Evidence such as this suggests that followers influence leaders, as well as vice versa. Most teachers, for example, would agree that the class shapes their behavior as much as they shape the class's.

Leaders or Situations?

We have noted that part of what the leader does can be seen as making up for something that is lacking in the situation. For example, if performance feedback is built into the job, there is no need for the leader to provide it. If the job is highly structured (for example, repetitive assembly-line work), then there is no need for the leader to structure the task any further. Indeed, the subordinate may resent it if (s)he does. This substitutability of leader and situation may account for many of the research problems. Sometimes considerate leadership helps, other times it does not. Perhaps the situation is already providing what is needed in the latter case. Steve Kerr and John Jermier (1978) have recently started work on a systematic review of such "substitutes for leadership." Their work certainly resolves some of the puzzles found in previous studies, and promises to enrich our broad understanding of when particular leader actions are, and are not, likely to make an impact.

Is Leadership Real?

Perhaps the broadest attack on the whole leadership notion has been proposed by Calder (1977), who suggests, essentially, that the whole thing is an attributional error, like those we reviewed in Chapter 3. Groups and individuals notice that their work is sometimes better, sometimes worse, and look around for a "cause" to which they can attribute the change. Since everyone believes that leaders have something to do with group performance, we "attribute" the performance change to the leader's actions. Leaders buy into the same belief and so does the organization, since it needs some justification for appointing some people as leaders, and needs to believe that it is in control of the situation. Thus if the shared belief is that, say, considerate leadership is most effective, the data will tend to bear it out. Conversely, if authoritarian leadership is believed to be effective, the data will confirm this. In this light, leadership behavior, group reactions to different leaders, and the hiring and firing of leaders can all be understood more as a complex ritual of confirming certain beliefs about leaders and their importance than as anything to do with real direct effects of leaders on followers. If we all believe that leaders matter, they will. And if we think good leadership is of a certain kind, the data will "prove" us right. It is worth considering the ritual of firing managers of losing baseball clubs in this light. You cannot fire the whole team, but something has to be done to reassure us that the club is being properly run. Firing the manager is a handy scapegoating device, even if managers do not in fact make much difference.

SUMMARY

As we said at the start of the chapter, leadership is complex, and not yet fully understood. Now that we have looked at the evidence, what are the take-home lessons? First, clearly, we should look very carefully at anyone claiming to have a sure-fire way to lead well. If such a method exists, it certainly has not yet reached the leadership researchers.

But acknowledging that we do not know everything is not the same as saying that we know nothing. There is good evidence that what leaders do makes at least some difference. There is also good evidence that doing the same thing, regardless of the situation, is not likely to be very effective all the time. To be effective, we need to strive for a match between what we do (or are) and the situation in which we find ourselves.

We have reviewed several models of how this match can be achieved. To Fiedler, matching is achieved by knowing our LPC score, and then getting into, or reshaping, situations so that their favorableness matches our LPC. To Vroom and Yetton, we choose from a range of decision-making techniques, some more participative, some less, in light of our evaluation of the need to protect decision quality and ensure acceptance by the group. The various approaches based on the Ohio State dimensions of consideration and initiating structure range from the "one best way," "high-high manager" model promoted by Blake and Mouton to more complex diagnoses based on the situation. Finally, path-goal theory suggests a set of diagnostic questions revolving around what it takes to motivate subordinates, and a set of leader responses aimed at filling the gaps and enhancing the subordinates' motivation.

As throughout the book, then, we see that the answer to "What makes a good leader?" is, "It depends." We have tried to summarize in this chapter some of the key features on which leadership depends, and how. You will certainly be forced, in your own work, to develop a range of leadership methods and a set of diagnostic questions for choosing one or another. You may well be exposed to training based on one or another of the theories reviewed here. This chapter has aimed (1) to sharpen the diagnostic questions you may ask and (2) add to the range of responses you have available. At the least, it should convince you that both elements are necessary. In leadership, if nowhere else, the search for the "one best way" is surely a fool's search.

DISCUSSION QUESTIONS: CHAPTER 7

1. What is the difference between "appointed" and "emergent" leaders? Which method of assigning leadership is commonly seen in:

a. Sports teams

b. Campus organizations

c. Musical groups

d. Military organizations

e. Discussion groups

What does this suggest about the relative advantages and drawbacks of the two methods of selecting a leader?

2. How can we tell whether a particular leader is "effective"? For each of the five groups listed in Question 1, indicate what measure or measures you would use to assess whether or not the group was being led effectively.

3. Modern views of leadership suggest that, to be effective, a leader must do two things: make a diagnosis of the situation and choose the best leadership response. Suppose that you have just taken a position as leader of a small research team working on semiconductor devices. Select one of the major leadership theories discussed in this chapter and describe:

a. What diagnostic questions you would ask

b. What leadership response you would make in light of the answers

4. Make a list of about a dozen people you think of as outstandingly effective leaders, past or present. Select from a variety of contexts: political, business, military, intellectual, athletic, artistic, personal, etc. Can you identify any qualities that all your examples have in common (other than the fact that they were effective)? What does this suggest about the common belief that "great leaders are born, not made"?

5. Retired military officers seeking new jobs often advertise themselves as having a proven track record of leadership. This seems to imply that leadership skills demonstrated in one context will work as well in a new context. Does this seem to you to be a well-founded claim? Why, or why not?

Chapter 8

Conflict and Conflict Resolution

How do you feel when you find yourself in situations like these?

Your roommate insists on playing the stereo late at night when you really want to get a good night's rest for an important quiz tomorrow.

Your quiz comes back with a grade of "C," although you thought you had done pretty well on it. When you check it, you realize that you read one of the key questions in a different way than the instructor did. The wording of the questions seems genuinely ambiguous to you, but the instructor disagrees.

Your date seems eager to see the basketball game, but you have your heart set on going to the jazz concert scheduled for the same evening. You don't know each other very well and, after a polite but terribly confusing discussion, you end up going out for pizza—which neither of you much likes, as it happens!

Early in your first job, your boss assigns you to work on a small but interesting technical problem, and gives you some strong suggestions as to how you should go about it. You happen to know a fair amount about the area, and are pretty sure that you could solve the problem much better using a different approach. But it *is* your first job, and you really want to get off to a good start with the boss.

For most of us, situations like these are uncomfortable, sometimes even seriously distressing. They each involve an element of "conflict" with another person, and we tend to think of conflict as something undesirable in our relationships. As a result, we tend to suppress it, to pretend that it is not happening.

The basketball-game-versus-jazz-concert example above suggests that suppressing conflict may not be a good way to deal with it. In the short run, neither you nor your date did what you wanted, and, one would guess, each person's unspoken resentment may get in the way of the later development of your relationship. Similarly, in the roommate example, your frustration about losing an important night's sleep may leave you looking for a way to get even later. If this goes on for long, you may both find yourselves looking for new roommates.

This chapter is not going to compete with "Dear Abby" in offering advice on dealing with disagreements with dates and roommates. The examples *do* suggest that "conflict" of one sort or another is a normal part of our everyday lives, neither good nor bad necessarily, but something we need to acknowledge and deal with. Our focus, of course, will be on conflict processes in organizational life. We will be concerned with questions like:

• What are the characteristics of a conflict situation?

• What factors tend to contribute to the occurrence of conflicts?

- What alternative ways of dealing with conflict exist?
- What are the consequences of dealing with conflicts in these different ways?

THE NATURE OF CONFLICT

In a general sense, we use the term "conflict" for situations in which we see some other individual or group as frustrating or being in the way of our (or our group) doing what we want. This definition covers a very wide range of situations, from the global to the personal. At the global level, there is a conflict between OPEC and the oil-consuming nations of the world: OPEC wants higher oil prices, the oil users want cheap oil, so their interests are in conflict. At the personal level, we could stretch the definition to cover the conflicts we feel inside ourselves; the "serious student" side of us wants to study for tomorrow's quiz, the "hell raiser" side of us wants to go out and party. We experience a conflict between the two parts of our personality.

One way to categorize conflict situations is in terms of what "actors" (individuals or groups) we are considering, and whether the conflict is within or between such actors:

Actors	Conflict within	Conflict between
Individual	Intrapersonal	Interpersonal
Group	Intragroup	Intergroup
Organization	Intraorganizational	Interorganizational
Nation	Intranational	International

We can generally think of a particular conflict as being *between* actors at one level, or *within* actors at the next higher level: interpersonal conflict (between two people) can often be viewed as intragroup conflict (within a group); intergroup conflict (between two groups) may well be intraorganizational (if both groups belong to the same organization). It is useful to keep this double perspective in mind when analyzing a given conflict situation, since it may suggest ideas for how the conflict can be managed. For example, seeing a conflict as *between* two departments of an organization focuses attention on the differences in their interests. Seeing the same conflict as *within* a single organization draws attention to their shared interests, such as the survival of the organization!

Notice also that our definition of conflict treats it in terms of the *perceptions* of the two parties, not in terms of any objective reality. In one sense, this is just a reminder of the important point that if people believe that something is real, their behavior will be shaped by it. In another sense, this is a reminder to check out whether or not there really is a conflict. Perhaps it is all a misunderstanding; your roommate thinks you would like some background music while you study, and is sacrificing his sleep, too. Or maybe he would be as happy listening on headphones, so that his interests and yours, while different, can both be achieved. Not all conflicts disappear when we check them out, but some do. It is worth keeping in mind that conflict behavior follows from a belief, not necessarily a reality, that one person or group is frustrating the other's interests.

An interesting implication of this perceptual view of conflict is that we often misjudge the amount or kind of conflict in a particular situation. We tend to think of conflict situations in win-lose terms: I win what you lose, and vice versa. This is true of simple games and bargains, but is often not true of more complex situations. For example, in dividing up a piece of work with a lab partner, you may both be trying to minimize your own inconvenience and effort, but there is no reason to assume that the same things are inconvenient or difficult for both of you. Perhaps one is better at wiring up the equipment, while the other is good at data analysis; perhaps one likes working in single long sessions, while the other prefers regular short sessions. Given these differences, it would not be efficient for the two of you to split fifty-fifty on everything—you would both be better off with a different deal. However, the preferred split may not be obvious to either of you since, as we noted in Chapter 2 on decision making, we are not very good at understanding which parts of a complex package really affect our overall evaluation of the package. Straight bargaining issue-by-issue might well seem like a sensible procedure, but would most likely get you to the undesirable fifty-fifty split.

Kenneth Hammond and his colleagues at the University of Colorado have explored such conflicts with the aid of computer-interactive graphics (Hammond, 1971). They try to separate conflict due to misunderstanding of the situation and of each other (which they call "cognitive conflict") from the more familiar conflict caused by having to split one thing that both parties want ("motivational conflict"). They have found that conflicts between, say, environmentalists and hydro engineers over particular water projects can be sharply reduced if each party understands his own and the other's weighting for different aspects of the projects considered. One party may not mind giving up Feature A, while the other really wants to eliminate it. Finding a design that eliminates this feature thus makes one party much better off, and the other only a little worse off (see Flack and Summers, 1971). Hammond's computer technology aims to find the areas where assymmetrical tradeoffs are possible, so that each party ends up relatively well satisfied. This cannot work in every area, but in a number of instances, Hammond has been able to reduce overall conflict considerably by clearing up the "cognitive conflict" elements. Essentially, what he seeks to do, and what traditional negotiators try to do, is to transform situations that the parties consider fixed or zero-sum games into positive sum games. That is, they change situations where one wins what the other loses into ones where both parties come out better off. We shall consider further examples of this later in the chapter when we look at bargaining and negotiation processes.

In summary, the main points we have considered thus far are:

1. Conflict is a normal, everyday occurrence, not inherently good or bad.
2. Conflict is found within and between all levels, from individuals to whole nations.
3. The central element of conflict is that at least one of the parties involved believes that the other is frustrating the first party's interests.
4. This belief does not have to be well founded for conflict behavior to occur.
5. We tend to think of conflict in win-lose terms, although it may well be possible to discover win-win solutions.
6. Such discovery may be helped by a developing computer-based technology aimed at clarifying the areas of misunderstanding (or cognitive conflict), and narrowing the areas of real conflict of interest (or motivational conflict).

We now turn to an examination of some factors that lead to confict.

THE CAUSES OF CONFLICT

Robinson Crusoe living alone on his desert island experienced no work-related conflict—except, perhaps, the intrapersonal kind. We need some other person or group around for a conflict to arise. Further, the potential for conflict requires that our work be in some way coordinated with another's. There is little cause for conflict between two researchers who simply share the same lab space, working on different projects, unless they have to share the same equipment. The first requirement for a conflict to arise, then, is that at least one of the parties feels a need for joint decision making with another (March and Simon, 1958).

One group of factors that set up potential conflict situations thus relates to the need for joint decision making. Major examples include:

Joint dependence on a scarce resource.   If two units need to use a particular piece of equipment (a computer, a wind tunnel) or service (a typing pool, a programming service) and the shared resource is in short supply, they need to make joint decisions on matters like priorities and schedules. A potential conflict arises. The commonest example of a shared organizational resource is money; shared dependence on a limited budget sets up the classic conflict situation. (Incidentally, the scarcity, not just the sharedness, of the resource is critical. Conflicts of this sort are likely to increase after cutbacks, or when the shared resource has not expanded in step with the needs of the users.)

Task interdependence.   The basic idea of an organization is to break up large jobs into smaller ones, so that each can be worked on by specialists. This in turn implies that coordination will be required to pull the small tasks back together, and this coordination requires joint decision making. In a manufacturing operation, for example, each department must complete its part of the work before departments later in the sequence can start theirs. One department may require parts and materials, assistance, or information from other departments in order to get its work done.

An important aspect of this interdependence is whether or not it is reciprocal (Walton and Dutton, 1969). If the interdependence amounts to a two-way street, with each party about equally dependent on the other, there is a built-in incentive to iron out any disagreements. However, if the interdependence is asymmetrical, problems arise. In relationships between line and staff departments for example, the staff group is dependent on the line people for information about operating problems, for cooperation, and for a chance to try out new ideas. The line group, on the other hand, can refuse to give this cooperation and, at least in the short term, be no worse off. (In fact, the line group may be better off in the short run, since the new ideas proposed by the staff group will often be disruptive initially.) This asymmetrical interdependence can generate problems in the necessary joint decision making between the two groups.

Another important asymmetry comes from differences in organizational power or prestige. For example, adequate patient care in a hospital clearly requires cooperation between doctors and nurses. However, the doctors have vastly more power and prestige, and tend to dominate joint decision making. The nurses' legitimate needs for cooperation can easily be neglected, leading both to poorer patient care and resentful nurses. Similar asymmetries arise in many settings where the cooperating parties differ in power or prestige. Some examples are the relationships between professionals and support technicians in research labs, between engineering and sales departments in manufacturing firms, between secretaries and bosses in almost every context. It is worth recalling the strategies noted earlier in Chapter 6 on power, by which those on the short end can even the balance. The lab assistant who does *exactly* what (s)he is told can ruin the researcher's experiment just as surely as one who disobeys flagrantly—but is much harder to punish. Such strategies shift the task interdependence back toward symmetry, and force the joint decision making to be genuinely shared.

Organizational level.   March and Simon (1958) have speculated that the felt need for joint decision making increases as one goes up the organization. They argue that departments are formed primarily because a cluster of activities is seen as needing coordination, which is typically achieved by placing the clusters under a single manager. This manager tends to see the activities under his or her control as in need of careful coordination. Therefore, the department itself is seen as more self-contained and in less need of coordination with other departments. The higher one goes in the organization, the more activities fall under each manager's jurisdiction and thus the more each sees a need for joint decision making. This argument makes sense, but I know of no clear empirical data showing that the phenomenon is widespread.

The three factors—joint dependence on scarce resources, task interdependence, and, perhaps, organizational level—lead to a perceived need for joint decision making between organizational units, and thus set the scene for possible conflicts. However, conflicts will not arise unless one of two further conditions is present: either the parties must be pursuing different interests and goals, or, if they share goals, they must have different solutions in mind.

In the nonexistent totally rational organization, neither of these conditions can arise. The overall organizational goal—for example, maximizing profit—is broken down into clear operational objectives for each department and each individual, and incentives are arranged so that each individual acts to achieve his or her subobjective. Joint decision making is then merely a matter of rational problem solving. The best schedule for use of the shared facility, for example, is jointly settled by working out which will best serve the overall objective. Rationality prevails.

In real life, organizations rarely work this way. The linkages between overall organizational goals, departmental objectives, and personal targets (for which we are rewarded) are often quite loose. Our efforts are much more likely to be focused on the latter than on the former. The head of the production department and the head of the sales department may both nod politely at the general idea that they share the goal of maximizing the profits of their employer, XYZ Corporation. But their behaviors are much more likely to be shaped by the specific objectives set for their two departments, which they need to achieve to earn their annual bonuses and enhance their chances for promotion.

These differences in real, operational objectives are likely to go hand in hand with differences in the way problems are perceived. Earlier (in Chapter 3), we saw that executives with different professional backgrounds saw different problems in the same factual description of an organizational case history. Mr. P, the production head, is likely to analyze the setting of a production schedule for next month in terms of its impacts on his department. Will the machines need resetting constantly, or can he set them to produce a given product and let them run? Will he be reassigning people all the time or have them working steadily at their best jobs? Will he be able to produce equal numbers of Part A and Part B, since B can be cut from the leftover sheets from making Part A? Setting up a good production schedule is a difficult job, and Mr. P considers himself good at it. Basically what he would like is to produce efficiently, and have the sales department get organized and sell what he makes.

Ms. S, the head of sales, does not see the world quite the same way. She knows that what keeps the customers coming back is that they can get the products they want, made exactly to their specifications, and delivered quickly. Good customers are hard to find, and it just takes one disappointment to lose them, sometimes for good. She doesn't understand why Mr. P has so much trouble producing the items her customers want. At least all his problems are inside one shop, and all his people are employees, while she has to travel all over the country and persuade, not order, the people she works with. In her ideal world, the sales department would set the production schedule and the production department would then go about making what had been promised. What could be simpler?

As the example suggests, it is not only the need for joint decision making (here, task interdependence, reflected in having to agree on a production schedule) that sets up the conflict situation. The two departments are also working toward different operational objectives, and they approach their joint decision making task with different definitions of what the central problem really is. Given the need for joint decision making, either goal differences or different problem definitions would be sufficient to produce conflict. Here both factors are operating, and conflict seems likely. We shall examine the form it might take, and its possible consequences, in the next section. First, however, we shall look briefly at a number of organizational devices that reduce conflict before it starts.

CONFLICT REDUCTION

The essence of the previous section was that conflict is likely when two parties feel that they have to make a decision jointly, but approach the decision either with different goals or with different definitions of the shared problem. The converse is that conflict is less likely when one or more of these elements are missing. Organizations have evolved a number of devices for eliminating or reducing the causal factors. For example:

Buffer inventories.   Establishing a buffer stock between two sequentially interdependent departments allows the two to operate more independently of one another. The attractiveness of this approach depends on factors such as cost and perishability of the items stored.

Loosened schedules.   Scheduling conflicts increase rapidly as schedules become tighter. Allowing a little slack, while costly, may be worth it in terms of reduced conflict.

Transfer pricing.   Some organizations set up internal price arrangements, with supplying departments selling their outputs to using departments. Such schemes can be costly to set up, but they decouple departments that otherwise would have to spend effort coordinating their activities.

Reduced common-resource dependence.   Conflicts associated with shared use of a common resource, such as a secretarial pool, a computer, or an item of research equipment, can be eased simply by giving each user department its own "dedicated" resource. Again, the duplication of similar equipment or activities may be costly, but so are extended conflicts.

Personnel transfer.   Conflicts stemming from strong personal identification with one department's problems and goals can be eased by exchanging or rotating people among departments. If successful, this produces a better understanding in each department of the other's problems and goals, and builds up a network of contacts between the departments.

Physical location.   Locating potentially conflicting groups physically close to one another may help establish the easy informal relationships between the two that facilitate conflict reduction. Alternatively, moving them well apart may help to keep them out of each other's hair. I suspect that part of the motivation for putting corporate R&D groups in some remote location away from manufacturing facilities is to keep them from continually meddling in production processes.

Sequential goal focus. Part of the goal conflict discussed above comes from the fact that each party involved has several different goals, or the same goals differently weighted. Cyert and March (1963) suggest that organizations reduce multiple-goal conflicts by attending to goals sequentially. One month the emphasis is on product quality and everyone focuses on this goal, putting other goals on the back burner. Later the emphasis shifts, perhaps to cost reduction or innovation. This strategy has the effect of simplifying complex goal structures (if only temporarily), making agreements easier to reach.

Budgetary procedures. Conflicts between departments over budget allocations are central to most organizations. Pondy (1967) has noted a number of common procedures that ease conflict in this area. For example, budget categories such as "cost reduction," "safety," and "expansion" tend to localize disagreements, because a given proposal is in competition with only a subset of the other proposals. Within categories, projects tend to be ranked only partially, with some of those not currently funded assigned into long-run plans (and thus up for reconsideration later). Such procedures tend to reduce the sharpness of straight head-to-head competition between all proposals, and perhaps ease the resentment of the losers.

Note that each of these devices represents a partial retreat from the aim of running the organization as the tightest possible ship, minimizing costs, scheduling as tightly as possible, or using every resource to the fullest. They represent what is referred to as "organizational slack." The examples suggest that "slack" is not at all the same thing as "waste." Slack buys a reduction of conflict, and may be money well spent!

CONFLICT BEHAVIOR

Despite the existence of conflict-reducing devices, some degree of conflict is a normal (indeed, a desirable) feature of organizational life. In this section we shall examine some important aspects of what conflicting parties actually do, and the consequences flowing from their behaviors.

Pondy (1967) suggests that, to understand conflict behavior, we need to consider the entire "conflict episode." The conflict episode runs from the causes of one party frustrating the other through their coming to *conceptualize* the conflict, their *interactions,* and the *outcomes* of the conflict, both *direct* (how the issue was resolved) and *indirect* (the aftermath of this particular episode, and how it affects later conflicts). We shall discuss each of these elements separately here while bearing in mind that in practice each interacts with and shapes the others.

Conceptualizing the Conflict

The simplest, though rarely the most accurate, way to think about a conflict is to assume that the parties understand the issues in the same way and are disagreeing only about who is to win and who is to lose (or where between these two points they will settle). In fact, as we have seen throughout this book, people rarely see any given issue in just the same way. Under conditions of conflict, differences in their conceptualization of the issue are likely to be sharpened. As the production-versus-sales example suggests, the parties are likely to see the issue in different ways. Even if they are cooperative, each is likely to phrase the matter as "How can I help the other department without sacrificing the efficiency of my department?" If relationships are less friendly, the conceptualizations may be more along the line of "Now what are those idiots trying to pull on me?" "It's time those people learned who's important in this organization." Or, "Now's our chance to get them for that dirty deal they pulled on us last month." Each of these conceptualizations might refer to the same joint decision, the setting of a production schedule, but they strongly suggest different ways of getting there.

The parties' conceptualizations of the conflict thus include the ideas of each as to what issues are at stake. They also include an understanding of what alternative actions are available, and what will be the consequences of each alternative for each party. The win-lose orientation implies that whatever is better for one party is worse for the other. This is not the only possibility. It may be possible to devise alternatives that are desirable for both; and it is nearly always possible to find an alternative that will damage the other, if we do not mind damaging ourselves in the process.

It is useful here to expand our thinking from the single dimension implied by win-lose into two dimensions defined by the gains and losses of each party, as shown in Figure 8.1. Here the win-lose dimension is the diagonal running from Point 1 (B wins, A loses) to Point 5 (A wins, B loses), with Point 3 representing a compromise between the two. One merit of this way of thinking is that it reminds us that we may have overlooked alternatives near Point 2 (where both parties gain) and we may be considering alternatives near Point 4 (where everyone loses).

Another use of Figure 8.1 is to describe the process of reaching a settlement of the conflict. Thomas (1976) suggests the label "distributive" for the diagonal running from 1 to 5, in that outcomes along this line define how the gains are to be distributed between the two parties. The other diagonal, running from 4 to 2, he refers to as the "integrative" dimension, in that it reflects the degree to which the solution achieved satisfies the concerns of both parties. The former reflects how the "pie" is to be divided, and the latter reflects how large the "pie" is.

Figure 8.1. Possible Outcomes of a Two-Party Conflict

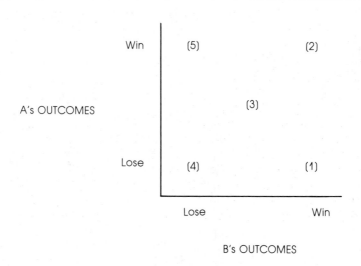

Suggesting that win-win solutions like Point 2 *may* exist is not the same as claiming that they always do, or that the parties will be able to find them. Indeed, some classes of conflict processes (known as "Richardson processes," after the scholar who first gave a detailed analysis of them: Richardson, 1960) have the disturbing property of driving the participants in the direction of Point 4. International arms races may be of this sort. Starting at a neutral point such as 3, if one party tries to get ahead (for example, A makes a move in the direction of Point 5), B reacts with a move in the direction of Point 1, and the joint outcome moves toward the even but ruinous solution represented by Point 4. Similar "escalations" are possible in organizations, for example, when two departments try to get ahead of each other by with-holding cooperation, triggering destructive counterattacks, and so on until most of their energies are spent trying to do the other in, rather than advancing their own interests. We shall have more to say on such processes when we discuss the dynamics of conflict.

Interactions

The parties are likely to approach the conflict with somewhat different understandings of what is at stake, and what ranges of possible out-comes are possible. We will assume that each sees important stakes involved, so that joint outcomes are likely to fall in the top right-hand quadrant of Figure 8.1. The crucial question is now where, within this range of joint outcomes, will the conflict get resolved? The way the two parties interact will clearly have an important influence on this outcome.

An important influence on the form of this interaction is the orientation the two parties bring to it. If both start with a competitive, hard-bargaining orientation, a compromise solution is the best that can be hoped for. Conversely, if both approach the matter with a problem-solving, collaborative orientation, an outcome satisfactory to each is more likely to be found. Unfortunately, as we shall see below, there is evidence that a bargaining orientation tends to drive out a problem-solving approach. Therefore, if either party starts with a bargaining orientation, the other is likely to be dragged down to the same level.

In a bargaining approach, each party's tactics are shaped by the power base (s)he has available. Recall the five types of power base suggested by French and Raven (1959): reward, coercive, legitimate, referent, and expert (see Chapter 6). The first two suggest such bargaining tactics as offering inducements (e.g., personal rewards or concessions on other issues) if the other party accepts one's position, or threatening punishments if (s)he does not. Legitimate power involves appealing to formal rules, contract terms, or simply "pulling rank" to induce the other to comply. Referent power can be used in bargaining to the extent that one party is personally attracted to the other, and may be particularly important in the informal negotiations by which many conflicts get settled. Finally, expert power can be used tactically if one party has inside knowledge or skills which the other does not. If I am bargaining with a technician about equipment scheduling, I am at a disadvantage if the technician knows the detailed maintenance needs of the machine and I do not. (Note that these power bases tend to shrink as the bargaining gets tougher. Personal attraction and trust in the other's expertise are likely to disappear; legitimate power is reduced to the extent that it is denied by either party; and rewards and coercion are reduced to their crudest form, as in shows of strength between unions and management.)

The problem-solving approach that allows collaborative solutions to be found is in sharp contrast to the bargaining approach. In problem solving the two parties need to exchange accurate information, both about the objectives they are pursuing and about the alternatives they are considering to achieve them. This requires a high level of trust between the two—trust that the other will give accurate factual information and not exploit the information given for a bargaining advantage. No one puts his or her own cards on the table unless the other player does so, too.

We have suggested that a bargaining mode of conflict resolution tends to drive out problem solving, despite the potentially higher payoffs to both parties of problem solving. Let us examine some of the dynamics by which this comes about, so that we can better see what is required to stop it happening.

Self-fulfilling prophecies.   Although the parties may approach a conflict with some predispositions, the situation is significantly defined by their initial interaction. If, for example, one party starts off by making an obviously extreme demand, the other is likely to react with an extreme opposite demand, and the situation becomes one of bargaining. An initial problem-solving approach is more precarious, because the other party may treat it as an opportunity for a bargaining advantage, forcing the first party to take a similar approach.

Escalation.   Once an adversarial, hostile negotiation is under way, the issues involved tend to escalate; more issues are drawn into the bargaining, larger stakes are involved, hostility increases, and trust disappears. This escalation process makes issues harder to resolve, while simultaneously making the solution process itself more difficult.

Cognitive simplification.   Under stress, people tend to think in simplified, black-and-white terms, to consider fewer alternatives, and to focus on fewer criteria. Therefore, to the extent that conflict is experienced as stressful, flexible, and creative, subtle, thinking is driven out and satisfactory solutions become more difficulty to reach.

Communication breakdowns.   As the conflict accelerates down this slippery slope, communication between the two parties may break down entirely. They become increasingly hostile to one another, trust diminishes, understanding of the other's point of view becomes vague, and personal animosity increases. Blake and Mouton (1961a) report an interesting experiment bearing on such breakdown. They asked the members of problem-solving groups that had been in competition to summarize, as objectively as they could, all the solutions the groups had generated to their problems. The experimenters found that group members had a much better comprehension of the solutions produced by their own groups than of those produced by their opponents. This was not simply because members were more familiar with their own group's ideas. They had ample opportunity to study all the ideas and rated their understanding of them as equal. Further, they had no awareness that they were distorting their opponents' positions and ideas. This suggests that communication breakdown can occur without either party being aware of it.

Representation.   When a conflict involves large groups, it is common to have the negotiations conducted by representatives of each side, rather than by the entire membership. Apart from reducing the number of people whose time is taken up, this tactic might allow a reasonable settlement to be found away from the public eye by experienced, level-headed people from each side. However, the tactic may backfire. The negotiators have two duties: to find a solution acceptable to both sides, and then to sell that solution to their own side. This second duty sets up pressures for the representatives to hold on to strong positions favorable to their groups because they do not want to look as if they have sold out to the opposition, or have been deceived or outmaneuvered. Another study by Blake and Mouton (1961b) demonstrated this "loyalty" effect. Elected representatives from groups that had been in competition were asked to rate, as objectively as possible, all the solutions that had been proposed by either side. Virtually all of them stayed loyal to their own group's position, even when doing so led to deadlock. Outside judges, however, had little difficulty in picking a clear-cut preferred solution. In fact, a negotiator has two settlements to make, one with the opponents, the other with his or her own group. It should not be too surprising that the latter interest often predominates.

What all this suggests, then, is that problem solving involves a rather precarious balance, which, once tipped, can easily degenerate first into bargaining and then into deadlock. What can be done to stop or reverse this degeneration?

THIRD PARTY INTERVENTIONS

If the parties are aware of the dynamic forces that have been sketched above, they may be able to stop the conflict from degenerating into a deadlock. However, these forces seem to be strong, particularly when the stakes are important to both sides. In such cases, third parties—outsiders not directly involved in the focal conflict—may be able to help. Various individuals can serve in this role: a respected colleague can help end a dispute between two individuals; a senior manager may be able to resolve a conflict between two lower-level department heads; a professional mediator can work to compromise and resolve a deadlocked negotiation between union and management.

We may distinguish among three roles an outsider can play, ranging from less to more formal (see Kochan, 1980):

The mediator.   A mediator is a neutral third party who works informally to try to bring the disputing parties to a settlement. The mediator has no real power other than the trust and respect of the parties involved. The mediator's main value is in keeping the lines of communication open between the parties, helping to focus on and clarify the issues, sometimes suggesting integrative, problem-solving solutions. Successful mediation seems to be more of an art than a science, and experienced mediators may operate in many varied ways, ranging from just being helpful listeners and clarifiers to actively proposing possible substantive settlements.

The factfinder. Factfinding is a rather more formal role than mediation, but it still does not involve the power to impose settlements. In collective bargaining, the factfinder typically holds hearings and makes formal, written recommendations on how the dispute should be settled. However, the parties involved are not required to abide by this suggestion, but may use, modify, or even ignore the recommendations.

The arbitrator. In arbitration, the most formal and the most powerful of the three outsider roles, the neutral party both decides and imposes a settlement on the disputing parties. In formal collective bargaining, arbitration may be either *voluntary* (the two parties agree to be bound by the arbitrator's decision) or *compulsory* (the arbitrator's decision is legally binding). In less structured settings, such as two department heads taking a dispute to their joint superior, the third party's decision is likely to be essentially binding, simply because of the relative power of the parties involved.

An alternative to conventional arbitration, known as "final offer" arbitration, has recently attracted widespread interest. The procedure can be best explained by referring to the "bargaining zone" model of negotiation, shown in Figure 8.2 (Walton and McKersie, 1965):

Figure 8.2.   A "Bargaining Zone" Model of Negotiation

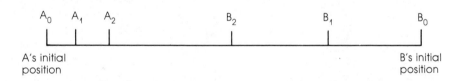

(Note that this is essentially a one-dimensional rendering of the two-dimensional outcome space of Figure 8.1 discussed earlier, and thus ignores the possibility that more satisfactory points may be found. We are here discussing only the "distributive" dimension.)

The "bargaining zone" model pictures the disputants as making a series of offers to one another, starting with their initial positions (A_0, B_0). It is assumed that each party becomes less satisfied with offers further from its own initial position. Each has a "target point" offer, which it regards as a desirable point at which to settle, and a more distant compromise point, its "resistance point," beyond which further compromise will be made reluctantly or not at all. If these "resistance points" are sufficiently far from each party's initial position that an overlap can be found, a "positive contract zone" is said to exist. In this instance there is a range of settlements acceptable to each party, and bargaining focuses on where within this zone the settlement will be made. If no such overlap exists, the parties have a "negative contract zone," and alternative ways must be found of resolving the dispute.

Now, suppose that an arbitrator were called in to resolve the dispute represented in Figure 8.2, where the two parties have bargained to the offers (A_2, B_2) and reached a stalemate. The arbitrator's tendency is obviously to try to find a settlement somewhere between A_2 and B_2, which, in this case, will likely result in a settlement closer to A_0 than to B_0, since B has moved more rapidly than has A. Notice the incentive system this sets up for the two parties. Anticipating conventional arbitration of this sort, each has an incentive to make a very strong initial demand or offer, and then to give ground very slowly. This makes a stalemate probable, and leaves the arbitrator with a very large gap to attempt to reconcile. In short, the prospect of conventional arbitration provides the parties with an incentive not to settle, and to adopt very tough negotiating tactics.

"Final offer" arbitration overcomes this incentive system in an interesting way. In contrast to conventional arbitration, the neutral party is not allowed to impose any "split-the-difference" solutions, but must select one or the other of the parties' final offers—either A_2 or B_2 in Figure 8.2, but not somewhere between. Under this arrangement, each party aims to be marginally closer than its opponent to the point the arbitrator will regard as reasonable. This sets up a powerful incentive for the parties to negotiate in good faith, and raises the probability that they will reach a settlement on their own, instead of resorting to arbitration. If, for example, B made no movement from its initial position, then A would win the whole ball game by offering only a mild concession. Since both parties understand this, each tries to outmaneuver the other by being more reasonable—which is exactly what successful negotiation is about! Studies of negotiation behavior both in the lab (Notz and Starke, 1978) and in the real world (Feuille, 1975) suggest that "final offer" arbitration does, in fact, lead to these desirable outcomes.

Third parties can thus play a number of useful roles in resolving conflicts. They may be able to offset the mechanisms of escalation, growing hostility, cognitive simplification, and communication breakdown that drive out a problem-solving approach and force the parties into adversary bargaining. Once the situation has become one of bargaining, third parties may be able to facilitate reaching a satisfactory settlement, by drawing on their interpersonal skills, the trust in which both parties hold them, or the power they may have to structure the negotiation process or to impose a settlement.

THE POSITIVE SIDE OF CONFLICT

Earlier in this chapter we hinted that some degree of conflict is not just a normal part of organizational life, but can even be desirable. We do not mean to suggest that an organization is healthy if every decision becomes the focus for bitter argument, if every personal relationship is shot through with suspicion and distrust, or if every action requires lengthy bargaining and negotiation. Such organizations may exist, but we do not expect them to do very well, or to last very long. At the same time, we should be suspicious of organizations in which none of these things happen. They may also be on the road to failure.

A balance needs to be found. Unfortunately, there is little solid research indicating just where the best balance is to be found for particular situations. We can at least suggest where some trade-offs have to be made:

Motivation. For most people a degree of competition or rivalry seems to be energizing; we try harder in games against a real opponent than when we are just practicing. However, few of us function well under intense, prolonged conflict; and it is all too easy to slide from trying to do well into trying to beat the other party. (Evidence on this point is discussed in Chapter 9.)

Innovation and adaptability. The emergence of a conflict can both signal that some change is needed and provide a mechanism for making the necessary change. For example, if the production department has always set the production schedule, and now finds itself in continual conflict with sales, it may signal that market conditions have shifted, and that some more formal joint planning needs to be done between the two departments. Note, again, that this process can go too far. Once the joint decision process is in place and formalized, it may itself become too rigid, and be an obstacle to further necessary change.

Communication. Conflict can open up communication channels, by requiring people who normally do not talk to one another to communicate in order to resolve the disputes. This increased communication can improve the quality of the shared decisions. However, as we have seen, if the conflict escalates, communication tends to break down in concealment, suspicion, and hostility, perhaps to the point where there is less contact between the parties than before the conflict episode.

New mechanisms. As these examples suggest, conflict can lead to new organizational arrangements, such as joint planning groups or formal grievance procedures. Again, these may be mixed blessings. They may allow difficult disputes to be resolved effectively, but they may undercut the informal, face-to-face procedures that operated before. Consider, for example, the elaborate procedures set up at some universities for resolving grievances between faculty and students. These procedures provide the student with protection against arbitrary faculty decisions, but they also make it more likely that even minor disputes will be dealt with formally, with all the implicit drawbacks of delay, time wasting, public records, and distrust.

Challenging ideas. As we saw in the early chapters of this book, we all have habitual ways of thinking about problems, approaches we use so routinely that we are not even aware of them. Creative thinking requires us to challenge these assumptions and habits. Active argument with people who hold other views forces us to do that. Evan (1965), for example, found that at least some of the highly productive R&D groups he studied were characterized by more conflict over technical matters than were less productive groups. In a similar vein, Mason (1969) has proposed the use of a formal adversary procedure, rather like a law court, in developing long-range plans, with one party formally assigned to challenge the other's approach. Out of such a formalized conflict, he suggests, we can hope to develop a synthesis (or, in our terms, an integrative solution) superior to the views of either party alone.

SUMMARY

We have suggested that some level of conflict between individuals, between groups, and between organizations is both normal and useful. Conflict arises when one party perceives another to be frustrating some valued interest. The perception may or may not be well founded, and we should generally expect the parties involved to hold different perceptions of what the conflict is about.

Conflicts tend to arise when two parties must make a joint decision (as when they are jointly dependent on a common resource, or must coordinate their work), and when each approaches the joint decision either with different goals or different solutions in mind. Conflict situations can be avoided by various devices aimed at weakening one or another of these factors: buffer inventories, loosened schedules, transfer prices, reduced resource interdependence, personnel transfer, physical location, sequential attention to goals, and budgetary procedures. Each of these devices reduces the probability of conflict, but at a cost to the organization.

Conflicts still arise, however, and we traced through some of the major aspects of the conflict episode from conceptualization to aftermath. The idea of a "joint outcome space" was used to suggest that conflicts are often not just win or lose (the "distributive" dimension), but may allow both parties to achieve (or fail to achieve) their goals (the "integrative" dimension). The interaction of the conflicting parties is shaped both by their orientation to the conflict and by the power base each has available.

An important feature of conflict interaction is that it can escalate; joint problem-solving approaches can be driven out by adversarial, hostile bargaining. Several mechanisms were discussed: tendencies for the expectations of each party to be forced on the other, with a bargaining orientation dominating; escalation of the issues involved; cognitive simplification; and communication breakdown. The pressures driving representatives of each side towards extremism were also noted. We concluded that joint problem solving, generally the preferred approach, tends to be driven out by bargaining.

Outside third parties can help to resolve conflicts by mediation, fact-finding, or arbitration. The "bargaining zone" model of negotiation was used to illustrate the difference between conventional and final offer arbitration. Finally, we reviewed a number of factors that make some level of conflict desirable in organizational life: its motivational impact, its role in innovation and adaptability, its effect in opening up communication channels and bringing new organizational mechanisms into being, and its role in stimulating creative thinking.

DISCUSSION QUESTIONS: CHAPTER 8

1. You conflict with a colleague over which of you will have access to a set of laboratory equipment to run some experiments. After a heated discussion you discover that both of you can run your experiments if you rearrange the schedules a little. Was the original conflict "cognitive" or "motivational"? Why is the difference important?

2. The conflict in Question 1 can be traced to the fact that you and your colleague are dependent on a shared, scarce resource (the

equipment). Suggest two other factors that can increase the need for joint decision making, and thus increase the possibility of conflict.

3. Need for joint decision making sets up the possibility of conflict, but actual conflict will not emerge unless the two parties are either pursuing different goals or see different solutions. How might these two elements develop in the situation sketched in Question 1?

4. Eight "conflict reduction" mechanisms—organizational devices that reduce the likelihood of conflicts arising—were identified in the chapter. Give an example of how each might be used to reduce the possibility of conflicts arising between faculty members in a university department.

5. We tend to think of conflict outcomes in win-lose terms: what one party gains the other loses. Win-win and lose-lose outcomes are also possible. Give an example of each kind of outcome for (a) a barroom brawl and (b) a war between two countries. For each kind of conflict, describe how a "Richardson process" might drive the conflict toward the lose-lose outcome.

6. Taking union-management negotiations as an example, show how each of the following processes might tend to drive out problem solving and make a bargaining orientation more likely:
   a. Self-fulfilling prophecies
   b. Escalation
   c. Cognitive simplification
   d. Communication breakdowns
   e. Representation

   What roles might an outsider play in this process, and what might (s)he do to improve the situation?

7. What is meant by "final offer arbitration," and how is it different from conventional arbitration?

8. From the viewpoint of overall organizational effectiveness conflict is not invariably a bad thing. Give examples of five different functions that are served by a moderate level of conflict.

Chapter 9

Groups

There are large and important differences between the way we learn an engineering discipline in school and the way we practice that discipline in the outside world. For most engineers, the basic shift from solving simplified, textbook puzzles to tackling complex, real-world problems is a source of great satisfaction. Engineers tend to be more interested in specific, concrete, working results than in abstract, theoretical solutions on paper. There is something immensely gratifying in seeing one's ideas turn into a real, working object, whether the object is something as grand as a new bridge or as humble as a new teakettle. (It also helps, of course, that we are paid in real money, not in grades, for the excellence of our designs!) For reasons such as this, most engineering students look forward eagerly to the time they can start practicing their profession.

One aspect of the shift from school to practice comes as a surprise, and often as a frustration, to young engineers: the predominance of group decision making in professional practice. In school, we mainly work as soloists: we study alone, are examined as individuals, receive individual grades. In professional practice, however, most key decisions are made in collaboration with other professionals. One individual may have the basic idea for the bridge (or the teakettle), but the idea will not become a reality until it has been checked over and modified by others. Suppose the new idea is, in fact, a design for a new teakettle. Even if the engineering design is excellent, the production department will want to check that it can be manufactured efficiently, the marketing department will want to check whether or not it fits a slot in the market, the legal department will want to check whether or not it infringes existing patents, the service department will be concerned about how easy it will be to repair, and so on. Even for this relatively simple product, it is unlikely that all the relevant expertise will be in any one person's head. The commonest method of bringing diverse expertise to bear on one issue is the decision-making group. The workings of such groups are the topic of this chapter.

The use of groups to make important decisions is, of course, not confined to engineering design. From the thesis examining committee to the National Security Council, from the Parent-Teacher Association to the grand jury, from the New Products Development Group to the editorial board of a professional journal—in virtually every area of our lives, important decisions are made by groups. Since group decision making is so important, it is not surprising that there has been a great deal of research on the subject. We cannot hope to do more than sample a few of the research topics here, emphasizing those of more relevance to engineering work. (Rossini's paper, Reading #4, discusses a range of additional issues relevant to group work. Good overviews of the major research themes are given in Cartwright and Zander [1968] and Hackman [1976].)

WHAT IS AN EFFECTIVE GROUP?

We must first clarify what we mean when we say a group is "effective." Suppose, as an example, we assemble a group to assess the impact microcomputers will have on our organization over the next five years. Suppose, further, we have some way of "objectively" evaluating the solutions developed for this problem; for example, we can compare the solutions against the recommendations of an expert panel, so that each solution could be given a score out of 100 points. Given such a scoring scheme, we could rate, first, the quality of the solutions developed by each of the group members working alone, and then the quality of the group solution working together. Where would we expect the quality of the group solution to fall in relationship to the spread of individual solutions?

The result suggested in Figure 9.1 is perhaps the best we could hope for. First, the group was able to come up with a single recommendation (as suggested by the convergence of the lines from solo to group solutions). Second, the group answer was better than the best individual answer (since the group convergence point is above the "best individual" answer). This is, however, not the only possible result. It is

Figure 9.1.   Solo and Group Solution Quality

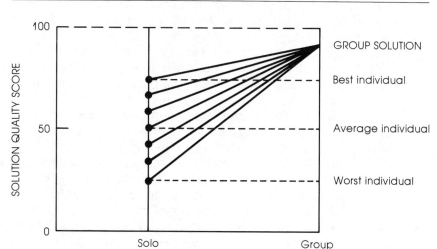

possible (and, in fact, reasonably common) to find group solutions falling all over the scale, even in the range below the score of the "worst individual" solution. Imagine, for example, that this least competent performer happens to be particularly stubborn and persuasive, and manages to talk the rest of the group out of their initial ideas, adding a few misjudgments as (s)he goes.

There is no guarantee that having a group work on a problem will produce answers good enough to justify the investment in time and effort. Remember that having n people work for an hour on a problem consumes n times as much person-power as does having one person work on a problem for an hour. Groups are not, *in general*, better or worse than their best, or worst, or average member. It depends on what sort of task they are working on, and how they work on it. The interaction of these "task" and "process" variables will be the major focus of this chapter.

It is worth emphasizing that we are mainly concerned here with "task-oriented" groups—those that come together to solve a problem, make a decision, or otherwise do work—and not with groups like parties or bull sessions, whose primary purpose is served merely by getting together. We shall, however, be concerned with the social and emotional side of groups to the extent that these factors affect task performance. A group that generates so much ill feeling among its members that they cannot work together is not going to be effective in its task. Even without reaching such a collapse, a group may be so torn apart after one meeting that its members become reluctant to meet again. Within a single group meeting, individuals may become angry or alienated to the point at which their feelings get in the way of effective functioning. Getting back at another group member may interfere with solving the problem. How much effort each individual contributes is likely to be affected by his or her feelings toward other group members. In short, even with our focus on the accomplishment of external tasks, we shall have to pay attention to the social and emotional side of group process.

As a final introductory comment, it is worth noting two related aspects of what might be called the "purely statistical" aspect of groups. Certain properties of groups arise simply because the group collects several opinions, not because of any interaction among the members. For example, suppose the microcomputer impact group was working on a simpler task, such as estimating the total cost of a particular set of computing equipment. On a task like this, we might expect individuals to make reasonable guesses, but with a random error, some guessing high, others low. In such cases, a little mathematics will readily show that pooling the individual estimates will yield, on the average, a better estimate than will any individual. In rough terms, the "true" parts of the judgments will tend to add together, while the "error" parts will tend to cancel out. In fact, as long as the individual errors are random and unbiased, the validity of the group average is a well-behaved function of the validity of the individual judgments and the size of the group. A family of such curves is shown in Figure 9.2. Note that, even for low-validity individual judgments, the average will ultimately reach assymptote at 1.0. This convergence is rapid for moderately valid individual judgments. Averages of a dozen or fewer such judgments are generally as valid as one can hope for. (See Hogarth [1978] for a fuller discussion of this point.)

A closely related statistical property of simply adding more group members can be seen when the problem requires recall of a single, clearly correct fact or the invention of a single, clearly correct insight. For example, a group is assigned the following problem: each member is asked to connect the nine dots in the diagram below using only four straight lines, and without lifting the pencil from the page (you might like to stop reading for a moment and see if you can solve this problem before you read on):

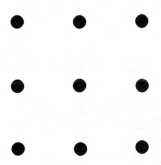

Most people will invent a constraint that makes this problem insoluble: they try to stay within the square formed by the outer layer of dots. The solution is simple once one realizes that this constraint is not imposed by the problem—but, as we saw in Chapter 3, we tend to get "locked in" to our initial way of seeing a problem. Once one realizes that the lines can continue outside the square, the solution becomes obvious. We could call these "ah-ha" or "eureka" problems.

Such problems have the simple statistical property that, if any member of the group sees the trick, the whole group will immediately agree. If each group member has an equal probability, p, of arriving at this insight, then the probability of the group achieving it is a simple function of group size (Figure 9.3).

Neither the improving validity of average judgments nor the improving probability of arriving at an insight has anything to do with subtle

Figure 9.2.   Validity of Mean of N Individual Judgments

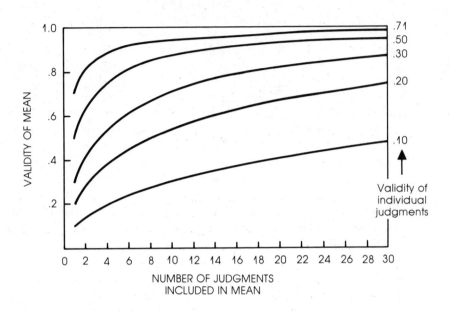

Figure 9.3.   Probability of a Group Solving a Eureka Problem

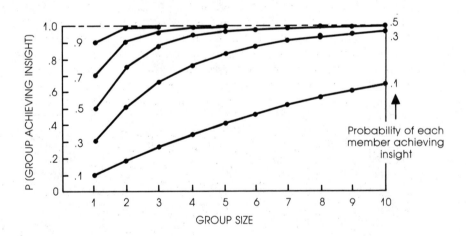

aspects of group functioning. They are simply statistical facts (although there is empirical evidence that real groups display these phenomena: see Collins and Guetzkow [1964]). We introduce them here simply as a reminder that we need to be careful when trying to assess group performance. We are not impressed if a group of six comes up with twice as many ideas as one individual. With more people involved, we would expect more output, we would hope for better solutions. The two simple statistical properties we have noted are a useful aid in asking our central question about how well groups perform: they remind us to ask, "Compared to what?"

THE EFFECTS OF WORKING WITH OTHERS

Perhaps the most obvious difference between group and solo work is simply whether or not other people are around. Working in a group may involve many different factors, such as cooperation, competition, division of labor, and status battles, but it invariably involves the presence of other people. In this section we shall look briefly at some of the research on how the presence of others affects our performance in various tasks. The phenomena themselves are of considerable interest. They are also subtle and complex, and serve to remind us of the care needed in moving from isolated research studies to practical applications in changed settings.

A little research history is a good place to start. In 1965, Robert Zajonc reviewed a number of studies on how the presence of others influences performance (Zajonc [1965]). He looked both at studies where the other people watched passively while the subject performed some task (i.e., the others were simply an audience) and at studies where the other people worked on similar tasks at the same time (i.e., the others were "coactors"). The studies included both humans performing human tasks, and other animals: rats eating alone or together, ants building nests alone or with others, and cockroaches learning to navigate simple mazes.

Zajonc's review turned up two interesting facts. First, our performance (and that of rats, ants, etc.) is often sharply affected by simply having other people around while we work. Second, the direction of the effect varies, with solo performance better for some tasks, worse for others. For example, a famous series of studies by Allport (1920) and Dashiell (1930) compared subjects working on various tasks either in isolated cubicles or seated around a table. On some tasks, such as canceling vowels from a sheet of text, or performing multiplication problems, the "seated together" subjects did better. For other tasks, such as problem solving or making judgments, the isolated subjects did better.

What makes the difference? Zajonc proposed a two-part explanation. First, he suggested, the presence of other people is a source of arousal: we become more alert, our body chemistry changes, our response patterns change. Second, when we are aroused, we tend to "emit dominant responses"—that is, we do habitual, well-learned things in preference to unfamiliar, novel things. Being aroused makes it easier to perform familiar tasks, but harder to learn new ones. (This arousal effect is well established, and is commonly used in practical settings. Football coaches, military leaders, and rhetoric trainers all know the importance of drill in establishing well-learned patterns of behavior before the big event. We fall back on habitual, well-learned behaviors when we are aroused.)

So far, so good. The implications of Zajonc's argument are reasonably straightforward. We should study alone, but take exams in crowds. Learning is inhibited by the presence of others, but once we have thoroughly learned the material, performance will be facilitated by having other people around.

Unfortunately, the story is not so simple. Another well-documented line of research suggests "social loafing," not "social facilitation." The phrase "social loafing" was invented by psychologist Bibb Latane as a summary for findings that follow.

If you pull as hard as you can on a rope, you (or, at least, the average person) will be able to exert about 140 lbs. of force. How much force will you and one other average person be able to pull? 280 lbs.? How much force will N average people be able to exert? 140N lbs.? In fact, careful studies of exactly this task (Ingham, 1974) have found that groups actually exert *less* force than this theoretical maximum, with the shortfall increasing with group size. For example, groups of size three pull at about 85% of the theoretical maximum, groups of size eight less than 50% of the maximum. The effect is known as the "Ringelmann Effect" in honor of the psychologist who discovered it in the 1920s.

What might cause the Ringelmann effect? One plausible explanation is that the individuals have trouble coordinating their efforts and pulling at the same time. A second possibility is that they try less hard in a group: social loafing. Ingham checked this by blindfolding his subjects and convincing them they were pulling with groups of different sizes, when in fact they each pulled alone. He found that people pulled less when they thought they were pulling with others—enough less to account for most of the shortfall. Social loafing thus accounts for most of the Ringelmann effect.

Imagine yourself in the following situation. You are sitting in a room waiting to participate in an experiment. You hear the experimenter, whom you just met, moving around in the next room. Suddenly you hear a loud scream and a crash, sounds of someone falling to the floor, followed by moans. Do you immediately rush in to help? As it turns out, most of us (70%) do—but only if we were in the waiting room on our own. If we were waiting with someone else, we are much less likely to offer help: only about 20% of us do. (Latane and Rodin, 1969.)

This finding is a little more scary than the rope-pulling experiment. When we are with other people "social loafing" shows up as a sharply lower probability of our offering help in what appears to be a life-or-death situation. There have been dozens of experiments along the same lines, using various different ambiguous events where help seems to be needed: apparent accidents, medical emergencies, thefts (where one might help the person stolen from), and events as simple as seeing someone drop a bundle of pencils in an elevator or hearing someone knocking to enter a room. (See Latane and Nida [1981] for a detailed review.) Over a very wide range of situations, settings, victims, and bystanders, the same effect emerges: we are much less likely to intervene if we are with others than if we are alone.

In his discussion of these "bystander intervention" studies, Latane suggests three factors that probably contribute to the social inhibition of helping. First, the situation is ambiguous, and the person offering help may appear foolish. Such embarrassment would be greater in front of an audience. Second, given the ambiguity of the situation, we tend to look to others (and they to us) for feedback about what is happening. If you see me not helping, you take it as a clue that help is not needed and do nothing, thus giving me exactly the same clue! Finally, being in a group spreads the responsibility for action over us all, rather than focusing it on the solitary individual. We may feel less individually responsible when we are in a group.

Something like this last explanation—the diffusion effect—may also account for the rope-pulling data (and comparable results for other simple tasks, such as individuals and groups being asked to shout as loud as they can). The pressure to act, and the rewards from acting, are spread out across the group, and thus act less powerfully on each individual as group size increases.

Can we tie together these various studies and explanations of how the presence of other people affects behavior? Can we predict whether the presence of others will lead to social facilitation or social loafing? Without pretending that we yet have any complete explanation of the effects, we can summarize what we know. Recall, first, that none of the tasks we have looked at in this section require any collaboration, sharing of ideas, or discussion of possibilities. They show only what happens to one individual's performance when other people are around, or the person believes they are.

There seems to be only one situation where the presence of others improves performance, and that is when we are required to perform, on our own, a simple, well-learned, solo task. In the other cases we have looked at, the presence of others tends to degrade performance. In learning or performing more complex tasks, the audience effect interferes with performance. Even when the task is simple and familiar, if it is a "group output" task (as in rope-pulling), working with others seems to dilute our motivation to put out our best efforts. When the task is ambiguous and out of the ordinary, as in helping a stranger in an emergency, the presence of others inhibits an individual's acting.

On balance, then, we would expect that groups will be at a disadvantage compared to individuals for most complex thinking tasks—the kind of work most often done by professionals. However, we should first look carefully at the type of task the group is working on, the understandings the members have, the pressures on them, and the rewards they anticipate from their participation.

GROUP TASKS

A wise and experienced observer of group process once suggested the following image of what happens in a heated group discussion. People bat around ideas like Ping-Pong balls on top of a table: clean, white, not dangerous, visible to everyone—the public game. Under the table, however, a second game is going on, a private game hidden from view. This under-the-table game is played with old, heavy, beaten-up bowling balls that get kicked around, stubbing toes, bruising shins, sometimes doing serious injury. The energies of the group are divided between the two games, so we will not understand what is happening in the group unless we can keep track of both.

The image may be overdramatic, but it reminds us vividly that there are two distinct dimensions of group processes. The "technical" dimension is the group's official work and the "social-emotional" dimension is the group members dealing with each other as human beings. The second dimension tends to be "under-the-table." In business meetings raising one's voice or otherwise showing emotion is regarded as taboo. "Let's look at this rationally," someone is sure to say, or "Let's keep personalities out of this, please." We are meant to be "cool," to show no emotion when our pet project gets turned down or we are snubbed.

This may not be the most effective way for groups to run. If Joe is still (privately) seething about the rejection of his pet project, he may look for reasons to turn down the next project presented to the group. His friend Jim, still feeling bruised from the snub he got five minutes ago, keeps quiet about some obvious weakness in a subsequent proposal, not wanting to risk another embarrassment. Since Jim is Joe's friend, Joe also keeps quiet out of loyalty. Thus another stupid project is launched. This sort of thing is not likely to increase the overall effectiveness of the group.

This is not to suggest that we would be better off expressing all our emotions openly in work groups. We do, however, have to pay attention to the social and emotional side of group work, if only to stop it interfering with the technical work. People experienced at chairing meetings become sensitive to these matters. For example, when you hear a phrase such as, "I don't care what you say, I still think . . . ," the speaker has probably passed the point of contributing to a rational exchange of ideas within the group. It may be a good time to move on to the next item of business, or to break for coffee.

To understand what happens in groups, then, we need to consider the two challenges the group has to overcome to operate effectively: the technical challenges and the social challenges. David Herold has proposed a useful scheme for assessing the complexity of each of these demands (Herold, 1979):

Technical demands.   Herold suggests that a group's task is technically complex if it has one or more of the following characteristics: it is "unprogrammable"; it is difficult; or the relevant facts or skills are widely dispersed around the group. A task is "unprogrammable" if it is unfamiliar to the members, if it varies unpredictably each time it appears, or if it has many alternative solutions (or, equivalently, if it is difficult to verify that a given suggestion is, in fact, a good solution). "Difficulty" simply means how much skill or effort is required and how many different operations the task requires. Finally, "information or skill dispersion" reflects how much collecting and sifting of information the group has to do, or how many different individuals have to contribute their special skills, for the group to reach a solution.

For example, consider a design team working on an unmanned space vehicle for interplanetary exploration. It is hard to imagine such a task being routine for any group: all sorts of possibilities have to be considered for each component, as well as for the whole system. The task is highly "unprogrammed." In addition, the task clearly requires a wide range of different specialist skills, and much hard work from the members. It is a "difficult" task. Finally, the relevant information and skills are not likely to be inside any one member's head; "information and skill dispersion" is high. The group faces a high level of technical complexity in designing the vehicle.

Social demands.   In Herold's scheme, the social demands on a group are complex if (1) there are grounds for serious disagreement and (2) the members care. The grounds for disagreement can arise either about means or ends. In "means" disagreement, the group has trouble agreeing how they should go about the task, who should do what, or how the parts are to be pulled together. In "ends" disagreement, the group has trouble agreeing what they are trying to accomplish, what criteria should be used in evaluating alternative solutions, or what the trade-offs should be among them. Neither of these types of disagreement will matter much unless the members care, unless they are "ego involved" in the task. "Ego involvement" can stem from a variety of sources, including involvement of highly valued skills (e.g., my professional reputation as a competent physicist), personally important stakes (e.g., my promotion, my department's budget), or involvement of strongly held beliefs or values (e.g., covering up an illegal act).

Again, an extreme example may clarify the issue. Several division managers and personnel specialists are charged with developing an affirmative action plan for hiring minorities and women in the company. First, the members are likely to be heavily "ego involved." The issue involves serious moral and social values, it has important implications for the way hiring will be done (and thus for the future of their departments), and, at least for the personnel specialists, important professional skills are involved. Second, disagreement can easily arise over both means and ends. One person thinks the company should hire only minorities and women until the proportions improve. Another thinks better targeted advertising will bring in a wide range of suitable applicants without forcing a change in the old selection method. One thinks that a 10 percent improvement in either category of employee would be a reasonable target; another thinks the aim should be 50 percent women in every job classification. With such strong disagreements on both means and ends, and such strong ego involvement of the members, we have no trouble rating the social demands on the group as highly complex.

These two dimensions of task demands may be combined to form the quadrants:

		Simple	Complex
SOCIAL DEMANDS	Complex	Type 4	Type 3
	Simple	Type 1	Type 2

TECHNICAL DEMANDS

This scheme can be useful in a number of ways. First, it allows us to make a diagnosis of the major issues facing the group and thus the sorts of problems that are likely to come up. For example, preparing a departmental budget might be a technically simple task for the people involved, but it is likely to raise complex social demands: a Type 4 problem. In contrast, a group of engineers assessing the potential for industrial solar heating has a Type 2 problem: technically complex, socially simple. This diagnosis leads directly to the second use of this scheme: deciding how to manage the group's work process. Such management is largely the role of the group's leader, and was extensively discussed in Chapter 7. Finally, the scheme may provide guidance as to the kinds of outside help that might be useful to the group. If social demands are complex, it may be worth investing in social skill training, team building, or self-conscious examination of the group's processes. On the other hand, if the major problem is technical complexity, it might make more sense to invest in hiring an outside subject-matter expert, or to pay more attention to the information-sharing and technical-evaluation sides of the group's activities. (See also Markus, Reading #1, and Conlon, Reading #8, in Part II.)

A slightly different view of group tasks is suggested by Steiner (1972). He distinguishes between "unitary" and "divisible" tasks. In unitary tasks, all group members do one thing (or the same thing). In divisible tasks, different members do different things. Most of the real-world tasks we have discussed so far are divisible tasks. They typically allow, or require, a division of labor into different subtasks that can be worked on separately. (Note, however, that group discussion tasks can go either way on this. Sometimes individual specialists work on different subtasks, sometimes everyone works on the whole problem.)

Steiner further splits unitary tasks. Some are "additive," in the sense that everyone does the same thing and the results are added together to make the group's output—for example, a relay race or a weaving shed. Other unitary tasks are labeled "disjunctive," emphasizing that the group's performance is equal to that of the best individual, such as a road race where the team is rated by its best individual, and the "eureka" problems discussed earlier, in which the whole group gets the answer if any individual does. A third type of unitary task is exemplified by mountain climbing and sequential production operations, where the group's success is determined by the performance of its weakest member. These are labeled "conjunctive" problems. Finally, some problems (such as group discussion) are "discretionary," in that they may be treated as either unitary or divisible, at the group's discretion.

This scheme gives some interesting insights into the range of tasks we have discussed already. For example, the rope-pulling task used to demonstrate the Ringelmann effect is clearly a unitary-additive task; the group's key problem is how to maintain the motivation of each individual so as to have maximum total effort. In contrast, the "bystander intervention" tasks were "unitary-disjunctive"; anyone offering help counted as an intervention. Most of the other group tasks we have considered were "divisible" (or at least "unitary-discretionary"); the group's central problem was to organize itself appropriately to face the various demands made on it.

The central point is that different tasks make very different demands on a group. To be effective, the group needs to be able to diagnose just what these demands are, and to organize to meet them. A classic demonstration is an experiment of Thorndike's (1938) comparing individual and group performance in two tasks: solving crossword puzzles and composing crossword puzzles. At first glance these two tasks appear to demand similar skills—ingenuity and wide vocabulary—but their crucial demands are different. Solving a crossword puzzle has a strong disjunctive character. If any member of the group solves a clue, the whole group is likely to agree and it becomes part of the group's answer. Composing a puzzle, on the other hand, requires a fitting together of many elements, a difficult thing to do except within a single mind. Sure enough, Thorndike's study found that groups outperformed individuals at solving puzzles, but individuals did better at composing them. The organization required for a group to create a new puzzle turned out to be too difficult. Even with all the range of ideas and possibilities a group can provide, the single individual turned out to be better suited for this task.

GROUP PROCESS AND REWARD STRUCTURE

The group's task is one important influence on the way the group operates. A second important influence is the way rewards are allocated for group performance. Consider, for example, the way grades are assigned in a class. Probably the commonest method is simply to grade each individual against some standard. However, if the instructor practices "curving," so that only some fraction of the class can get an A, some other fraction a B, and so on, an element of competition is introduced. A third method is to assign grades to groups (or even whole classes) on the basis of their collective performance, with each member getting the same grade. These group grades can themselves be based on an outside standard or on comparison with other groups.

These different reward systems are likely to affect the way class members go about the task of learning the course materials. How would you react under each arrangement to another class member who asked to borrow your notes, or to have some tricky point explained? Under *individual* grading, you might help if you had the time, since helping would have no effect on your own grade. However, if the grades are "curved," you have an incentive not to cooperate, because improving the other's performance damages your own chance of a good grade. In group grading, the incentive is to cooperate with a member of your own group, since this also helps you. Similarly, helping a nongroup member depends on whether or not the groups are in competition with one another.

The effects of these four reward systems—individual, competitive, cooperative, and cooperative with outside competition—have been extensively studied in group research. As one might expect, the results of these studies have varied widely. Sometimes one system, sometimes another, seems to lead to best overall performance, depending on a range of other factors such as type of task, size of group, characteristics of members, and how long the group works together. However, pulling together some hundreds of findings from these studies, a recent review (Johnson et al., 1981) suggests the following important results:

1. Overall, cooperative reward systems promote achievement and productivity better than do competitive systems.

This is obviously a most important conclusion, particularly since many of the reward systems in current use, both in the classroom and in the work organization, are competitive. A great deal of careful research, however, suggests that cooperative systems are more effective. This may not be true for very simple, unitary tasks, where Johnson et al. found roughly equal support for either reward system, and another, less complete, review (Schmitt, 1981) found a small superiority for competitive rewards. For all other sorts of tasks, however, the balance of the evidence is clear: cooperative rewards are better, especially for small groups with highly interdependent tasks.

2. Overall, cooperative reward systems promote achievement and productivity better than do individualistic systems.

Again, the balance of the evidence is clear, though it is possible to find a few exceptions. Johnson et al. found 146 relevant experimental results, of which 108 showed cooperation better; only six showed individualistic better; and forty-two showed no difference.

3. Individual reward systems produce much the same effects as do competitive reward systems. Cooperative reward systems produce much the same effects regardless of whether or not there is external competition.

The critical comparison seems to be between cooperative systems (whether or not they involve competition with an outside group) and other systems (individual, or competition between individuals). Overall, with the exceptions noted, cooperative systems do better.

These results have important implications for organizational life. Perhaps the central one is that we should take groups seriously, not just in assigning tasks to them, but in rewarding all the members for accomplishing their task. We are, as a society, strong on the virtues of individualism—and, as the third conclusion implies, we tend to interpret individual and competitive rewards in much the same way (though they are logically distinct). However, when we face complex tasks (social or technical, or both), the real payoff comes if working together is emphasized, rather than working against one another. Even when the task does not demand coordination or division of labor between the members of a group, there are plenty of opportunities for cooperation to help group performance. Information sharing, tutoring, and encouraging one another are such opportunities. The evidence strongly suggests that, in all but the simplest tasks, emphasizing these activities by cooperative reward arrangements leads to superior performance.

A second aspect of reward for group members has been studied under the label of "group cohesiveness"—roughly, how attractive the group is to its members. Research has, however, been somewhat muddied by a failure to distinguish between different kinds of cohesiveness. As Cartwright (1968) has pointed out, one can be strongly attracted to a group either because one is attracted to the other members or because one is attracted to the group's goals and tasks. For example, I might want to join the Astronomy Club because I like the other members, in which case, the group might be highly cohesive but do very little astronomy (low productivity). If I join because I want to learn about astronomy, we would expect high cohesiveness to go with *high* productivity. From the viewpoint of the individual member, two different rewards are implied by high cohesiveness: either the individual is rewarded simply by becoming a member of the group, or (s)he is rewarded by the group's performance. High cohesiveness can be associated with either high or low productivity, depending on what forms the basis for the attractiveness of the group to its members. (High cohesiveness is also an element of "groupthink," a phenomenon we shall discuss later in this chapter.)

In summary, we have seen that the way a group works is affected in a rather complex way by the external reward system. Overall, the empirical evidence strongly suggests that cooperative reward systems, with or without external competition, generally lead to higher group productivity than do either competitive or individualistic reward systems. The rewards associated with membership in highly attractive ("cohesive") groups are ambiguous in their effects on productivity. We can expect performance to be higher in cohesive groups only if that cohesion is based on task accomplishment. If cohesiveness is based on attraction to other members, productivity is unaffected (or is perhaps negatively affected) by a high level of cohesiveness.

GROUPS AND RISK TAKING

In 1961 a small bombshell was dropped on group decision researchers by a master's thesis done at MIT by J. A. F. Stoner. This study, and its subsequent refinement by Wallach, Kogan, and Bem (1962), suggests that decision-making groups may have the remarkable property of biasing their members toward making riskier decisions than each member would make alone. For obvious reasons, this finding attracted a lot of attention. Given the range of important decisions that are made by groups, it is a little worrying to think that such decisions might be biased towards gambling and high risk taking. In the past twenty years, a good deal of effort has gone into finding out whether and when such a bias might be found.

Stoner devised a number of situations called "choice dilemmas" in which the decision maker is confronted with a "safe" choice of moderate value and a "risky" choice that will be of high value if it works, and of low value if it does not. In one dilemma, a middle-aged engineer is told by his doctor that he has a serious heart disease which, untreated, will confine him to a wheelchair for the rest of his life. An operation is available, but it is risky. If it works, he will be completely cured; if not, he will die. Does he want the operation?

Given such a choice, most of us would ask, "What are the chances of the operation working out?" If it is certain to succeed, we will take it; if it is certain to fail, we will not. In between, there is some probability of success at which we are just balanced between having the operation or refusing it. The more we feel inclined to take a chance, the lower the odds are that we will take.

Stoner developed a dozen such "choice dilemmas," with different situations but the same basic structure. In each situation, he had people select the lowest acceptable odds for the risky option. They first worked on their own, then in a small group instructed to reach a consensus. (In both cases, they were asked to advise the central character in the story.) The startling result was that most of the groups made riskier recommendations than did the average of the individuals in the group. The phenomenon was labeled "risky shift."

Let us look more carefully at this result. As shown in Figure 9.4, individuals in a particular group have some range of opinions on how risky to be in a particular situation. Presumably, when asked to reach a consensus, they argue and persuade one another until their opinions more or less converge. But why should this convergence be, as Stoner found, generally on the risky side of the group average?

Several possible mechanisms have been suggested. One, the "diffusion of responsibility" argument, suggests that people making solo recommendations feel personal responsibility for the result, and thus

Figure 9.4.   Individual and Group Choice in a Risky Decision

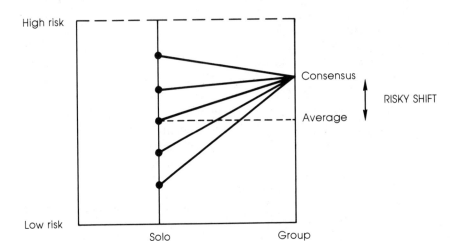

act cautiously. In the group, this pressure is diffused among the members, so the average becomes riskier. Another possible mechanism is that risk takers have all the persuasive arguments, like "Go on, don't be chicken" or "Are you a man or a mouse?" so their opinions are weighted more than those of the more cautious group members. A third, related, suggestion is that, at least for student groups it is more socially acceptable to act boldly—there is a norm for risk taking. Social norms operate more strongly in social situations than in solo decisions, hence, risky shift.

In the twenty years since Stoner's experiment, these and other explanations have been studied in a wide range of ingenious experiments, using different measures of risk, different types and sizes of groups, gambling for real money, and different decision procedures. Infuriatingly, the results refuse to fall into any neat patterns. Sometimes you get risky shift, sometimes cautious shift, sometimes no shift at all. For example, Blascovich et al. (1975) found risky shift (groups riskier than individuals) in playing blackjack; groups tended to bet more at any given odds. But Knox and Safford (1976) found exactly the reverse for individuals and groups betting on horse races.

Unfortunately, the best we can conclude at this point is, it depends—and we do not yet know on what it depends. A very recent study (Felsenthal, 1979) indicates only that the whole phenomenon, while intriguing, is situation specific. Sometimes individuals will find higher levels of risk acceptable when they choose on their own than when they choose in groups; sometimes they will find the reverse. All we know is that we need to be careful about this side of group functioning. Groups may well be biased about risk (as compared to the average of their members), but we cannot be sure in which direction. Active research on the question continues.

GROUPS AND CREATIVITY

Creativity is the ability to generate solutions that are both novel and effective, a talent we all have to some extent. Most of us wish we had more of it, or could find ways to nurture and stimulate what we have. In this section, we shall look briefly at what creativity is and whether groups can be used to stimulate it.

There is something profoundly mysterious about the instant of creation, the moment when everything falls into place and a new hunch comes into our minds. Memoirs of highly creative scientists, composers, and mathematicians all describe ideas "just appearing" to them, often at inconvenient moments. This is not to suggest that creative people just wait for inspiration. On the contrary, good ideas seem to come only after one has wrestled with a problem intensely, gathered information, mulled it over, and struggled to find a solution. What then seems to happen (Campbell, 1960) is that one's unconscious mental processes try out many possible alternatives and combinations, finally surfacing a very few for the conscious mind to consider. (Incidentally, these unconscious processes often seem to work best when the conscious mind has moved onto something quite different, hence the stories of creative eccentrics leaping out of bed, or the bathtub, to record their sudden insights.)

In short, creativity seems to require two things: (1) a prior immersion in the problem in all its aspects in order to generate many relevant ideas, and (2) an evaluation or verification phase to decide which, if any, of the ideas generated are any good. Can working in groups help either or both of these processes?

Generating Ideas

One technique aimed at stimulating the first, idea-generating phase is group *brainstorming* (Osborn, 1941). The basic rules of brainstorming are:

1. To try to generate as many ideas as possible, regardless of quality
2. To combine, modify, or build off ideas suggested by others
3. To withhold criticism or evaluation of ideas suggested.

Suggestions are scribbled quickly on flip charts, or the session is tape recorded. The basic idea is that something new and useful will come out of the intense, uncensored interaction of people pouring out ideas around the central topic.

There is no question that groups operating under these rules do produce a lot of ideas. However, so do individuals working under the same rules who pool their lists later. In fact, several studies (Dunnette et al., 1963; Lewis, Sadosky, and Connolly, 1975) have found that more and better ideas are produced by pooling individual brainstorming outputs than by brainstorming in groups. Brainstorming itself seems to work, but pooling is more effective than interaction. Of course, one might still want to use a group method, if only to ensure that everyone works on the problem for an adequate length of time. Thinking is hard work, and a bit of social encouragement may keep people from drifting off into some other activity.

A second group technique aimed at enhancing creativity is called synectics (Gordon, 1961). This technique uses a carefully structured series of phases through which the group works under the direction of a specialist leader. The core of the technique is a process in which the problem is approached obliquely by divergent, analogical thinking. Suppose a group wished to design a more effective watertight door for a submarine. Using synectics instead of the usual engineering approach, they might be asked to consider analogies from nature (e.g., how fish mouths work), mathematics (e.g., discontinuous functions), or mythology (e.g., heroes guarding a vital bridge). They might be asked to role-play the component, acting out what a door might feel like struggling to keep the water out, or they might be encouraged to turn the problem inside out, thinking about ways to make an opening as nonwatertight as possible. In short, where brainstorming seeks new ideas from the unfettered flow of possibilities, synectics provides a much more structured set of procedures for stimulating novel approaches to the problem.

Evaluating Ideas

By one means or another, a group has managed to produce a number of promising ideas to solve a problem. Now, how good is the group at sifting through them and selecting the best? This is a much more familiar task for a group, and much of what we have already said applies. The broad picture is that, while there are benefits from having a group evaluate ideas, the cost can be high. First, a significant fraction (sometimes 100 percent) of the participants' work can be taken up with the social demands of the group, that is, the "maintenance" functions. Second, the evaluations expressed may be shaped by factors other than a candid assessment of the merits of a given idea. (I may express more approval for a poor idea suggested by my friend or my boss than I would for a good idea suggested by my rival.) Third, groups exert pressures toward conformity, so that some of the divergence of multiple views is censored. Finally, groups seem to be "solution oriented" rather than "problem oriented"; much group discussion focuses on the merits of different answers, even when it is unclear what the question is (Maier and Hoffman, 1960).

Is it possible to enjoy the benefits of group discussion without incurring these costs? Two techniques that seem to offer some hope basically operate by exchanging opinions and ideas by a method other than face-to-face interaction. In one of these, the Delphi technique (Dalkey and Helmer, 1963), the "group" members never even meet in the same place (this has obvious advantages, especially if they happen to live on opposite sides of the country!). They "interact" by responding anonymously to questionnaires. The results are summarized by a coordinator and sent back to the participants, who then respond again, weighing the views and responses of the others. After a few (perhaps three or four) rounds, opinions generally converge enough for a consensus to emerge.

A second technique for operating without face-to-face interaction is called the "nominal group" technique. The members work in the same room, but instead of talking, they write their ideas on a pad of paper. These ideas are then pooled by each member contributing a single idea at a time for the coordinator to record on a flip chart in open view; each member contributes one idea in a round robin until all ideas have been recorded. Once all the ideas have been summarized, group discussion proceeds in the usual way. Finally, a private vote is used to arrive at a decision.

The nominal group technique seems to have a number of advantages over interacting groups. Idea generation is separated from evaluation. Working in the presence of others may motivate hard work and ensure that a wide range of ideas and opinions surfaces. Premature closure is discouraged by the time-management requirement. Since there is little interaction, less effort is required to manage the social side of the group. Crucially, all the ideas generated are placed publicly before the group, separated from the people who proposed them, so that the confusion between supporting one's friends and supporting the ideas of one's friends is reduced. There is a growing body of experimental evidence supporting the effectiveness of the technique (see Delbecq et al. [1975] for a useful review), and we may expect to see it more widely used in the future.

To sum up, a number of alternatives to the traditional interactive group have been tried, and described here, for different aspects of creative problem solving. Brainstorming and synectics have focused on idea generation, while Delphi and nominal groups have focused on idea evaluation. Each of these techniques appears to have a useful place in deciding how groups might be designed. They do, at least, serve to remind us that there is nothing sacred about the traditional format for meetings: that is, merely putting a number of people around a table and letting them thrash the problem out. This section has proposed some alternatives.

GROUPTHINK

The term "groupthink" was invented by Irving Janis (1972) to describe a particularly worrying phenomenon in decision-making groups. He studied a number of important historical decisions that had turned out particularly badly, and asked: How could intelligent, well-informed, and experienced people collectively come to such stupid decisions? The examples he examined were of famous historical blunders (e.g., the British government's decision to try to appease Hitler before the Second World War; the U.S. government's attempt to invade Cuba at the Bay of Pigs in 1961), but "groupthink" also seems a real danger in the decisions we might ourselves face.

The core of groupthink is the tendency of group members to suppress disagreements and strive for concurrence in a decision rather than weigh up information about several alternatives. Groupthink is more likely when a highly cohesive group faces a crisis decision under directive leadership. In these circumstances loyalty and support seem more important to group members than criticism and search. Outside information is tuned out, and individuals suppress both their own doubts and doubts expressed by other members. An "illusion of unanimity" is created: though members later recall their own doubts, they tended not to express them at the time, since they saw no one else expressing theirs. A strong "us versus them" feeling develops, with "us" as invulnerable and morally correct, and "them" as malicious and stupid. The group process focuses entirely on maintaining agreement, not on finding a good solution. Not surprisingly, some poor decisions can emerge.

SUMMARY: ASSETS AND LIABILITIES OF GROUPS

Even from this very selective sampling of what is known about how groups work, it is clear that groups are highly complex animals. To pull things together a little, we shall adopt a device suggested by Norman

Maier (1967) and try to list the assets and liabilities of groups as problem-solving and decision-making entities, and the factors that could operate as either assets or liabilities.

Assets. Groups have some obvious advantages over individuals. They generally have more information available to them, and more approaches to the problem. On statistical grounds alone, the independent judgments of several experts are likely to give a more valid average than the judgment of a single individual; and where a single insight will solve the problem, the chance of one member having this insight increases with the number of members. Beyond this, pooling of judgments, information, or approaches opens the possibility of improving solutions beyond what any single member can achieve.

A second major asset of groups is that, once a decision is made, group members are more likely to understand and accept it than they would if they were merely told of a decision reached by someone else. This is an important asset. As we noted in Chapter 2, decisions need to be implemented before problems are really solved. Good implementation is more likely when the implementers understand and accept what they are to do. Having been part of the decision-making process makes this more likely.

Liabilities. Groups also have some liabilities. First, they run up the payroll cost of solving the problem, since the time and effort of more than one person is involved. Second, working in a group means that "social maintenance" work needs to be done, to keep the group functioning at at least a minimal level. Further, to be effective, effort must be exerted to control the social process to prevent domination by any single individual, to minimize pressures toward conformity, to check the tendency to adopt solutions too early, and to prevent substantive disagreement from degenerating into other orientations such as winning or losing, or supporting our friends and knifing our enemies.

The mere fact of working with other people has effects on performance, as we saw in our brief review of the "social facilitation" and "social loafing" research. We tentatively concluded that these effects will, in most situations, come down on the liability side, with social loafing a real threat to group productivity.

Swing factors. The most interesting group phenomena we have looked at are those that could be either assets or liabilities, depending on the situation and how it is managed. The sorts of demands the task places on the group are one such "swing factor." Some tasks make complex technical demands on the group, others make complex social demands. To be effective, the group needs to address each of these two demands.

For example, focusing on interpersonal processes in a group whose central task is of high technical complexity is likely to be ineffective or distracting. Similarly, careful diagnosis of the task requirements for interdependence of the members' work ("divisible" versus the various forms of "unitary" tasks) is necessary for the group process to be managed effectively.

A critical aspect of group management is the choice of cooperative or competitive reward systems. We saw that cooperative systems appear more effective for most tasks, though competitive systems may be slightly more effective for very simple unitary tasks. A second aspect of matching process to task turns on the development of group cohesiveness. Here care is needed to develop the relevant basis for cohesiveness. Cohesiveness based on attraction to other members is less likely to lead to group effectiveness than is cohesiveness based on shared goals.

Group handling of risk is a "swing factor" in two senses. First, it is hard to predict whether groups will shift toward risk or caution compared to their average member (though it is likely that they will do one or the other, not merely average out). Second, it is not always clear which shift would be desirable. We might want to encourage boldness in a planning group with a stodgy, play-it-safe record, and caution in a group with the power to start wars or send people to jail.

Operating on these "swing factors" raises the possibility that desired group outputs can be encouraged by directly managing the way the members interact. In attempts to produce creative solutions to difficult problems, we saw that techniques have been developed for generating ideas (brainstorming and synectics) and for screening them (Delphi and nominal groups). These techniques, whatever their track record, certainly represent a conscious decision to design and manage what the group does. Examples of "groupthink" in crisis situations suggest what can happen if no steps are taken to manage group processes deliberately. In one sense, this task of managing the group process is the core of what we mean by "leadership," as we saw in Chapter 7. Other aspects of the process are taken up in Rossini's paper, Reading #4, on working in interdisciplinary groups, and in McCall's paper, Reading #6, on the particular problems that arise in leadership of professionals.

DISCUSSION QUESTIONS: CHAPTER 9

1. For some kinds of tasks groups might be expected to produce better answers than individuals, for statistical rather than psychological reasons. Suggest two examples of such tasks, and explain why the group is more likely to produce a good answer.

2. What is meant by "social facilitation"? What is meant by "social loafing"? When would you expect each effect to dominate the other in affecting the performance of a group?

3. What is the difference between the "task" or "technical" and the "social-emotional" or "interpersonal" aspect of a group's functioning? Classify the following remarks, heard in a group discussion, as to which aspect of the group's activities they probably represent:

    a. "The ultimate collapse load on that pillar should be over twenty tons."

    b. "Why don't the production people ever give us enough lead time on this item?"

    c. "I feel that dealing with customers is properly a marketing activity."

    d. "I think it's time we quit bickering and came to some firm decisions."

    (Be careful: people often use "I feel" when they are expressing thoughts, and "I think" when they are expressing feelings!)

4. Herold's classification of group tasks rates them in terms of the complexity of the technical and social demands they present. Give an example of a task that you would rate as:

    a. Technically simple and socially simple

    b. Technically simple and socially complex

    c. Technically complex and socially simple

    d. Technically complex and socially complex

    For each example, imagine you were the chairperson of the group. What problems would you expect, and how would you deal with them?

5. Considerable evidence suggests that groups working under cooperative reward systems are more productive than those working under competitive or individual reward systems. Cooperative reward systems are, however, relatively rare in the organizational world. Why do you think this is? Describe how you might set up a cooperative reward system for a research group that had previously operated under a competitive system. What effects on the members' behavior would you expect from the new system? How might it affect their feelings about belonging to the group?

6. What is meant by "risky shift" in the context of group decision making? Is it a well-established, stable phenomenon? If not, why is it worth knowing about?

7. What is "brainstorming"? Would you expect to generate more ideas if you "brainstormed" as a group or if you "brainstormed" individually and then pooled the results? What other techniques are available for enhancing group creativity?

8. List three interpersonal processes that might lower a group's performance in evaluating ideas. Describe how these processes are overcome in (a) the Delphi technique and (b) the nominal group method.

9. What is "groupthink"? Under what circumstances would you anticipate that "groupthink" would occur, and what might you do to try to prevent it?

10. What is meant by "a camel is a horse designed by a committee"? Does this seem to you to be a fair overall assessment of the effectiveness of groups? Why, or why not?

Chapter 10

Organizational Structure and Goals

Suppose that you decide one Saturday morning that you need a new bookcase, and that it might be fun and economical to build it yourself. You measure the area of wall where it will go, figure out the materials and tools you need, and head for the hardware store. By Sunday evening it is finished and ready for books—not quite as professional as the one you could have bought at a furniture store, but serviceable, and a source of modest satisfaction, quite apart from the money you saved.

As you sit admiring your handiwork, it occurs to you that building bookshelves might not be a bad way to earn a living. Working with wood and tools is fun. The results should get better with a bit of practice, and, judging from the prices you see advertised, there is money to be made. You start to think about a small business, yourself and a few employees, with a small workshop, building custom-made bookshelves. It might be an attractive alternative to working for someone else.

Before you call a lawyer to set up your company, it might be worth thinking a little further about what you are getting into. First, you will have to be a lot more efficient if you want to make any money building bookshelves. Your weekend project probably did not save enough money to pay you the minimum wage for your time. To achieve this efficiency, you will have to subdivide the work and buy special machinery for each part. One employee will do nothing but rough sawing; another will plane and sand the boards; another will assemble the pieces; another will finish and stain. The specialization of jobs and equipment is the key to efficiency (although it may not be the best way to design satisfying jobs: see Brass, Reading #3).

What does this leave for you to do (other than carry the profits to the bank)? Chances are that you will never touch a piece of lumber again; you will be too busy. You have moved from being a craftsperson to being a manager. You design the products, contact customers for orders, arrange financing with the bank, negotiate with raw-material suppliers, hire employees, deal with the payroll, assign production schedules. You do everything but build bookcases.

What has happened is that all the planning and organizing activities that you did in your head when you were working on your own have become a real job, a separate specialty. In building the organization you started by taking apart all the separate activities that go into making bookshelves; someone now has to put them back together again. In one sense this person is pure overhead; (s)he makes no product, but shows up on the payroll anyway.

Although this is oversimplified, it provides one useful way of looking at an organization. At the bottom are the employees who actually make the product, deliver the service, or deal with the customers. The rest of the organization is "administrative overhead," a coordinating machine that directs the work of the first-line employees. When we talk about "organizational structure," we are talking about this coordinating machine. To some extent it is consciously "designed" (see Wolf, Reading #2); to some extent it emerges as the participants go about their business.

THE IDEA OF STRUCTURE

It is not easy to give a brief, satisfactory definition of the term "organizational structure." The word "structure" itself is derived from the Latin word for "to arrange," and that is what we have in mind. How is the organization "arranged"? Think of all the ways we could answer that question. We could talk about its legal arrangements: is it a corporation or a partnership, profit or nonprofit, etc.? We could talk about its economic arrangements: its suppliers and customers, its markets, its profitability. We could talk about its interpersonal arrangements: who is friends with whom, what are the groups or cliques, who the isolates are; its physical arrangements—where the offices and plants are, who has which office. Each of these would tell us something about how the organization was "arranged," but not really anything about its "structure."

When organizational scientists talk about "structure" they usually have in mind the regularities of work and work relationships: who does what work, who directs whose work, and how are the different activities coordinated with one another? One way of representing this is the familiar box-and-lines diagram known as the "organization chart." The boxes on these charts generally represent jobs (not people, it should be noted). The lines represent what are called "reporting relationships" —roughly, who is whose boss. Most descriptions of the formal structure of an organization start with such a chart and its supporting documents, such as detailed job descriptions and procedure manuals.

The organization chart is thus something like an electrical wiring diagram, in that it shows the components of the device and their interconnections. It is, however, an incomplete description. What people actually do is only roughly captured by reading their job descriptions; the way they relate to one another is vastly more complex than a "reporting relationship." Indeed, organization charts may be so poor a reflection of reality that many organizations pay almost no attention to them. They are used in this chapter as helpful descriptive devices, which describe only a limited part of the complex patterning of regularities we call "organizational structure."

THE GEOMETRY OF ORGANIZATIONAL CHARTS

We suggested in chapter 5, "Communication," that organizations can usefully be thought of as arrangements for minimizing, not maximizing, communication between members. If, for example, the organization has n employees, we need a total of $n(n-1) \div 2$ communication links to connect everyone with everyone else. This number soon gets large, and total interconnection is impractical for organizations of any great size, because communication would be a full-time job.

In fact, most organizations are structured in a hierarchy with far fewer communication links. Such hierarchies face an interesting trade-off between height and width. For example, suppose every employee (except those at the base) has a given number of immediate subordinates, s (that individual's "span of control"). If s is large (ten or twelve), then an organization of a certain total size will be shorter and flatter than will the same number of employees arranged under a smaller value of s. Looked at the other way, if the number of levels in the structure is fixed, larger s values generate larger organizations. For example, a four-level organization quickly goes from very small to very large as s increases: it has one employee at the top, s employees at the next level, s^2 at the next, and s^3 at the lowest level. Thus, in a four-level organization:

Span of control, s:	3	5	7	9
Total employees, n:	40	156	400	820

Increasing the span of control by a factor of three (from three to nine) increases total employees by a factor of more than twenty (from forty to 820). Note also how many of the possible communication links are eliminated by the hierarchical arrangement. The small organization (s = 3) uses thirty-nine of the 780 possible links (about 5 percent), while the largest one (s = 9) uses 819 of the possible 335,790 links (about .24 percent). Finally, the smaller organization has thirteen of its forty employees in "administrative overhead" (i.e., not directly engaged in production), about 32 percent, while the larger one has only about 11 percent in these roles.

The sensitivity of these structural dimensions to changes in span of control led early organizational researchers to extensive exploration of the mathematical aspects of the matter, and even to attempts to discover an optimal value for s (Graicunas, 1937). In retrospect, these efforts seem rather silly. The underlying question is the number of subordinates a supervisor can effectively supervise, and the answer varies from one situation to another. (Do the employees know their jobs? Are they all in the same place?) However, it is worth bearing in mind that important structural dimensions like size, shape, number of levels, and span of control are logically interrelated, and that tradeoffs between them need to be made. We shall return to the effects of different tradeoffs later in this chapter.

DIMENSIONS OF STRUCTURE

In addition to the terms we have been using already, four other dimensions commonly appear in discussions of organizational structure: differentiation, specialization, formalization, and centralization (Kimberly and Evanisko, 1979).

Differentiation

There are advantages to having different parts of the organization work on different aspects of the business. In the example of the bookcase company, the differentiation came about in two ways: horizontally, by splitting out the different activities concerned with making the product, and vertically, by splitting out management from production activities. In large-scale organizations, both of these processes are extensive. Suppose, for example, our bookshelf company has grown into a giant with thousands of employees. Horizontal differentiation might now take one of several forms. We might group activities by *function*, with different departments for preparing lumber, sawing, assembly, finishing, and so on (and, in a company this size, a legal department, a sales department, perhaps even a computer center). Alternatively, we might set up departments to match the *customer groupings*, such as institutional furniture or domestic furniture. A third alternative would be to group by *product*, putting all our bookcase expertise in one department, and all our chair people in another.

Other groupings might make sense; for example, groupings based on *process* (e.g., if we got into using plastic laminates for some products instead of wood, and wanted to use special machinery effectively) or by *geography* (e.g., if we had plants all over the country, each producing for a local market).

Different types of differentiation can be used in the same structure. For example, a large company may specialize by region, but maintain functional or product groupings within each region. Sometimes the same activity appears in two different groupings, as when an activity like operations research is split between one central, corporate group and other groups attached to operating divisions.

Vertical differentiation refers to the splitting of different activities as one moves up the hierarchy. For example, both the first-level supervisor and the executive vice president are managers, but their activities and responsibilities are different. In tall organizations, one would expect to find more extensive differentiation of activities along the vertical dimension than one would find in flatter organizations. In general, those closer to the production level of the organization are more oriented towards the day-to-day, immediate problems of running the organization, while those higher in the organization pay more attention to long-run, strategic matters affecting the whole organization.

Specialization

Structures that are highly differentiated, especially in the horizontal sense, tend to need employees with highly specialized skills and areas of expertise. The relationship between differentiation and specialization need not be close, however. For example, within the various alternative departmental structures for our furniture company, we might have more specialization or less. Each employee in the department might be trained to perform adequately on any of that department's machines, or there might be one specialist for each machine. In research groups, there is a similar range between generalists and specialists (and advantages for each). In general, we refer to structures as "specialized" or "unspecialized," depending on which type of job predominates.

Formalization

There is an old U.S. Army saying about the three possible ways of doing anything: the right way, the wrong way, and the army way. What is being referred to is the army's tendency to have a detailed set of instructions, procedures, and rules for every task, no matter how trivial. There is an "army way" to make up one's bed, an "army way" to shave, an "army way" to write computer programs. Organizations in which procedures and rules are extensively specified are highly "formalized," in the sense we are using the word here. Such formalization tends to reduce flexibility and initiative, but also leads to adequate performance of routine tasks.

Centralization

Highly centralized organizations are those in which most decisions are made at the top. Decentralized organizations allow more flexibility to lower-level managers. Again, we can see that tradeoffs are involved. In a decentralized structure, the people making the decisions are likely to be well informed about what is going on in their areas, but less so about the overall organization and what is happening elsewhere. Highly centralized organizations overcome this, but at the cost of having a relatively small number of managers making most of the decisions, and thus working on highly filtered information and probably generating long decision delays.

LINE AND STAFF FUNCTIONS

A simple organizational hierarchy has difficulty dealing with professional specialists. Increasing "differentiation" of management functions tends to increase the number of specialized employees such as lawyers, computer specialists, and personnel experts, but these technical specialists are not hired for their management skills. They provide skills the organization needs, but they are not directly concerned in its day-to-day operations. How can they be fitted into the hierarchy?

The traditional solution has been to create what are called "staff" positions, distinguished from the "line" positions that actually manage the organization. The staff specialists provide advice and support to the line managers, but do not have any authority over them. They are, in an old phrase, "on tap, but not on top." The terms "line" and "staff" apparently come from the military: "line of command" is the chain of officers authorized to give orders (connecting the general at the top to the troops at the bottom), and "staff" personnel are outside this chain. They give advice, not orders.

This solution carries a large potential for trouble. Two seasoned observers of organizational life suggest that "there is probably no area of management which causes more difficulties, more friction, and more loss of time and effectiveness" (Koontz and O'Donnell, 1964: 262). In highly formalized organizations, procedures manuals fill page after page to spell out the authority and duties of the various line and staff positions—and still there are grey areas where disputes and conflicts occur.

An example shows how conflicts arise. Suppose you are a young operations researcher working in the industrial engineering department (a "staff" department) of a large organization. Your interest is in production problems—scheduling, line balancing, and layout. You go to the production supervisor to try to sell your services. How well do you think you will do?

Note, first, that "selling your services" is precisely what you have to do. In a general sense, you and the production supervisor are both interested in improving production. But that does not mean that you will be welcomed with open arms. In practical terms, you are a disturbance, an interruption, perhaps even a threat. Production supervisors are busy and cost conscious; talking to you takes time, and perhaps money if your time is billed to the production budget. You are probably seen as an impractical theoretician, full of book-learning but knowing nothing of the complex reality of getting the product out the door. Somehow you must convince the supervisor that things could perhaps be done better without suggesting that they are currently being done badly. Like most of us, production supervisors react badly to suggestions that their hard-won skills are inadequate.

You manage to steer around these difficulties and reach an agreement on a project. Now you need to collect data, time certain activities, keep new records. All these activities cause at least some disruption and suspicion on the shop floor. Merely using a stopwatch to time an activity can lead to trouble; the workers may suspect that time standards and pay rates are being reset, an obviously sensitive matter. Collecting the information you need may put an additional burden on people who are already busy. Your project will probably be a mystery to most of the employees, so there will often be suspicion: is my job, or my paycheck, or my familiar way of doing things, threatened?

Finally, consider your own motivations. What results are likely to satisfy you, or to advance your career? The production supervisor is probably most interested in a straightforward, short-term project that will enhance weekly production figures. You, on the other hand, are more oriented toward doing something sophisticated, a longer-term project that uses advanced methodology and will impress your boss and your colleagues. Even the language you use can get you into trouble; a phrase like "optimizing a stochastic throughput parameter" can kill a project instantly.

This picture, though overdrawn, suggests some of the difficulties that can arise between line and staff people. (Webber [1967] describes such conflicts in more detail, and offers several useful practical ideas on how to overcome them.) To some extent, the difficulties stem from decisions made in designing the organization's structure, and they can be reduced by careful specification of the boundaries and relationships between the staff and line functions. To an important degree, however, a potential for conflict is built into line and staff relationships. Professional orientations, reward structures, time orientation, problem formulations, even personality types, are likely to differ between the two areas, and cannot be solved merely by adding detail to the procedures manual, or by assigning this responsibility to one role and that authority to another. Much of the working out must be done, not by the formal structure of the organization, but directly between the people involved.

STRUCTURAL TRADEOFFS AND CONSTRAINTS

Thus far we have discussed some basic structural ideas of organization, noting some simple combinatorial properties of hierarchies (the relationship between span of control, number of levels, size and shape) and four important dimensions of structure (differentiation, specialization, formalization, and centralization). We now need to examine more closely how these dimensions relate to one another. In this section we shall look at a set of issues internal to the organization that tend to shape and limit the structural possibilities. We then examine the effects of technology and of external forces.

Implicit in the discussion of structural dimensions is the idea of a tradeoff, perhaps even a dilemma, which takes various forms. In the case of the "geometry" of the organization chart, the tradeoff is clear. We cannot have both close, detailed supervision (small span of control) and quick, effective communication from the shop floor to the chief executive (small number of levels), without giving up the advantages of a minimal hierarchy. Related tradeoffs confront us when we look at the other structural dimensions. If we differentiate departments by function, we lose the benefits of differentiation by product or customer. Many kinds of specialists are professionals. They value their autonomy and are hard to second-guess on technical matters. They are likely to respond poorly to being told how to do their jobs (high formalization) or what decisions to make (high centralization).

In a broad sense, the central structural dilemma is between flexibility and control. We want each employee to have the skills and motivation to do his or her job well, to respond appropriately and flexibly to the facts of the situation. On the other hand, we do not want anarchy. Somehow, all the individual activities need to fit together to work in harmony. This demands some degree of control and accountability. Ideally, we want each individual to work both adaptably and predictably, but the more we achieve one the less we achieve the other.

Max Weber, the German scholar whose ideas on power and authority were discussed in Chapter 6, described the way tradeoffs are made in the form of organization known as a classic bureaucracy. In a bureaucracy, Weber argued, the basic concern is with coordinating and controlling activities by means of legal authority. This leads to an organization characterized by:

1. Specialized tasks and standardized procedures
2. Centralized decision making and unity of command
3. Standard procedures and extensive written records
4. Hiring, firing, and promotion based on objective standards

5. A clear hierarchy of jobs with clear statements of duties and boundaries for each

6. Full-time, career employment based on contracts

7. Impersonality; employees and clients are dealt with by the rules, not on the basis of their personal characteristics.

(Today we tend to use the term "bureaucracy" to mean endless red tape, mindless rule-following, and other undesirable organizational characteristics. To Weber, "bureaucracy" was the pinnacle of administrative rationality, the way to overcome the abuses of power, favoritism, and capriciousness he saw in nineteenth-century organizations. Note, by the way, what an appropriate term "bureaucracy" is: A "bureau" is a cabinet for storing papers, and the organization Weber describes certainly depends, above all else, on the written record: the contract, the procedure manual, the written examination. It is exactly this impersonal, going-by-the-book, proper-procedure way of doing things that we are objecting to when we use the word "bureaucracy" in the scornful sense.)

To Weber, then, the central problem of administration is control: how to obtain machine-like reliability of the employees' activities. Several later scholars have pointed out, however, that this emphasis on control tends to be self-defeating. Merton (1957), for example, pointed out "following the rules" produces rigid, defensible behavior that is not always effective. When problems arise, the employee seeks reassurance in still more careful adherence to the rules, producing still less effective problem solving, and so on. Gouldner (1954) suggested another self-defeating loop. He saw that rules are likely to be translated into minimum performance standards, and that these will soon become maximum standards. Such performance will, in fact, not be acceptable, supervisors will supervise more closely, interpersonal tensions will rise, and the whole idea of "impersonality" goes out the window.

A crucial problem for a bureaucracy is how to deal with experts. The line-staff distinction may work when expertise *supports* the main work of the organization, but not when it is the substance of this work. The machine model may be reasonably effective (though not very humane) for organizing simple unskilled work. It may, for example, be "a good way to run a railroad," where coordination is the crucial problem. It is hard to see, however, how the model could be applied successfully to running an R&D laboratory. The bench-level Ph.D. researcher, after all, is employed precisely because (s)he knows more about some subject matter than anyone else in the organization. How can someone less expert set up the detailed job rules and performance standards that bureaucracy requires? Apart from professional demands for autonomy, the "expert" knows more than the rule maker. At some level, the higher administration just has to "take their word for it."

Elements of organizational structure cannot be fitted together on a mix-and-match basis. One cannot gain the advantages of rigid, formalized procedures *and* the advantages of flexible, adaptive behavior. Emphasizing one drives out the other. In fact, emphasizing one may be self-defeating, driving the system from reasonable to unreasonable levels of the target variable. In short, internal constraints and tradeoffs make only some of the theoretical variety of organizational structures viable. Further constraints arise from the nature of the organization's work, and from its environment.

THE IMPACT OF TECHNOLOGY ON STRUCTURE

A classic bureaucracy might be a good way to run a railroad, but it would be a poor way to run an R&D laboratory. What makes the difference? There are clearly many differences between the two settings; different people, different salary levels, different educations, different kinds of work. One potentially important difference that has attracted considerable research attention is the "technology" of the work. Researchers interested in this are have raised the question of "technological determinism." They ask, To what extent are organizational structures determined by the technology of the work done? We shall look briefly here at some of the findings bearing on this question. (See also Markus, Reading #1.)

We first need to be clear about what we mean by "technology," distinguishing particularly between *product* and *production* technology. The two need not go hand in hand. For example, highly sophisticated *products* (e.g. a communication satellite) can be assembled by primitive methods (a group of technicians working with hand tools). Conversely, very unsophisticated products (e.g., sliced bread) can be produced by highly sophisticated production methods (automated, computer-controlled processes). Our interest here is on the structural implications of production technology: roughly, "the techniques used by organizations in work-flow activities to transform inputs into outputs" (Porter, Lawler, and Hackman, 1975), or "who does what with whom, when, where, and how often" (Chapple and Sayles, 1961).

Several interesting category schemes have been proposed for analyzing different types of production technology. Thompson (1967) stresses the impact of different processes on the interdependence between people operating them. He distinguishes between:

1. **Long-linked technologies,** in which one worker's output is the next worker's input, as in assembly lines and machine shops
2. **Mediating technologies,** in which the primary activity is the bringing together of previously separate elements, as in employment agencies (job seekers and employers), banks (lenders and borrowers), and universities (students and teachers)
3. **Intensive technologies,** in which a variety of techniques and skills are brought to bear on a single problem or client, as in large construction projects and hospital emergency rooms.

Note that all three kinds of technology can be found within a single organization. For example, universities are categorized as primarily using a mediating technology, though we could also find aspects of long-linked technology (e.g., the freshman calculus sequence) and intensive technology (e.g., the dissertation committee).

Perrow (1967) proposed a second classification of production technologies. His scheme turns on two questions: (1) how frequent are exceptional cases? and (2) how well understood is the process of finding solutions for these exceptional cases? These questions suggest a 2 × 2 classification of technologies, as in Figure 10.1.

Figure 10.1.   Perrow's Classification of Technologies

FREQUENCY OF EXCEPTIONS

	Low	High
PREDICTABILITY OF SOLUTION SEARCH — Low	Craft	Nonroutine
PREDICTABILITY OF SOLUTION SEARCH — High	Routine	Engineering

Again, several different technologies may be found within a single organization. For example, the manufacture of electric motors is fairly *routine* (at least for standard models). Designing motors, although often complex, is pretty well understood (it is an *engineering* technology). Dealing with customers may be *nonroutine*. Certain parts of building motors require skilled workers whose expertise appears in no textbook (*craft* technology). All four of Perrow's categories thus show up in a single plant.

Thompson's and Perrow's schemes have proved tricky to use in field studies. A third approach, suggested by Woodward (1965), has been more useful for empirical studies, although it is basically restricted to manufacturing organizations. She distinguishes three types of production technology:

1. **Unit and small batch:** production of single items or small batches of items, typically to direct customer orders (e.g., made-to-order suits; large or technically-complex equipment).

2. **Mass production and large batches:** typically by assembly line, as in automobile manufacture and large batches of standard products.

3. **Process production:** e.g., oil refineries, chemical plants, and other continuous-production systems such as large-scale paper production.

Using this scheme, Woodward studied some one hundred manufacturing firms in England. She found a number of differences in their structures associated with differences in the technologies used. Going up the scale from unit to process technologies, one finds more levels of management, a higher ratio of managers to total employees, and a lower ratio of labor to total costs. Other measures peak in the middle of the range. The span of control of the first-level supervisor is higher in mass production than in either unit or process production; organization is less flexible, communication more often written, management more specialized (and, incidentally, human relations poorer) in mass-production firms than in either unit or process technologies.

We should not lean too heavily on these findings. Attempts to replicate them on other samples (e.g., Hickson, Pugh, and Pheysey, 1969) have not been very successful, and there is reason to think that they may apply primarily to smaller firms (only thirteen firms in Woodward's sample had over 1,000 employees). However, this pioneering study does put some meat on the abstract idea that technology and structure are interrelated. For example, in an oil refinery, most of the day-to-day production decisions are built into the equipment, leaving the production workers mainly with monitoring and maintenance duties. On an automobile assembly line, production decisions are shaped by the structure of the line itself, but worker effort, raw material supplies, and troubleshooting are vital. Building "one-off" heavy equipment requires skilled workers using unspecialized equipment flexibly and adjusting to the needs of a specific customer. It is not likely that the same organizational structure will serve each of these systems equally well.

This is not to say that technology creates structure or that there is any strict "technological determinism." Experiments at Volvo with alternatives to the assembly line for automobile manufacture suggest that technology can be adapted to fit with other interests. (In this case, the interest was in increasing worker performance by shifting to small groups. See Katz and Kahn [1978] for an interesting review of these experiments, as well as Markus, Reading #1). However, it does appear that production technology is tied to structure in important ways, especially for those parts of the organization that are directly coupled to the production process.

THE IMPACT OF ENVIRONMENT ON STRUCTURE

In the two previous sections we have seen that organizational structure is shaped, first, by requirements of consistency with other structural elements, and second, by requirements of consistency with the technology of production. Other shaping factors—"environmental factors"—come from outside the organization.

Organizations exist in continuous interchange with their environments. People, things, energy, and information flow in and out: employees, clients, suppliers' salespeople; raw materials, finished products, scrap, tools, equipment; electricity, gas, waste heat; by telephone lines, radio, printed pages, drawings. These interchanges with the environment are the core of what is called the "open systems" view of organizations.

Organizations develop specialized structural elements to deal with these flows. The personnel department specializes in the flow of employees through selection, training, and recruitment. The purchasing department acquires the materials and equipment necessary for operation. Sales and marketing deal with the disposal of products to customers. R&D both creates and collects information. Most of these flows are two-way, both into and out of the organization. Sales, for example, deals with the flow of product or service to the customers, and also with the flow of market-need information into the organization.

To some extent, then, organizations need to adapt to their environments if they are to stay in business. It is obvious that organizations fail when either their raw materials or their markets dry up. No university can survive without students, no oil refinery without oil, no meatpacker whose customers turn vegetarian, no buggy-whip manufacturer whose customers turn to cars. Subtler issues, however, emerge when we start to look at the multiplicity of adaptations that are demanded, and the range of options possible for each.

If an organization has been functioning for some time, we can assume that it has met, at least minimally, the major demands made on it by its environment. The major threat to its survival is change, and, of course, all environments change to some extent all the time. It is possible to adapt to change by staying flexible, monitoring the environment, and responding quickly. The most difficult aspect of the environment, however, is unexpected change—in a word, uncertainty. It is not hard for a utility company to plan for steady growth in demand. It may even be able to cope with declining demand. What is really hard is dealing with an unexpected, large-scale shift to, say, solar heating. Uncertainty, not just predictable change, poses the crucial environmental challenge to an organization's survival.

There are two conservative strategies for coping with uncertainty. One can try to insulate oneself from it or try to reduce it. Organizations use both strategies. They deal with uncertainties in their supplies of critical raw materials by trying to negotiate long-term contracts, or by building up stockpiles. If this fails, they may buy out the supplier. They reduce the uncertainty of customer tastes by advertising aimed at developing predictable preferences, or they shift to more predictable markets. Such illegal activities as price-fixing agreements with competitors can similarly be seen as uncertainty-reducing tactics. Thompson (1967) argues that these strategies operate to allow the "technical core" of the organization to operate in a stable, low-uncertainty environment by buffering it from its external environment, or by reducing the uncertainty in that environment.

An alternative strategy is to be flexible, that is, to structure the organization so that it can respond quickly and effectively to the unexpected. The machine-like bureaucratic structure does not appear very responsive in this sense. A rather different organizational structure, known as the "organic" structure, seems much more promising for highly uncertain environments.

The terms "mechanistic" and "organic" were suggested by Burns and Stalker (1961) to describe the contrasting structures they found in a study of twenty British manufacturing firms. "Mechanistic" structures are similar to classic bureaucracies: centralized, highly formalized, complex hierarchy, standardized jobs. The "organic" organizations tended to be more decentralized, to have less rigidly defined jobs, to have a great deal of lateral (as opposed to vertical) communication, and to pay less attention to rank, more to the task. Interestingly, neither pattern of organizing was superior overall. Firms were successful to the extent that they organized to suit their environments, with mechanistic ones more successful in stable environments and organic ones more successful in unstable, high-uncertainty environments.

As with the Woodward studies, later work suggests that Burns and Stalker's conclusions are on the right track, but may be a little too broad. Lawrence and Lorsch (1967) looked more carefully at the scientific, market, and techno-economic aspects of the environment. Their findings suggest that uncertainty in each of these environmental sectors is reflected in the structure of the part of the organization directly in contact with it, but not necessarily in the organization as a whole. Where uncertainty is high, the relevant portion of the organization becomes highly differentiated, with many different subsystems specializing in different aspects of the environment. This in turn sets up the need for integrating mechanisms beyond the coordination provided by the usual hierarchy. Joint planning groups, individuals officially assigned as "coordinators," or even formal integrating units provide these integrating needs.

In summary, both Burns and Stalker and Lawrence and Lorsch found that firms need to adapt to the uncertainty of their environments if they are to be effective. Something close to the bureaucratic, machine model seems to be effective in stable, low-uncertainty environments. In unstable, high-uncertainty environments, more flexibility is required, at least for those parts of the organization in contact with the environment. This flexibility is achieved by deemphasizing rigid job assignment and centralized coordination via the hierarchy in favor of decentralized structures, more flexible job assignments, and lateral integration.

PROJECT AND MATRIX ORGANIZATION

High-technology organizations, such as aerospace firms, need to maintain high levels of expertise in disciplinary and functional areas. This is best achieved by grouping together the relevant specialists such as airframe specialists, engine specialists, and control systems specialists. On the other hand, their business comes in the form of discrete projects or products, typically large one-off projects with short lead times like a feasibility study for a particular space mission, or a design for a new commercial plane. These projects require the work of many different specialists, often on a crash basis.

When such projects arise only occasionally, it is possible to cope by maintaining the basic functional structure, assigning individuals temporarily to project teams. Such teams typically involve a core project management team, responsible for the project as a whole, plus specialists who join and leave the team as the need for their expertise arises. However, when projects make up the bulk of the firm's business, this project team approach becomes less satisfactory since the specialists rarely spend time in their expertise groups. In response to this problem, a number of organizations have developed what is called "matrix structure," in which individuals are members both of functional divisions and project or program teams. See Figure 10.2.

In matrix structure each individual has reporting responsibilities to both a project manager and a division manager. The former focuses on managing the project, including planning, scheduling, customer contact, and budgeting. The latter deals with such matters as training, promotion, support facilities, and technical expertise. (See Shannon [1972] and Galbraith [1973] for discussion of practical details.)

Figure 10.2.   A Matrix Structure

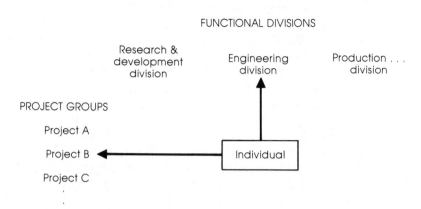

The matrix structure replaces the single coordinating hierarchy with two such structures. This has advantages in terms of flexibility (e.g., ease of reassignment of people from one project to another) and coordination (because work is coordinated in two different ways). It also has costs. Communication is increased beyond that required by the minimal hierarchy, and, because individuals have two bosses, there is a danger of conflicting instructions and loyalties. To be effective there must be good coordination between functional and project managers. However, despite the potential for difficulties, there are numerous examples of companies, especially those in high-technology, rapid-change, large-project environments, in which some form of matrix structure has been used effectively.

THE INFORMAL ORGANIZATION

On the campus where I teach there are paved paths connecting one building with another and small areas with benches for people to sit and talk or eat lunch—a perfectly normal campus layout. However, there are also unofficial paths and unofficial picnic-places: a worn strip across the lawn from the library to the computer center, a favorite shady spot on a small hill where you can spread a blanket and watch the passersby. Overlaid on the "official" design—the network of paved paths—is an "unofficial" pattern of paths that people actually use in getting around the campus. The campus designers seem to prefer their nice, orderly "official" paths; but, where this system does not fit, people make the paths they find useful.

Much the same thing happens to organizational structures. On the one hand is the neat, rational, "official" structure of the organization chart—the "formal structure." Overlaid on this is the pattern of connections people actually use in doing their work. There are patterns of friendships and useful contacts in other departments, such as a friendly secretary in the payroll department who can straighten out an expense statement, or a softball teammate who happens to be an expert program debugger. The pattern of these informal relationships is known as the "informal organization."

"Informal organization" is not a label for an alternative way of organizing, a casual, friendly alternative to the bureaucracy. It is an overlay, not a replacement, to the official structure. It is a map of what people actually do, just as the official structure is a map of what people "officially" do. Both maps capture an important aspect of how the organization works. In fact, the "informal organization" is not even a single map, but several different maps, each of which can be overlaid on the formal structure. One could, for example, trace out the patterns of friendship between employees of a company, and learn something by laying out this pattern on top of the organizational chart. A related, though somewhat different contrast might emerge if one looked at maps of who talks to whom; or of who is considered influential in what areas; or to whom people go for technical advice or bright ideas. Each of these maps captures something different about how the organization actually functions. The contrasts between each of them and the "official" map, the organization chart, are often very informative.

Anyone who has worked in an organization knows that much of what goes on is not shown on the organization chart. However, it was not until the 1930s that organizational researchers paid much attention to informal patterns of work behavior. The stimulus was a large-scale experiment that failed. In the early decades of this century research on organizations had stressed (1) formal procedures and structures and (2) design of jobs and work environments. The general (if unstated) assumptions were close to those of F. W. Taylor's "scientific management," which basically treated workers as machines. Jobs were carefully designed for efficiency, workers were trained to perform them in the most efficient way, cash incentives provided the motivation, and a proper work environment kept the "machines" humming.

The experiment that failed was conducted at the Hawthorne plant of the Western Electric Company, mainly from 1928 to 1933. The initial effort was to determine the effects of such variables as lighting, heating, and rest periods on worker performance—the "physical environment" in which the workers performed. As the experiment proceeded, however, it became clear that there was no straightforward relationship between these variables and work output. For example, output increased when illumination was increased, but increased again when illumination was reduced.

The researchers (Mayo, 1933; Roethlisberger and Dickson, 1939) finally realized that the physical effects of their manipulations were less important than the psychological effects. Specifically, they set up a special group of women assembly workers to work in a room separate from the main work area, under special, relatively democratic supervision, and who were obviously being studied carefully. This special treatment seems in itself to have had more of an impact than did the changes in illumination and other physical surroundings. (The study, incidentally, has given us the term "Hawthorne effect" for the changes in behavior that come from the awareness of being studied. This certainly happened, and still happens, but is a minor part of the Hawthorne results.)

The results have been widely misquoted and misinterpreted. Some writers have claimed that they show that "money does not matter," although, as Lawler (1973) has pointed out, a substantial part of the productivity change can be tied to changes in pay. Others have claimed the studies as showing the importance of forming teams to raise production. Again, the data do not confirm this. In a later part of the study, intact work-groups of men changed their production hardly at all, regardless of what the researchers manipulated. They had a strong group, but, as it happened, a group that was suspicious of management "rate-busting" tricks.

What the Hawthorne studies showed, and a great deal of later research has confirmed, is the importance of informal organization. A work group is not just a number of individuals who happen to work for the same boss. They have patterns of friendship, communication, respect, influence on one another, norms about behavior, shared stories (true and false), and traditions. A division on an organizational chart is not just a rational clustering of activities. It is overlaid and interwoven with ties of friendship and suspicion, loyalty and distrust, ambition and resignation. The organization chart is a very sketchy and incomplete map of the territory. The cluster of other maps we refer to collectively as the "informal organization" also tells us important features of that territory—information we need to know if we are to navigate successfully.

ORGANIZATIONAL GOALS, ORGANIZATIONAL EFFECTIVENESS

Earlier in this chapter we described the formal structure of an organization as a machine for coordinating the work of those at the bottom of the organization, the production employees. It makes as much sense to describe the organization from the top down, as a machine for carrying out the purposes of those at the top. In both cases we tend to think of individuals at the top of the hierarchy pursuing broad goals and objectives, while those lower down focus on more specific subobjectives. The chief executive pursues overall profitability; the middle manager worries about getting the product shipped; and the blue-collar employee machines *this* specific component to *that* specific engineering drawing.

This rational view of organizations in terms of nesting of goals and objectives within the hierarchy has had a powerful influence on organizational researchers (and on management practice, in Management By Objectives, or MBO). It has been especially popular for researchers interested in the measurement of organizational effectiveness, that is, in how well a given organization is performing. The logic is straightforward: goals say what the organization is *trying* to do, measurement will discover what it is *actually* doing, and a comparison of the two will show how *well* it is doing.

Unfortunately, this approach has some severe practical problems. First, overall goal statements tend to be vague and general. A university, for example, generally has in its charter some goal statement such as "providing undergraduate and graduate education, and conducting research." This leaves open real questions such as quality versus quantity, balance between graduate and graduate, or what kind of research is appropriate. Further down the organization one is likely to find more specific objectives. A department head may well have numerical objectives, e.g., "X percent growth in graduate degrees by the year 1985." However, it is often not clear how these objectives relate to the official overall goals. Nor will people necessarily tell you what all their objectives really are, particularly when their personal goals are tied in with the organization's performance. Stated goals can be a misleading approach to understanding what an organization is doing, or to how well it is doing it.

Another group of organizational researchers, trying to get away from the problem of goals, have used ideas from systems theory to attack the effectiveness problem. Yuchtman and Seashore (1967) start with the fact we noted earlier, that organizations are in continuous exchange with their environments. To be effective, they must earn enough by their outputs to be able to acquire the inputs they need to stay in business. Thus, Yuchtman and Seashore argue, one may assess an organization's effectiveness by looking at its ability to secure scarce and valued resources from its environment. An organization that can acquire everything it needs to grow and prosper is doing well; an organization that cannot is doing badly.

This is an elegant approach, and gets around many of the difficulties with the goal-based approach. However, it has turned out to be rather difficult to apply in practice. A university might be able to acquire money (certainly a "scarce and valued resource") by bribing members of the state legislature. Or an industrial firm might increase its profits (and thus its ability to buy scarce raw materials) by illegal collusion with its competitors. Neither would fit our common-sense idea of an effectively run organization.

My own view (see Connolly, Conlon, and Deutsch, 1980) is that we should give up the idea of trying to achieve single, overall measures of how effective an organization is. Organizations are complex. Their interchanges involve many different groups of people, each of whom may reach an assessment of effectiveness, and be able to do something about it. The same company may be wonderful to work for (effective from the perspective of its employees), pay only modest dividends (not too effective from the perspective of investors), have a splendid record on controlling environmental pollution (effective to the Sierra Club), and be a poor performer in terms of civil rights (low effectiveness as judged by the NAACP). There may be some way to consolidate all these different assessments into a single score, but it is hard to see what it is. For now, it is probably better to think, as Larry Hrebiniak (1978) suggests, of effectivenesses, not of a single measure of effectiveness.

SUMMARY

This chapter has covered a lot of ground from the initial discussion of setting up a small bookshelf plant, in which the shift was made from coordinating all the activities in one person's head to setting up a formal structure to do so. "Structure," as represented in an organization chart, mainly serves to identify how the various activities are broken down and how they are coordinated by a hierarchy of reporting relationships. This hierarchy can be described in terms of its "geometry"—number of levels, spans of control—and in more global terms such as differentiation, specialization, formalization, and centralization. These dimensions are not independent, but are linked together by logical as well as practical constraints. We discussed line and staff relationships as an important example of how structure shapes, but does not define, behavior.

Any structure is in part shaped by internal constraints. The particular form known as "bureaucracy" represents a collection of tradeoffs aimed at maximizing control of employee activities. This design has a machine-like logic, and is characterized by high levels of differentiation, specialization, formalization, and centralization.

In addition to the internal constraints, structures are shaped by the technology used in production, and by factors outside the organization, known collectively as "the environment." We discussed three typologies of production technology: Thompson's long-linked, mediating, and intensive types; Perrow's routine, nonroutine, craft, and engineering types; and Woodward's unit, mass, and process types. For the last, at least some evidence suggests that technology and structure are linked, particularly for those parts of the organization closely tied to the work flow.

External factors affect structure because people, things, energy, and information flow continuously into and out of the organization. Organizations must adapt to the uncertainties of these flows, either by buffering themselves or directly reducing the uncertainty. Bureaucratic, mechanistic structures seem less effective in highly uncertain environments than are "organic" structures characterized by less centralization, less formalization, more flexibility, and more horizontal integration. Under the combination of technological and environmental factors found in industries such as aerospace, novel structures such as project and matrix arrangements have proved successful.

Real organizations are only partially described by their formal structures. We must also consider the patterns of informal structuring known collectively as the "informal organization," including patterns of friendship, influence, information flows, norms, and traditions. As was first demonstrated by the Hawthorne studies, these factors have an important influence on actual behavior in the organization.

Finally, we considered organizational effectiveness, the measurement of how well an organization is performing. Several problems were noted in the traditional approaches to this issue, which are based either on the organization's goals or on how it deals with its environment to maintain its inputs. Instead, we presented a view based on multiple assessments of effectiveness. Numerous groups, inside and outside the organization, assess effectiveness in their own terms, and try to influence the organization to conform more closely with their views. The idea that there can be a single measure of overall effectiveness should be abandoned in favor of a whole set of effectiveness measures, generated by each of the multiple constituencies with which an organization has to deal.

DISCUSSION QUESTIONS: CHAPTER 10

1. An organization's "structure" is often represented by an organization chart. What exactly is shown on such a chart? What aspects of the organization's structure does it leave out?

2. What is meant by an individual's "span of control"? For a three-level organization, what happens to (a) the total number of employees, and (b) the percentage of employees in "administrative overhead," when the span of control changes from four to eight?

3. What aspects of an organization's structure are described by the following terms:

   a. Differentiation

   b. Specialization

   c. Formalization

   d. Centralization

   What would be the probable impact of the change outlined in Question 2 on each of these four aspects?

4. Scientists and engineers are frequently employed in "staff" rather than "line" positions. How does this affect the kinds of work they do? If you had been employed in a staff role in your specialty for five years since leaving school, what changes would you face in moving into a line job such as chief of inspection and testing?

5. Weber uses the term "bureaucracy" to describe administrative excellence; we tend to use it as a term of abuse. Identify five aspects of bureaucracy that led Weber to admire this mode of organizing, and show how each has come to be seen as a drawback (at least if overdone).

6. Give examples to illustrate the differences between the following classes of production technologies:

   a. Long-linked, mediating, and intensive

   b. Routine, craft, engineering, and nonroutine

   c. Unit, mass, and process

   What major differences in organizational structure would you expect to be associated with each kind of technology?

7. What is meant by the following terms in describing an organization's reactions to environmental uncertainty? Give an example of each type of reaction.

   a. Buffering the technical core

   b. Adopting an organic structure

   c. Subsystem differentiation

8. What is the difference between "project" and "matrix" forms of organizing? How does each differ from more traditional forms of organizing?

9. What is meant by the "informal organization"? Give an example of how the structure of the informal organization can shape activities more strongly than does the formal structure. How might a manager be able to use an understanding of the informal organization to his or her advantage?

10. What problems should you expect if you were to try to assess an organization's performance by comparing its actual achievement with its official goals? What alternative approach might you take? Describe how you would use your approach to assess the effectiveness of an R&D laboratory.

References

Ackoff, R. L. "Management Misinformation Systems." *Management Science* 14 (1967):147–56.

Adams, S. J. "Inequity in Social Exchange." In *Advances in Experimental Social Psychology.* Berkowitz, L., ed. New York: Academic Press, 1965.

Allen, T. J. "Communications in the Research and Development Laboratory." *Technology Review* 70 (1967):1–8.

_____, and Cohen, D. I. "Information Flow in Research and Development Laboratories." *Administrative Science Quarterly* 14 (1969):12–19.

Allport, F. H. "The Influence of the Group upon Association and Thought." *Journal of Experimental Psychology* 3 (1920):159–82.

Ashour, A. S. "The Contingency Model of Leadership Effectiveness: An Evaluation." *Organizational Behavior and Human Performance* 9 (1973):339–55.

Blake, R. R., and Mouton, J. S. "Comprehension of Own and Outgroup Positions under Intergroup Competition." *Journal of Conflict Resolution* 5 (1961):304–310.(a).

_____. "Loyalty of Representatives to Ingroup Positions during Intergroup Competition." *Sociometry* 24 (1961):177–83.(b).

_____. *The Managerial Grid.* Houston: Gulf Publishing, 1964.

Blascovich, J.; Ginsburg, J. P.; and Howe, R. C. "Blackjack and the Risky Shift. II: Monetary Stakes." *Journal of Experimental Social Psychology* 11 (1975):224–32.

Bruner, J. S., and Taguiri, A. "The Perception of People." In *Handbook of Social Psychology,* G. Lindzey, ed. Cambridge, Mass.: Addison-Wesley, 1954.

Burns, T. "The Directions of Activity and Communication in a Departmental Executive Group." *Human Relations* 7 (1954):73–97.

_____, and Stalker, G. M. *The Management of Innovation.* London: Tavistock Publications, 1961.

Calder, B. J. "An Attribution Theory of Leadership." In *New Directions in Organizational Behavior*, B. M. Staw and G. R. Salancik, eds. Chicago: St. Clair, 1977.

Campbell, D. T. "Blind Variation and Selective Retention in Creative Thought as in Other Knowledge Processes." *Psychological Review* 67 (1960):380–400.

Cartwright, D. "The nature of group cohesiveness." In *Group Dynamics*, by D. Cartwright and A. Zander, 3d ed. New York: Harper and Row, 1968.

_____, and Zander, A. *Group Dynamics*, 3rd ed. New York: Harper and Row, 1968.

Chapple, E. D., and Sayles, L. R. *The Measure of Management*. New York: Macmillan, 1961.

Cherry, C. *On Human Communication*, 2d ed. Cambridge, Mass.: MIT Press, 1966.

Collins, B., and Guetzkow, H. *A Social Psychology of Group Processes for Decision Making*. New York: Wiley, 1964.

Connolly, T. "Communication Nets and Uncertainty in R&D Planning." *IEEE, Transactions on Engineering Management*, 1975, EM-22, 50–54.

_____. "Information Processing and Decision Making in Organizations." In *New Directions in Organizational Behavior*, B. M. Staw and G. R. Salancik, eds. Chicago: St. Clair, 1977.

_____.; Conlon, E. J.; and Deutsch, S.J. "Organizational Effectiveness: A Multiple-Constituency Approach." *Academy of Management Review* 5 (1980):211–18.

Cyert, R. M., and March, J. G. *A Behavioral Theory of the Firm*. Englewood Cliffs, N.J.: Prentice-Hall, 1963.

Dalkey, N., and Helmer, O. "An Experimental Application of the Delphi Method to the Use of Experts." *Management Science* 9 (1963):458–67.

Dashiell, J. F. "An Experimental Analysis of Some Group Effects." *Journal of Abnormal and Social Psychology* 25 (1930):190–99.

Dearborn, D. W. C., and Simon, H. A. "Selective Perception: A Note on the Departmental Identification of Executives." *Sociometry* 21 (1958):140–44.

Deci, E. L. "The Effects of Externally Mediated Rewards on Intrinsic Motivation." *Journal of Personality and Social Psychology* 18 (1971):105–115.

_____. "The Effects of Contingent and Noncontingent Rewards and Controls on Intrinsic Motivation." *Organizational Behavior and Human Performance* 8 (1972):217–29.

Delbecq, A. L.; Van de Ven, A. H.; and Gustafson, D. H. *Group Techniques for Program Planning*, Glenview, Ill.: Scott, Foresman, 1975.

Dunnette, M. D.; Campbell, J. P.; and Hakel, M. D. "Factors Contributing to Job Satisfaction and Job Dissatisfaction in Six Occupational Groups," *Organizational Behavior and Human Performance* 2 (1967):143–74.

Dunnette, M. D.; Campbell, J. P.; and Jaastad, K. "The Effect of Group Participation on Brainstorming Effectiveness for Two Industrial Samples." *Journal of Applied Psychology* 47 (1963):30–37.

Edwards, W. "Dynamic Decision Theory and Probabilistic Information Processing." *Human Factors* 4 (1962):59–73.

Einhorn, H. J. "Learning from Experience and Suboptimal Rules in Decision Making." In *Cognitive Processes in Choice and Decision Behavior,* Wallsten, T. S., ed. Hillsdale, N.J.: Lawrence Erlbaum Associates, 1980.

Evan, W. M. "Conflict and Performance in R&D Organizations." *Industrial Management Review* 7 (1965):37–45.

Evans, M. G. "The Effects of Supervisory Behavior and the Path Goal Relationship." *Organizational Behavior and Human Performance* 5 (1970):277–98.

Felsenthal, D. S. "Group versus Individual Gambling Behavior: Reexamination and Limitation." *Behavioral Science* 24 (1979):334–45.

Feuille, P. "Final Offer Arbitration and the Chilling Effect." *Industrial Relations* 14 (1975):302–310.

Fiedler, F. E. *A Theory of Leadership Effectiveness.* New York: McGraw-Hill, 1967.

_____. "The Leadership Game: Matching the Man to the Situation." *Organizational Dynamics* 4 (1976):6–16.

Flack, J. E., and Summers, D. A. "Computer Aided Conflict Resolution in Water Resources Planning." *Water Resources Research* 7 (1971):1410–14.

Fleishman, E. F., and Peters, D. R. "Interpersonal Values, Leadership Attitudes, and Managerial 'Success'." *Personnel Psychology* 15 (1962):127–43.

Florman, S. C. *The Existential Pleasures of Engineering.* New York: St. Martin's Press, 1976.

Fox, F. V., and Staw, B. M. "The Trapped Administrator: Effects of Job Insecurity and Policy Resistance on Commitment to a Course of Action." *Administrative Science Quarterly* 24 (1979):449–71.

French, W. L., and Raven, B. "The Bases of Social Power." In *Studies in Social Power.* Cartwright, D., ed. Ann Arbor: University of Michigan, Institute for Social Research, 1959.

Galbraith, J. R. *Designing Complex Organizations.* Reading, Mass.: Addison-Wesley, 1973.

Gibb, J. R. "Defensive Communication." *Journal of Communication* 11 (1961): 141–48.

Goodman, P., and Friedman, A. "An Examination of Adam's Theory of Inequity." *Administrative Science Quarterly* 16 (1971):271–88.

Gordon, W. J. J. *Synectics.* New York: Harper and Row, 1961.

Gouldner, A. W. *Patterns of Industrial Democracy.* Glencoe, Ill.: Free Press, 1954.

Graicunas, V. A. "Relationships in Organizations." In *Papers on the Science of Administration,* Gulick, L., and Urwick, L., eds. New York: Columbia University, Institute of Public Administration, 1937.

Gross, B. M. *Organizations and Their Managing.* New York: Free Press, 1968.

Grove, B. A., and Kerr, W. A. "Specific Evidence on Origin of Halo Effect in Measurement of Morale." *Journal of Social Psychology* 34 (1951):165–70.

Hackman, J. R. "Group Influences on Individuals." In *Handbook of Industrial and Organizational Psychology*, Dunnette, M. R., ed. Chicago: Rand-McNally, 1976.

Haire, M. "Role Perceptions in Labor-Management Relations: An Experimental Approach." *Industrial Labor Relations Review* 8 (1955):204–216.

_____, and Grunes, W. F. "Perceptual Defences: Processes Protecting an Original Perception of Another Personality." *Human Relations* 3 (1958):403–412.

Hall, D. T., and Nougaim, K. E. "An Examination of Maslow's Needs Hierarchy in an Organizational Setting." *Organizational Behavior and Human Performance* 3 (1968):12–35.

Hammond, K. R. "Computer Graphics as an Aid to Learning." *Science* 172 (1971):903–908.

Hamner, W. C., and Hamner, E. P. "Behavior Modification on the Bottom Line." *Organizational Dynamics* 4 (1976):3–21.

Herold, D. M. "The Effectiveness of Work Groups." In *Organizational Behavior*, Kerr, S., ed. Columbus, Ohio: Grid, 1979.

Hersey, P., and Blanchard, K. H. "Life Cycle Theory of Leadership." *Training and Development Journal* 23 (1969):15–21.

Herzberg, F. "One More Time: How Do You Motivate Employees?" *Harvard Business Review* 46 (1968):54–62.

Hickson, D. J.; Hinings, C. R.; Lee, C. A.; Schneck, R. E.; and Pennings, J. M. "A Strategic Contingencies Theory of Intraorganizational Power." *Administrative Science Quarterly* 16 (1971):216–29.

Hickson, D. J.; Pugh, D. S.; and Pheysey, D. C. "Operations Technology and Organizational Structure: An Empirical Reappraisal." *Administrative Science Quarterly* 14 (1969):378–97.

Hogarth, R. M. *Judgment and Choice: The Psychology of Decision.* New York: Wiley, 1980.

_____. "A Note on Aggregating Opinions." *Organizational Behavior and Human Performance* 21 (1978):40–46.

Hollander, E. P. *Leaders, Groups and Influence.* New York: Oxford University Press, 1964.

House, R. J., and Mitchell, T. R. "Path Goal Theory of Leadership." *Journal of Contemporary Business* 5 (1974):81–97.

Hrebiniak, L. G. *Complex Organizations.* New York: West Publishing, 1978.

Janis, I. L. *Victims of Groupthink.* Boston: Houghton Mifflin, 1972.

_____, and Mann, L. *Decision Making.* New York: Free Press, 1977.

Jennings, D.; Amabile, T. M.; and Ross, L. "Informal Covariation Assessment: Data-based vs. Theory-based Judgments." In *Judgment Under Uncertainty: Heuristics and Biases*, Kahneman, D., Slovic, P., and Tversky, A., eds. New York: Cambridge University Press, 1982.

Johnson, D. W.; Maruyama, G.; Johnson, R.; and Nelson, D.; and Skon, L. "Effects of Cooperative, Competitive, and Individualistic Goal Structures on Achievement: A Meta-analysis." *Psychological Bulletin* 89 (1981):47–62.

Jones, E. E. "The Rocky Road from Acts to Dispositions." *American Psychologist* 34 (1979):107–117.

Katz, D., and Kahn, R. L. *The Social Psychology of Organizations,* 2d ed. New York: Wiley, 1978.

Katz, E., and Lazarsfeld, P. *Personal Influence.* New York: Free Press, 1955.

Kerr, S. "On the Folly of Rewarding A, While Hoping for B." *Academy of Management Journal* 18 (1975):769–83.

_____; Schriesheim, C. A.; Murphy, C. J.; and Stogdill, R. M. "Toward a Contingency Theory of Leadership Based upon the Consideration and Initiating Structure Literature." *Organizational Behavior and Human Performance* 12 (1974): 62–82.

Kerr, S., and Jermier, J. M. "Substitutes for Leadership: Their Meaning and Measurement." *Organizational Behavior and Human Performance* 22 (1978): 375–403.

Kimberly, J. R., and Evanisko, M. J. "Organizational Technology, Structure and Size." In *Organizational Behavior,* Kerr, S., ed. Columbus, Ohio: Grid, 1979.

Knox, R. E., and Safford, R. K. "Group Caution at the Race Track." *Journal of Experimental Social Psychology* 12 (1976):317–24.

Kochan, T. A. "Collective Bargaining and Organizational Behavior Research." *Research in Organizational Behavior* 2 (1980):129–76.

Koontz, H., and O'Donnell, C. *Principles of Management,* 3d ed. New York: McGraw-Hill, 1964.

Kotter, J. P. "Power, Dependence and Effective Management." *Harvard Business Review* 55 (1977):125–34.

Latane, B., and Rodin, J. "A Lady in Distress: Inhibiting Effects of Friends and Strangers on Bystander Intervention." *Journal of Experimental Social Psychology* 5 (1969):189–202.

Latane, B., and Nida, S. "Ten Years of Research on Group Size and Helping." *Psychological Bulletin* 89 (1981):308–324.

Latham, G. P., and Locke, E. A. "Goal-setting: A Motivational Technique That Works." *Organizational Dynamics* 8 (1979):68–80.

Latham, G. P., and Yukl, G. A. "A Review of Research on the Application of Goal Setting in Organizations." *Academy of Management Journal* 18 (1975):824–45.

Lawler, E. E. *Motivation in Work Organizations.* Monterey, Calif.: Brooks/Cole, 1973.

_____; Porter, L. W.; and Tannenbaum, A. "Managers' Attitudes Towards Interaction Episodes." *Journal of Applied Psychology* 52 (1968):432–39.

Lawrence, P. R., and Lorsch, J. W. "Differentiation and Integration in Complex Organizations." *Administrative Science Quarterly* 12 (1967):1–47.

Leavitt, H. A. "Some Effects of Certain Communication Patterns on Group Performance." *Journal of Abnormal and Social Psychology* 46 (1951):38–50.

Lewis, A. C.; Sadosky, T. L.; and Connolly, T. "The Effectiveness of Group Brainstorming in Engineering Problem Solving." *IEEE Transactions on Engineering Management,* 1975, EM-22, 119–124.

Lowin, A., and Craig, J. R. "The Influence of Level of Performance on Managerial Style: An Object-Lesson in the Ambiguity of Correlational Data." *Organizational Behavior and Human Performance* 3 (1968):440–58.

Maier, N. R. F. "Assets and Liabilities in Group Problem Solving: The Need for an Integrative Function." *Psychological Review* 74 (1967):239–49.

_____, and Hoffman, L. R. "Quality of First and Second Solutions in Group Problem Solving." *Journal of Applied Psychology* 44 (1960):278–83.

March, J. G. "Bounded Rationality, Ambiguity, and the Engineering of Choice." *Bell Journal of Economics* 9 (1978):587–608.

_____, and Simon, H. A. *Organizations.* New York: Wiley, 1958.

Maslow, A. H. "A Theory of Human Motivation." *Psychological Review* 50 (1943):370–96.

Mason, R. O. "A Dialectical Approach to Strategic Planning." *Management Science* 15 (1969):B403–B414.

Mayo, E. *The Human Problems of an Industrial Civilization.* New York: Macmillan, 1933.

McCall, M. W. "Power, Authority and Influence." In *Organizational Behavior,* Kerr, S., ed. Columbus, Ohio: Grid, 1979.

McCall, M. W.; Morrison, A. M.; and Hannan, R. L. *Studies of Managerial Work: Results and Methods.* Greensboro, N.C.: Center for Creative Leadership, 1978.

McClelland, D. C. *The Achieving Society.* Princeton, N.J.: Van Nostrand, 1961.

_____, and Burnham, D. H. "Power Is the Great Motivator." *Harvard Business Review* 54 (1976): 100–110.

Mechanic, D. "Sources of Power of Lower Participants in Complex Organizations." *Administrative Science Quarterly* 7 (1962):349–64.

Merton, R. K. *Social Theory and Social Structure,* 2d ed. Glencoe, Ill.: Free Press, 1957.

Miller, G. A. "The Magical Number Seven, Plus or Minus Two." *Psychological Review* 63 (1956):81–97.

Miller, J. G. "Information Input, Overload, and Psychopathology." *American Journal of Psychiatry* 116 (1960):695–704.

Mintzberg, H. *The Nature of Managerial Work.* New York: Harper and Row, 1973.

Murray, H. A. "The Effect of Fear upon Estimates of the Maliciousness of Other Personalities." *Journal of Social Psychology* 4 (1933):310–29.

Nord, W. R. "Beyond the Teaching Machine: The Neglected Area of Operant Conditioning in the Theory and Practice of Management." *Organizational Behavior and Human Performance* 4 (1969):375–401.

Notz, W. W., and Starke, F. A. "Final-Offer versus Conventional Arbitration as a Means of Conflict Management." *Administrative Science Quarterly* 23 (1978): 189–203.

Odiorne, G. S. *Management By Objectives.* New York: Pitman, 1965.

Osborn, A. F. *Applied Imagination: Principles and Procedures of Creative Thinking.* New York: Scribner's, 1941.

Oskamp, S. "Overconfidence in Case Study Judgments." *Journal of Consulting Psychology* 29 (1965):261–65.

Penner, D. *A Study of Causes and Consequences of Salary Satisfaction.* Crotonville, N.Y.: General Electric Behavioral Research Service, 1967.

Perrow, C. "A Framework for the Comparative Analysis of Organizations." *American Sociological Review* 32 (1967):194–208.

Petrock, F., and Gamboa, V. "Expectancy Theory and Operant Conditioning: A Conceptual Comparison." In *Concepts and Controversy in Organizational Behavior*, Nord, W. R., ed. 2d ed. Pacific Palisades, Calif.: Goodyear, 1976.

Pfeffer, J., and Salancik, G. R. "Organizational Decision Making as a Political Process: The Case of a University Budget." *Administrative Science Quarterly* 19 (1974):135–51.

Pondy, L. R. "Organizational Conflict: Concepts and Models." *Administrative Science Quarterly* 12 (1967):296–320.

Porter, L. W.; Lawler, E. E.; and Hackman, J. R. *Behavior in Organizations.* New York: McGraw-Hill, 1975.

Read, W. H. "Upward Communication in Industrial Hierarchies." *Human Relations* 15 (1962):3–16.

Richardson, L. F. "Conflict Escalation." In *Arms and Insecurity: A Mathematical Study of the Causes and Origins of War*, Rashevsky, N., and Trucco, E., eds. Pittsburgh, Pa.: Boxwood Press, 1960.

Roethlisberger, F. J., and Dickson, W. J. *Management and the Worker.* Cambridge, Mass.: Harvard University Press, 1939.

Rogers, E. M. *Diffusion of Innovations.* New York: Free Press, 1962.

Ross, L. "The Intuitive Psychologist and His Shortcomings." In *Advances in Experimental Social Psychology*, Berkowitz, L., ed. vol. 10. New York: Academic Press, 1977.

Shannon, R. E. "Matrix Management Structures." *Industrial Engineering* 4 (1972):19–27.

Staw, B. M. "Motivation in Organizations: Toward Synthesis and Redirection." In *New Directions in Organizational Behavior*, Staw, B. M., and Salancik, G. R., eds. Chicago: St. Clair Press, 1977.

———. "Rationality and Justification in Organizational Life." *Research in Organizational Behavior* 2 (1980):45–80.

Steiner, I. D. *Group Processes and Productivity.* New York: Academic Press, 1972.

Stogdill, R. M. "Personal Factors Associated with Leadership: A Survey of the Literature." *Journal of Psychology* 25 (1948):35–71.

———. *Handbook of Leadership.* Glencoe, Ill.: Free Press, 1975.

Strauss, G. "Tactics of Lateral Relationship: The Purchasing Agent." *Administrative Science Quarterly* 7 (1962):161–68.

Strodtbeck, F. L., and Hook, L. H. "The Social Dimensions of a Twelveman Jury Table." *Sociometry* 24 (1961):397–415.

Tannenbaum, R., and Schmidt, W. "How to Choose a Leadership Pattern." *Harvard Business Review* 36 (1958):95–102.

Thibaut, J. W., and Riecken, H. W. "Some Determinants and Consequences of the Perception of Social Causality." *Journal of Personality* 24 (1955):113–33.

Thomas, K. W. "Conflict and Conflict Management." In *Handbook of Industrial and Organizational Psychology.* Dunnette, M. R., ed. Chicago: Rand McNally, 1976.

Thompson, J. D. *Organizations in Action.* New York: McGraw-Hill, 1967.

Thorndike, R. L. "On What Type of Task Will a Group Do Well?" *Journal of Abnormal and Social Psychology* 33 (1938):409–13.

Tversky, A., and Kahneman, D. "Judgment under Uncertainty: Heuristics and Biases." *Science* 185 (1974):1124–31.

Vroom, V. H. "Can Leaders Learn to Lead?" *Organizational Dynamics* 4 (1976): 17–28.

———, and Yetton, P. W. *Leadership and Decision Making.* Pittsburgh, Pa.: University of Pittsburgh Press, 1973.

Wahba, M. A., and Bridwell, L. G. "Maslow Reconsidered: A Review of Research on the Need Hierarchy Theory." *Organizational Behavior and Human Performance* 15 (1976):212–40.

Wallach, M. A.; Kogan, N.; and Bem, D. J. "Group Influence on Individual Risk-taking." *Journal of Abnormal and Social Psychology* 65 (1962):75–86.

Walster, E.; Aronson, E.; and Abrahams, D. "On Increasing the Persuasiveness of a Low Prestige Communicator." *Journal of Experimental Social Psychology* 2 (1966):325–42.

Walton, R. E., and Dutton, J. M. "The Management of Interdepartmental Conflict: A Model and Review." *Administrative Science Quarterly* 14 (1969):73–84.

Walton, R. E., and McKersie, R. B. *A Behavioral Theory of Labor Negotiations: An Analysis of a Social Interaction System.* New York: McGraw-Hill, 1965.

Ward, W. D., and Jenkins, H. M. "The Display of Information and the Judgment of Contingency." *Canadian Journal of Psychology* 19 (1965):231–41.

Webber, R. A. "Innovation and Conflict in Industrial Engineering." *Journal of Industrial Engineering* 13 (1967):48–57.

———. "Perceptions of Interactions between Superiors and Subordinates." *Human Relations* 23 (1970):235–48.

Woodward, J. *Industrial Organization: Theory and Practice.* London: Oxford University Press, 1965.

Yuchtman, E., and Seashore, S. E. "A System Resource Approach to Organizational Effectiveness." *American Sociological Review* 32 (1967):891–903.

Yukl, G.; Wexley, K. N.; and Seymore, J. D. "Effectiveness of Pay Incentives under Variable Ratio and Continuous Reinforcement Schedules." *Journal of Applied Psychology* 56 (1972):19–23.

Zajonc, R. B. "Social Facilitation." *Science* 149 (1965):269–74.

Zalkind, S. S., and Costello, T. W. "Perception: Some Recent Research and Implications for Administration." *Administrative Science Quarterly* 7 (1962):218–35.

Part II
Contributed Papers

Socio-Technical Systems: Concepts and Applications

M. Lynne Markus

Massachusetts Institute of Technology

Engineers, especially industrial engineers, tend to think of organizations as technical systems. They focus on the way materials flow within a plant, how different operations are sequenced and scheduled, how individual jobs are designed and how they fit together, and so on. Social scientists, on the other hand, tend to think of organizations as social systems. They focus on how people feel about their jobs, how they get on with fellow workers, how work norms develop, the effects of leaders, and so on. The two approaches have developed more or less independently. Each has its particular strengths, but neither gives a complete picture of the way organizations work.

In the past few years, researchers have started to develop ways of thinking about and changing organizations that consider technical and social systems ideas simultaneously: the "socio-technical systems" approach. The basic belief of this approach is that the social and the technical aspects of work settings are interdependent; changes in one have important implications for the other. Lynne Markus elaborates briefly on this key principle, and considers the value of the approach to engineers whose job it is to organize and improve other people's work settings. A typical assignment is discussed in detail. The example emphasizes a more general point: that introducing technical change without first considering the social system can lead to consequences very different from those the designer had in mind.

For much of American business, this is an era of aging physical plant, changing workforce demographics and values, and increased international competition. These pressures intensify the continuing desires of managers to monitor and improve the productivity of workplaces in both the office and the factory. Ready to fill managers' needs are countless vendors of productivity improvement approaches and automated solutions, from the office of the future to factory-floor robotics. Managers and technical specialists need ways to evaluate and choose from among the many proffered solutions.

The socio-technical systems (STS) approach is one of many methods for improving workplace productivity. It differs sharply from more widely used approaches in almost every point of philosophy and action. It can be used in both white- and blue-collar settings, although, within the office, it has been used more frequently for clerical than for managerial operations. It is appropriate in settings that will stay largely labor intensive and manual, in those that have already been automated, and in those that are about to be automated. The STS approach is difficult and time consuming to apply, but the results in many applications have been so successful that the approach warrants careful understanding and evaluation by managers and engineers charged with improving productivity.

This chapter describes the STS approach, its history, goals, and technique, and contrasts it with a well-used method of productivity improvement. An example is presented to illustrate the benefits of the concepts that underlie the approach. Finally, some general conclusions are drawn about the relevance of STS to managers and engineers.

THE SOCIO-TECHNICAL SYSTEMS APPROACH

The STS approach originated in Great Britain in the 1950s. A group of professionals, many of them trained in psychiatry, turned their attention to problems in the postwar industrial sector. One of their first projects was to investigate the disruptions caused by the introduction of assembly line technology in coal mines, which had been traditionally worked by teams of miners performing the entire coal-getting process and sharing a common pay packet. The new technology divided up coal-getting into a number of specialized jobs and destroyed traditional patterns of interaction among the workers. In spite of the new machinery, output fell and worker dissatisfaction rose, with incidents of outright hostility occurring among workers and between workers and managers.

The investigations of the STS researchers uncovered a number of naturally occurring experiments, in which the miners had tried to adapt the new technology to their traditional patterns of working together. Payment schemes as well as the division of labor were involved in these attempts. Compared to the assembly line work organization, these team-oriented work structures resulted in much higher output and worker satisfaction. Based on these and other studies in many different industries (e.g., metal-working, textiles) and in many different countries (India, Norway, and the United States), proponents of the STS approach developed a methodology for redesigning existing workplaces which has also been applied to the design of new production facilities. Subsequently, the approach was adapted to white-collar settings, especially clerical operations. Most recently, practitioners of the method are using it in conjunction with classical systems analysis techniques to develop and implement computerized information systems.

Evaluating the STS Approach

The STS approach can be contrasted with more widely used methods on the dimensions of goals and techniques. Because sharp contrasts often provide the clearest insights into different methods, this chapter will compare STS to a method with which it is most dissimilar: classical industrial engineering. You may feel that the comparison is unfair, because industrial engineering (IE) is really a collection of methods rather than a unified approach or because IE is rarely practiced in precisely the form described here. The purpose of the comparison is not to show why STS is better than IE, but to show how STS is different.

Goals

Simply put, the STS approach has as its goal to bring a workplace into alignment with the environment in which it operates and to bring the technical aspects of the workplace into alignment with the social aspects. In contrast, the objective of classical IE is to optimize the operations of a technical system subject to constraints imposed by the human beings who must operate it. Let's examine these points in more detail. First we need definitions of technical system, social system, socio-technical system, and environment.

The *technical system* is more than just machinery, like a production line. Still less is it an isolated tool, like a hammer or a computer. Rather, the technical system is the total set of knowledge,

skills, and devices that people have accumulated for accomplishing a particular goal. The *social system* consists not only of individual people with their individual differences in attitudes, desires, and abilities, but also of the patterns of interaction and communication which they develop among themselves while applying a technology to achieve a goal. The *socio-technical system*, therefore, is the whole comprised by the technical and social systems operating together as they actually do in the workplace. It is an organized pattern of activities in which people try to achieve certain goals by applying technology. But just as the technical system cannot really operate independently of the social system, a socio-technical system cannot operate independently of its surrounding context. If they are to continue to function, work settings must carry out transactions with customers, suppliers, labor markets, regulators, and so forth, collectively referred to as the *environment*.

The STS approach aims to achieve a state of match or balance, first between the social and technical systems, then between the socio-technical whole and its environment. In this state of balance, the needs or dictates of neither member of each pair takes precedence, if the whole is to be fully effective. Therefore, the highest performing socio-technical systems will be neither those in which the technology is designed around the needs of people nor those in which the social relations are designed around the dictates of technology. Both sets of needs and constraints must be considered and adjusted simultaneously, a process which suggests its name: the principle of *joint optimization*. Similarly, the demands of the environment should not be the major design consideration for a socio-technical system, nor can the well-functioning socio-technical system impose its preferred mode of operation on the environment.

In contrast, the classical IE approach aims to optimize technical systems to the greatest extent possible given that the people who operate them have needs for rest and social interaction and have limitations in strength, intelligence, memory, and other attributes. This approach does consider both social and technical systems, but subjugates the needs of the first to the dictates of the second. According to STS proponents, such a procedure of single criterion optimization, however constrained, will produce an organization which is less productive and less humanly satisfying than an organization in which social considerations are maximized jointly with technological ones.

Technique

This distinction between single criterion optimization and joint optimization may strike one as splitting hairs. But it leads to real differences in technique. Technique refers to the specific steps performed and the procedures for the sequence, timing, and assignment of responsibility for each step.

For purposes of evaluation, any productivity improvement approach can be dissected conceptually into three major steps or phases: analysis, design, and implementation. *Analysis* refers to the concepts used to describe the workplace as it exists currently, to uncover problems in operation which should be remedied and to identify opportunities for change and factors that may facilitate change. *Design* refers to the specific recommended changes in the way the workplace is organized or configured. *Implementation* refers to the process of making the recommendations workable, of getting them used in the work setting.

Analysis

Socio-technical systems practitioners have developed a structured method for analyzing existing or planned socio-technical systems as a basis for redesigning them or setting them up de novo. The method, described below, requires detailed attention to social factors which are given only cursory treatment in the classical IE approach.

One version of the STS analytic method (Cummings and Srivastva, 1977) entails nine steps:

1. Initial scanning
2. Identification of unit operations
3. Identification of key process variances
4. Analysis of the social system
5. Workers' role perceptions
6. Maintenance systems
7. Supply systems
8. Environment and strategic plans
9. Proposals for change.

In the initial scan, analysts identify broad characteristics of the system and its environment and the main problems facing it. The key decision at this stage is to define the *boundaries* around the system, that is, to decide what activities and jobs will be considered inside or outside the operation in question. Initial scanning covers organizational structure, geographic layout, objectives, the major inputs (physical and informational), processes, and outputs.

The second step identifies major self-contained phases in the production process, where materials or information undergoes recognizable transformations in state or location. These are called *unit operations*. This type of analysis is especially difficult in white-collar operations where many processes are invisible, but it forms an essential basis for understanding key *variances*, which are deviations from standards or specifications.

In step three, analysts identify the major controllable and uncontrollable variances that arise from the material being processed or from the processing itself. Matrices are drawn to show the interrelationships among them, and variances most critical to the socio-technical system are identified.

The goal of the social system analysis is to provide a basis for designing or redesigning people's jobs. Tables are prepared showing how various job roles currently control key variances. Payment schemes are described and reviewed. The spatial locations of people, their patterns of work-related communication in time, and their authority and responsibility relationships are outlined. This step is preparatory to assessing the degree to which current jobs achieve people's social and psychological needs, as viewed by the jobholders themselves.

Next, the processes that support the primary unit operations are analyzed; these are systems concerned with maintenance and supply. The purpose is to determine to what extent roles inside the primary system should incorporate these supporting tasks and how variances arising from them should be controlled.

A similar analysis takes place with respect to the wider environment of the socio-technical system. Its purpose is to identify policies and plans that will affect the socio-technical unit and to design into the unit ways to manage external events.

Finally, proposals for change are generated and tested through thorough discussion before specific recommendations are made. The final recommendations are evaluated against criteria related to the social and technical objectives of the unit under analysis.

The STS analytic model as described above is most appropriate for production departments in which continuous processing technology is employed, but several variations have evolved for service and clerical units. The strength of the model is that it gives explicit attention to social aspects of the workplace and the degree to which jobs meet social and psychological needs of workers. In contrast, the IE approach excels in the analysis of technical systems, through such techniques as short interval scheduling, work measurement (time study), systems and procedures (e.g., forms design), management engineering, and work simplification. The quality of specific technical recommendations produced through these techniques may, in fact, exceed those of the STS method. But where the IE method suffers is in the development of an overall social-plus-technical framework into which piecemeal recommendations can be integrated.

Design

Underlying the proposals for change produced by the STS analysis method are principles of *job design,* which differ sharply from those of classical IE. A favored STS job design approach is called autonomous work groups or *self-regulating work systems.* In autonomous work group designs, each small group of workers operates as a team with total responsibility for a clearly defined work task or product. Sometimes the purview of the work team will include all the maintenance and supply activities necessary to make the team self-supporting. Occasionally, the team members will also take on responsibility for many tasks frequently assigned to managers, such as scheduling, assigning people to specific tasks, interviewing and training new workers, performance evaluations, and goal setting. In some cases, autonomous teams take on so many managerial functions that there is no need for formally designated supervisors or leaders of individual teams. This reduces the number of managers and the number of levels in the managerial hierarchy needed in facilities.

In contrast to the STS approach, which focuses on designing *clusters* of job roles around particular processes, the classical IE approach designs *individual* job roles in ways that make each jobholder relatively autonomous. A variety of rationales underlie this focus on individual jobs. First, each job is made simpler, so replacement workers are easy to train. Second, limited sets of required skills make workers less valuable, so they can be paid less. Third, jobs that do not require much cooperative activity enable individual performance to be measured and rewarded, reducing managerial fears that workers are colluding to restrict output.

If this depiction of the classical engineering approach to job design sounds too harsh, it is supported at least in part by research evidence. A study by James Taylor (1977) showed that a sample of engineers most frequently used the job design criteria (in descending order of use) of:

Assigning each employee a specific group of tasks as a full-time job

Assigning each employee one particular task as a full-time job

Assigning each employee one particular task and rotating employees at intervals.

Less frequently used were the criteria more consistent with the STS philosophy:

Assigning each employee a whole production process as a full-time job

Assigning groups of employees to specific groups of tasks and allowing them to assign the individual tasks informally among themselves.

Taylor also found that engineers ranked "maximizing throughput per unit of time," "efficient use of machine resources," "making jobs as simple as possible to perform," and "reducing manpower" more important than "providing more job satisfaction" as "considerations for breaking technical processes into human tasks that result in greatest product quality at lowest cost" (1977).

Implementation

The STS approach differs from the classical IE approach in two key implementation aspects. First, STS relies heavily on *worker participation* throughout the cycle of analysis, design, and implementation. Second, STS does not try to nail down all contingencies through a rigid socio-technical design, but rather concentrates or provides a flexible and adaptive workplace framework which the workers will articulate and evolve over time.

In the earlier description of the STS analytic model, one very important fact was omitted. The analysts are themselves a small team composed of workers and managers and special consultants who may or may not have engineering backgrounds. One of the basic principles of the approach is that the people who do the work have a great deal of knowledge about processes, their variances, and how to control them. If they sometimes lack the "big picture," this is often because the limited scope of their jobs does not allow them to see and influence the objectives of the work system. Forming an *action group* with people representing a variety of perspectives often overcomes these obstacles to effective worker participation. The action team conducts the analysis, formulates hypotheses for redesign, proposes these to managerial decision makers and other employees for review, revision, and decision, and then oversees their implementation, initially on a trial basis.

The use of trial periods and *operational experiments* is another hallmark of STS. This allows the organization to avoid massive, disruptive change. Redesign proposals are tried out in small parts of an organization, bounded off from the rest to minimized problems if the change should not work as expected. If the change is unsuccessful, it can be dropped without too much expense or "loss of face," and other proposals from the action team can be tried. If the change is successful, the utility of the proposal can be demonstrated to other parts of the organization, enhancing its chances of easy acceptance.

In contrast, IE requires the services of experts from outside the work setting to perform the analysis and the redesign. Yet standard organizational practice rarely permits these specialists to implement their ideas directly. Instead, the plans are turned over to local management who may poorly understand them, the underlying rationales, or ways in which they can be modified to fit unforeseen circumstances without destroying their effectiveness.

This last point becomes especially critical since the designs produced through the classical IE approach are carefully crafted to cover almost every detail. All duties are assigned so that no slack time exists, all responsibilities are identified so that jurisdictions are clear. But if one piece of this plan fails to fit the work setting, perhaps because of conditions the engineer failed to consider, its very completeness and specificity make it all the harder to modify.

In contrast, STS recognizes the simple fact that a redesign of jobs is nothing other than a new technical system: it requires the social system of the workplace to infuse it with life, to make it "go." Consequently, design proposals are purposely left somewhat *underspecified;* the minimum specifications for a self-regulating system are spelled out, but no more. The process of making the plan workable is left to the discretion of the work team, who adapt it to changing circumstances and to their own increased knowledge about the operation of the socio-technical system.

The STS approach does not do away with industrial engineers or the need for their special skills. Rather, it provides a framework in which they can contribute together with those who work in the system. The theme of *industrial democracy* clearly runs through the approach; STS proponents believe that people have the right and the responsibility to influence the structure of their working lives.

To illustrate the advantages of the STS approach, an extended example has been prepared, describing a problem facing many medium to large-sized organizations in all sectors of the economy, public or private, manufacturing or service. The background data about the problems and organizational issues are ones that you yourself might compile through a little leg-work and interviewing, if you were assigned to one of the many staff teams trying to improve the productivity of computer software development. After this description follows the outline of a thorough, realistic, and sensible approach that you might actually take if you did *not* use the STS method. (We know this approach to be thorough, realistic, and sensible, because it is now being taken around the country by a number of real design teams!) The last part of the example presents some of the things that could go wrong with your solution because you failed to take into account key socio-technical concepts of environment and social system.

THE SOFTWARE DEVELOPMENT PROBLEM AT COMPUPHILE

Background

Compuphile Corporation is a large organization that has been using computers since the late 1950s. Like many similar companies, over the years it has built up a large staff of computer professionals to program the applications software necessary to make the computer do useful work for managers and engineers. Over the same time period, internal demand for software has grown so fast that the computer professionals cannot keep up. Currently, a two-year backlog exists, which means that it will be two years before the programmers will be able to start to build a program requested today, and then it may take two years or more to complete it. Compuphile managers are understandably upset when they are told that they may expect to see a needed application in four or five years.

The head of programming at Compuphile would like to find a way to satisfy his customers within a more acceptable time frame. One potential solution might be to purchase software "ready made" from other companies or software vendors. But because Compuphile is very large and quite different from most other companies, the programming manager rightly feels that this solution will not work. Packaged software would have to be tailored to Compuphile's special needs ("we might as well build it from scratch"), or else Compuphile managers would have to change their unique procedures to fit the packages (unfeasible because of the number of people involved). So the head of programming is looking for ways to improve the productivity of his systems development group.

Traditional Approach to Designing a Solution

Let's suppose that you are a member of a team charged with the responsibility for designing a technology to improve the software development process. Where would you begin? You'd probably start by describing how systems development takes place now at Compuphile and identifying leverage points for improving the process.

The systems development process consists of several phases. Initially, someone who wants a system contacts a systems analyst to document needs and requirements. At Compuphile, these analysts are people with data processing backgrounds, but they are organizationally located within the departments of computer users. The systems analyst documents the potential user's needs in a standard format and prepares a preliminary design of a computer-based system sufficient to meet these requirements. He or she then estimates the costs of building and operating such a system and the benefits that would derive from it, in terms of savings, avoided costs, increased revenue, and/or intangible value to the organization.

At this point, the systems analyst conducts informal discussions with people in Compuphile's centralized programming group to determine whether they will have the time to devote to this project if it is approved. This hurdle passed, the analyst condenses the already voluminous documentation into a two-page report and submits it to a management committee, which will approve or reject the proposal on the basis of its cost and value to Compuphile. If and when the project is finally approved (usually after several go-arounds with the steering committee), the project will then be turned over to the central programming group, which performs a detailed system design, programs or "codes" this design, debugs it (removes errors), and then tests it with typical data before turning it over to the client for acceptance testing.

If the client identifies a problem with a system during acceptance testing, the system is sent back to central programming, where it will be revised and recoded until it "works right." When the client feels the system does what it is supposed to, the system is accepted and put into "production," which means that it is run on a regular basis (e.g., weekly) on the computers in Compuphile's corporate data center. After this, the system has entered the phase of its life cycle known as "maintenance." During this phase, if the client identifies any major bugs in the system or desires any changes, improvements, or enhancements to it, a miniature version of the entire system development life cycle (requirements analysis, preliminary design, cost-benefit analysis and approval, detailed design, coding, debugging, testing, and acceptance) must be performed for each change request. Maintenance work is performed by groups of programmers within central programming separate from those who develop new systems.

Project Strategy

After this overview of the software development process at Compuphile, you decide to focus your efforts to improve the productivity of system development on the activities of the central programming group. You do this largely on the advice of the people who assigned you to this project in the first place, who are managers in the central programming group. They believe that they have no ability to influence the systems analysts and clients who reside outside their organizational domain.

Having identified the central programming group as your focus for analysis and problem solving, you proceed to use work study methods to collect statistical data. You also interview people about their perceptions of the process. You rapidly discover why programming is such a labor-intensive activity.

First of all, the technology of programming can be most simply described as uncertain. There are almost an infinite number of ways to program any medium-sized problem. And programmers with similar levels of experience may exhibit enormous variation in the quality and quantity of their output. Some researchers have found differences on the order of thirty to one in such measures as program length, speed of execution, and coding time among programmers working on identical tasks.

Second, the biggest part of software costs occurs after the initial development, when the software is "up and running." The entire front end of the process, up to acceptance testing, accounts for only about 30 percent of the life cycle time. Since systems usually last for years once developed, the lion's share of life cycle time occurs when the system is operational. Less obviously, the *cost* of maintenance is proportional to the length of the operational phase, because clients' requirements frequently change over time, requiring reprogramming. Furthermore, some people believe that the cost of maintenance exceeds the cost of comparable new development, because of the time required to learn what previous programmers did and to make the necessary changes without introducing new bugs.

Third, a major reason software maintenance is so difficult and time-consuming is the lack of good documentation (written descriptions, augmented with graphical and tabular material, of how the program works, analogous to an automobile operation and repair manual). You are told that programmers hate to do documentation almost as much as they hate maintaining someone else's programs. It is possible to ensure that they document a system when it is first built, simply by refusing to accept the system without it. But whether the documentation is good or not is another story. Further, it is impossible to guarantee that initial system documentation will be kept up-to-date by subsequent maintenance programmers. (Many factories have analogous problems keeping machinery repair manuals up-to-date.) Paper documentation is bulky and difficult to index; simple changes must frequently be recorded in several places on multiple documents. Once documentation gets out-of-date, updating it becomes a massive undertaking, equivalent in some people's way of thinking to building a new system.

Finally, you discover inefficiencies in the ways Compuphile programmers produce lines of code. Programmers at Compuphile develop programs in virtually the same way that students in university programming courses do (except, of course, for all the extra paperwork). In other words, even if the programmers are developing programs that will later execute during production runs in an on-line mode, the programmers must use the "batch" mode to develop the programs. They sit at their desks, plan their work (ideally), begin on preprinted coding forms, then turn these in for keypunching. After checking for keypunching errors, they submit their decks to be run by computer operators on data center computers. While they are waiting the several hours until they get the results of their runs, they are (one hopes) working on documentation, coding or debugging another section of code, or programming other work. However, you and others observe them spending a fair

amount of time engaged in what industrial engineers call "idle time": walking to and from the keypunch area and the data center, reading *Computerworld* and talking with other programmers.

The Designed Solution

Inspiration strikes you and your teammates as you review the data you have collected on the technology of computer programming at Compuphile. You see a way to improve the process by simultaneously standardizing program development, reducing programmer idle time, and automating program documentation. The solution you come up with (and which a number of other teams are currently coming up with) might be called an application development tool (ADT). Each programmer will have at his or her desk a computer terminal at which he or she will be able to write, run, debug, and test programs. Because the terminal will be located at the programmer's desk, there will be no time wasted walking to other locations, and, since the programmer will have little excuse to leave the desk, idle chatting with other programmers will be reduced. Because the system will be on-line, waiting time for results will be dramatically reduced, so that programmers will get more work done in one day.

But the real benefits of the ADT will come from the controls and checks it builds into the programming process. Using the terminal will require the programmers to use specially developed software that guides and constrains their choices about how to build programs. It may, for example, require the programmer to input a written description of the program before any code will be accepted, thus ensuring that documentation gets done. (This strategy was employed in the one real ADT described in computer science literature.) It may also, for another example, store already programmed "modules" of code to perform frequently repeated, general-purpose programming tasks (such as sorting a list of numbers or calculating sales tax), and then require the programmer to supply only the code required to string these modules together in the proper sequence or the parameter values necessry to tailor the modules to specific needs. This would prevent expensive duplication of effort.

Once the documentation and code are stored in the computer's memory, it should be much easier to maintain programs using the ADT. As with program development, documentation of maintenance changes will have to be input before the changes, and the ADT will "prompt" the programmer to change the documentation in all the necessary places by means of automatically maintained cross-indexes. Because the documentation is stored in electronic, not paper, form, there is no need to retype the old documentation, and all "copies" of the documentation are simultaneously made up-to-date and consistent.

The people who chartered your project team proclaim your solution excellent and approve the necessary funds for development. Eventually, the ADT is built, installed, and the programmers are trained to use it. You confidently await the reports of your success; you expect lines of code per programmer day to increase, time to deliver a working system to a client to decrease, the cost of maintenance programming to decrease, and programmers to be delighted with their technological marvel.

Consequences of the Design

But after a while the results begin to accumulate, slowly at first, later more dramatically. The ADT is not all it was cracked up to be. What follows are two scenarios of the unanticipated negative consequences that might have occurred if such an ADT were implemented at Compuphile. At this point, the example is purely hypothetical, and it is unlikely that all of the negative results would occur in any one company. The scenarios illustrate some major considerations that were neglected in what appears to be a very thorough analysis and design effort.

In the first scenario, you find that the number of lines of debugged code per programmer day increased, as you expected. Consequently, development projects were being turned over faster to the users for acceptance, and more jobs are being put into production. Unexpectedly, clients began sending more systems back for reprogramming, and programmers began expressing dissatisfaction with the system by quitting in droves.

Analysis of the Relationship Between the Socio-Technical System and the Environment

These negative consequences, which may have occurred even though the ADT *succeeded* in accomplishing its goals of improving the speed of system development and maintenance, can be traced to the environment of the central programming facility: clients and systems analysts. Here's the explanation. With the new programming technology, more systems were being rejected at acceptance testing, revealing a structural problem that has always existed in the system development process at Compuphile. Systems analysts, located in client departments, are rewarded for achieving goals important to their bosses. In the case of systems development, that goal is speed. Since analysts are data processing people by training, they have always tended to take short-cuts by reducing the time they spend clarifying client needs. They rush ahead to develop a preliminary technical design that can be turned over to the central programming group.

In the past, it was often two years or more before the programming group finished their tasks, by which time the clients' original needs had changed, requiring reprogramming of the system. (This happened even when the original requirements specifications were correct.) So deficiencies in the "specs" were rarely discovered under the old development technology, because clients blamed the slowness of central programming and their own changed needs. Usually, projects were just quietly scrapped, with no questions asked, even after several hundred thousand dollars had been spent programming the wrong system.

With the ADT, central programming was able to deliver systems much faster, in about six months, so systems analysts stepped up the pace of their work, with even greater temptation to shortcut the analysis phase. When clients had the opportunity to review a delivered product within a reasonable time frame, during which their needs had not changed, it became all too clear that central programming was coding the wrong specs and that the analysts were at fault. Clients at Compuphile have always perceived the technically trained systems analysts as members of central programming in spite of the true organizational reporting relationship, so they naturally blamed central programming for the "new" problem.

To have avoided these negative consequences stemming from the separation of clients and systems analysts in the environment of central programming, the ADT design team should have performed its analysis to include environmental interactions and should have developed the ADT to address problems at the environmental interface. In socio-technical systems parlance, the design team failed to "bound" (put boundaries around) the problem properly.

Analysis of the Social System/ Technical System Relationship

A very different aspect of the increased number of systems in production was responsible for discontent among the programmers. This aspect is a mismatch between the ADT and the social system within central programming. The ADT allowed the same number of programmers to produce more systems. Initially, no one worried about the fact that fewer programmers could handle the demand for software, because such a large backlog existed. But as the backlog decreased, the number of systems requiring maintenance programming increased. Programmers were shifted from new program development, the much preferred job, to maintenance programming. As mentioned earlier, maintenance programming is the bane of data processing specialists, except for a few who thrive on knotty problems. But the ADT reduced or eliminated much of the desirable development work, leaving the not-so-desirable maintenance. At Compuphile, programmers who shifted to maintenance work from new program development invariably quit within six months. The excellent job market for people with their skills facilitated the exodus.

The negative consequences discussed so far have been predicated on the assumption that the ADT achieved its goals of greater productivity in software development and maintenance. But what if the ADT failed to achieve its goals, again for reasons relating to the match between the new technical system and the social system within central programming? Consider a second scenario of consequences.

Perhaps the number of lines of code per programmer day *did* increase, but the length of time to deliver a tested system to a client did not decrease. Investigation revealed that debugging and testing were taking *longer* with the new system, in spite of the fact that the code was easier to read and understand and was better documented. Belatedly, it became obvious that under the old batch method of program development, programmers were using their "idle" time between runs to help their colleagues debug code. It is always easier to spot the bugs in someone else's code than in one's own. With the ADT, programmers had no reason to leave their desks, and old patterns of helping and interaction broke down. It became an admission of failure to invite another programmer over to one's terminal to offer advice, whereas offering advice had been more casual before, as one looked over another's shoulder on the way back to one's desk.

If this were not bad enough, turnover within the central programming group increased from its original level of 25 percent (common in the data processing industry) to an alarming 45 percent six months after the ADT was installed. Exit interviews with departing employees revealed their dislike for the fact that the ADT collected and analyzed productivity measures on individual programmers. Supervisors, armed with new performance data, had stepped up their feedback and control attempts. In addition, a number of programmers reported leaving because the ADT required them to program in a new higher-level language used only by Compuphile. They feared this would erode their existing skills in COBOL and reduce their attractiveness on the job market.

Implications of the Systems Development Example

In spite of the careful and systematic efforts of your project team, the solution you designed created at least as many problems as it solved. If you had been guided in your analysis and design efforts by the STS philosophy, you might have avoided some of the more obvious dysfunctional consequences of your ADT. In particular, the STS approach would have alerted you to the issue of how you placed boundaries around the central programming group as the target of your intervention. The need to design thoroughly the relationships between central programming and its environment would have been obvious. Further, you would have been directed to explore carefully the existing social relationships among programmers and the ways in which the climate of the old work setting had encouraged teamwork and job satisfaction.

It should be noted that you would have derived these benefits from the STS method even if you had employed only the concepts and perspectives of the analysis and design methods without the STS implementation procedures of worker participation in the design process and minimum design specification. It is quite possible that both the design of your ADT and programmer acceptance of it would have been much better had you been willing and able (with the approval and support of top management) to undertake the full STS approach. This would have required you to change your role in the process from one of outside expert to one of consultant and resource to the action team of inside experts.

CONCLUSION

This chapter has only scratched the surface of the STS approach, briefly illustrating the key concepts and methods and demonstrating the value of using these in an actual situation. To round off this overview, we will mention two recent uses of the approach and summarize its limitations and strengths.

STS was used in the design and start-up of a new paint manufacturing plant for a large corporation. The corporation had identified the need for a new plant, and management was committed to experimenting with the STS approach for several reasons. First, management believed that jointly optimizing the social and technical systems would produce a work setting in which technical performance (product cost and quality) would be better than in other plants. A relevant fact was that the cost of low-quality paint was high, up to $20,000 per batch, and the quality could be adequately controlled only by workers exercising skilled judgment; electronic control instruments could not entirely substitute. Therefore, it was important to develop an organizational culture in which workers took responsibility for the product. Second, management believed that workers would be more satisfied with their jobs, since they would have influence on important decisions, and that this would make the facility less susceptible to union organizing attempts. Management hired external STS consultants and trained internal ones to lead teams of managers through the exercise of laying out the plant. The first workers were hired and trained in the concepts of autonomous work teams. These workers then helped interview, hire, and train the remaining workers. When the plant was running, it produced higher quality paint at lower cost with better measures of

employee satisfaction (absenteeism, turnover, questionnaire responses) than any of the company's other facilities. The plant also remained nonunion, to the satisfaction of the managers. The results are described in detail in Poza and Markus (1980).

A large high-technology company used STS to redesign the clerical procedures and computerized applications for processing the company's payroll. Currently, all the payroll processing for the company's tens of thousands of employees in dozens of locations is done at a single headquarters location, a fact that runs counter to the very decentralized way in which the company does everything else. Although the rationale for change is great, management is rightly concerned about the massive dislocations that change in such a sensitive function could produce. Consequently, this company is willing to invest time and money to ensure that the employees help design the new system that they will have to make work.

As both of these examples imply, the major drawback to the full STS method is the time and cost associated with it. In several STS case studies carefully documented by Taylor (1978), it is clear that it may take eighteen months or more for action teams to produce acceptable proposals for redesign, meeting once or twice a week while continuing to do their regular jobs. The salaries of action team members and the fees of any outside consultants must be paid throughout this period and may amount to a considerable sum. And there are also benefits forgone if management waits to make changes until the action team has concluded its work.

On the other hand, like most situations in which careful planning is done, STS implementations are often easy and successful right from the start without the painful, nonproductive adjustment processes that accompany ill-planned changes. The STS method often results in major improvements with little or no disruption of work, a considerable achievement. Further, many benefits of the STS method can probably be achieved without the use of the implementation strategies if engineers and other experts are trained in STS analysis methods and design principles. But this limited approach has drawbacks, too, and the decision to abbreviate the STS approach should be carefully considered.

Another potential limitation of STS is that successes with it have been reported more commonly in new plant startup situations than in cases involving the redesign of entrenched practices. But this is not a very serious limitation, since changing things already in place is probably more difficult no matter what approach is used. The strength of STS is that it provides an integrated approach to changing existing settings that has been known to work in some cases when all else has failed.

A third limitation is that STS embodies values and prescriptions that may not be appropriate in all work settings. STS proponents believe that workers have the right and responsibility to help design their working lives. These ideals may be very much out of place in highly autocratic cultures. On the other hand, the experience with STS has frequently been that people more than live up to their work design responsibilities, even in work settings where they have historically been left out of decision making.

All in all, these limitations of the STS approach are not very severe in comparison to its strengths. The method has demonstrated success in simultaneously improving productivity and job satisfaction of employees. It is appropriate in a wide range of settings involving manual operation and partial or total automation. It can be used when changes in the technical system are prohibitively expensive, as in an older steel mill, as well as when designers have the luxury of building a new technical system from scratch, as in new plant design. And finally, because STS bases its change methodology on a coherent integrated philosophy of effective work settings, people who use it are less likely to create new problems in the process of trying to remedy old ones. This makes the socio-technical systems approach a useful one for engineers and managers struggling to cope with technical and organizational change.

REFERENCES

Bostrom, Robert P., and J. Stephen Heinen. "MIS Problems and Failures: A Socio-Technical Perspective. Part I: The Causes." *MIS Quarterly,* September 1977.

_____. "Part II: The Application of Socio-Technical Theory." *MIS Quarterly,* December 1977.
Reviews STS approach and applies it to the development of computerized management information systems.

Cummings, Thomas G., and Mary Lynne Markus. "A Socio-Technical Systems View of Organizations." In *Behavioral Problems in Organizations,* by Cary Cooper. Englewood Cliffs, N.J.: Prentice-Hall, 1979.
Summarizes the key concepts underlying the STS method.

Cummings, Thomas G., and Srivastva, Suresh. *The Management of Work: A Socio-Technical Systems Approach.* Kent, Ohio: Kent State University Press, 1977.
Gives the history of the STS method, describes the method in detail, presents two detailed cases of its application in a blue-collar and a white-collar setting.

Lawler, Edward E. "The New Plant Revolution." *Organizational Dynamics,* Winter 1978.
Describes and discusses the use of the STS method in the design of several new manufacturing facilities.

Poza, Ernesto, and Markus, M. Lynne. "Success Story: The Team Approach to Work Restructuring." *Organizational Dynamics,* Winter 1980.

Presents a detailed case study of the use of the STS method in a new paint manufacturing plant.

Taylor, James C. "Job Design Criteria Twenty Years Later." Los Angeles: UCLA, Institute for Industrial Relations, 1977.

Presents results of study showing criteria used by engineers and systems analysts to design jobs.

_____. "Studies in Participative Socio-Technical Work System Analysis and Design: Service Technology Work Groups." CQWL-WP-78-1-A, CQWL-WP-78-1-B. Los Angeles: Institute for Industrial Relations, 1978.

Describes STS intervention in the Central Stores and Employment Division Departments of a large scientific laboratory.

Walton, Richard E. "The Diffusion of New Work Structures: Explaining Why Success Didn't Take." *Organizational Dynamics,* Winter 1975.

Reviews some of the early new plant STS experiments and analyzes the failure of their managing companies to spread the benefits to other facilities.

Organizational Design

Gerrit Wolf

University of Arizona

Organizational design addresses the problem of organizing people to achieve an effective organizational outcome. Traditionally, design has focused on formal influence structures, job descriptions, reporting relationships, etc.—the familiar elements of the "organization chart." Effectiveness has been considered primarily in terms of product quantity and quality.

A more contemporary view treats organizational design as the problem of specifying strategies for generating and distributing information within the organization so as to facilitate effective decision making. This view expands the concept of design to include not only one-way channels of communication between people (as in the supervisor-subordinate relationships), but also interaction within groups of people, interactions between people and computers, and interactions between people in the organization and the external environment.

Gerrit Wolf reviews both the traditional and the modern approaches to organizational design, and shows how the latter expands both the problems that can be dealt with and the tools that are used in solving these problems. Design strategies are outlined for different types of organizations. In particular, we show how designing for organizations with a strong science and technology component (R&D laboratories, engineering departments, MIS departments, etc.) is different from designing for less technological organizations (e.g., production, sales, or service-oriented activities).

Converting materials into products, information into reports, and problems into solutions requires the organizing of jobs and people. Organization is needed because more than one job and one person are needed to change input to output, and because there is no one automatic or natural way to organize. Some constraints need to be recognized. Although an architect can design many different houses, some basic rules must be followed in all cases.

To understand the process of organizing, we start with an example. An engineer invents a piece of equipment, called a *modem*, which allows two computers to talk to each other. This modem is smaller, faster, and cheaper than comparable products. He advertises the product in a trade journal and receives ten orders. With these orders, he buys the electronic parts and assembles them in his basement. The products are sent to the ten customers who ordered them. We now have a business.

But, from a design perspective, we do not have an organization. An organization is needed if more than one person is needed to handle the functions of financing, manufacturing, marketing, R&D, budgeting, personnel, and a design to integrate all these functions. How many people are needed? What jobs are they to have? How do they relate to each other? At issue is uncertainty about means and about ends. The design of the organization depends on the amount of uncertainty, which can vary according to two major issues.

The first is the extent to which the organization understands how means are related to ends. For example, how is price related to sales, cost to sales, sales to competitors' sales, sales to financing, production technique to costs, etc.? These relationships can be well understood, or not even well known. The second issue concerns the degree of agreement among the relevant actors inside and outside the firm. For example, will the FCC sanction the modem, will the telephone company prevent its use, will the financial community lend money, will the employees give loyalty to the firm? The interests of the relevant parties may be similar or in conflict. If, for the sake of exposition, we treat these two issues as dichotomous rather than continuous, the crossing of the two yields four approaches, which focus on the kinds of decisions required, the firm's design, and performance criterion for success.

First, if means-ends relations are understood and there is certainty and agreement about ends, the decisions are programmed, the design is traditional, and the performance criterion is efficiency. This is the bureaucratic concept of organizational design, in which computation from operations research methods is combined with rational interpersonal relations. This design requires a stable environment that cannot disrupt the internal working of the organization. (See Chapter 10.)

Second, if means-ends relations are uncertain, but there is agreement about ends, the decisions involve problem solving, the design of the organization is informational, and the performance criterion is a solution. This is a contemporary information-processing conception of design, appropriate in rapidly changing environments. Search, problem solving, and discussion are combined to increase information-processing capabilities. If the changing environment became more predictable because of the design features, one would expect a reversion to traditional design features.

Third, if means-ends relations are certain but there is a disagreement about ends, the decisions involve conflict resolution, the design of the organization is a political structure, and the performance criterion is effectiveness. This is a political concept of design appropriate in an environment with diverse interests. Negotiating, bargaining, and compromise are the focus. Conflict may be mistaken for uncertainty about means and ends, and may therefore be dealt with inadequately by the informational design features. Also, conflict may be denied because of the effort needed to deal with differences among workers, management, owners, suppliers, buyers, and regulators, and the traditional design mistakenly used.

Fourth, if means-ends relations are uncertain and there is a disagreement about ends, the decisions require creativity, intuition, and inspiration. The design is flexible and the performance criterion is innovation. This concept of design is eclectic and appropriate in chaotic environments, particularly those in which opportunities and resources are declining. The creative solution may come from a strong leader or from a strong group. Failure to address the uncertainties will hurt the firm.

All organizations face the two basic issues of means-ends uncertainty and disagreement over ends. The four approaches described above have been used to characterize the design of whole organizations (Thompson and Tuden, 1959). Here they are used to characterize different parts of an organization at different times. Organizations differ in how many of their problems fall in each of the four categories. The balance of the chapter details the design features found useful in each category.

For example, in the firm producing modems, the manufacture of the modems and the development of budgets, calling for computational decisions and a bureaucratic design, falls in approach one. The marketing of the product is basically an approach two problem, in that it consists of problem-solving decisions (assessing the number of customers, distributors, advertising, and pricing). The financing and staffing of the organization, which require bargaining, compromise, and negotiation, fall in approach three. The development of new products, requiring innovation, is an approach four problem.

Each function has a dominant-problem approach, and also has secondary problems that require use of the other approaches. For example, when red tape overloads the hierarchy in the traditional approach, communication increases across the hierarchy, which is an approach two design feature, as we shall see. This means that each part of the organization is a mixture of the four approaches, providing complexity, as well as having a dominant approach, a desired simplicity.

A design feature first focuses either on technological dependence among jobs or on communication among people. Second, a design feature focuses on horizontal technical or communication process, or it emphasizes the vertical controlling relationship among jobs or people. These distinctions become clear in the specific contexts of each of the four approaches to organizational design.

DESIGN OF THE TRADITIONAL ORGANIZATION

The design of a traditional organization assumes a stable environment. Manufacturing is the function that is typically designed traditionally because production can be isolated from the outside environment through buffers. The four features of a traditional design are work process, specialization, formal procedures, and hierarchy. Work process and specialization relate jobs horizontally, and formal procedures and hierarchy organize work vertically.

Work process and formal procedures define the technology, and hierarchy and specialization define relations among people. Shown in table form, the design features of a traditional organization appear thus:

	Technology	People
Horizontal relations	Work process	Specialization
Vertical relations	Formal procedures	Hierarchy

Each of the four is described separately. All four are necessary to form a complete design. The origins of the design can be found in the scientific analysis of Frederick Taylor shortly after the turn of the century (Taylor, 1911), and in Weber's analysis of bureaucracy in Germany (Weber, 1947).

The philosophy behind these four design features is that the planning of work can and should be separated from the doing of the work. Workers labor, managers plan the work. This separation of "mind" and "body" is efficient as long as the production process is well understood and the workers accept it. At the turn of the century matching worker skills to the job and paying for performance were sufficient motivation. Today the system may work if, in addition, the employees get something more from the job than pay and feel respected by management (Roethlisberger and Dickson, 1939).

Work Process

Two dimensions have been used to order or classify work processes. One dimension describes the job in isolation and the other describes interconnections among jobs. Together they classify a range of work procedures.

The job itself varies from routine work to nonroutine work. Routine work has been described as having repetition, simple rules, fragmented tasks, few exceptions, and no variety, as prescribed by the traditional approach (Taylor, 1911). At the other end of the continuum we find nonroutine work, with less repetition, variety, complex rules, many exceptions, and whole problems to solve (Hackman and Lawler, 1971). Routine work was made the ideal by Frederick Taylor, who at the turn of the century analyzed the coalminer's job and found the correct and routine way to perform it, regardless of worker. Taylor assumed workers would be motivated only by the economic gains from productivity. Nonroutine work has become the ideal of job enrichment specialists, who note that routine work is unmotivating (turnover, destruction, drugs, for example, become problems), while challenging work is naturally motivating.

Job interconnections vary from few to one-way to two-way interdependencies (Woodward, 1965; Thompson, 1967). The special order craftsperson, R&D researcher, or job shop operator are examples of independent jobs, where tasks are done in small batches. Mass production using an assembly line typifies the one-way connection of jobs. Continuous process chemical, electrical, and nuclear plants demonstrate the two-way interdependent work process involving feedback loops.

Historically, there has been a negative correlation between job challenge and job interconnection. The more interconnection among jobs, the larger the policy manual specifying what is required of each job; and the more rules, the more routine the job. This correlation was associated with widespread use of the assembly-line technology and increases in the size of the organization. Where there is continuous process technology and creative variation on the assembly line, the correlation disappears. Also, decentralizing the organization into divisions changes the nature of the relationship of job challenge and job interconnection, described below.

There are variations in job type, even within a given technology. For example, batch process may exhibit a wide variety of work, as in an R&D lab, or be as routine as a car repair shop or, in most cases, a doctor's office. Mass production may be designed as at Ford, where people are immediately replaceable and interchangeable, or as at Volvo, where people are skilled and work in teams on a whole section of a car. Continuous process may be as routine as monitoring the valves and dials in an oil refinery or as challenging as solving problems in a nuclear power plant.

If (foolishly) only the work process constraint were used to design an organization, work would be routinized because uncertainty would minimized. The industrial engineering approach, following in the steps of Taylor, uses sophisticated technology and time-and-motion studies to routinize the work and eliminate the inefficiencies of the laborer. Personally, however, the engineer looks for challenging problems to which his or her professional skills can be applied. Therefore, work process cannot be used as a design constraint without simultaneously specifying the skill levels of the employees.

Specialization

The more complex and nonroutine the job, the more specialized are the skills required to do the job. These skills are developed through training, which can (1) take place on the job, (2) be taught by the organization, or (3) be a requirement of admission to the job. A technician can receive junior college training and/or receive on-the-job apprenticeship. An engineer requires four or more years of college training and on-the-job experience to reach high levels of responsibility.

Training builds skills and knowledge into the person, as opposed to a strategy of building information into the work process or information support system. Training people rather than simplifying the job tends to build in the employee a commitment to the academic discipline, a commitment that may be at odds with the goals of the organization. The organization pays a price for expertise in terms of employee independence from the organization's goals of profit or service. Professionals may press for a functional departmental structure in which their expertise is further supported, but the organization loses some flexibility.

Engineers are in high demand because of the technical nature of most operations and because engineers leave the field so quickly. A professional who shows adaptability moves up in the organization to become a manager. A professional who does not adapt may find that training has a half-life of five years in this rapidly changing society. (See Daryl Chubin, "Career Patterns of Scientists and Engineers," Reading #5.)

The organizing problem is to what extent the firm should invest in expensive professionals as compared with other features available to it.

Formal Procedures

Formal procedures consist of written documents of many kinds, such as job descriptions, performance evaluations, attendance rules, budgets, order forms, sales and tax forms, financial reports, pay schedules, and operating procedures. Various disciplines of human resource management, accounting, finance, and operations management have standard ways of developing, using, and implementing these written documents. The documents represent what is known about connections of means and ends.

To be of use, the information in the documents needs to be internalized by relevant employees in the firm. If substantial parts of the documentation do not become internalized, the documents either become irrelevant to controlling the behavior of employees or too much time is spent consulting them.

The purpose of the formal procedures is to standardize and routinize what needs to be done. Reference to procedures should save time and contribute to producing acceptable behavior. The written procedures are like a computer program for handling routine tasks. Unlike a computer program, all events and behavior cannot be formalized, and even if they could be formalized, a negative reaction of employees to red tape would undercut their effectiveness.

Hierarchy

Hierarchy is a necessary and powerful constraint in controlling information flows (Simon, 1969). With no hierarchy among n employees, there would be $n^2 - n$ two-way communication channels. The figure can be cut in half by making all communications one-way. However, if a person receives instruction from only one supervisor, the number of communication channels is reduced to $n - 1$. Hierarchy minimizes the number of necessary channels. Without hierarchy, large organizations would be impossible because the number of nonhierarchical channels grows by the square of n, the number of employees.

The $n - 1$ channels may be distributed in a flatter or taller hierarchy and the number of subordinates for each superior—the span of control—may be large or small. The traditional approach thought there was an optimal number of levels and span of control. Empirical evidence finds weak relationships between these variables and either attitudes or performance (Porter and Lawler, 1965).

For hierarchy to work, three conditions must be satisfied: (1) the authority structure of hierarchy must be accepted by all members, especially those at lower levels; (2) the instructions from on high must be appropriate to the job setting; and (3) the decisions required of the hierarchy must be handled in real time. These conditions increasingly fail in today's complex society.

The acceptance of authority has been called the process of legitimation. A position does not so much command authority as it is given authority by those who submit to it. While acceptance of authority is the condition of employment, the administration of authority may be handled in different ways: personally or impersonally; participatively or not; arbitrarily or consistently. Failures of authority are usually due to an inappropriate style for the particular subordinate, job, or problem (Vroom. and Yetton, 1973; Fiedler, 1976; House, 1971). Authority succeeds with the right conditions. If the superior is of high status, and part of a highly accepted normative belief structure, a subordinate will comply with instructions that violate a personal set of values (Milgram, 1962).

A second failure of authority is incompetence due to lack of expertise, or inability to get the information, feedback, and expertise from others. Hierarchy has the intrinsic problem of finding out what is going on down below. Subordinates do not deliver bad news because it could cost them their jobs or promotions. While hierarchy speeds instructions, it inhibits the corrective forms of feedback (Leavitt, 1978). The catch is that the person in authority may not realize there is a problem in getting feedback and think that his/her authority is effective because subordinates accept the authority.

The last failure of hierarchy is that it can handle only so many decisions per unit of time. The hierarchy can become overloaded with decisions as they get pushed up the hierarchy (Galbraith, 1973). Certainly the hierarchy can be trimmed so that one level does not have more decisions to make than another, but in large bureaucratic organizations we see red tape stretching decision making out to the point of reducing efficiency.

DESIGN OF THE ORGANIZATION AS AN INFORMATION SYSTEM

When the hierarchy becomes overloaded, when the technology becomes complex, and when the organization cannot be buffered from the environment, uncertainty is produced in means-ends relations. What is needed are design features that manage this uncertainty (Lawrence and Lorsch, 1969). The four features of an information system approach are slack goals, lateral relations, computers, and departmentation (Galbraith, 1973). Slack and computers are technological; lateral relations and departmentation concern communication between people. Computers and lateral relations focus on horizontal relations; slack and departmentation emphasize vertical relations.

While these four features form a system, there is a tradeoff among them so that one can be substituted for another. The marginal cost becomes a criterion for selecting a feature. The goal of all four is to reduce the uncertainty in means-ends connections in the process of converting inputs into outputs.

The four features can be summarized with the following table:

	Technology	Persons
Horizontal relations	Computers	Lateral relations
Vertical relations	Slack-goals	Departmentation

Computers

The use of computers to manage, store, and manipulate information can be viewed as part of the historical process begun in the Industrial Revolution of mechanizing work process, or as a different way of constraining work, a way that points to a new work revolution.

The parable of the spindle (Porter, 1962) illustrates the difference between machine design to control behavior versus constraint design to control information flows. In the parable a restaurant has a problem with the waiters and the cooks. The waiters find the cooks unresponsive to their orders, not knowing when the order will be filled and if it will be filled correctly. The cooks find the waiters too demanding and unappreciative of the cooks' pride in quality. The control of mechanistic design calls for detailed job descriptions, training in interpersonal behavior, and close supervision. The information-processing approach improves the information flow by inserting a communication device between waiter and cook: a spindle, which clusters orders for the cook's convenience. If the spindle is full, the waiter knows the cook cannot handle another order just now. The spindle acts as a physical recording of the order. Memories are not taxed, face-to-face confrontation is decreased, quality of information is increased, and cook and waiter are free to do their own jobs as they see fit.

The computer's impact is revolutionary because it has the potential for minimizing the routine work of people and aiding employees in productive ways for nonroutine work. The repetitive task, whether it be inventory control, purchase ordering, letter typing, ticketing, etc., can be done more quickly, accurately, and reliably by computer than by people. People are then left to plan and create strategies and tactics, with the aid of the computer-generated alternative scenarios. Computers are now used extensively in routine tasks at lower levels of the organization. The use of computers at high levels as decision-support systems has a way to go.

Behavioral problems arise with the increasing use of computers: (1) user incompetence, misuse, and defensiveness and (2) power and politics with shifts in information access.

The decision process for different types of decision makers has been modeled or simulated: stockbrokers, physicians, and admissions officers. Based on what we know about the relative abilities of human versus the computer to process information (see Connolly, 1977), the model of the decision maker always performs better than the decision maker. This fact is threatening to many managers. What they have trouble understanding is that if information is computable, the computer can do it more quickly and reliably. What information should be given to the computer, how to put it in computable form, and how information should be combined require human thinking before the computer can run. This division of labor between computer and human is not well understood. It is a creative and challenging division of labor to those educated in computer usage, and an Orwellian threat to the traditional manager (or doctor) who perceives himself as the following: omni-potent, irreplaceable, omniscient.

Galbraith (1973) recognized the computer as a design constraint. It is one of four constraints whose purpose is to increase the availability of timely information. Up until this recognition, designers had emphasized that authority structures were the only means of dealing with uncertainty. It was said that structure followed strategy (Chandler, 1962). The computer provides a means of dealing with strategy and the environment without changing authority structures directly. In practice, structures adapt to the new information access and distribution.

A case study demonstrates the interconnection of information systems, authority, and politics. In the early days of computing, over a decade ago, a firm wanted to spend big money and buy the best available machine. The stated reason was that the computer would be able to provide instant answers to almost any question that an employee could ask, whether it be about company policy or the technicalities of his or her job. A consultant advised the firm that the objective could be achieved for a fraction of the cost of the computer and its necessary personnel. The firm hesitated taking the consultant's advice because his solution was not as prestigious as having its own computer.

However, the firm did try the consultant's suggestion, which was to hire two college graduates as "gofers," give them an office with several phones, and announce to everyone that the gofers' office would get answers to any technical or policy questions phoned in. The gofers were instructed that they did not even need to leave the office because it was an empirical finding that any answer could be found within four phone calls. Call the person most likely to know and ask that person whom to call if he or she cannot help.

The human information system worked well for six months, when it had to be abandoned because it worked *too* well. Employees quit using it because they feared the power of the gofers, who came to know who asked questions and who had answers. The gofers became the center of an information network that gave them high potential power. Clearly, information access is not neutral relative to power bases in the organization.

Lateral Relations

The three problems of hierarchy—resistance, blindness, and overload—can be overcome by designing specifically non-hierarchical lateral channels. These channels can be between pairs of employees or between permanent or temporary groups from different departments. They may emerge informally as people strive to get the job done. A wise designer legitimizes useful lateral relations and designs new lateral relations as a way of getting information to the right place at the right time.

Resistance to hierarchy and authority can be countered by coopting lower level employees into higher level policy groups. Examples are putting students on college policy committees, or requiring union and worker representatives on corporate boards of directors. Chrysler, in the United States, and the largest German firms by codetermination law provide for worker inputs and influence on the management of the firm. The cooptation does not give veto or absolute power to the workers, but does give a setting for new ideas and information to be brought to bear on policy.

Authority blindness is overcome by the manager following the principle that those who have the best information need to be consulted even if they do not directly participate in the decision. For example, setting up a liaison meeting between two employees, one from engineering and the other from the operations department, serves several purposes. The two employees have first-hand information needed to solve recurring problems, and their bosses' time is freed to work on more important problems. Much of a manager's time is spent relaying information and problems from one manager to another. The hierarchical channels can become extended and overused with trivial problems. Having lower level employees meet and solve problems at their level saves managerial time and improves the quality of the solution.

Another lateral relation is the integrator or managerial assistant for high level management. This role does not have the formal authority to order subordinates to comply, but instead talks with all relevant parties, gathers information, understands positions, clarifies positions to others, and persuades. The managerial assistant can be found in the public sector in a senator's office as well as in the private-sector large firm. The person is often young, highly trained, and skilled in a discipline. The expertise is a base from which to persuade people. The position also is a valued training opportunity for developing excellent young talent.

The overloading of authority can be reduced by using teams and task forces in addition to liaison and integrator roles. A task force is a temporary group composed of three or more people from different departments or areas. The expertise of the individuals relative to the problem is the main criterion for membership. When the problem is solved, the task force is dissolved. The manager gets the expertise needed and is relieved of time commitment to work on other matters. A team is like the task force in composition but has permanence because the problem that is the reason for its existence recurs. Besides expertise, interpersonal skills are required. Without group problem-solving skills, teams fail. These skills can be personal qualities of the participants, such as tolerance for ambiguity and ability to confront conflict, or group skills, such as group problem-solving techniques.

Slack

Goals are an individual's or organization's expression of intention, of what they are trying to achieve. These intentions are primary characteristics of a person or organization because intentions direct and guide behavior and reduce uncertainty, on the one hand, and on the other act as justifications, rationalizations, and interpretations of what has happened (Weick, 1969). The interconnection of individuals' goals and organizational goals specifies a hierarchy. Slack resources such as additional time, money, and effort influence individual and organizational goals and, in turn, performance.

Two goal properties—goal level and acceptance—relate positively to performance. Goal level specifies the quantity or quality performance standard. As it increases, the achievement of the goal becomes harder, requiring greater commitment. Goal acceptance is the degree of commitment to the goal. These two goal properties combine multiplicatively, as follows:

Performance = Level × Acceptance

This model says there is an increasing effect of goal level at greater amounts of acceptance, and vice versa.

The model seems to say that a person or firm should shoot for the moon, but trying for the maximum is not indicated because goal level and acceptance are negatively related via the variables of slack resources and plans. The greater the slack resources and the more extensive the plans, on the one hand, the easier it is to reach the goal and therefore the lower the level of the goal, and, on the other hand, the higher the acceptance of the level. Formally, we have

Acceptance = Plans and Slack

Level = C − Plans − Slack

Therefore, if we arbitrarily set the constant C equal to 1 we have

Level = 1 − Acceptance

which says that the more slack resources and plans the higher the acceptance and the lower the level. Substituting, we then have

Performance = Level × (1 − Level)

Therefore, an optimal level of goal difficulty should be moderate at .5. Deviation from the .5 level yields lower performance.

Research on achievement motivation (Atkinson, 1964) and goal setting (Locke, 1968) supports the model for individuals. Many organizations use management by objectives (MBO) to implement the model. Superior and subordinate together set specific goals and, if these goals are moderately difficult—that is, challenging—the subordinate's performance will be optimized. When all superiors and subordinates participate in MBO, we have a vertical hierarchy that has been negotiated. MBO, based on the goal model, differs extensively from the work process approach, which ignores available resources, and from hierarchy, which assumes instructions will be implemented regardless of their difficulty. MBO complements work process and hierarchy approaches by increasing the likelihood that goals will be implemented.

Research on slack resources shows that organizations use slack as a strategic option for managing uncertainty (Galbraith, 1973). One can adjust performance levels directly or run overtime schedules or use furloughs to indirectly adjust levels. One wants to get the performance levels near .5. The classic example of slack is the scheduling of machines in a batch or job shop operation. The scheduling problem turns out to be as complex as designing an artificial player to win at the game of chess (Simon, 1969). The problem is handled practically by using rules of thumb to schedule machines. Even if it were possible, the cost of planning the optimal machine scheduling would be prohibitive.

In this section, we have not discussed goal conflict among people or groups. The political approach below focuses on this issue.

Departments

After an organization grows out of its entrepreneurial childhood, basic areas of production, finance, marketing, and personnel grow in size. It becomes reasonable to organize the employees within each function into a department. Other functional departments that may emerge are R&D, and engineering and planning, often serving as support. Which are primary or line departments and which are support or staff departments depends on the organization's mission.

The functionally designed organization benefits from the expertise found in each department. Division of labor within a department provides the firm with specialists. These specialists keep their expertise by interacting with fellow experts. The department is the setting in which disciplinary knowledge is fostered and developed. The departments are linked to the president's office. Therefore, the hierarchy is flat when the departments are seen as units. The larger the organization, the taller the hierarchy.

The functional departments also produce a liability. Expertise in departments generates a functional blindness, an inability to understand other departments, a superior attitude toward other departments, and competition with other departments. These are negative factors because the departments are dependent on each other to create organizational performance.

These liabilities are accentuated as the organization grows with the addition of new products or services. Functional departments are committed to expertise in their areas, not to the product or service. Therefore, the divisional organization, product department, was developed to overcome the liabilities of functional departments. Divisional boundaries organize communication and information according to products, whether they be goods or services. This arrangement is in contrast to the departmental functional organization. It arises when the firm produces multiple lines or if there is great geographical dispersion, as in an international firm (Galbraith, 1973).

The divisional units overcome the intergroup conflict and communication problems that arise between functional departments. Employees within a unit are committed to the production of a product. Coordination is driven by this commitment to delivering the completed product. Time delays are decreased because conflicts among operations, quality control, R&D, or marketing are decreased. While the uncertainty due to conflict based on departmental self-interest is reduced, the potential expertise is sacrificed. For example, a functional firm may have mechanical, electrical, and industrial engineers in an engineering department. The self-contained units firm decentralizes each engineer to a different product and requires the engineer to be a generalist. The development of the specific expertise is lost. Another example is the difference between a functional firm with a computer department and a divisional firm that decentralizes the computing operations among the product lines. The division or product manager is a generalist, while the department manager is an expert.

The organization can gain the benefits of the functional and the divisional constraints by designing boundaries that make up a matrix organization, a structure often used in project-oriented firms. Both functional and project structures are explicitly defined. An employee is a member of both a functional department and a project division. The name "matrix" comes from the graphical representation where the columns are departments, rows divisions, and a cell locates an employee, who is responsible both to the functional manager and to the divisional manager. The simplicity of hierarchy is lost and the firm must work out the responsibilities of the two managers for planning, training, performance appraisal, and promotion. Working out the responsibilities can be a problem, but the benefits may be the only way of accomplishing organizational goals. The matrix organization was first developed by NASA to accomplish the man-on-the-moon mission. This mission required the expertise of engineers and scientists and the achievement of project completion within a rigid time frame.

Large firms find another form of the matrix organization the way to retain expertise and product timeliness. For example, IBM has functional organization for a home office staff and divisional organization for its worldwide operations. Plans, not people, receive the scrutiny both of experts at the home office and of divisional managers in the field. A five-year planning process is a complex annual dialectic between the home office and the division. In this confrontation, the departmental expertise of personnel, finance, engineering, and R&D departments are brought to bear on the plans, needs, and requirements of the product divisions, such as the small equipment division (typewriters), the minicomputer division, and the large frame computer division. Conflict is made explicit and encouraged between parties. This openness is in contrast to the within-person stress found in the dual responsibility matrix organization at NASA.

DESIGN OF THE ORGANIZATION AS A POLITICAL SYSTEM

Design of the organization as a political system is the management of the conflicting interests and goals held by the important actors in the firm (Blau, 1964). The prior two design approaches assumed there was a consensus. One might naively assume that if the hierarchy were properly designed, there would be no conflict of interests because people higher in the hierarchy, all the way up to the chief executive officer, could specify and demand adherence to the goals as set from the top. Conflicts emerge among departments because their interests differ. For example, manufacturing wants to maximize productivity, while marketing wants to maximize sales. Also, conflicts occur at the boundaries of the organization in relation to resource dependencies related to supplies, labor forces, and finances (Pfeffer and Salancik, 1978).

The four features of the political design are:

	Technology	People
Horizontal relations	Incentives	Bargaining
Vertical relations	Mediation	Governance

The interconnection of the design features is much more problematic than in the previous approaches. Little is known about the substitutability or conjunctive relationships among them. An example is the relationship between incentives and bargaining. Changing the incentives from individual to group incentives increases the need to bargain in order to allocate the group's rewards. Similarly, an increase in democratic governance may decrease the likelihood of unions and the need to bargain with labor.

We turn now to a description of each design feature, bearing in mind their interconnections.

Incentives

The consequences or payoffs from actions or strategies by various employees may not be the same to all employees, nor the same for every combination of actions. The structure of payoffs can vary from perfectly opposed, partially opposed, unrelated, partially congruent, or completely congruent. The perfectly opposed is called constant-sum or win-lose conflict, the partially opposed or congruent is called nonconstant sum or partial conflict, and completely congruent payoffs are called cooperative or win-win structures. (See Chapter 8.)

The naive application of payoff structures says all payoffs between firms are win-lose and all payoff structures within firms are win-win. The realistic view is that there are partial conflict structures between and within firms. An oligopoly market is an example of a partial conflict between firms. The relationship between a supervisor and a subordinate (Zahn and Wolf, 1981) or between two departments are examples within the firm. Partial conflict is particularly difficult to handle if it has a Prisoner's Dilemma structure (Rapoport and Chammah, 1965), characterized by each person preferring to compete rather than cooperate, but preferring the other to cooperate rather than compete. The result of these two preferences is that if both parties compete they are both worse off than if they both had cooperated. But there is no assurance that both will cooperate.

To increase the likelihood of cooperation, one needs to decrease the incentives for competition. For example, group bonuses in addition to individual pay may increase the cooperative group effort. In sports, an athlete may be offered incentive bonuses for team victories. In business, employees may have a profit-sharing plan.

Bargaining

If the payoff or incentive structure cannot be changed, one can focus on clarification of the strategies and perception of the strategies. Several examples demonstrate the process.

Bargaining over wages between labor and management is an example of bargaining in a constant-sum payoff structure. One kind of strategy is a tough or hard strategy that demands as much as possible, giving in only slowly. A soft strategy, by contrast, gives in quickly. A third strategy is to view the situation as having multiple issues, e.g., benefits, hours, and working conditions as well as wages. In this case, one could be tough on some issues or soft on others.

The final solution needs to be fair to each side. Failure to strike a bargain can be costly to both sides.

Another bargaining situation is the non-constant-sum situation. For example, the manufacturing department prefers to produce the old modem rather than the new smart modem. The old one is easier to produce because manufacturing has the experience. Marketing, on the other hand, prefers to sell the new modem because the demand is greater. The two departments need to coordinate their strategies. Failure to do so leaves the firm with too many of the old modems unsold and too few new modems available for sale. This bargaining problem is called "the battle of the sexes," characterized by a man and a woman choosing between going to the play or going to the sports event. Going separately is least desirable. One solution is that they go to the play tonight and to the sports event tomorrow night. This is coordination, analogous to the coordination required by manufacturing and marketing.

In any case, if bargaining is going to work, each side needs to realize that something must be given up in order to gain something else. If bargaining does not work, one can turn to the previous design feature, i.e., changing the structure of the payoffs, or one can use mediators or governance to resolve the conflict. (See Chapter 8.)

Mediation

In this design feature, a third party is used as a judge to resolve the conflict. Mediation combined with strong adversial debate by the parties in conflict has been used by major firms in the development of goals, consequences, and strategic plans.

One example of this in a multidivision firm is to have long-term planning proposals generated at the bottom of the firm in departments. For each proposal the corporate level generates a set of critiques and counterarguments. Reports and presentations of the department and the corporate level are presented to the executive to whom the department reports. This executive acts as judge or mediator, who works a solution from the sharply conflicting views.

This adversary process is called "the devil's advocate" procedure. It was used by President John Kennedy during the Cuban missile crisis (Allison, 1971), for whom members of the executive branch decision group prepared position papers and arguments. The reason Kennedy used this procedure was that conflict had been smothered in the executive group when decisions were being made in the Bay of Pigs invasion of Cuba a year earlier. The adversary process guaranteed that all points of view would be heard.

Governance

With this design feature the formal political process is used to manage conflict. Representative political process of governance uses committees to make decisions: membership on the committees is determined by democratic vote. The use of representative committees is extensive in Europe. However, although it has a long history in the United States it is limited to relatively small firms, particularly worker-owned ones (Wolf, Ronan, and Leatherwood, 1982).

Three kinds or classes of committees are used in firms: strategy committees, compensation committees, and working conditions committees. The strategy committee could be the board of directors. In Europe large firms are required to have workers represented on the board. In the United States, the Chicago-Northwestern Railroad is one of the largest worker-owned firms. It naturally has workers represented on the board.

Boards of directors have been analyzed as mechanisms for gaining resources through cooptation. Putting a minority, whether it be banker or worker, on the board diffuses the demands of the minority while gaining commitment.

The formal structuring of committees reflects informal coalitions that form and reform over differing issues in the firm. From this perspective, the organization is a set of coalitions, headed by the dominant coalition. Working conditions are addressed in Europe in works councils. In this country, compensation and work conditions are dealt with in firms that use Scanlon plans. Scanlon committees decide how to split profits and how to improve working conditions to increase profits.

The purpose of the committees is to provide an arena in which goal conflicts can be addressed and resolved. Instead of assuming away or suppressing goal differences, conflict is directly addressed. Similar behavior problems that face teams and task forces are part of formal committees. There are issues of status, decision procedures, and group cohesiveness.

THE FLEXIBLE ORGANIZATIONAL DESIGN

Situations that are so complex that it is hard to separate means from ends, to identify means or ends, or to evaluate means and ends may require a design different from the prior three. Such a situation is characterized by random matching of problems, choices, and decision makers. In what March (1972) calls the "garbage can" situation, problems are looking for decision makers, choices or solutions are looking for problems, and decision makers are looking for choices. The complexity of the situation inhibits a rational matching of problems, solutions, and decision makers. Complex

situations often occur in an R&D department or in the strategic development of the firm.

March claims that organizations need "to supplement the technology of reason with the technology of foolishness; they need to act before thinking." We look at four features of a flexible firm that places action first or combines action with thinking to learn about means and ends. The four features are professionalism, learning groups, experimenting manager, and leadership. Learning groups and professionalism focus on horizontal relationships; an experimenting manager and leadership focus on vertical relations. Professionalism and experimenting managers use technological aids; learning groups and leadership focus on the outcomes of designing new problems and new solutions. Graphically, we have:

	Technology	People
Horizontal relations	Professionalism	Learning groups
Vertical relations	Experimenting manager	Leadership

Professionalism

We have noted specialists in the traditional design. In complex situations we can also have professionals, e.g., doctors, lawyers, engineers, and scientists, all possessing similar characteristics. Professionals are committed more to their profession than to the firm for which they work. The work of a professional is organized around projects or cases, which are worked on by a group of relative strangers for a definite period of time. Project groups change continuously over time as the problem changes and are, therefore, temporary. Structure evolves based on expertise and skill, not on authority.

The implication of professionalism as a feature of a flexible design is that the technology is not hardware, but knowledge accessible by experts. While the professionals may design and use computer technologies that facilitate the basic work, often the basic work is the delivery of a service to a client. Developing the client who needs to play a role in delivering the service is critical. Unlike manufacturing, where the technological core can be buffered from the customers, delivery of service needs to combine the professional role with the client role. Thus, it is the service of the client that creates the need for a flexible design.

Learning groups. Learning groups originated since World War II. Founded by Chris Argyris and associates, they focus on small groups as an area to change and improve personal communication. The first phase, in the 1950s and '60s, was the development of laboratory training or T groups by the National Training Laboratory for small groups of managers (Argyris, 1962). In the late '60s and early '70s the focus was broadened to encompass team building in the whole firm (Argyris, 1970). Phase three, into the 1980s, emphasizes multilevel learning on particular kinds of problems for top executives (Argyris, 1982). A technology is associated with learning groups in all three phases. The learning group does not have a leader, but a facilitator who is an expert. The group members need to be relatively free of abnormal personal problems. The task of the group is to question basic assumptions of the group members about authority and rationality. It needs to cut through defensiveness, biases, and blinders of individuals to do this. Each member must operate through norms of openness, trust, and honesty, which are reinforced by the facilitator. The group members learn to act as coequal teachers and students in improving communication, creativity, and problem solving.

Experimenting manager. Research design is the technology used to assess the effect of a program, policy, or project. Campbell (1969) and his students have proposed that managers work with or act as research methodologists to design ways to evaluate the success of a project. When a situation is complex and one does not know what will work, the experimenting manager tries something and evaluates how well it works. Doing something is consistent with normal managerial behavior (Minzberg, 1973). Evaluating the effect of the decision using scientific methods is new to many managers.

Connolly (1977) focused on organizational conditions that promote and inhibit the use of the experimenting approach by managers. If potential negative information can spoil a career, the experimenting approach will be avoided. The organization needs to reward truth as much as performance.

Leadership. Much has been written on leadership, but there is little agreement about the role of a leader in highly complex situations in which there is uncertainty and disagreement. One view is that the leader does many things: defines problems, sets new goals, creates a new climate, presents an illusion, at least, that what was chaos is no more, and makes tough allocation decisions that cut budgets. Lee Iacocca of Chrysler appears to fit this mold—the right person in the right place at the right time (Fiedler, 1976). (See Chapter 7.)

An alternative view is that the leader must involve the organization members in a redesign of the organization. A review and audit must be done of the design features used and their effects. New features need to be considered in relation to other features. The leader energizes the organization to find a new organizational form. The head of Mitsubishi in Japan comes closest as an example (Pascale and Athos, 1981).

The strong leader in the right place generates many negative side effects that many may accept as necessary evils. The energetic leader avoids the side effects by drawing on the resources of the employees rather than finding employees expendable. In either case, the leader who understands the opportunities available in the traditional, informational, political, and flexible approaches is much likelier to perform well than the leader who understands little.

CONCLUSION

Portfolio. The designer has many choices to make and some questions to consider to help make the choices. Each of the four design approaches has four features. From this set the designer needs to select a portfolio of features that constitute the design. Here are considerations in the selection of a feature:

1. Is it appropriately responsive to the uncertainty in means-ends connections or disagreement about ends?

2. Does one need a permanent or temporary fix? For example, increasing slack is temporary, while a computer system is relatively permanent.

3. Does the feature fit well with other features from the same approach now being used? For example, does hierarchy fit the technology?

4. Does the feature fit well with features from other approaches? For example, does a group incentive scheme fit with assembly line technology?

The manager-designer needs to think of the firm or part of the firm as presented with a *distribution* of problems based on the actual or perceived uncertainty of means-ends relation or disagreement about ends. The design features allow the manager to respond to the distribution. As the distribution changes shape, the portfolio of design features may need to shift. Monitoring the distribution of problems and adjusting the features on the portfolio are the job of the manager-designer.

Implementation. The selection and implementation of a feature is a problem in organizational change. Problems in unfreezing, changing, and refreezing the firm can be extensive. See Edward Conlon, "Managing Organizational Change," Reading #8, to understand the difficulties in making any change.

REFERENCES

Allison, G. *Essence of Decision.* Boston: Little, Brown, 1971.

Argyris, C. *Interpersonal Competence and Organizational Effectiveness.* Homewood, Ill.: Irwin, 1962.

_____. *Intervention Theory and Method.* Reading, Mass.: Addison-Wesley, 1970.

_____. *Reasoning, Learning and Decisions.* New York: Wiley, 1982.

Atkinson, J. W. *An Introduction to Motivation.* New York: Van Nostrand, 1964.

Blau, P. W. *Exchange and Power in Social Life.* New York: Wiley, 1964.

Campbell, D. "Reforms as Experiments." *American Psychologist* (1969).

Chandler, A. *Strategy and Structure.* Garden City, N.Y.: Anchor, 1962.

Connolly, T. "Information Processing and Decision Making in Organizations." In *New Directions in Organizational Behavior,* Barry Staw and Gerald Salanick, eds. Chicago: St. Clair Press, 1977.

Fiedler, F. A. *A Theory of Leadership*. New York: McGraw-Hill, 1976.

Galbraith, J. *Designing Complex Organizations*. Reading, Mass.: Addison-Wesley, 1973.

Hackman, J. R., and Lawler, E. E. "Employee Reactions to Job Characteristics." *Journal of Applied Psychology* (1971):259–86.

House, R. J. "A Path Goal Theory of Leadership Effectiveness." *Administrative Sciences Quarterly* (1971):321–32.

Lawrence, P., and Lorsch, J. W. *Organization and Environment*. Homewood, Ill.: Irwin, 1969.

Leavitt, H. *Managerial Psychology*. Chicago: University of Chicago Press, 1978.

Locke, E. A. "Towards a Theory of Task Motivation and Incentives." *Organizational Behavior and Human Performance* (1968): 157–89.

March, J. "Model Bias in Social Action." *Review of Educational Research* 42 (1972): 413–29.

Milgram, S. "Behavioral Study of Obedience." *Journal of Abnormal and Social Psychology* 67 (1962):371–78.

Minzberg, H. *The Nature of Managerial Work*. New York: Harper and Row, 1973.

Pascale, R. T., and Athos, T. *The Art of Japanese Management*. New York: Simon & Schuster, 1981.

Pfeffer, J., and Salancik, G. *The External Control of Organizations*. Evanston, Ill.: Harper and Row, 1978.

Porter, E. H. "The Parable of the Spindle." *Harvard Business Review* (1962):58–66.

Porter, L. W., and Lawler, E. E. "Properties of Organization Structure in Relation to Job Attitudes." *Psychological Bulletin* (1965): 23–51.

Rapoport, A., and Chammah, A. *The Prisoner's Dilemma*. Ann Arbor: University of Michigan, 1965.

Roethlisberger, F. I., and Dickson, W. J. *Management and the Worker*. Cambridge, Mass.: Harvard University Press, 1939.

Simon, H. A. *The Sciences of the Artificial*. Cambridge, Mass.: NI Press, 1969.

Taylor, F. W. *Principles of Scientific Management*. New York: Harper, 1911.

Thompson, J. P. *Organizations in Action*. New York: McGraw-Hill, 1967.

_____, and Tuden, A. "Strategies, Structures, and Process of Organizational Decision." In J. D. Thompson et al., *Studies in Administration*. Pittsburgh: University of Pennsylvania Press, 1959.

Vroom, V., and Yetton, P. *Leadership and Decision Making*. Pittsburgh: University of Pennsylvania Press, 1973.

Weber, M. *The Theory of Social and Economic Organization*. New York: Oxford, 1947.

Weick, K. *The Social Psychology of Organizing*. Reading, Mass.: Addison-Wesley, 1969.

Wolf, G.; Ronan, W.; and Leatherwood, M. *Categorizing Work Management Systems*. Working paper, University of Arizona, Department of Management, 1982.

Woodward, J. *Industrial Organization Theory and Practice*. London: Oxford, 1965.

Zahn, L., and Wolf, G. "Leadership and the Art of Cycle Maintenance." *Organizational Behavior and Human Performance* (1981): 26–49.

Job Design and Redesign

Daniel J. Brass

Pennsylvania State University

Many of the jobs currently found in organizations are poorly designed. From the individual worker's point of view, such jobs are unsatisfactory for various reasons: they lack challenge, demand less skill than the individual offers, allow little opportunity for learning and growth, are excessively repetitious, and so on. From the organization's point of view, the costs of ill-designed jobs show up in poor product quality, employee dissatisfaction, absenteeism, tardiness and turnover, high grievance rates, and even direct sabotage. Badly designed jobs, then, are not just inhumane: they lead directly to low productivity and profitability.

Daniel Brass reviews briefly the history of job design from the "scientific management" of the early twentieth century to the present day. The major focus is on the techniques that have been developed only in the past few years. These move beyond ideas of "job enrichment," which emerged during the 1960s, and are now approaching the point where the job designer can move with some confidence in taking a new or existing job and redesigning it so as to be better both for the individual employee and for the organization. The concepts, tools, and procedures available to the job designer are reviewed, and the procedure is illustrated by means of a concrete example. The last part looks at the evidence now available for the effectiveness of the new techniques, and assesses the likely future prospects of this area of work.

During the Great Depression of the 1930s, Mrs. Clare Brass, known for miles around as "Grandma" Brass, began selling her homemade pies to friends and neighbors to make up for the money Grandpa Brass was losing in the stock market. Using her own secret recipe, which had been handed down through several generations but never written down, her pies were soon in great demand. Grandma Brass had to set up a larger kitchen in the old shed behind the house and put her grandchildren to work.

Although the pie making involved several distinct tasks—mixing the dough, rolling out the crusts, mixing the fillings, filling the pans, baking—the coordination of these activities presented no problem. Grandma Brass did them all herself, and the grandchildren ran errands to the store for ingredients or made deliveries around town. Although the price of the pies was rather high, Grandma Brass used only the finest ingredients, and took great pride in establishing a reputation as the finest pie maker in the state. When she won a blue ribbon at the World's Fair, orders began arriving from all over the country.

Orders exceeded production capacity, so Grandma Brass hired her oldest grandson, Dan, who was eager to learn the business. The work was then divided up; Dan was allowed to mix the ingredients and watch the ovens. This required some coordination, but, with only the two of them, they simply communicated informally. But even the two of them working together could not keep up with the demand, and soon five new assistants were hired. When two more assistants were hired, coordination problems began to arise, and Dan began spending more of his time supervising and training.

Over the years, the Homemade Pie business continued to grow. More workers were hired. To facilitate training, each worker was assigned a small specialized part of the pie baking. More

attention had to be given to coordination, and Dan soon began writing down everything his grandma had taught him. Standardized procedures were developed and written down to insure that all the pies were made the same, and to make the coordination of all the specialized tasks easier.

In 1972, a corporation was formed, Pies, Inc., with Dan as president and chairman of the board. Dan had a vision of a Grandma Brass Homemade Pie as a pie that everyone could afford, a pie that would be readily available in every grocery store in the country. To realize this dream, work analysts and industrial engineers were hired along with architects to design a modern efficient pie-making factory. The factory, completed two years ago, incorporates all the most modern technology and is considered by many engineers to be one of the most efficiently designed production systems in the country. With all these changes in production, Dan expected to realize even higher profits even though the retail price of the pies was much lower.

However, the first two years of operation of the factory did not result in the high rate of production, or profits, expected. The factory layout appears to be technologically sound; however, the workers (many of them college students) do not seem to be motivated to do a good job. They seem to be alienated from their work; many of them constantly complain, and several instances of sabotage have occurred. Many grocery stores have discontinued their orders due to production mistakes; apple pies in boxes marked "cherry," pies with a crust missing, or no filling. In addition, the company has had major problems with turnover of workers and high absenteeism rates, not to mention tardiness.

Dan, under pressure from stockholders, has begun an intensive investigation of the problems. Results of a wage analysis show that the workers are receiving above-average wages, and the medical coverage and other fringe benefits are the best in the area. Incentive plans, whereby the workers earn additional money for producing more than the standard number of pies, were instituted after the first year of operation. This increased production slightly, but the quality of the pies continued to decrease, and absenteeism and turnover have continued to rise.

A job analysis indicates thirty-two different production jobs in five basic departments: (1) dough making, (2) crust, (3) filling, (4) baking, and (5) boxing. These departments are the result of attempts to specialize jobs along functional lines. The procedures for making the pies have been scientifically analyzed and broken down into their smallest component parts. Each worker performs only one small part of the overall process. Time and motion studies have resulted in a highly standardized procedure for performing each task, and the equipment and machinery have been designed to prevent any deviations from the prescribed methods. This high degree of specialization and standardization has helped defer the cost of training new employees; any job can be taught to a new worker or substitute in a matter of hours. This has been particularly important with the high turnover and absenteeism rates.

In the dough department, four workers control machines that combine the flour, salt, shortening, and water, in that order. Another worker handles a machine which mixes the ingredients. Other workers divide the mixed dough into patties, the "weighers" make sure each pattie is exactly 10 ounces, and other workers place the patties on a conveyor belt that transports the dough to the crust department.

In the crust department, the lower crust workers roll out the patties as they go by on the conveyor belt. Every

other dough pattie is rolled out by an upper crust worker. Still other members of the crust department are responsible for placing pie pans on the belt, one pan for every two rolled-out dough patties that go by on the belt. A select few "panners" are responsible for placing one of the dough patties in the pans—the lower crust of the pie.

About half of the workers in the filling department mix the ingredients, while the other half ladle the mixtures into the lower crust of the pies as they go by on the conveyor belt. Both the "mixers" and the "fillers" are highly specialized; each worker handles only one particular filling. Thus, there are "apple fillers," "lemon mixers," "blueberry fillers," etc. A good filler can easily fill 3,500 pies a day.

The bakers no longer do any actual baking. They simply place the second rolled-out dough pattie on top of the filling, forming the upper crust. Other workers in the baking department must perform the task of pressing an initial (A for apple, B for blueberry, etc.) into the upper crust without squashing the filling, before the belt carries the pies into large ovens.

When the pies come out the other side of the ovens, they are cooled down as they go through the "cooling room." They are then ready to be boxed. The boxers simply note the initial on the pie and place it in the appropriately marked box.

In addition to these production jobs, each department has a group of quality control personnel. They are responsible for inspecting the product after each stage, and removing any "errors." To catch all the mistakes, the number of quality control inspectors has steadily increased during the first two years of operation. They now comprise almost 20 percent of the work force.

Many of the supervisors are work analysts and industrial engineers—

specialists in seeing that the workers perform their duties in the prescribed manner. They are responsible for writing detailed manuals describing the specific motions to be performed in completing each job. Their engineering backgrounds are also extremely helpful in correcting malfunctions in the machinery and the conveyor belts. Some of the workers' attempts to sabotage or "shut down the line" have been averted because of the supervisors' expertise.

The supervisors are almost unanimous in their opinion that the type of workers being hired is the cause of the problems. They have indicated to Dan that college students these days are lazy, unwilling to accept responsibility, and untrustworthy. They come to work late, pay little attention to what they are doing, watch the clock all day, and want to leave early. The supervisors believe that some of the older workers are union organizers trying to unionize the plant.

The supervisors have recommended that they be allowed to supervise the workers more closely (this would require hiring some additional supervisors), and that the workers who can't keep up with the belt be fired. As one supervisor said, "What these young kids need is a good kick in the pants! Then maybe they'll start working and stop complaining. They say the work is boring and the belt moves too fast, but they still have time enough to think up ways to sabotage it. They ought to be happy that they have jobs."

This example illustrates how an organization and individual jobs might be designed using a traditional job engineering approach. The scenario might have sounded familiar to you; you may have worked in an organization with a similar design, and your own job activities and responsibilities may have been similar to those described. Many organizations today use such an approach. In fact, if you were asked to redesign the pie-making operation, you might find it difficult to suggest an alternative plan. However, there are a variety of different ways in which jobs might be designed. And, while there is almost unanimous agreement that the way in which jobs are designed is of great importance to organizations and workers, there is little agreement on the best way to design jobs. In fact, there may be no "best" way.

We will focus on various theories and methods for the design of jobs. As noted, the design in the pie-making example follows traditional job-engineering methods. As you read and consider other approaches, take time to apply them to the pie-making example—redesign the pie-making jobs and evaluate the advantages and disadvantages of each approach.

TRADITIONAL JOB ENGINEERING

The foundations of traditional job engineering can be found in the writings of such men as Adam Smith (Smith, 1910) and Frederick Taylor (Taylor, 1911). The approach focused on designing jobs to achieve maximum efficiency of motion in the least amount of time. Such analyses later became known as "time and motion" studies.

Perhaps the most important principles of job engineering concern the division of labor and standardization of the work process. In a classic example, Smith described how the task of making pins could be broken down into eighteen distinct subtasks: eighteen workers, each doing only one distinct subtask, can produce at a much greater rate than when each of the eighteen men performs the entire task of making a pin. Soon, the principle of division of labor became a cornerstone of job engineering. In essence, the principle states that the greatest efficiency of production can be achieved when the overall organizational task is divided so that each worker performs one small sub-task or specialized job.

Frederick Taylor, sometimes called the father of time and motion studies, was among the earliest writers to advocate standardization of the work process. Taylor's approach consisted of scientifically analyzing a job to determine the one best way—most efficient in terms of time and motion—to perform the task. Once this method of performing the task was determined, it became standard operating procedure. That is, all workers performing the same task did it in exactly the same manner. In another classic example, Taylor described the efficiency of scientific analysis and standardization. A pig-iron worker named Schmidt, following Taylor's specifications, was able to improve his production from 12½ tons per day to 47½ tons per day.

The two principles seemed to go hand in hand, and today one readily associates a highly specialized, standardized job with traditional job engineering. Perhaps the overwhelming majority of production jobs today are designed following these principles, and several advantages have been identified in connection with using this traditional job engineering approach. Specialized, standardized jobs:

1. Allow workers to learn the job quickly, thereby decreasing training costs

2. Allow workers quickly to become experts at performing the same sub-task over and over

3. Make hiring easier, since almost anyone can quickly learn the simplified, standardized procedures for performing the job

4. Require less supervision because procedures are preprogrammed

5. Allow for the maximum use of equipment and machinery because, when a worker performs a variety of tasks, equipment involved in one task lies idle when the worker is performing other tasks

6. Ensure that the results of production —the parts—are uniform and interchangeable. One might also add that the workers, performing the same subtask, are also uniform and interchangeable, thus minimizing the organization's dependency on the idiosyncracies of individual workers.

Some of the possible disadvantages of this traditional job engineering approach are described in the pie-making example. Workers may become dissatisfied with performing the same small, routinized task over and over. Specialized, standardized jobs become boring. Workers make mistakes. They are not involved in their work or challenged by it. There is no sense of achievement in performing the task well. Product quality decreases while absenteeism and turnover increase.

A Crisis In Job Design?

Are we to assume that such problems automatically result from traditional job engineering? Are such problems widespread today? Are we being asked to give up efficiency in order to have happier workers? Questions such as these have been asked by many managers and researchers, and the answers have been the subject of numerous debates.

On the one hand, an abundance of evidence suggests that there *is* a crisis. The General Motors' Vega plant at Lordstown, Ohio, has been frequently singled out as the ultimate of modern job engineering. The average task took 36 seconds to complete, and each worker repeated his or her assigned task almost one hundred times per hour. But the plant was plagued with strikes and sabotage. Paint was scratched, upholstery cut, and tools welded into internal compartments to cause unidentifiable rattles. Absenteeism rates reached 20 percent on Mondays and Fridays, and the turnover rate approached 25 percent. The organization was forced to hire regular, full-time workers, whose job it was to fill in for absentee workers.

And there is evidence to suggest that the problem in job design is not restricted to blue-collar, assembly line workers. Seashore and Barnowe (1972) have suggested that collar color doesn't count. An American Management Association survey reported in the *Wall Street Journal*, 29 May 1973, found 52 percent of 2,821 executives questioned were dissatisfied with their work. Even scientists and engineers may not be immune from specialized, standardized work. Engineers often work in a large drafting room and may be subject to factory-like rules and regulations. Recently, a research chemist, working for a major pharmaceutical company, indicated that everyone was so *specialized* that he only handled one small aspect of each research project. While the projects changed, he did pretty much the same thing over and over.

Work in America (1973), a report from U.S. Department of Health, Education, and Welfare, summarized the results of their investigation:

> Significant numbers of American workers are dissatisfied with the quality of their working lives. Dull, repetitive, seemingly meaningless tasks, offering little challenge or autonomy, are causing discontent among workers at all occupational levels. . . . The redesign of jobs is the keystone of this report.

On the other hand, many have criticized behavioral scientists and the popular media for creating a crisis that, according to them, does not exist (Gainor, 1975; Fein, 1973). Siassi, Crocetti and Spiro (1974) found that automobile workers were not dissatisfied or bored with their work. Analysis of trends from 1958 to 1973 by the Survey Research Center of the University of Michigan would tend to support this "no crisis" position. These analyses show no significant decline in job satisfaction, and that more than 80 percent of the work force are satisfied with their jobs (Quinn, Stains, and McCullogh, 1974).

Obviously, the degree to which a crisis in job design exists is debatable. Regardless of the conflicting survey results and opinions, many major corporations (AT&T, Texas Instruments, ICI, Volvo, Polaroid, General Foods, Dow Chemical) have undertaken projects to redesign jobs. Saab has promoted their redesign efforts through advertisements that state, "Bored people build bad cars. That's why we're doing away with the assembly line" (Kossen, 1978).

REDESIGNING JOBS

Job Enlargement and Job Rotation

Both job enlargement and job rotation are redesign strategies that focus on adding variety to the job to reduce boredom. In job enlargement, the job of a worker is enlarged by assigning the worker several tasks rather than one. For example, instead of just installing the right rear tire mount, an auto worker might also be responsible for installation of the rear bumper and tail lights. The object is to add more tasks so that the job becomes more interesting. In job rotation, workers rotate, or trade off, among several different tasks. For example, the auto worker may work on tire mounts for an hour, then rotate to bumpers for an hour, and then to tail lights for another hour.

Both job enlargement and job rotation have been supported by research in activation theory. Activation theory is based on neuropsychological research that suggests that performance is poor when stimulus inputs to the brain are low. An optimum level of performance is achieved when these sensory inputs are neither extremely low nor extremely high (Scott, 1966).

Although these redesign strategies are common in many manufacturing plants, they are sometimes criticized because they are seen as simply adding more routine, boring tasks to the job. Critics note that the enlarged job may soon become just as boring and monotonous as the previously nonenlarged (or rotated) task. For example, at IBM the job of wiring 2,331 small wires within a calculator panel was formerly done by several employees. One connected all the black wires, another all green, another all yellow, etc. The panel moved from person to person on an assembly line. Those jobs were reassigned so that each employee now wires a whole panel, all 2,331 wires (Wharton, 1954).

A more successful attempt at job enlargement was undertaken at Maytag (Kilbridge, 1960). Before the redesign, the assembly of a washing machine water pump, which involved twenty-seven different parts and a variety of tools and operations, was performed by six different workers. The company reported decreased labor costs per pump when they did away with the six-person line and each worker assembled an entire pump.

Job Enrichment—Individual Approaches

Herzberg's OJE. One of the first approaches to "enriching" jobs was based on the dual-factor theory and research of Frederick Herzberg (1968). Herzberg suggested that a worker's satisfaction with his or her job was the result of two, independent sets of factors. The first set, "hygiene factors," included salary, company policy, working conditions, supervision, and interpersonal relations. According to Herzberg, these factors were primarily related to the worker not being dissatisfied with his or her job. They would not, however, lead to a worker being involved in the work or motivated to do a good job.

The second set of factors, which became known as "motivators," included the work itself, recognition, achievement, advancement, and responsibility. Herzberg argued that jobs must be redesigned or "enriched" so that workers had opportunities for responsibility, recognition, and meaningful work. Adding these "motivators" to a job would result in increased motivation on the worker's part. Herzberg now prefers to refer to this redesign strategy as "orthodox job enrichment" (OJE) (1974). Although the dual-factor theory has received severe criticism, the success of applications of OJE have been widely publicized (Paul, Robertson, and Herzberg, 1969; Ford, 1973), and Herzberg is often credited with initiating attention to the motivating potential of the design of jobs.

The Hackman-Oldham Model. Perhaps the most complete and well-researched model of job redesign is that developed by Hackman and Oldham (1980), presented in Figure 1. Building on the previous work of Turner and Lawrence

Figure 1.   The Hackman-Oldham Model

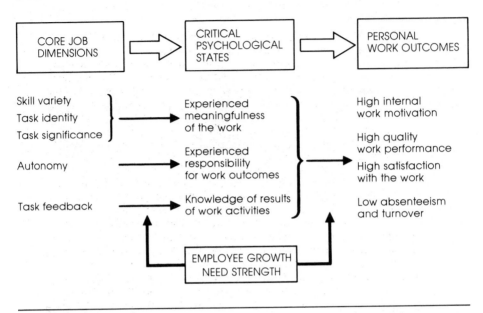

From: J. R. Hackman and G. R. Oldham, "Development of the Job Diagnostic Survey," *Journal of Applied Psychology*, 1975, 60, p. 161.

(1965) and Hackman and Lawler (1971), Hackman and Oldham have identified five core job dimensions:

1. **Skill variety:** The degree to which a job requires a variety of the individual's different skills and talents in carrying out the work activities. Note that this job dimension does not merely involve doing a number of different activities, but stresses that the activities involve a variety of skills and talents.

2. **Task identity:** The degree to which an individual's job requires the completion of a "whole" and identifiable work process; completing the whole job rather than just performing bits and pieces or only one small part.

3. **Task significance:** The degree to which the individual's job has a sub-

stantial impact on the lives and work of other persons within or outside the organization.

4. **Autonomy:** The degree to which the individual's job provides independence and discretion in scheduling the work and in the procedures for carrying it out.

5. **Task feedback:** The degree to which an individual receives clear information concerning his or her work performance directly from doing the task itself. Note that this core job dimension stresses feedback obtained from the actual performance of the job, rather than feedback provided by supervisors, quality control inspectors, or co-workers.

Any job can be described as having high or low degrees of each of these five core job dimensions. According to the model in Figure 1, high degrees of these core dimensions will result in a worker experiencing certain critical psychological states. A worker will experience a feeling of meaningfulness when his or her job is high on skill variety, task identity, and task significance. When a good deal of autonomy is present, a worker will feel responsible for the outcomes of his or her work. Task feedback leads to a knowledge of the results of his or her efforts.

As with Herzberg's OJE, the Hackman-Oldham approach attempts to create jobs that are inherently motivating to workers. Hackman and Oldham refer to this personal outcome as internal work motivation (see Figure 1), which occurs when an individual's feelings are closely tied to how well he or she performs on the job. Good performance leads to good feelings and self-rewards, which act as an incentive to continue performing well. Poor performance is accompanied by bad feelings and increased effort to perform better.

For workers to be highly internally motivated, the three psychological states must be present. First, if the worker does not have knowledge of the results of his or her work, the worker has no basis for feeling good or bad. Second, if the worker feels that the quality of the work is dependent on some external factor such as the machinery, the procedure manual, the boss, or other workers, he or she will not feel personally responsible for work, whether it is good or bad. Finally, even if the worker has sole responsibility for the job and has ample information about his or her performance, the work must also be meaningful. If the work seems unimportant or makes little difference, it is not likely that internal motivation will result. In other words, workers experience positive feelings

and motivation toward their work when they are aware (knowledge of results) that they are personally responsible (experienced responsibility) for performing well on a job that they care about (experienced meaningfulness). A job lacking any of the three (meaningfulness, responsibility, or knowledge of results) can be viewed as incomplete and unlikely to produce the desired outcomes.

According to the Hackman-Oldham model, other outcomes, in addition to high internal work motivation, are also likely to occur when the critical psychological states are present. A great deal of accumulated research has consistently shown that workers who describe their jobs as high on the core job dimensions also report high levels of satisfaction with their work (Hackman and Oldham, 1980; Dunham, 1979). That is, they respond positively to such questions as, "Generally speaking, how satisfied are you with your job?" (Hackman and Oldham, 1975). Other specific facets of satisfaction, e.g., satisfaction with pay, supervisors, company policy, or co-workers, are not included in the model. This is because a redesign effort, following this model, focuses on the relationship between the worker and his or her job. It would not be expected that satisfaction with pay, for example, would change following a redesign effort.

High *quality* work performance is also seen as a positive outcome resulting from enriched work (see Figure 1). The rationale for including quality work performance is that it will naturally result from high internal work motivation. When a person feels good about performing well, and bad when performing poorly, he or she will naturally strive to do high quality work. The *quantity* of work performance is not necessarily expected to increase, particularly if producing in great numbers or at high speeds makes it necessary to reduce the quality of performance. When doing research in an organization, it is often difficult to obtain concrete measures of job quality or quantity. Researchers may be forced to rely on general ratings made by supervisors, or to report only satisfaction and internal motivation measures. Presently, the results concerning performance and enriched jobs are mixed.

As with performance measures, it is often difficult to obtain absenteeism and turnover measures, or to sort out legitimate absences due to illness from absenteeism or turnover that is the result of dissatisfaction with the actual work. Although it might logically follow that increased satisfaction with the work and high internal motivation would lead to a decrease in absenteeism or turnover, current research results are inconclusive. Some studies have shown that low levels of the core job dimensions are associated with high absenteeism, although one study found that absenteeism increased following the redesign of jobs (Hackman, Pearce, and Wolfe, 1978).

Individual differences. Hackman and Oldham have been careful not to suggest that job enrichment, following their model, is appropriate for every worker in every organization. People are different; some workers may prefer to have a challenging, enriched job, others may not. The model suggests that the *growth need strength* (GNS) of each employee may be the determining factor. By growth need strength is meant the degree to which an individual has a high need or desire for growth, personal accomplishment, and learning. The model suggests that GNS will moderate the relationship between the nature of the work and the outcomes noted. Workers with high GNS will respond more positively (higher internal work motivation and satisfaction with the work) than will workers with low GNS, who may be more concerned with the amount of pay they receive, job security, or the other people they work with. Having a job with a great deal of skill variety, autonomy, feedback, etc., may make little difference to low GNS workers.

The research results concerning GNS as a moderator have not always been conclusive. Some research has shown a positive relationship between the core job dimensions and work satisfaction without attempting to account for individual differences. Other research, incorporating the GNS consideration, has found a more positive response for high GNS individuals than for low GNS individuals. Based on the current state of the research, it is probably reasonable to expect that, on the whole, workers will respond from neutral to positive to an enriched job (Dunham, 1979).

Assessing the Need for Redesign

Assume that you are the manager in the pie-making plant. You are asked for your opinion as to the cause of the problems. As you first read through the case you may already have made a diagnosis or assessment. Chances are that your intuitive diagnosis did not focus on the design of the jobs. Research has shown that we often focus on the characteristics of the *person* in attributing cause of behavior, and give insufficient attention to the characteristics of the *situation* (Jones and Nisbett, 1971). For example, the supervisors in the case believe that the cause of the problems is the type of workers being hired.

Rather than relying on feelings or hunches, we need some systematic way to diagnose the situation—in this case, to determine if the cause of the problems involves the design of the jobs. One systematic way of assessing the possible need for job design is the use of a questionnaire like the *Job Diagnostic Survey* (JDS), which was constructed by Hackman and Oldham to measure the job characteristics included in their model and the outcomes that may result from job redesign (Hackman and Oldham, 1980).

Two forms of the JDS are available. The longer form includes questions that tap the critical psychological states noted in the model. Because these psychological states are, by definition, internal to persons and not directly changeable, most researchers and practitioners use the shorter form. The shorter form of the JDS focuses relatively more attention on the more objective core job dimensions. Some examples of these questionnaire items, taken directly from the JDS, are included in Figure 2. Before reading further, you may want to examine these questions and rate the jobs of the workers in the pie-making case. You may also want to rate a job that you have had in the past, e.g., a summer job, or the job that you may hold presently.

The five questions in Figure 2 represent only a small subset of the questions on the JDS used to measure skill variety, task identity, task significance, autonomy, and feedback from the job. Other questions, used to measure the same dimensions but stated slightly differently, are also included. The scores on items used to measure the same dimension are averaged together to improve the reliability of the responses. Because the ratings on all questionnaire items are always subject to individual biases, the best way of assessing the core job dimensions is to obtain ratings of the same job from several different sources. For

example, the person performing the job, the immediate supervisor of that person, and a disinterested observer frequently will each make independent ratings of that person's job. These three independent ratings are combined to provide a more accurate assessment of the job dimensions.

Using the scores for each job dimension (on a scale from 1 to 7), an overall measure of job enrichment, the motivating potential score (MPS), can be calculated according to the following formula:

$$\text{MPS} = \frac{[(\text{skill variety} + \text{task identity} + \text{task significance})/3] \times \text{autonomy}}{\times \text{task feedback}}$$

Note that the formula reflects the model. Skill variety, task identity, and task significance are added together to form the meaningfulness construct. A high score on one of the three can compensate for a low score on one of the other two dimensions. However, if autonomy or task feedback is missing (or if the three dimensions composing meaningfulness are all missing), the MPS score would be zero, regardless of the other scores, because the formula is multiplicative.

The JDS has been administered to a wide variety of job holders. Recently, Oldham, Hackman, and Stepina (1979) have published national averages based on a sample of jobs (6,930 employees in fifty-six different organizations). Figure 3 shows a profile for the core job dimensions both for the national average and for a subset of professionals, which includes scientists and engineers. You may want to develop your own profile for a past summer job, or for one of the jobs in the pie-making case.

Using the scales from the JDS (from a low of 1 to a high of 7), the lowest possible MPS would be 1 and the highest possible score would be 343 (7 cubed). The lowest MPS for an actual job observed

Figure 2. Questionnaire Items from the Job Diagnostic Survey (JDS)

Please describe your job as objectively as you can.

1. **To what extent does your job involve doing a "whole" and identifiable piece of work?** That is, is the job a complete piece of work that has an obvious beginning and end? Or is it only a small part of the overall piece of work, which is finished by other people or by automatic machines?

1 ———— 2 ———— 3 ———— 4 ———— 5 ———— 6 ———— 7

My job is only a tiny part of the overall piece of work; the results of my activities cannot be seen in the final product or service.	My job is a moderate-sized "chunk" of the overall piece of work; my own contribution can be seen in the final outcome.	My job involves doing the whole piece of work, from start to finish; the results of my activities are easily seen in the final product or service.

2. **How much variety is there in your job?** That is, to what extent does the job require you to do many different things at work, using a variety of your skills and talents?

1 ———— 2 ———— 3 ———— 4 ———— 5 ———— 6 ———— 7

Very little; the job requires me to do the same routine things over and over again.	Moderate variety.	Very much; the job requires me to do many different things, using a number of different skills and talents.

3. **In general, how significant or important is your job?** That is, are the results of your work likely to significantly affect the lives or well-being of other people?

1 ———— 2 ———— 3 ———— 4 ———— 5 ———— 6 ———— 7

Not very significant; the outcomes of my work are **not** likely to have important effects on other people.	Moderately significant.	Highly significant; the outcomes of my work can affect other people in very important ways.

4. **How much autonomy is there in your job?** That is, to what extent does your job permit you to decide **on your own** how to go about doing the work?

1 ———— 2 ———— 3 ———— 4 ———— 5 ———— 6 ———— 7

Very little; the job gives me almost no personal say about how and when the work is done.	Moderate autonomy; many things are standardized and not under my control, but I can make some decisions about the work.	Very much; the job gives me almost complete responsibility for deciding how and when the work is done.

5. **To what extent does doing the job itself provide you with information about your performance?** That is, does the actual work itself provide clues about how well you are doing—aside from any feedback co-workers or supervisors may provide?

1 ———— 2 ———— 3 ———— 4 ———— 5 ———— 6 ———— 7

Very little; the job itself is set up so I could work forever without finding out how well I am doing.	Moderately; sometimes doing the job provides feedback to me; sometimes it does not.	Very much; the job is set up so that I get almost constant feedback as I work about how well I am doing.

Figure 3. Average Scores on Core Job Dimensions

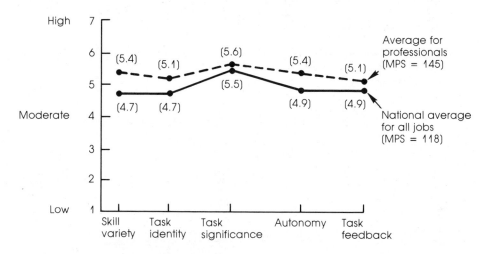

and reported by Hackman and Oldham was 7 for the job of typist in an overflow typing pool. The typists in this particular pool simply waited at their typewriters until one of the regular typing pools became overloaded. Hackman and Oldham also report observing an autonomous organizational development consultant with an MPS of over 300. As Figure 3 indicates, the national average MPS is around 118, while the average for professional jobs is 145.

Implementing principles. Following a systematic analysis of jobs and a determination that job redesign may be required, an organization may institute a change program aimed at improving MPS. Because the critical psychological states are not directly accessible to manipulation, most such efforts have concentrated on the core job dimensions. Hackman et al. (1975) have suggested some implementing principles that may be useful in a wide variety of settings. Figure 4 summarizes the steps and the particular job core dimensions which may be affected.

Combining tasks. This principle is similar to job enlargement in that it involves combining several tasks to create larger whole tasks for individual workers. Assigning a larger whole task to a worker should increase task identity, and the assumption is made that performing several tasks will require more skill variety than performing one small task.

Forming natural work units. A similar approach to increasing task identity is to group smaller, fractionated tasks together into meaningful, natural jobs to be assigned to individuals. What is required is some logical, intuitive basis for grouping the tasks. For example, a typist might be assigned all the work from a particular department, or all the correspondence for one geographical area. The emphasis is on a "natural" work unit, one that makes sense to the worker and with which he or she can identify. This increases the individual's "ownership" of the work and thus increases task identity and task significance.

Establishing worker-client relationships. In connection with the above two principles, natural work units can often be formed around the clients or receivers of the product or services.

Figure 4. Implementing Principles and Possible Effects on Core Job Dimensions. Adapted in part from: J. R. Hackman, G. R. Oldham, R. Janson, and K. Purdy, "A New Strategy for Job Enrichment," **California Management Review**, Summer 1975, p. 62.

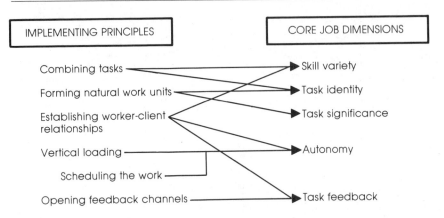

Establishing worker-client relationships involves identifying the client, determining the most direct contact possible between the worker and the client, and establishing a system whereby the worker can receive evaluative feedback from the client. One example of this approach was applied in a theme amusement park. Customers to the park are given "Good Job" slips when they enter the park. When the customer sees a worker working hard, or receives particularly courteous service or help from an employee, the customer can award the worker a "Good Job" slip.

When workers have direct relationships with clients of their work, three core job dimensions may increase. Direct feedback from customers may increase task feedback. Skill variety may increase because client relationships involve the use of interpersonal skills (establishing relationships is now part of the job). Autonomy may also increase because workers have personal responsibility for deciding how to handle clients.

Vertical loading. This principle involves redesigning the job so as to include aspects that are normally performed by persons vertically higher in the organization hierarchy. For example, this may involve allowing employees to set their own performance goals, do their own quality control inspections, handle exceptional cases or problems which are normally referred upward to supervisors, or make decisions about how and when to do the work. Vertical loading may involve an analysis of the job functions of the immediate supervisor of an employee to determine which functions might easily be handled by the employee rather than the supervisor. Vertical loading should have a major effect on increasing autonomy.

Scheduling the work. A particular form of vertical loading allows employees to schedule when they are going to work. This was particularly successful in a mental health institution where the staff had to be rotated through shifts to provide adequate staffing twenty-four hours a day, seven days a week. The monthly scheduling of the staff had been a major responsibility of a high-level administrator, who personally considered it a major headache. Employees were continually asking the administrator for special schedules to accommodate personal business and activities, and, after the monthly schedule was posted, the administrator was the recipient of numerous complaints. The administrator retired, and the next month's schedule was posted with blank spaces next to each of the staff members' names. Each member was responsible for scheduling his or her own work hours. The staff preferred this system and it has continued without problems for more than two years.

Another form of self-scheduling, called "flextime," is now being used by nearly 1,000 U.S. companies and involves over 300,000 employees (Stein, Cohen, and Gadon, 1976). Flextime allows workers to set their own working hours within certain limits agreeable to the employer. Usually there is a core period of time, from 9:30 A.M. to 3:00 P.M., when everyone is expected to work. Arrival and departure times, however, are flexible, perhaps from 7:00 to 9:30 A.M. and from 3:00 to 7:00 P.M. Workers may also be allowed to schedule the length and starting times for breaks and lunch periods, as long as their total working time adds up to the required number of hours. Such corporations as John Hancock, Smith Kline, and Hewlett-Packard have reported enthusiastic employee response to such programs.

Opening feedback channels. This approach emphasizes providing employees with direct, immediate, and regular feedback about their performance. This may involve employees keeping personal performance charts, the use of sophisticated equipment such as computers to print out performance data, allowing workers to perform their own quality control inspections, or, as previously noted, establishing direct client relationships. Such methods should increase task feedback.

Job Enrichment—Group Approaches

The Hackman-Oldham model, described above, is designed primarily to apply to individual workers performing jobs that are more or less independent of each other. Instances may arise when workers are highly interdependent or when the "whole" task is too complex to be assigned to one individual. In such cases, a group approach to job redesign may be more appropriate than an individual approach. Several approaches to group job design have been offered under the labels of socio-technical systems (see Lynn Markus, "Socio-Technical Systems," Reading #1), autonomous work groups, and quality of work life projects. Much of the writing in this area consists of chronological reports of actual job redesign projects, rather than any systematic model or framework such as that offered by Hackman and Oldham for individual job enrichment (Rice, 1958; Trist et al., 1963; Susman, 1976; Davis and Taylor, 1979; Cummings and Srivastva, 1977).

However, many similarities across group redesign projects exist, and many overlaps with the individual approach are noted. Most projects center around the creation of self-managing or autonomous work groups. The autonomy and responsibility of the group are stressed, but most group approaches also include assigning the group a whole, meaningful task and designing direct feedback systems. In other words, the core job dimensions and the critical psychological states may be equally relevant to both the individual and group redesign approaches.

The key to a group job redesign approach may be that the individual can satisfy certain needs (experience meaningfulness, for example) through membership in a group. Although the individual may not be able to complete the entire job on his own, the group of which he is a member can complete the task and the individual members may experience the same feelings of closure. Likewise, Katz and Kahn (1966) note that not every person need make all the decisions about his work in order to experience a feeling of autonomy. Moreover, the group decision-making approach has the advantage of not overwhelming the individual with responsibility he or she is unprepared to accept.

In addition to establishing responsibility for outcomes of meaningful work, a group job redesign effort requires that attention be given to establishing satisfactory interpersonal relationships among group members. Satisfactory relationships among group members, according to several group redesign researchers, involves more than friendship among members (Rice, 1958; Trist et al., 1963; Bucklow, 1972; Engelstad, 1972). The critical variable may be the degree of mutual support among members in performing the group task. The idea is one of *task support*—members of the work group cooperate with one another in achieving the task requirements. Each group member is willing and ready to pitch in to help get the job done. Everyone is available to help when problems arise.

There may be a high correlation between task support and mutual friendship within the group, but it is suggested that support in performing the group task is the key variable in establishing satisfactory group relationships. As Rice notes, when the value attached to group membership becomes an end in itself, the group and their social activities may become more important than the task. When this happens, task performance suffers, and the result may be unsatisfactory relationships among members (Rice, 1958).

Building upon the identified core dimensions of individual motivating tasks, while focusing upon the group as the unit of analysis, the following elements are suggested as characteristics of a motivating group task:

1. **Skill variety.** The degree to which the successful completion of the group task involves the use of a variety of skills and talents of the group members

2. **Task identity.** The degree to which the group task is a whole and meaningful job, rather than just a minute piece of the overall organizational task

3. **Task significance.** The extent to which the completion of the group task has an important impact on others, including persons within and outside the group and the organization

4. **Autonomy.** The degree to which the group, in and of itself, has discretion and freedom in deciding how they will carry out the work (pace, scheduling, procedures, etc.)

5. **Task feedback.** The extent to which the group receives direct and reliable information concerning its performance

6. **Task support.** The degree to which group members actively support and cooperate with one another in completion of the group task.

For individuals to experience meaningfulness, responsibility, and knowledge of results obtained as a result of the above dimensions, they must feel as if they are included in, or belong to, and are viable members of the group. That is, if an individual worker does not feel as if he or she is a member of the group, it is unlikely that the worker will experience the critical psychological states even when the group task is designed to increase autonomy, task identity, feedback, etc. Therefore, feelings of belonging may be considered a critical psychological state in the group redesign process. This psychological state is referred to as "experienced membership."

It is likely that task support will be instrumental in achieving experienced membership. That is, when co-workers are active in their support of a worker, when they are ready to pitch in and help when problems arise, the worker has ample evidence that he or she has been included in the work group. If co-workers are nonsupportive and unwilling to help, if a worker is told to solve his or her own problems and not to expect help or assistance from others, it is unlikely that the worker will feel as if he or she is a member of a cooperating, interdependent work group. Figure 5 summarizes the core dimensions and psychological states for group task redesign.

Implementing Group Redesign

The model of group redesign shown in Figure 5 has not been systematically tested. However, many descriptions of actual group redesign projects are available for analysis. The following implementing principles represent a summary, abstraction, and labeling of similar steps common to many group redesign projects. In addition, the suggested effects of these principles are related to the model suggested in Figure 5.

In general, most group task redesign projects have the following prescription for the formation of autonomous or self-managing work groups:

Employees who perform interdependent tasks are grouped into a common work unit that is relatively differentiated from other work units. The group is *given responsibility for the work process and provided feedback and rewards for group performance.*

Designating a whole task. Tasks that constitute a meaningful whole for the workers are put together. Davis (1957) has suggested that this include all four of the activities inherent in productive work: production (processing), auxiliary (supply, tooling), preparatory (set-up), and control (inspection). Given these sets of activities, the tasks chosen to comprise a whole unit of work should be interdependent. Task interdependence may be of two forms: simultaneous or sequential (Emery, 1959). Simultaneous interdependence occurs when the completion of a task involves two or more workers performing the task at the same time. For example, the operation of a particular machine may require simultaneous coordination of two workers. Sequential interdependence involves tasks that are carried out in sequence: Task A must be completed before Task B can begin. In general, both Task A and Task B would be included in the "whole" task, dependent on the time lag between performing the two tasks. The shorter the time lag between the two tasks, the greater the necessity to include them both in the same work unit.

The determination of interdependent tasks often involves a systematic analysis of the workflow process. One way to do this is to construct a giant matrix, with all the organization's tasks listed across the top and down the side of the matrix. Workers or analysts then fill in the boxes according to the extent to which two different tasks are interdependent or require cooperation between the workers performing them. Tasks that are highly interdependent, have short time lags between them, and require a good deal of cooperation between workers are grouped together (Susman, 1980).

Figure 5.   Model for Group Task Redesign

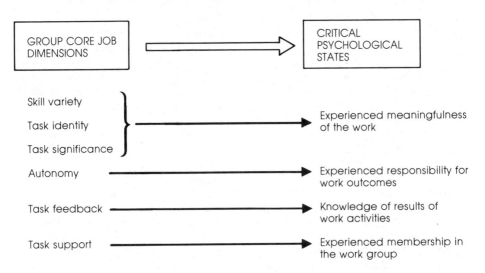

Once interdependencies have been analyzed and tentative groupings of tasks have been determined, feedback and reward possibilities must be evaluated to some degree. The end result of a grouping of tasks should be able to be easily evaluated so that performance feedback and rewards based on performance can be provided to the workers. This criterion can usually be met if all interdependent tasks are included within the grouping. If, however, an evaluation of performance can be made only after additional tasks are completed, those additional tasks should probably be included within the unit. It is important that workers performing a group of tasks feel that, as a group, they are completing a whole, meaningful unit of work. Such a feeling can only be achieved when evaluation and performance feedback does not depend on the completion of additional tasks that are not included within the grouping (Cummings and Srivasva, 1977).

The designation of a whole and meaningful unit of work may be the most important, and the most difficult, step in group task redesign. This step will not only have an obvious effect on task identity and experienced meaningfulness, but it will also indirectly affect autonomy and feelings of responsibility. For example, if all interdependent tasks are not included within the same unit, the workers in that unit will not feel that they have control over the entire process, since the evaluation of the end product will depend on work completed outside the group.

Group formation.   Once a group of tasks that constitutes a meaningful whole has been designated, a group of workers to perform these tasks can be formed. This involves consideration of the necessary skills involved in completing the whole task, the ultimate size of the group, and status and skill differentials within the group.

Size.   According to several group redesign practitioners, the number of workers making up the group should be no more nor less than the number needed to successfully complete the whole task efficiently. If the whole task can be easily completed by one worker, an individual approach to redesign can be undertaken. If the whole task is too complex for one worker, or involves costly inefficiencies when assigned to one worker, a group redesign may be more appropriate. For example, the different skills used in the construction of an automobile may be too complex for any one worker. In addition, assigning each worker the responsibility for making an entire car would involve tremendous capital expenditures for tools and machinery, much of which would lie idle as the individual worker completed different parts of the overall task.

The size of the work group will depend on the particular skills required to complete the whole task. If there are too few workers, a skill necessary to the completion of the task may be missing. The workers will not only not experience the completion of the entire task, and consequent task identity and meaningfulness, they will also experience a feeling of failure. Too many group members, on the other hand, may result in some members feeling unneeded—of making little or no significant contribution toward the accomplishment of the task. Task significance, task identity, and meaningfulness are low for unnecessary workers. Not contributing to the overall completion of the task, they cannot feel that they are having any significant impact on others within the group.

Skill and status levels.   Rice (1958) suggests two related proposals on the level of skill of the group members: (1) the range of skills required of group members should be such that all members can comprehend all the skills necessary for the completion of the whole task, and (2) tasks requiring comparable

skills should provide some opportunity for interchange of tasks among group members. These two conditions make it possible to rotate jobs in the group, and may increase skill variety. Members who are skilled in a variety of within-group tasks are able to provide task support when difficulties arise in a particular task.

In many group redesign projects, skill variety through job rotation and task support are encouraged by the use of a skill evaluation pay plan. Workers are paid on the basis of how many tasks they can perform. The greater the number of tasks they can perform, the higher their salary. When salary is based on skill level, training plays a key role. In at least one group redesign project, workers were guaranteed the right to a specified amount of training time per week as part of the negotiated union contract (Susman, 1980).

Rice also suggests that skill level and any accompanying prestige or status within the group should be more or less undifferentiated, thereby simplifying job rotation and preventing any feeling that one task or worker is insignificant in relation to the others. In some group redesign projects, old job titles and role designations, which conveyed relative status, were abandoned in favor of new labels.

Self-selection.   In several group redesign projects, workers were allowed to select each other in forming groups, within the limits imposed by skill requirements. Workers often selected each other on the basis of skill levels rather than friendship (Rice, 1958; Trist et al., 1963). Worker self-selection increases autonomy and is likely to lead to high levels of task support and feelings of membership.

Self-selection also implies that a group member may choose to move to another group if he or she does not find the group satisfactory. Workers who are not initially chosen to be included in any group, or new workers recently hired by the organization, are sometimes placed into training groups until they have acquired the necessary skills to be chosen by a work group. In some instances, members of working groups assess and choose from a number of job applicants (Sims and Manz, 1980).

Vertical loading. Vertical loading increases the autonomy of the group and is at the heart of most group redesign projects. Groups are given control over the pace of work, scheduling, work techniques—all decisions that concern their immediate work process—given the normal technical and economic restrictions. In one group redesign effort (Sims and Manz, 1980), workers within a group made out their budget, assigned jobs within the group, kept timekeeping records, quality control statistics, daily inventories, qualified workers to move to higher skill levels and higher pay, negotiated between-group transfers, and, in general, made all decisions concerning production. Such groups have autonomy to the point that members often think of themselves as self-contained businesses trying to make a profit.

Spatial arrangements. A key concept in much of the literature on work group autonomy is the idea of definable physical boundaries. The task should be easily definable in terms of a whole task, and the process of completing the whole task should also take place within an easily definable physical area. Equipment and persons required to complete the whole task should be located within easily definable boundaries, which differentiate the whole task and the work group from other whole tasks and their related work groups. In other words, each group

should have its own territory for which it is responsible. Such an arrangement should permit increased opportunities for autonomy and increased feelings of control and responsibility.

Emery (1972) notes that the degree to which a work group is capable of responsible autonomy is a function of the extent to which its work task is an independent and self-contained whole. He further suggests that the primary role of a supervisor, given the formation of an autonomous work group, is to manage the immediate boundary conditions of the workers. The supervisor's role is not to control the activities of the autonomous group but, rather, to supply needed material inputs to the group, thereby reducing any interdependence across boundaries that separate different groups. Inventory buffers are often maintained between groups so that one group is not dependent on another for necessary parts or equipment.

Furthermore, there must be proximity; workers within a group must be located close enough to each other that job rotation and task support are possible. Physical work space that isolates individual workers makes job rotation and task support more difficult.

Feedback on group performance. For the group to know how well it is performing, feedback based on group performance must be available. Economic, quality, and quantity data, normally reserved for supervisors and managers, are provided to group members. For example, at Volvo, computers flash hourly production rates onto display screens, providing instant feedback to work groups (*Wall Street Journal*, 1 March 1977). In other cases group members are encouraged to keep their own group records on production and quality control. In keeping with the overall group emphasis, feedback is generally presented in terms of group performance, rather than individually.

Group payment plan. Because the whole task is performed by the group, several organizations shift from an individual to a group payment plan when undergoing group task redesign. That is, the group is paid as a group on the basis of group performance. Such a payment plan may be a major factor in encouraging task support. When the wages of individual group members are dependent on completion of the entire group task, it is likely that members will pitch in and help others when problems with particular tasks arise.

The group payment plan is not inconsistent with the skill evaluation pay plan, previously noted. Individuals might be paid a base salary, based on their skills, and receive incentive or bonus wages in addition to the base salary. These incentive wages would be directly linked to both the quantity and quality of group performance.

Figure 6 summarizes the group task redesign implementing steps and their possible effects on the core job dimensions.

Successes . . . and Failures

In a recent survey of *Fortune's* top 1,000 industrial firms, 48 percent of those responding indicated that they were involved, or were soon to be involved, in job redesign efforts (Reif, Ferrazzi, and Evans, 1974). Scores of redesign projects have been reported in the literature. However, as is often the case, the evidence on the effectiveness of job enrichment is often qualitative and is probably reported only when companies are successful in their efforts.

Perhaps the most publicized job redesign project occurred at the Volvo plant in Sweden (Gibson, 1973; Gyllenhammar,

1977; *Time,* 6 September 1974). Following successes in limited job redesign efforts in truck assembly and upholstery departments, and with a top management philosophy to improve the quality of working life, Volvo designed their new Kalmar plant around autonomous work groups rather than the traditional assembly line. Kalmar's employees are grouped into teams of fifteen to twenty-five workers. Each team is responsible for a major segment of the auto assembly process: electrical wiring, door assembly, instrumentation, finishing, etc. Platformlike trolleys, guided by computer, move the auto body, chassis, and subassemblies from one group to another. Teams have considerable autonomy; as a result, the plant has fewer supervisors than a conventional auto plant. Volvo credits the job redesign with decreasing absenteeism (from 35 to 15 percent, in some cases) and turnover, and increasing the quality of the product.

In the United States, General Foods designed and constructed a pet food plant in Topeka, Kansas, around the principles of challenging jobs, teamwork, and skill development (Walton, 1972, 1977; *American Machinists,* 12 November 1973). Following group redesign ideas, self-managing teams of seven to fourteen workers were created. A basic feature of the Topeka plant was a skill evaluation pay plan that included only four different pay rates: (1) starting level; (2) single level (skilled on one job); (3) team level (skilled on all jobs within the team); and (4) plant level (skilled on all operator jobs within the plant). Employees received pay increases not for production, but for developing new skills. The Topeka plant also eliminated such status symbols as assigned parking spaces, differences in office size and decor, separate eating facilities, etc. Initial reports on the redesign effort

Figure 6. Summary of Implementing Principles and Possible Effects on Core Job Dimensions for Group Task Redesign

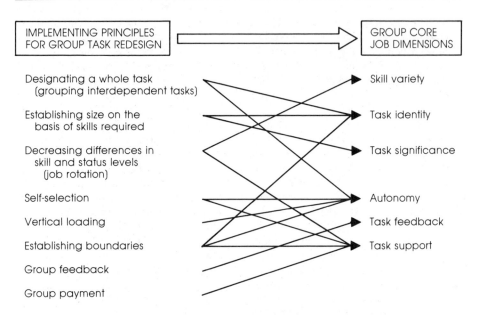

were highly favorable; overhead costs 33 percent lower than other plants, quality rejects reduced by 92 percent, a 91 percent reduction in absenteeism compared to industry averages, and the best safety record of any General Foods plant.

Successes in nonmanufacturing jobs have also been reported. Bankers Trust of New York reported substantial decreases in the number of check forgeries, misfilings of checks, and customer complaints following an individual approach to redesigning the jobs of check verifiers (Kraft and Williams, 1975). Gomez and Mussio (1975) also report a successful individual job enrichment of clerical jobs in a civil service setting.

Texas Instruments reported a reduction in turnover from 100 percent to 10 percent when janitorial workers were given increased autonomy and responsibility. Cleanliness improved, and the number of workers needed was reduced

from 120 to 71 (Herrick, 1971). On the other hand, Motorola found that more workers were needed when they individually redesigned the jobs of assembly workers. However, the company also reported greater productivity, higher quality, and lower work costs (*Business Week*, 4 September 1971).

These examples are impressive, but failures of job enrichment efforts have been reported (Frank and Hackman, 1975). Some of the reasons for failures and pitfalls to avoid in undertaking redesign have been noted by Hackman (1975).

Lack of diagnosis. Successful early reports of job redesign have sometimes led companies to institute programs that are not needed or that do not relate to their actual problems. Low employee morale or high absenteeism and turnover may be the result of low wages and fringe benefits, poor relations among co-workers or supervisors, or unhealthy working conditions. Job redesign will not "cure" such problems. Such problems may, in fact, prevent employees from responding positively to enriched jobs (Oldham, Hackman, and Pearce, 1976; Oldham, 1976).

Individual differences. Not all workers want challenging jobs. A group of Detroit auto workers spent a month observing and working within a group redesign framework at a Saab plant in Sweden. Most preferred the traditional U.S. assembly line. As one worker said, "If I've got to bust my ass to be meaningful, forget it; I'd rather be monotonous" (Goldman, 1976). Job enrichment programs are doomed to failure if they are aimed at workers who do not want enriched jobs.

Reif and Luthans (1972) have suggested that workers may prefer to look outside the organization for meaningful activities. It is interesting to note the extent to which the core job dimensions are present in leisure activities. For example, one might consider golf as an example of an individually enriched activity; or football might be viewed from a group redesign perspective. For many people leisure activities may provide meaningfulness, responsibility, and knowledge of results.

Managerial resistance. First-level managers and supervisors may resist job redesign efforts that make them give up their normal supervisory and control functions. Some managers may feel that employees cannot handle increased autonomy, others may simply resist changes because they fear they will no longer be needed once jobs have been enriched. Many redesign efforts do offer real threats to supervisory job security. To avoid managerial resistance, it may be necessary to enrich the

manager's job, too, or provide managers with new job functions (such as boundary maintenance).

Top management philosophy. Many job redesign practitioners emphasize the importance of top management in redesign efforts. If the values, philosophy, and overall climate of the organization are not supportive of the change, redesign will eventually fail. Top management must be committed to giving workers more autonomy and control of the work process. For example, *Business Week* (28 March 1977) reported that a change in top management at the General Foods Topeka plant had led to removal of much of the autonomy and self-management of the work teams. However, it should be noted that several employees of the Topeka plant disputed this report at the 1981 Quality of Work Life Conference in Toronto.

Creeping bureaucracy. Although changes are made in the jobs of lower-level workers, traditional bureaucratic structures may eventually creep in and destroy redesign efforts. For example, following standard company practice, job planners wrote detailed, standardized descriptions of the new jobs in their enrichment program, and these descriptions were passed down to the employees through company foremen (Hackman, 1975). When rigid bureaucratic procedures that operate from the top down are not changed along with job redesign, they may effectively weaken any attempt to improve the quality of working life.

Organizational choice. Many of the advantages and disadvantages of job redesign, as well as the contingencies associated with different approaches, have been noted. The organizational choice of which to use will depend on a number of considerations. But the organization does have a choice (Trist et al., 1963). Although it is commonly felt that technology dictates job design, many redesign projects have been undertaken with little or no change in the technology (Sims and Manz, 1980; Trist et al., 1963). There are costs involved with redesign, just as there are costs associated with absenteeism, turnover, and poor product quality. Rather than propose "one best way" to design jobs, we endorse a strategy of awareness and understanding of the various alternatives. Only then can a determination be made as to which approach, or combination of approaches, might best meet the needs of the organization and the employees.

REFERENCES

Boyer, R. K., and Shell, R. L. "The End of the Line at Lordstown." *Business and Society Review*, Autumn 1972.

Bucklow, M. "A New Role for the Work Group." In *Design of Jobs*, L. E. Davis and J. C. Taylor, eds. Middlesex, England: Penguin, 1972.

Business Week
4 September 1971   "Motorola Creates a More Demanding Job."
4 March 1972   "The Spreading Lordstown Syndrome."

Cummings, T. G., and Srivastva, S. *Management of Work: A Socio-technical Systems Approach*. Kent, Ohio: Kent State University Press, 1977.

Davis, L. E. "Toward a Theory of Job Design." *Journal of Industrial Engineering* 8 (1957): 305–9.

_____, and Taylor, J. C. *Design of Jobs*. Santa Monica, Calif.: Goodyear, 1979.

Dowling, W. F. "Job Redesign on the Assembly Line: Farewell to Blue Collar Blues." *Organizational Dynamics*, Autumn 1973.

Dunham, R. B. "Job Design and Redesign." In *Organizational Behavior*, S. Kerr, ed. Columbus, Ohio: Grid, 1979.

Emery, F. E. "Characteristics of Socio-technical Systems." Tavistock Institute of Human Relations, Doc. no. 527, 1959.

_____. "Characteristics of Socio-technical Systems." In *Design of Jobs*, L. E. Davis and J. C. Taylor, eds. Middlesex, England: Penguin, 1972.

Engelstad, P. "Socio-technical Problems of Process Control." In *Design of Jobs*, L. E. Davis and J. C. Taylor, eds. Middlesex, England: Penguin, 1972.

Fein, M. "The Myth of Job Enrichment." *The Humanist*, September–October 1973.

Frank, L. L., and Hackman, J. R. "A Failure of Job Enrichment: A Case of the Change That Wasn't." *Journal of Applied Behavioral Science* 11 (1975):413–36.

Gainor, P. "Do Blue Collar Workers Really Have Blues?" *Detroit News*, 5 January 1975.

Garson, B. "Luddites in Lordstown." *Harper's*, June 1972.

Gibson, C. H. "Volvo Increases Productivity Through Job Enrichment." *California Management Review*, Summer 1973.

Goldmann, R. B. *A Work Experiment: Six Americans in a Swedish Plant*. New York: Ford Foundation, 1976.

Gomez, L. R., and Mussio, S. J. "An Application of Job Enrichment in a Civil Service Setting: A Demonstration Study." *Public Personnel Management*, January–February 1975.

Gooding, J. "Blue-collar Blues on the Assembly Line." *Fortune*, July 1970.

Gyllenhammar, P. G. *People at Work*. Reading, Mass.: Addison-Wesley, 1977.

Hackman, J. R. "Is Job Enrichment Just a Fad?" *Harvard Business Review*, September–October 1975.

_____, and Lawler, E. E. "Employee Reactions to Job Characteristics." *Journal of Applied Psychology* Monograph 55 (1971): 259–86.

_____, and Oldham, G. R. "Development of the Job Diagnostic Survey." *Journal of Applied Psychology* 60 (1975):159–70.

_____, and Oldham, G. R. *Work Redesign*. Reading, Mass.: Addison-Wesley, 1980.

_____; Oldham, C. R.; Janson, R.; and Purdy, K. "A New Strategy for Job Enrichment." *California Management Review* 17 (1975): 57–71.

_____; Pearce, J. L.; and Wolfe, J. C. "Effects of Changes in Job Characteristics on Work Attitudes and Behaviors: A Naturally Occurring Quasi-experiment." *Organizational Behavior and Human Performance* 21 (1978): 289–304.

Herrick, N. Q. "The Other Side of the Coin." Paper delivered at Twentieth Anniversary Invitational Seminar of the Profit-Sharing Research Foundation, 17 November 1971, Evanston, Ill.

Herzberg, F. "One More Time: How Do You Motivate Employees?" *Harvard Business Review* 46 (1968):53–62.
_____. "The Wise Old Turk." *Harvard Business Review* 52 (1974):70–80.

Jones, E. E., and Nisbett, R. E. "The Actor and the Observer: Divergent Perceptions of the Causes of Behavior." In *Attribution: Perceiving the Causes of Behavior*, E. E. Jones et al., eds. Morristown, N.J.: General Learning Press, 1971.

Katz, D., and Kahn, R. L. *The Social Psychology of Organizations*. New York: Wiley, 1966.

Kilbridge, M. D. "Reduced Costs Through Job Enlargement: A Case." *Journal of Business*, October 1960.

Kossen, S. *The Human Size of Organizations*. San Francisco: Canfield, 1978.

Kraft, W. P., and Williams, K. L. "Job Redesign Improves Productivity." *Personnel Journal*, July 1975.

Oldham, G. R. "Job Characteristics and Internal Motivation: The Moderating Effect of Interpersonal and Individual Variables." *Human Relations* 29 (1976):559–69.

_____; Hackman, J. R.; and Pearce, J. L. "Conditions Under Which Employees Respond Positively to Enriched Work." *Journal of Applied Psychology* 61 (1976):395–403.

_____; Hackman, J. R.; and Stepina, L. P. "Norms for the Job Diagnostic Survey." *JSAS Catalog of Selected Documents in Psychology* 9 (1979):14.

Paul, W. J.; Robertson, K. B.; and Herzberg, F. "Job Enrichment Pays Off." *Harvard Business Review* 47 (1969):61–78.

Quinn, R. P.; Stains, G. L.; and McCullough, M. R. "Job Satisfaction: Is There a Trend?" Manpower Research Monograph no. 30. Washington, D.C.: U.S. Department of Labor, 1974.

Reif, W. E., and Luthans, F. "Does Job Enrichment Really Pay Off?" *California Management Review*, Fall 1972.

Reif, W. E.; Ferrazzi, D.N.; and Evans, R. J. "Job Enrichment: Who Uses It and Why." *Business Horizons*, February 1974.

Rice, A. K. *Productivity and Social Organization: The Ahmedabad Experiment*. London: Tavistock, 1958.

Scott, W. E. "Activation Theory and Task Design." *Organizational Behavior and Human Performance* 1 (1966):3–30.

Seashore, S. E., and Barnowe, J. T. "Collar Color Doesn't Count." *Psychology Today*, August 1972.

Siassi, I.; Crocetti, G.; and Spiro, H. R. "Loneliness and Dissatisfaction in a Blue Collar Population." *Archives of General Psychiatry* 30 (1974):261–65.

Sims, H. P., and Manz, C. C. "Conversations with Autonomous Work Groups." Symposium presented at Fortieth Annual Meeting, Academy of Management, 14 August 1980, Detroit.

Smith, A. *The Wealth of Nations*. London: Dent, 1910.

Stein, B.; Cohen, A.; and Gadon, H. "Flextime: Work When You Want To." *Psychology Today*, June 1976.

Susman, G. *Autonomy at Work: A Socio-technical Analysis of Participative Management*. New York: Praeger, 1976.

_____. "Conversations with Autonomous Work Groups." Symposium presented at Fortieth Annual Meeting, Academy of Management, 13 August 1980, Detroit.

Taylor, F. W. *The Principles of Scientific Management*. New York: Norton, 1911.

Time magazine. "Volvo's Valhalla," 16 September 1974.

Trist, E. L.; Higgin, G. W.; Murray, H.; and Pollock, A. B. *Organizational Choice*. London: Tavistock, 1963.

Turner, A. N., and Lawrence, P. R. *Industrial Jobs and the Worker*. Boston: Harvard, 1965.

Wall Street Journal

29 May 1973   " 'White-collar Blues' Turn Up in a New Study of Businessmen's Job Attitudes."

1 March 1977   "Auto Plant in Sweden Scores Some Success with Worker Teams."

Wallick, F. "Work with Dignity." *The Humanist*, September–October 1973.

Wharton, D. "Removing Monotony from Factory Jobs." *American Mercury*, October 1954.

Work in America. Cambridge, Mass.: MIT Press, 1973.

Working on Interdisciplinary Teams

Frederick A. Rossini

Georgia Institute of Technology

Suppose you were the director of a large university or research institute, and had to assign researchers to work on the following problems:

- A new idea for a multi-beam x-ray machine
- An effective safety device for passenger cars
- A transportation plan for a major American city.

What sorts of people would you assign to each project? For the first project, you might decide on a medical doctor, an electrical engineer, and perhaps a mathematician; in the second perhaps a mechanical engineer, a psychologist, and an economist; in the third you might select a sociologist, a geographer, a real-estate specialist, perhaps a lawyer. In each case, you would be putting together a group of highly trained professionals with very different backgrounds and skills, very different ways of looking at the world—and, probably, very decided opinions about how the particular research problem should be approached. There is clearly no guarantee that they will be able to work together effectively (or even work together at all).

Problems that demand the collaboration of diverse specialists seem to be growing in frequency and importance. Frederick Rossini outlines the problems they commonly face and what can be done to make them more effective. He starts by distinguishing three rather different forms of collaboration: cross-disciplinary, transdisciplinary, and inter-disciplinary—the latter typically presenting the most difficult form of collaboration. He then considers the impact on such interdisciplinary groups of the organizational setting in which they work; the way the group is managed; the communication structure linking the members of the group together; and the way in which the different participants structure their specialized knowledge. The final section considers how these factors can be taken into account in actual group work, looking particularly at how the social and intellectual processes of the group can be integrated into a usable final product.

THE IMPORTANCE OF INTERDISCIPLINARITY IN RESEARCH AND DEVELOPMENT

Research and development (R&D) has been steadily increasing in importance and complexity in the developed world. It plays a major role in the development of new concepts, products, and processes. And it involves many dimensions, such as the magnitude of projects, the administrative problems arising from coordinating the efforts of a number of diverse units, the technical complexity of artifacts and processes involved in R&D, and the intellectual complexity of contemporary science and technology.

We focus here on one aspect of the intellectual complexity of science and technology: interdisciplinarity. Interdisciplinarity involves the presence of a number of academic and professional disciplines in a single R&D activity. Different disciplines can participate in research or development in several alternative modes that involve different relationships among the disciplinary components and lead to differences in their interrelation or integration. In *multidisciplinarity*, the disciplinary contributions are performed independently and joined externally—much like creating a book from articles related to the same theme, each of which stands apart from the others. In *transdisciplinarity*, a single overarching intellectual framework serves to unite the components. This situation really doesn't occur in practice since existing transdisciplinary frameworks, such as general systems theory, do not currently serve as serious bases for R&D. *Interdisciplinarity* falls between those two extremes. Here the components of a report or artifact are linked internally and substantively without the presence of a transdisciplinary framework. The interrelationship can be lik-

ened to a "seamless garment" as compared to the "patchwork quilt" of multidisciplinarity (Rossini et al., 1981). Jack Nilles (1975) has described interdisciplinary research as "the joint, coordinated, and continuously integrated research done by experts from different disciplinary backgrounds, working together and producing joint reports, papers, recommendations . . . so tightly interwoven that the specific contribution of each researcher tends to be obscured in the joint product."

Interdisciplinary research is steadily becoming a more important activity. The reasons for this lie both in technological and societal need and in intrinsic intellectual interest. The need occurs because many of the most pressing societal problems cut across existing academic and professional disciplines and their institutional embodiments. Issues in microelectronics R&D, global strategy, and water problems involve a range of disciplines if they are to be dealt with in their full complexity. Likewise, a wide range of questions of great intellectual interest, relating to the study of such areas as values and ancient cultures, are of similar scope. One important form of interdisciplinary policy-related research, technology assessment, is discussed by Alan Porter, in "Assessing the Social Impacts of New Technologies," Reading #7. The practical importance of interdisciplinary research is widely recognized, yet many researchers are skeptical of its performance and the quality of its output. In evaluating interdisciplinary research, the usual criteria for valid and useful research are augmented by the need for integration of disciplinary components.

There are many significant examples of interdisciplinary work. The discovery by Watson and Crick of the double helix structure of DNA (Watson, 1968) involved contributions from genetics and x-ray structural analysis. Individually these contributions would have produced nothing. Skillfully integrated, they brought about a major discovery.

Widely known, but not usually recognized as an example of interdisciplinarity, is the process of preparing an environmental impact statement (EIS), which is required in the United States for all major actions by the federal government. Consequences of assessed projects and programs are wide ranging. They include environmental, psychological, institutional, social, technical, legal, political, and economic impats. These consequences cannot be studied effectively in isolation since they interact extensively. For example, a new dam may bring ecomnic benefits to farmers in a particular region; these economic gains may increase their political clout; and so on. To cover such a wide range of impacts, an EIS must be collaborated on by a wide range of experts in different fields.

Even such an apparently mundane development as the coated stainless steel razor blade came from an interdisciplinary group of scientists and engineers at the Gillette Company. The team included chemists, physicists, and metallurgists, as well as mechanical and electrical engineers. This group was establisted to undertake a long-range study of the properties and uses of razors and razor blades.

These examples indicate the importance of interdisciplinarity in R&D. Below, we will explore problems in performing successful interdisciplinary work to explain why effective interdisciplinarity is difficult to achieve, offer some of the keys to successfully leading or working on interdisciplinary teams, and warn of a number of the pitfalls to avoid. Perhaps we will also be able to communicate some of the interest and excitement of interdisciplinary work.

EDUCATIONAL AND ORGANIZATIONAL PROBLEMS, OR, WHY PRACTITIONERS OF INTERDISCIPLINARITY OFTEN FLY BLIND

The primary source of training for R&D personnel is the educational system, from first grade through graduate school. The secondary source of training is on-the-job instruction and experience. Beginning in first grade, with the split between reading and math, formal instruction is almost totally divided into disciplinary areas. As the subject matter becomes more sophisticated, the divisions become finer and finer. By the time they receive their Ph.D.s, solid state physicists have difficulty communicating with high energy physicists— and *theoretical* solid state physicists have difficulty communicating with *experimental* solid state physicists. Organic chemists and physical chemists are on different intellectural wavelengths. Behavioral psychologists cannot understand psychoanalysts, and vice versa.

Nowhere is the fine-grained approach to knowledge more evident than in graduate research training. Students almost always work for one professor and in one discipline. Even when the student works in a research group, each individual thesis is typically a discrete part of the professor's research program.

Thus the educational system struggles endlessly against interdisciplinarity. There are only rare exceptions to this dismal picture of disciplinary isolation. Occasionally a course involves a team project where not only are a number of individuals jointly responsible for the output, but the project itself is sufficiently broad to cut across disciplines. Similarly, a small number of research projects are genuinely interdisciplinary. Such projects often produce problems unheard of in the usual academic context, problems both social and intellectual. The basic difficulty is that, to complete the project, researchers must successfully cope with many people and many disciplines for which their training has usually not prepared them. Despite many opportunities for discouragement, some students and researchers revel in the intellectual and social challenges of interdisciplinary projects. Generally, however, formal education offers almost no preparation for interdisciplinary work.

The other source of training is on-the-job training and experience. In most academic institutions, discipline-bound organizations and rewards are a way of life. Similarly, many corporate and government R&D organizations are organized along disciplinary-based divisions. For example, Oak Ridge National Laboratory has a chemistry division, an analytical chemistry division, a physics division, a solid state physics division, etc. Even where divisional lines can be crossed, strict time accounting procedures, such as the need to charge each minute of time to a particular project, may mean that problems that cross disciplinary lines will be dealt with as *multi*disciplinary rather than as *inter*-disciplinary, with the corresponding loss of integration in their solution.

In the meantime, the major social problems that cut across disciplines do not go away. Drug abuse is a chemical, medical, social, and psychological problem, among other things. War and peace involve not only technology, economics, and institutions, but also environmental, social, and psychological considerations. The development of solar energy likewise requires contributions from many disciplines. The demand for interdisciplinary solutions to problems will not abate. Yet few if any researchers have the least bit of relevant formal training.

Recognizing the necessity and desirability of interdisciplinary research, many groups have begun with the "wouldn't it be nice if . . ." attitude. Yes, it would be nice if chemists, biologists, economists, and political scientists were to work together on an interdisciplinary research project and produce an integrated output. But this will not occur merely by wishing it so, as many participants in interdisciplinary projects have discovered. The habits, values, and standards of research training work against it.

Even when projects were successful, the personal and professional costs have been high. In one project, viewed as successful by participants and sponsors, five divorces occurred in the project team. The project was not the sole cause, but it certainly exacerbated preexisting marital problems. In another successful project, four participants, faculty members at a university, were denied tenure and, in effect, fired. Their work on the project was very good, it just didn't count toward gaining tenure. A project that failed in a relatively inhospitable environment destroyed the professional upward mobility of its principal investigator, a personal and professional tragedy for him.

By now you may ask: "Is interdisciplinarity worth all of this?" My answer is a qualified yes. I believe interdisciplinarity is necessary for R&D and will increase in importance. The qualification is that you must look before you leap. You need some insight into the conditions under which interdisciplinary work can be performed successfully. Next we will discuss various factors that may lead to successful interdisciplinary work, how to evaluate it, and make some general observations for guidance.

LOOKING AT THE ORGANIZATION

What kinds of R&D organizations provide the most effective home for interdisciplinarity? What organizational conditions should you look for if you are planning an interdisciplinary project or want to join an organization where interdisciplinary work is possible?

The first thing to check is the attitude of the organization's management. If interdisciplinarity is discouraged, you can write the organization off. If management claims to be neutral or favorable, look for subunits where interdisciplinary projects have been performed and try to learn about their success. It may be that some subunits of an organization provide favorable sites for interdisciplinary work, while others are totally inhospitable.

Beyond what the organization says about itself, there are some other indicators of potential for interdisciplinarity. Most organizations have internal divisions. If an organization is too small for divisions (e.g., the International Research and Technology Corporation or the Futures Group), it is a prime candidate for interdisciplinary activities. If there *are* divisions, their basis can give some clue to how well interdisciplinarity fits within the organization. Typically, disciplinary divisions (remember Oak Ridge National Laboratory) are a signal that disciplines are important. Problem-oriented (urban studies, international affairs, energy) divisions or departments signal a greater likelihood of interdisciplinary capability—especially when these divisions are staffed by specialists from a variety of disciplines. Oak Ridge National Laboratory has an energy division that is so staffed. A caveat here is to determine whether a multidisciplinary rather than an interdisciplinary

approach is being followed. This can be determined in part by reading their reports to see if the disciplinary contributions are woven together or discrete.

Another consideration is the flexibility of divisional barriers and the ease with which an individual who is attached to one division can work on a project in another division. The greater the flexibility of an organization in using its personnel, the greater its potential for sound interdisciplinary work. Find out whether the organization requires a charge number for every minute of professional time spent (as SRI International does). If so, unscheduled interaction, almost invariably a part of interdisciplinary work, will be difficult, and the potential for interdisciplinarity will be weakened. Finally, rewards must be available, in practice as well as in principle, for the successful performance of interdisciplinary work. Without rewards beyond mere survival in the organization, only deeply committed persons are going to take the risks that interdisciplinarity involves.

Now let us look at specific types of organizations. The university department, with its strong disciplinary orientation, is probably the worst home for interdisciplinary work. Running a close second is the large industrial or government lab that is organized into disciplinary divisions; organizational and accounting procedures are likely to hamper the formation and functioning of teams composed of members from various divisions (Rossini et al., 1981).

At the other extreme, one type of organization stands out as favorable to interdisciplinary research: the small, flexible research unit where interdisciplinary work is facilitated and rewards are made available for successful work. Good examples are contract research organizations that have no divisional boundaries (two were mentioned above) and university institutes or programs with problem area emphasis (such as MIT's Center for Policy Alternatives or the Science and Public Policy Program of the University of Oklahoma). However, in such small, flexible units it may be difficult to retain and reward qualified people.

In academic institutions, departments have almost exclusive control over important rewards, e.g., tenure. The process of review by which retention, tenure, and promotion are determined is in the hands of disciplinary-minded colleagues. An engineer who engages in interdisciplinary, policy-related research is judged by engineers on the basis of his or her performance as an engineer, not as a policy analyst. Not surprisingly, engineers have often found policy analysis irrelevant to the practice of engineering, and thus the performance of the engineer-turned-policy-analyst is considered unacceptable as engineering, whether or not the work on the interdisciplinary project was outstanding or poor, or whether or not his or her papers dealing with policy issues were important or trivial. Coauthored papers, as many are in interdisciplinary research, present another barrier to evaluation.

You may wonder why an individual cannot be evaluated on the basis of performance by persons knowledgeable in the problem area rather than in a specific discipline. Supporters of the status quo argue that the disciplines have proven their value over long periods of time, and that interdisciplinary and team research, whatever their merits in the abstract, are all too often a convenient refuge for weak performers who cannot make the grade in the highly competitive world of academic research.

All this leaves the academic interdisciplinary researcher vulnerable to the unfavorable judgment of his or her peers. In professional schools, the situation is sometimes more favorable. Yet academia has been the graveyard of much interdisciplinary work.

Why dwell on the problems of interdisciplinary research in academia? The answer is, that future researchers, including those who will be involved in interdisciplinary research, are still being trained in this environment by professors who must face the pressures described above. Indeed, the lack of a natural training site helps make interdisciplinary work the difficult undertaking it is.

MANAGING INTERDISCIPLINARITY

We now narrow our focus from the larger organization down to the particular project—which, in interdisciplinary work, is always a team project. Such projects are complex in that different intellectual frameworks and value systems are represented by the team members. Getting persons with diverse mind-sets to collaborate fruitfully to perform highly complex tasks is the responsibility of the manager of the project, who must not only see to it that the work meets the usual quality standards, but also that it is an *interdisciplinary* output, one in which the disciplinary contributions are linked internally. The task of managing multidisciplinary work is much less difficult; what is needed is simply to obtain some worthwhile products and staple them together in logical order.

To discuss the attributes of an effective manager of interdisciplinary projects, we begin by discussing three abstract types of R&D managers (Hill, 1970): democratic/facilitating, authoritarian, and laissez faire.

As the name implies, the democratic/facilitating manager involves the members of the team in making decisions that involve substantive and procedural issues relating to the project. Team meetings are held when needed, and all channels of communication among team members are open. The leader listens to the team members, offering support and assistance freely, and accepts their advice without hesitation when it fits the case. The team members feel that they are part of the project. On the other side of the coin, however, such a leader is ready and willing to make final decisions after having received input from the team members. Sometimes these decisions go against the view of the majority, but this is part of the leadership role. The leader does not make decisions capriciously or vindictively. It is necessary to balance the goals of the project with the interests and needs of the individual participants, but when all is said and done, the project should achieve its goals, if possible on time and within the budget.

The authoritarian leader puts the emphasis on the role of the leader. His or her control is nearly absolute. Such an individual makes all the important decisions, minimizing input and participation from the team. The team member is reduced to an intellectual flunkey. This may lead to irritation and disgust. Still, professionals being what they are, assignments will most likely be carried out, though perhaps grudgingly. Some will leave the team; others may become alienated and perform perfunctorily. Authoritarian leadership might be effective for a project requiring the performance of isolated tasks (the antithesis of interdisciplinary research). It is not likely to elicit the joint, cooperative performance of a team of sophisticated researchers that will lead to a well-integrated outcome.

The authoritarian leader can at least get some results, but the third type, the laissez faire leader, has difficulty even here. This leader's procedure is to be passive, give some vague initial ideas to the team, and then sit back and see what happens. Usually, either nothing happens, or some widely disparate results, which may or may not be germane to the project, occur. In either case, in the final period of the project's life the project leader faces a difficult situation. (S)he must take the pieces produced willy-nilly by the team members and put together a cohesive report. In real projects, laissez faire leadership has led to late reports that were either unsatisfactory or required an enormous effort from the team leader. Feeling let down by the uninstructed and unguided team, the leader often experiences intense frustration, coupled with the threat of career failure. Leadership of interdisciplinary projects is a risky business!

The message for team leaders—and for those who work with them—is clear. The most effective interdisciplinary leader is one who communicates with his or her team, preferably in close physical proximity, and shares decisions with them. However, this flexibility and openness should not involve any weakness in making "bottom line" decisions, even unpopular ones. When closure is needed or a decision must be made, the leader should make it, simply and decisively.

Both authoritarian and laissez faire leaders lack one of the two critical attributes of a democratic/facilitating leader. The authoritarian is delighted to make decisions, but unwilling to share them. The indecisive sharing of the laissez faire leader leaves colleagues puzzled and without direction. While both styles often fail in a team context, superhuman individual efforts have been known to save projects.

TEAM MEMBERS—PROFILE AND BEHAVIOR

Some generally desirable qualities of participants in interdisciplinary projects were described by Samuel Estep, a law professor at the University of Michigan, in a discussion with the author. Based on his experience as a member of technology assessment teams, Estep suggested that effective participants are well versed in the intellectual culture of research, possess open, curious minds, and are imbued with common sense. They have stable egos and are able to accept attacks on their ideas without interpreting them as personal attacks. They are also able to question their own basic values and intellectual assumptions. Their internal organization and self-discipline are complemented by a hard-nosed results orientation. They are not afraid to ask simple or stupid questions, not frightened by terminology, nor easily dissuaded from a thought-out position. They work well with other people, and can accept responsibility for their mistakes and learn from them.

These qualities belong to a flexible and resourceful individual who can see through and around the institutions and conventions of the researcher's world, and who is not afraid of breaking new intellectual ground. Such persons wish to understand the fundamentals of a problem as it exists without trying to mold it to fit the tools of their intellectual training. For example, such a person, although an economist, might revel in understanding the technical aspects of the coal liquification process (s)he was studying. Ideally, these persons are not wedded to specific formulations or solutions of problems. They want to learn from others and are equally comfortable as leaders in their areas of expertise or as followers where others' knowledge is greater.

The interdisciplinary researcher's overriding motivation should be to solve the problem at hand in its full complexity. This entails the realization that the quality of the final research product depends on the group and its range of capabilities, rather than on the individual. In interdisciplinary research, the persons responsible for the various disciplinary components of research throughout the life of the project are collectively called the "core team." In a small to medium-size project the core team members essentially perform the entire research. On large or complex projects, the core team members may each be the leader of a research team performing one component of the project. Thus the linkages across disciplines are forged at the top of the hierarchy (as will be discussed later).

The most effective number of members for a core team depends on the project. However, upper and lower bounds can reasonably be set. Except on the smallest projects, teams below three individuals do not allow an appropriate range of capabilities and dynamic interaction for an effective project. Above seven, the sheer number of communications links becomes hard to manage. On technology assessment projects of around five person-years of effort, we found that core teams of from three to five were most effective for integration among the disciplines (Rossini et al., 1981). Larger teams proved workable if great care was taken to ensure the effective interaction of the members.

Surprisingly, there is evidence that the core team should be composed of as wide a range of disciplinary participants as is consistent with the project, rather than of persons with cross-disciplinary backgrounds or who are expert in "systems" (Rossini et al., 1981). That is, when studying nuclear energy production, a team made up of a nuclear engineer, an economist, a political scientist, an ecologist, and a health physicist may be superior to one composed of five systems analysts. It may be that persons who are "interdisciplinary" in themselves or who adopt a nominally cross-disciplinary approach, such as systems analysis, may not be well attuned to problems in integrating disciplines since they have "solved" these problems within themselves. Still, the evidence on this point is inconclusive, so each project and group of participants needs to be examined individually.

Finally, for effective integration the participants should learn, up to a point, to speak each other's languages. Since conceptual frameworks, observation categories, theories, and techniques vary widely among disciplines (and within most disciplines as well), a minimum common basis of mutual understanding is required for the core team to deal with all parts of the project. This basis should include, but not necessarily be limited to, the basic concepts of each field, essential observational categories, and key dynamic linkages. It is helpful to know, for example, that an economist usually develops models, while an ecologist usually gathers field data. During the process of learning about one another's intellectual frameworks and intellectual values, the core team members will also learn the personal characteristics, work habits, and other qualities of their colleagues that will increase mutual understanding, hopefully to the benefit of the project.

PROJECT BOUNDING

Bounding a project consists of setting its limits and form (Armstrong and Harman, 1977). While this is a crucial component of all R&D work, it is more so in interdisciplinary projects because of the number of persons and disciplines involved. Clearly, the less complex the project on either of these dimensions, the less critical the bounding. In bounding, as in life, extremes should usually be avoided. One extreme is closing out options near the beginning of a project, and thus being unable to respond to new information and changes during the course of the study. This opens up the study to irrelevance, that is, asking and answering the wrong questions. One project (Grad et al., 1975) dealing with assessing technology to eliminate pollution due to automobiles, neglected energy costs and had its analysis vitiated as its report was released just after the Arab oil embargo of 1973. The other extreme is leaving the bounds totally open till the end of the project. This condition results in a rich but unfocused study. As one project leader found at the end of such a study, the task of integrating the plethora of material he had obtained consumed him for a year. It was a truly frustrating experience.

It has been found that the effective bounding of a study as judged by its participants correlates with interdisciplinary integration. This finding is intellectually plausible in general since bounding helps pull a study together and give it focus and direction.

What then is effective bounding? It consists of determining the general direction and focus of the project in its early phases. More specific bounding occurs as the project proceeds, without losing the ability to make a major change in direction should improbable occurrences make this necessary. Closure occurs progressively until the end of the project. If the bounding decisions involve the active participation of the core team, there is a steady flow to closure. Arbitrary imposition of rigid bounding by the team leader, higher management, or sponsor before startup may decrease project effectiveness.

Up to a point, team time spent in bounding is fruitful, but bounding should not serve as a substitute for substantive work. As in so many areas of project management and methodology, the all-too-rare quality of good judgment is the primary requisite.

PROCESS FEATURES—
INTRATEAM COMMUNICATION
AND ITERATION

Intrateam communication lies at the heart of any group project, and is especially important in interdisciplinarity. We discussed earlier the elements that make possible a common group basis for understanding various intellectual frameworks. Below, we consider the patterns of communication among core team members.

There are two extreme types of communication patterns for a project group. The first is the "all-channel" pattern: everyone talks to everyone else (see Figure 1a). The number of channels rises rapidly as the number of team members increases. The second is the "hub-and-spokes" pattern: each team member communicates with the team leader and with no one else (see Figure 1b).

Intermediate configurations are possible in which some of the channels are not used and/or the channels used are of differing strengths. Figure 1c shows an intermediate case that was used in one well-integrated and successful interdisciplinary study. It indicates both unused channels and the varying strength of the channels that are used. In a large team this may be the most effective compromise. There is evidence, however, that the "all-channel" pattern is the most effective for interdisciplinary integration, followed by the intermediate and "hub-and-spokes" patterns, in that order. The evidence is especially striking for the last phase of the project, when the final report is prepared. Here, the more

Figure 1.   Communications Patterns in Interdisciplinary Projects

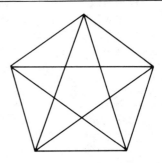

a. All-channel pattern for a five-member core team

b. Hub-and-spokes pattern for a five-member core team

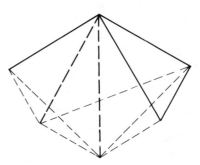

Strength of channel:

——————————— Strong

— — — — — — — Intermediate

– – – – – – – – Weak

c. Intermediate case used in a successful and well-integrated interdisciplinary study

communication, the better. Interdisciplinary projects have been observed that were apparently well integrated with a high level of communication until the end phase. Because of lack of funds or for personal reasons, intrateam communication decreased at that point and the final report was written by one or two individuals, essentially in isolation. The result was a final report which lacked integration. Similarly, improved communication at the end of a project may improve its integration although intrateam communication had not been strong up to that point.

On large projects the core team members act as the leaders of research groups rather than as individual researchers. This leads to a hierarchy of communication, as shown in Figure 2, that presents three options for a two-level communications pattern integrated by "all-channel' communication within the core team. For still larger projects, such patterns can be extended to many levels, with integration taking place on more than one level. However, the larger the project, the greater the information load on the ultimate core team members if the project is to be effective.

The communication network is used in the process of iterating, or redoing the study. Iteration is common in large impact assessment studies where relatively little of the knowledge used is original. A typical pattern consists of an initial "quick-and-dirty" run-through to set the bounds of the study's content and form. This is followed by an iteration in which the study is conducted in depth. The final pass would be designed to study areas that had not been covered or that needed additional work, and finally to integrate the study. A bit of "folk wisdom" among technology assessment practitioners is that the first task of any assessment is to write the final report. The report is, of course, iterated to completion during the rest of the study. A

Figure 2. Hierarchical Communications Pattern: Core Team as Research Managers and Integrators in All-channel Pattern

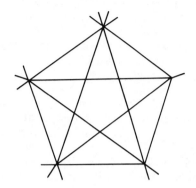

a. All channel with spokes

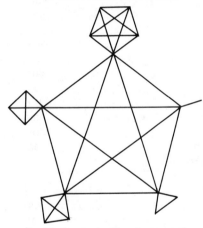

b. All channel with all channel

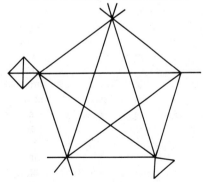

c. Combination

primary effect of iteration is to integrate the study by pulling its disparate components closer and closer together in subsequent revisions.

The situation is similar in fundamental research (e.g., the discovery of the structure of DNA), where a relatively high proportion of effort goes to the generation of new knowledge. Of course, writing the final report is not sensible because of the high level of uncertainty that exists. Thus, iterations have to be determined on the basis of earlier results to a greater extent than in assessment-like studies. Here the overall direction of the study has a greater (but typically not large) probability of changing radically as the research unfolds.

Iteration has potential for increasing the validity, utility, and integration of any interdisciplinary project. Validity is increased because knowledge gaps can be eliminated and work rechecked, utility because it can be better shaped to a desirable form, and integration because the study may be woven together through successive iterations.

FRAMEWORKS FOR INTELLECTUAL AND SOCIAL INTEGRATION OF INTER-DISCIPLINARY PROJECTS

Thus far we have dealt with the factors that contribute to the success of interdisciplinary projects. Now we consider four ideal types of possible social and intellectual frameworks within with projects can be integrated (Rossini et al., 1981; Rossini and Porter, 1979). Because these frameworks are presented as ideal types, few projects fit any of them perfectly. But in many projects attempts at integration take on features of one or more of these types. No single approach is ideal for every situation, since each framework has its own strengths and weaknesses.

The first approach is *common group learning* (a good example is described in Kash et al., 1973). The most important aspect of this framework is that the output of the project is the common property of the group. In essence, this approach tries to eliminate specialization by making each core team member equally knowledgable in the entire project. Typically, after the project is bounded, each core team member works on that part of the study closest to his or her own expertise (the economist on economics, the engineer on engineering, etc.). After this first phase, the results are critiqued by each team member and are discussed in common by the group. The second phase of the project is the further development of each component analysis through critique by the group. This time the individual components are given to another team member, someone who is usually not an expert in the area (the economist on engineering, the engineer on economics, etc.). This process is iterated until most of the team has worked on most of the parts of the project. Common group learning is illustrated schematically in Figure 3a. The strength of this approach is its marvelous ability to bring to bear the totality of expertise in the team on each aspect of the project. At the same time, it has the weakness that depth of analysis cannot be maintained because each individual must master the technical details of parts of the project in which he or she has no expertise. This difficulty means that common group learning is most appropriate for projects where the level of technical competence (as opposed to intellectual acumen) is not a barrier to the team members. As the competence requirements for the project rise, the use of common group learning becomes less helpful. There are a number of projects, such as those dealing with analysis of nontechnical policy issues, where the advantages of common group learn-

Figure 3. Four Social and Intellectual Frameworks for Integrating the Components of Interdisciplinary Research

LEGEND

○ Individuals who possess particular expertise

☐ Repositories of knowledge other than individuals

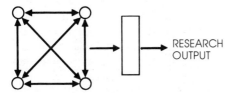

1. Intensive group interaction   2. Common group knowledge

a. Common group learning

1. Model created by certain individuals   2. Individuals contribute information to the model and use it in establishing findings

b. Modeling

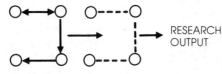

1. Pairwise interaction at boundaries between component experts   2. Better informed and interrelated analysis

c. Negotiation among experts

1. Pairwise interaction only between the leader and other individuals   2. Leader acquires composite knowledge and synthesizes findings

d. Integration by leader

ing can be brought to bear without its weaknesses.

A second approach to project integration is *modeling* (examples are Harvey and Menchen, 1974, and Enzer, 1974), usually with a large computerized model or series of linked models. The model can be developed specifically for the project, imported intact from some external source, or imported and modified by the project team. Models have the virtue that each participant can input information to the model. Thus the model serves as an integrating framework for the various analyses, thereby incorporating the task of integration into the structure of the model. This is illustrated schematically in Figure 3b.

Yet it is precisely the structure of the model that may be seriously deficient as an integrating framework. It is difficult to conceive of a model that can incorporate with equal facility a wide range of qualitative and quantitative information. It is easy to dispute the unique structure of some model from a point of view that finds it irrelevant to the problem at hand. In addition, in almost every case, computerized models favor quantitative information over qualitative material to a significant degree. They can deal well with technical and economic considerations, but not with social and institutional ones. Thus, given a wide intellectual range of participants or a broadly defined problem, a model could generate problems instead of solving them. However, as the problem focus narrows to emphasize quantitative details that integrate easily, a model becomes a more plausible approach to integration. In any event, models may be used in specific component analyses or to integrate parts of a complex project. Models have a great deal to contribute in simplicity and rigor, and should not be ignored.

A third framework for integration is *negotiation among experts* (a useful example is in Changnon et al., 1977). This approach is similar to common group learning in that analyses are critiqued and iterated. It differs in that it preserves expertise. After each team member performs the component of the project in which he or she is most expert, the results are critiqued by the group with each group member attempting to relate his or her perspective to the analysis. The iteration is performed by the expert who attempts to relate the critiques of the other team members to the analysis. Negotiation among experts is illustrated in Figure 3c. Iterating this process ideally leads to an integrated result. The real weakness of this approach

is that, since the expert is the last court of appeal, the critiques may be rejected or shoved aside, resulting in a multidisciplinary, rather than an interdisciplinary, result.

The final approach to be discussed is *integration by leader,* illustrated in Figure 3d (Harkness, 1976, is an example of this type). This is the classic "hub-and-spokes" pattern, with communication allowed only between the team member and the team leader. While this procedure may sound absurd, it has actually been used in a number of interdisciplinary projects for reasons such as lack of funds to support member communication or the physical dispersal of the team members. An advantage, if it can be called one, is that the burden of integration is localized. Unfortunately, in projects of reasonable size the burden of integration is greater than one person can bear. The demands that integration places on a single individual typically result in a collection of fragments, a multidisciplinary project. In one instance where integration by leader was attempted, the team members felt unprofessionally treated by being unable to communicate with one another and rebelled; the leader felt frustrated. Integration by leader is not a very good candidate except in small projects where the leader's expertise covers a considerable portion of the intellectual range involved.

These four ideal types do not exhaust the potential for integrative frameworks, but they do cover a goodly range of the possibilities. It is a sound idea to develop a strategy for integration on each project. Such a strategy may incorporate some of these ideal types with emphasis on fitting the framework to the project. Conscious attention to integration should improve the chances of achieving it.

DEALING WITH THE USER

The simplest type of user community is found in disciplinary academic basic research. It consists of the homogeneous group of basic researchers interested in the same problem area. With similar intellectual world views and vocabularies and a common problem focus, communication by mailing preprints and through journal literature is economical and straightforward. Technical terms can be used with impunity, and much information that would have to be explained to the uninitiated can be left unsaid.

When the project deals with applied research or the translation of basic research into applications, the user community becomes broader and less homogeneous, and hence more difficult to communicate with. Common interests and vocabularies are replaced by a wide range (Caplan et al., 1975). Likewise, when the project is interdisciplinary, the number of potential user communities increases (Berg et al., 1978).

This spread in potential user communities for interdisciplinary projects requires conscious attention on the part of the project team to the users' interests, needs, and capabilities. (We are, of course, assuming that the project is not dedicated to a single user.) The first step in ensuring the effective utilization of the project's results takes place at the beginning of the project and consists of identifying the potential user groups. Contact with the groups is the next step. Ultimately, the project team should learn the information needs of the user groups and the level and formats in which they can most usefully receive this information. In some cases, such as some forms of basic research, these are rather obvious and require only cursory attention, but in many instances in applied and policy work, where the users are not themselves producers of information, it is important to contact the user groups to lay the groundwork for their ultimate use of project results.

Through interaction with the producers, the users often become familiar with and supporters of the project. At the same time the users act as critics of the team's efforts. On a project dealing with offshore oil and gas resources, contact was maintained throughout the project with environmentalists and the oil industry (Kash, 1977). Ongoing contact not only makes the work more useful, but also makes it more valid as well. Since the final outcome is not surprising to the users, who are fully familiar with the thrust of the project, it is readily assimilated into their world. The format is in good part user determined, thus overcoming a principal obstacle to effective use.

This general strategy merits some detailed discussion. First, the distinction among basic research, applied research, policy research, and development is important. In the first case, the user groups are composed of individuals who can grasp parts of the project, and who could be participants as well as users. Convention dictates publication of results in the open journal literature. Applied research users are more diversified. They include groups who can exploit the application, such as development groups, other applied research groups, financial backers, and basic researchers who feed on problems generated in an applied context. Users of policy research are still more diversified. They are made up of other researchers and persons involved in and affected by the policy issue under study. In terms of interests, needs, and ability to assimilate technical information, the range of these groups can be quite extensive. Thus the potential for diversification of output, both in media of presentation and technical depth, appears most critical here. Finally, development is intended for large-scale production or ultimate users. The important point is to understand user needs and interests, and from these to select the appropriate level of technical depth and desirable formats.

Contact with users is costly in time and money, and alternate presentations of results may draw effort away from the substantive thrust of the project. Thus there exists a trade-off that is especially acute in the cases of policy and applied research. There are no hard and fast rules for how much effort should be allocated to utilization. One thing is clear, however: if no explicit attention is given to this problem, the work may be useless, and, if it is not knowledge acquired for its own sake, a failure.

EVALUATING INTER-DISCIPLINARY WORK—WHAT DOES IT TAKE TO SUCCEED?

The form of integration sets interdisciplinary work apart from other kinds of research. To evaluate interdisciplinary research, we must determine how well integrated the output of the project is. Three sources of evaluation for integration are peers, performers, and users.

Peers are individuals comparable to the members of the project team in training and experience. They are in a position to offer a judgment about the project's overall quality without having a stake in the outcome of the evaluation. Advisory committees (where these exist) may be composed at least in part of peers. Likewise, peers are used by funders and journal editors to critique project proposals and results. They may

play both a formative role in shaping the ongoing study and a judgmental role in evaluating the integration of the final product.

Performers can offer information and observations about the process that produced the final project output. They may offer insight into the causal mechanisms leading to the integration of the project. Although users may not have great insight into the technical quality of a project, they can state how well it meets their particular needs. If these needs require an integrated output, some insight into integration is available here. However, user evaluations are the weakest input into the evaluation of integration. Users can only say whether the output was sufficiently integrated to meet their needs. Performers are best at evaluating the integration of the process that is causally connected with integrated output.

A number of types of integration are reflected in project output (Rossini et al., 1978). Editorial integration is the most basic form; the output possesses a logical flow, moving from introduction through body of work to conclusions. Another type is conceptual/terminological integration, in which the same vocabulary is used consistently throughout, thereby avoiding isolated vocabularies and varied usages.

While these two types of integration provide a basis for a coherent project output, systematic integration incorporates the concept of interdisciplinary integration. It emphasizes the existence of a single framework, explicit or implicit, within which the project is oriented. It also includes consideration of internal linkages among the project's disciplinary components which weave them together into a "seamless garment." The constellation of these three types of integration approximates well the notion of interdisciplinary integration.

Interdisciplinary integration can be most reliably determined by agreement among peers, producers, and users. Ranking on an ordinal scale by the evaluators provides an indication of degree of integration and the basis for an overall comparison among a number of projects, if this is desirable.

Serious evaluation of interdisciplinary research is still an ideal. The problems of doing interdisciplinary work are so great that little thought or conscious design is presently being expended in evaluation. Where evaluation is undertaken, it is desirable to design it as part of the process so that data can be recorded on the spot without having to rely on memories later. Collecting the same types of process and output data for several comparable projects allows a comparative evaluation of similar projects under differing process conditions, and thus more evidence of factors that contribute to integration.

CONCLUSION

Interdisciplinarity is important and becoming more so as societal need and intellectual opportunity present problems whose solutions do not lie in the province of a single discipline. The need for interdisciplinarity is growing at a rate that outstrips the ability of R&D and educational institutions to cope with it. Because of the current mismatch between institutions and needs, interdisciplinary work is often practiced in an unstable environment, creating institutional, intellectual, and personal tensions. In closing, we offer some practical guidance for participants and managers of interdisciplinary R&D in the present situation.

For the organization, two major objectives are (1) to lower the internal barriers to cross-disciplinary collaboration and (2) to provide adequate rewards for such collaboration. The first objective can be achieved by following one of two strategies. On the one hand, interdisciplinary units can be created that contain within them personnel from a wide range of disciplinary backgrounds. In the university environment, these appear as institutes or programs. Unfortunately, these units usually lack control over their academic personnel who remain responsible to their disciplinary departments. In R&D labs or contract research organizations interdisciplinary groups are usually tied to a problem area, e.g., energy. Here too there is the possibility that if the organization is structured in quasi-disciplinary divisions, these will have greater long-term staying power than the interdisciplinary project units that cut across them.

The second approach to cross-disciplinary collaboration is breaking down the barriers between disciplinary units so that interdisciplinary projects may be organized and run through disciplinary units. This involves streamlining personnel and budget transfer mechanisms. It also collides squarely with the second concern—rewarding participants in interdisciplinary projects.

Lack of reward is a significant stumbling block to successful interdisciplinary research. Only the most dedicated professional can work productively in the absence of reward, or under threat of a negative reward. However, in many academic departments rewards accrue only for disciplinary contributions, and team efforts are viewed with suspicion, since disaggregating individual contributions is an uncertain business. As long as control of tenure rests with disciplinary departments, interdisciplinary work is at best a chancy undertaking. Even when cross-disciplinary institutes and programs exist, their lack of control over promotion and tenure blunts their effectiveness. Superficially, the problem of adequate reward appears to be solved readily outside of academia. Successful performance of duties leads to reward. However, problems may arise. One difficulty is the jealousy of a manager when he sees his unit's R&D funds being paid to persons in other units, decreasing both his direct cost budget and overhead recovery. The "keep-it-in-the-unit" mindset militates against collaborative work across unit boundaries. A second difficulty arises when a cross-disciplinary problem-oriented unit is created. In many cases the colleagues of the individuals in the unit progress more rapidly through the ranks of the larger organization because they remain in the usual career path. If the problem-oriented unit is dissolved, its members seem to fit in the spots they came from, rather than at higher levels in the organization. As all this suggests, the problem of providing adequate rewards for successful participation can be a serious inhibitor of interdisciplinary work.

For the individual participants, the emphasis is on their being both teachers and learners, persons who will use the project to grow in understanding both of the area being researched and in the intellectual frameworks of the other project participants. At the same time they will have to communicate their own intellectual world to their colleagues. They should have a genuine interest in the project at hand and in interdisciplinary research. It is also a good idea to anticipate some personality problems in the course of a project. Disputes are likely when individuals *talk by one another* in their intellectual analyses, not to mention the usual dislikes and rivalries that crop up in any team effort. Individuals may find that interdisciplinary research puts them under inordinate strain. Psychological problems are possible. Tasks are almost invariably more complex and take longer than anticipated. Personal and intellectual interaction becomes more critical and demanding. Yet, in spite of these difficulties and pitfalls, interdisciplinary projects often offer a sense of accomplishment accompanied by the exhilaration of discovering new intellectual worlds and perceiving the connections among them.

For the interdisciplinary team's leader, important objectives are developing and maintaining strong intrateam communication, making sure that an adequate, but not excessive, information base is developed in the process of bounding the project, and ensuring that iteration occurs to the extent necessary to weave the various components together. In the last analysis, the team leader is responsible for making the bottom-line decisions that determine the direction of the project. Although team participation in decisions is helpful and usually to be encouraged, the leader's role remains crucial in making timely and decisive decisions.

It is clear that the present R&D and educational environments are not designed for interdisciplinary work. Education, especially at the critical level of research training, is disciplinary in character; cross-disciplinary work is usually frowned upon. In addition, the main scholarly production of the neophyte researcher—the thesis—is an individual, disciplinary product. Thus, in general, the educational system does everything in its power to discourage interdisciplinary work. Likewise, most R&D organizations are structured to reinforce the prejudices of the educational system. All this at a time when the social and intellectual needs for interdisciplinary work are so great!

The solution, I believe, lies in revising graduate training in research to allow another option in addition to the present system. This alternative would allow the student to be trained broadly in a number of areas as well as in an area of depth concentration, with the option of doing the thesis project in a group context. Such measures attack the root causes of the problem and in the long run should alter our concept of R&D. Secondary measures such as the establishment of permanent, long-lived, cross-disciplinary units in academic and R&D institutions would add solid reinforcement to the basic strategy of educational change. A progressive society deserves that its educational institutions be in tune with its legitimate R&D needs, and the difficulty of achieving interdisciplinarity in R&D presents an outstanding case of a present mismatch.

REFERENCES

Armstrong, J. E., and Harman, W. W. *Strategies for Conducting Technology Assessments.* Palo Alto, Calif.: Stanford University, 1977.

Berg, M. R., et al. *Factors Affecting Utilization of Technology Assessments Studies in Policymaking.* Ann Arbor: University of Michigan, Institute of Social Research, 1978.

Caplan, N., et al. *The Use of Social Science Technology in Policy Decisions at the National Level.* Ann Arbor: University of Michigan, Institute of Social Research, 1975.

Changnon, S. A., Jr., et al. *Hail Suppression: Impacts and Issues.* Urbana: Illinois State Water Survey, 1977.

Enzer, S. *Some Impacts of No-Fault Automobile Insurance: A Technology Assessment.* Middletown, Conn.: Institute for the Future, 1974.

Grad, F. P., et al. *The Automobile.* Norman: University of Oklahoma Press, 1975.

Harkness, R. C. *Technology Assessment of Telecommunications/Transportation Interactions.* Menlo Park, Calif.: SRI International, 1976.

Harvey, D. G., and Menchen, R. W. *The Automobile—Energy and the Environment: A Technology Assessment of Advanced Automotive Propulsion Systems.* Columbia, Md.: Hittman Associates, 1974.

Hill, S. C. "A Natural Experiment on the Influence of Leadership Behavior Pattern on Scientific Productivity." *IEEE Transactions on Engineering Management.* EM-17 (1970): 10-20.

Kash, D. E. "Observations on Interdisciplinary Studies and Government Roles." In *Adapting Science to Social Needs.* Washington, D.C.: American Association for the Advancement of Science, 1977, pp. 147-78.

_____ et al. *Energy Under the Oceans: A Technology Assessment of Outer Continental Shore Oil and Gas Operations.* Norman: University of Oklahoma Press, 1973.

Nilles, J. "Interdisciplinary Research Management in the University." *Journal of the Society of Research Administrators* 6 (1975): 9-16.

Rossini, F. A., and Porter, A. L. "Frameworks for Integrating Interdisciplinary Research." *Research Policy* 8 (1979): 70-79.

Rossini, F. A., et al. *Frameworks and Factors Affecting Interaction Within Technology Assessments.* Report to the National Science Foundation, grant ERS 76-64474. Atlanta: Georgia Institute of Technology, 1978.

_____. "Interdisciplinary Integration Within Technology Assessment." *Knowledge* 2 (1981):503-528.

Watson, J. D. *The Double Helix.* New York: Signet, 1968.

Career Patterns of Scientists and Engineers

Daryl E. Chubin

Georgia Institute of Technology

A surprisingly high proportion of science and engineering students come to the end of their educational programs without ever having given much serious thought to their professional careers. Having chosen a major, and perhaps a specialty within it, we work busily through a largely prescribed sequence of courses, putting off any serious career planning until we get close to graduation and start looking for a job. Given how one job tends to shape our skills and interests for the next one, we may find ourselves firmly set on one career path when we would really have preferred another.

Daryl Chubin offers some background information needed for sensible career-planning decisions in the scientific and technological professions, looking first at what might be called the "demography" of such careers: What are the major options? What sorts of people typically choose each option? How are they trained? And what sorts of organizations do they join? The second section looks at the individual's career as it unfolds within an organization. What are the organizational incentives and constraints? How do these differ by employment sector, professional role, and career stage? How do these factors affect the individual's creativity, performance, and satisfaction? Finally, since most of us can look forward to professional careers stretching well into the twenty-first century, what can we expect the future to bring in terms of changing career patterns? Obviously, we are not suggesting that it is possible (or even desirable) to make firm plans for the rest of one's professional life. It is, however, useful to have some background on what the options and major consequences are.

Those who think we are living in a state of some cyclical depression are wrong: The old world can never be put back. [The United States] is the first nation to evolve from adolescent growth into a new scientific and technical maturity in a service economy we do not yet fully understand.

—Derek de Solla Price (1978)

Over a quarter of a century has passed since the Russian satellite Sputnik was launched into space. During this period an ideology of science and technology has grown and gravitated to the center of American life. Seen after World War II as an "endless frontier," American science and technology have become big, expensive, and not always synonymous with the public interest. Massive doses of federal money and an eager market for technical manpower and its products in the 1960s gained the United States parity with the Soviet Union.

Today, however, the American public has little more than the fleeting comfort of pride in capturing the lion's share of Nobel prizes, and has a keener awareness of the failings of science. A cancer cure, eradication of the threat of nuclear war, and the preservation of our natural environment elude us. Costs and risks, as well as benefits, accompany technological advances. Likewise, federal funding for research and development (R&D) and the training of technical manpower lead to some unhappy choices. No ideology or rhetoric of science can escape the harsh economic, political, and social realities facing us in 1981. For as the cost of science and technology has soared, so has the public's clamoring for accountability. Worse yet, the market for the selling of expertise has turned generally bearish, converting the oversupply of newly trained scientists into an army of the underemployed.

This picture may seem gloomy, but it describes the changing economic, political, and social climate in which American scientists and engineers have embarked on and pursued their careers. For many newly minted Ph.D.s the post-Sputnik period represented a psychological cycle of great anticipation and even greater despair. The 1980 Ph.D. in physics or mathematics was among the first-grade students who announced their intention to be "a scientist" in response to the question of "What to be when you grow up?" These students were weaned on the physical sciences, versed in the old and new maths, and headed for graduate school. For those who survived the Vietnam War and declining support of graduate departments thereafter, receipt of the Ph.D. in 1980 was another rude awakening.

How does one launch a brilliant career when jobs in science are scarce and those that are available offer deflated remuneration in an inflated economy? Why does one remain in an organization when the monetary rewards of employment are scarce? Why do scientists continue to do research (or discontinue it) when nobody seems to be paying attention? How do scientists decide when it's time for a change in employer, or primary activity, or program of research? And how does the future for engineers differ from that which scientists face?

These are some of the questions we will try to address here. First, we present a demography of the labor force in science and engineering. What are the trends in the size and distribution of this population? Second, we examine the organizational contexts that give meaning to careers. Where does this technical labor force work and what does it do? Third, we consider the performance of technical work. Who evaluates it, how is it rewarded, and how do we measure the experience behind the numbers of years and papers? Finally, we look tentatively into the future, suggesting the prospects for careers in science and engineering—how they are apt to change—to the end of the twentieth century.

A DEMOGRAPHY OF THE SCIENTIFIC LABOR FORCE

Growth of the scientific labor force in the United States has been a foregone conclusion for twenty years. The annual production of new Ph.D.s has more than tripled since 1960, to a present rate of over 30,000. During the same period engineering and science Ph.D.s—which include mathematics, physical sciences, and life sciences—have grown at a slightly slower rate. Today, they represent one-third of the Ph.D.s granted, compared to one-half in 1965.

Ph.D.s alone, however, do not constitute the scientific labor force. In many fields, the doctorate-as-terminal-professional-degree is a fiction. Certainly in engineering, computer science, and even traditional disciplines such as physics, career success does not depend on a Ph.D. A master, or even a baccalaureate, of science degree is sufficient. A Ph.D. is required primarily for the purpose of teaching at the college or university level. That so many scientists earn this degree reflects the traditional "drawing power" of the academic sector and the centrality of the teaching role in a science and engineering labor force that now exceeds 600,000. Yet roughly half of these persons possess a Ph.D. and two-thirds of them are employed in the industrial sector. The tradition is changing.

A Question of Gender

Foremost among the changing traditions in the science and engineering population is the increasing proportion of women. Still, only 10 percent of the Ph.D.s in science and engineering are women. Until equal opportunity ("affirmative action") legislation required employers to assess the composition and employment history of their labor force, little attention was paid to gender. Since 1973, however, the National Research Council (NRC), among other governmental and private organizations, has compiled detailed employment statistics that help to corroborate anecdotal accounts of discrimination and success. Some of these statistics bear repeating here, some are reported later.

Table 1 shows the distribution of doctorates awarded to women in 1968 and 1977 by broad field. Clearly, both numbers and percentages have grown rapidly, though women are a solid minority of Ph.D. recipients. Whereas the trend is clear, what lurks behind the numbers is even more telling. First, on the average, women scientists at receipt of the doctorate show evidence of greater academic ability—as measured by college grades and high school test scores—than men and, in recent years, have completed their Ph.D.s as fast as or faster than men. Greater selectivity of women students may be at work here. That is, the perception of science as a masculine profession and cultural stereotypes of what constitutes "women's work" no doubt discourage female students who have the aptitude to earn a graduate degree from pursuing one. Those who do persevere, defying both cultural stereotypes and social pressures, are a select group who surpass the performance of their male counterparts.

Second, and more disconcerting, all other NRC findings suggest that doctoral women scientists in the academic sector lag behind men in salary, faculty rank, and tenure status. Specifically, women are most likely to be assistant professors, men full professors. In 1980

Table 1. Women Receiving Doctorates in Sciences and Engineering, 1968 and 1977

Field	Number	Percent of doctorates awarded, 1968	Number	Percent of doctorates awarded, 1977
Physical sciences	232	5.0	431	9.9
Life sciences	510	13.8	957	20.1
Social sciences	552	15.8	1,830	28.1
Engineering	12	0.4	74	2.8
Total	1,306	8.9	3,292	18.0

Source: National Research Council, Summary Report, 1977. Reprinted in Science and Technology: A Five-Year Outlook, Washington, D.C., National Academy of Sciences, 1979, chapter 10.

less than 10 percent of all professors, but 52 percent of all instructors, were women (who constitute 26 percent of full-time instructional faculty). In twenty-five major institutions surveyed, women were seven times more likely than men to be at the lowest rank of instructor/lecturer. For all ranks, 72 percent of the men, but only 46 percent of the women, are tenured. And this disparity seems to be increasing! Third, in relation to the pools of new women Ph.D.s (see Table 1), chemistry and mathematics—classified as physical sciences—employ far lower proportions of women faculty than do other fields. Indeed, in the 1974–75 academic year, only 2 percent of full-time staff in chemistry departments were women, although 10 percent of the chemistry Ph.D. recipients were women.

The Academic Stereotype and Nonacademic Employment

From these data alone, it appears that opportunities within science vary considerably by gender, field of training, and sector of employment. On the one hand, we may be encouraged by reports that the number of women employed full-time as scientists and engineers in academe increased 5 percent in 1978 compared to 2 percent for men. In that same year, women engineers increased 19 percent. On the other hand, women still occupy less than 3 percent of the engineering positions in all academic institutions.

Looking at the industrial sector, the Bureau of Labor Statistics finds that industries with high concentrations of science and engineering personnel, such as petroleum refining and electrical equipment companies, employed 17 percent more workers from 1965 to 1977, but only 4 percent more from 1970 to 1977. And remarkably, by 1979, chemistry and chemical engineering graduates, at all degree levels, constituted over half the professionals employed in American industrial research!

As Table 2 indicates, industry, government, and nonprofit employers combined offered a smaller percentage of jobs to new Ph.D.s in 1977 than they did in 1969. The greatest increase occurred in postdoctoral study, which, of course, reflects the shortage of permanent (tenure-track) positions on college and university faculties. It is not unusual to hear about an experimental physicist who took a one-year "post-doc" at an accelerator site only to remain in that research position six years later. How

Table 2. Employment Plans of New Doctorate Recipients (by Percentage), 1969 and 1977

Fields of employment	Engineering, Mathematics, and Physical Sciences		Nonsciences	
	1969*	1977	1969*	1977
Postdoctoral study	20	28	2	4
Academic	31	25	80	70
Industry, government, and nonprofit	42	38	7	15
Other and unknown	6	9	11	11
Total	100	100	100	100

*From unpublished NRC tables.
Source: National Research Council, Summary Report, 1977. Reprinted in **Science and Technology: A Five-Year Outlook**, Washington, D.C., National Academy of Sciences, 1979, chapter 10.

likely is it that this valuable member of an experimental team will abandon the security of a million-dollar-per-annum research grant (which pays his salary) to accept an assistant professorship at an institution with no accelerator of its own and that cannot guarantee him tenure? In terms of his research, opting for the latter would be foolish. In terms of advancement and reward, the choice may not be so clear-cut.

The prevalence of an "academic stereotype" has discouraged pursuit of a scientific career outside of full-time, tenure-track academic employment. But this image of the Ph.D. researcher evaluated according to a single standard of written productivity (published papers) has never accurately captured the diversity of what scientists and engineers do, where they do it, and how they and others feel about it. To clarify our notions of our own career opportunities and decisions, we need answers to more detailed questions. How do organizations shape careers? What are the constraints that scientific personnel encounter? How do scientists and engineers choose the work roles they play? And how have these constraints and roles changed as science has become

bureaucratized, team oriented, and increasingly (at least in the industrial sector) profit motivated?

SCIENTISTS IN ORGANIZATIONS: WORK CONTEXTS AND PROFESSIONAL ROLES

The heading above is borrowed from a classic book by two social psychologists, Donald Pelz and Frank Andrews, first published in 1966, revised in 1976. Pelz and Andrews present an impressive assortment of findings relating scientists' behavior to the organization of research laboratories. Their findings underscore the importance of work context in the performance of professional "roles"—jobs and duties seen as indispensable for achieving the goals of an organization. Scientists and engineers are, after all, employees—highly skilled and creative perhaps, but employees nonetheless. Employees build careers in the sense of playing a sequence of roles defined by an organizational ladder of positions, titles, and responsibilities. The connection between the scientists' performance and the expectations of the employing organization cannot be overemphasized. Whereas the organization sees a range of roles played in concert at a given point in time, the scientist sees a niche for his/her expertise, a step toward career goals.

Because scientists and engineers are professionals, their work roles require the application in some form of specialized knowledge to clients' problems. What complicates the performance of roles, however, is the definition of both the problems and the clients posing them. These definitions differ by employment sector: in the words of Pelz and Andrews, satisfactory performance of a role depends on "the 'fit' between a scientist's abilities and the setting in which he works."

Who, then, is the scientist's client? In academe, we might say "the student." Indeed, this is the only sector where teaching is a formal role. However, after years of conforming to the maxim "publish or perish," many a faculty member has published *and* perished. Was their student clientele dissatisfied? Probably not; any member of a college or university faculty quickly learns that his/her job entails more than one role—certainly more than teaching. The research role is highly valued, for it brings visibility and the trappings of success—name recognition and research funds—to faculty members and the employing institution alike.

By contrast, in industry both one's role and clientele differ. Profit making is so highly valued that meeting deadlines and supervising the production of a quality item, whether it is hardware or design, is likely to be the path to organizational success and career advancement.

Individual Decision Making and Organizational Wisdom

The fit between role expectations and role playing is often poor. Take, for example, the "role conflict" between teaching and research. The Ph.D. is known as a research degree; it certifies the recipient as a competent, nominally creative researcher. Yet fully half of those with Ph.D.s never publish; presumably they do no research, but fulfill their employers' expectations by satisfactorily executing another role. Many faculty were tenured in the 1960s in just this way. Some departments and whole institutions support a faculty that is 70 percent tenured. What happened in the 1960s could not be sustained in the 1970s. Effective teachers who were not also productive researchers "perished." Whether they fled the academic sector is difficult to trace. Clearly, their careers were disrupted. Today we call them "tenure casualties," a glib summary of the lack of fit between a professional and his/her academic employer. Fortunately, there are other roles, other sectors, and other clients.

What emerges from numerous studies of job choice is the conclusion that scientists may act "rationally" in selecting a sector of employment and one role as primary among others, but that the system or market may not respond in kind. Professionals, of course, are recruited for positions; this is no assurance that they will become "acculturated" to local demands of an employing organization. They may become disgruntled with the nature of their work or the sluggishness of their advance up the organizational ladder. Often a proven researcher is promoted to a full-time administrative role that substitutes paperwork such as proposal writing and budget balancing for "bench" science. Since organizations tend to attribute exceptional qualities, such as leadership, to successful junior employees, promotions can be the undoing of the precocious scientist. Attributions based on faulty measures and dubious predictions of future performance have been called the "bogus wisdom" of an organization—or at least of its upper management echelon. The upshot is that a gifted scientist or engineer may take an administrative role for which (s)he has no training or aptitude and in which he or she fails miserably. Such a career "failure" dramatizes the irrationality of employers as much as, if not more than, the decision making of the neophyte scientist.

Nor is the neophyte scientist simply released into the job market. Typically, (s)he is guided or sponsored by a faculty supervisor or mentor who uses a personal network of research and other colleagues to identify promising job leads for the student. Such leads usually follow the mentor's orientation to the kind of scientific work to which (s)he personally is inclined and to which (s)he deems the student best suited.

Types of Scientists/Engineers

By the time the neophyte is certified (by degree) and marketable, he or she has begun to develop an identity and to become committed to a particular kind of employer and role. Three types of scientist that have been empirically distinguished are the public, the private, and the organizational scientist. The public scientist has a commitment to pure science and coincides with the academic stereotype. The private scientist stresses applications of science and thrives in the for-profit, private sector. The organizational scientist is most attuned to the needs of his/her employer. In contrast to the public scientist, who has a "cosmopolitan"—national or international—reputation and network of colleagues, the organizational scientist is a "local" who derives influence and satisfaction by excelling in the more immediate environment, be it academic, governmental, or industrial. The organizational scientist is also most apt to spurn or outgrow the research role and embrace administration. Both public and private scientists may be tapped for a fourth scientific role, that of "gatekeeper." This responsibility includes journal editing and peer review decision making for research funding and fellowship competitions. The gatekeeper wields power by filtering information; the most direct route to such an influential position is the visibility afforded by published research. Consequently, the research and gatekeeper roles are closely tied.

Gatekeeping is pivotal for the effective execution of all professional roles. To gain and maintain a competitive edge—in people, research, job opportunities, etc.—any organization needs gatekeepers, each specializing in information derived from particular sources and shared only with certain others. It is within networks and among gatekeepers that the informal transactions of science and engineering take place.

Informal strains can develop when identity, employer, and role are inconsistent. Although all local employers exact a measure of devotion from their employees, even the most cosmopolitan scientist routinely takes on a local task, such as head of a search committee or chair of a campuswide group, to demonstrate loyalty. For loyalty and expediency are easily confused; a few may be "stars" but none are free agents. They, and the institutions that recruit and employ them, trade on the reputation of the other. It is a marriage of convenience that may give careers a sense of duty and continuity that is misleading if not utterly false. Nevertheless, to some extent, all scientists and engineers are of the "organizational" type.

At the same time, dissatisfactions with employers can be offset by the incentives and rewards employers provide. This is especially so in industry.

Because the firm is geared to the commercial development of research, its laboratories favor knowledge that can become profitable (for example, through patents), and are often biased against long-range programs unless they also yield short-term results. For the scientist who is instrumental in such organizational successes, status and financial gain move hand-in-hand. As one ascends the many rungs of the career ladder of the firm, salaries and titles change. In addition, greater involvement, if not autonomy, in substantive work decisions accrues.

For the academic counterpart of the industrial scientist, status and remuneration are trade-offs. The salary scale is more modest in the university, the career rungs fewer. After attaining a full professorship, remaining local challenges lie solely in administration—department head, dean, etc. Usually this transition to full-time administration marks the end of the scientist's or engineer's research productivity and, for that matter, most teaching activity. What is gained when these roles are forsaken is salary. Academic administration pays, if not well, then noticeably better than do orthodox faculty positions.

For the active researcher, local remuneration can be supplemented by cosmopolitan service. One need not assume formal gatekeeping roles; consultantships to private companies help to compensate for the public scientist's relatively modest salary. Advising government agencies and peer reviewing as a panelist deciding which proposals should be funded or designated as high priorities provide a sense of "good citizenship," prestige, and free travel plus expenses rather than remuneration for the service rendered.

Interestingly, as biomedical researchers approached the threshold of genetic manipulation in the late 1970s, an unprecedented number took a page out of the industrial R&D manager's handbook. They founded their own firms to produce and market the fruits of recombinant DNA technology: insulin, interferon, and other "gene therapies." Alternatively, with the urging of a persistent few government science advisers, Harvard University and Monsanto entered into the first academic-industrial agreement to capitalize on the best of these two sectors. Under such a collaboration, the basic ideas of university-based researchers can be translated into profitable mass-produced applications by industry. Although the two institutions will not "share and share alike," the arrangement is far more equitable and sensible than most like to admit. If such arrangements are emulated—Exxon and the American Association for the Advancement of Science, the largest scientific society in the United States, are spearheading the effort—the distinctions among scientists' identity, expectations, and roles may blur, heralding novel and interesting career patterns. The $1,000-a-day consultations that some medical school molecular biologists now provide to genetic engineering firms are becoming common. Owning stock in the Biogens and Genentechs will be as attractive as the renown of receiving the Nobel prize. And why not? There's certainly more than one path to glory in science and technology.

Conclusions on Individual-Organizational Fit

To enhance the satisfaction and productivity of scientists and engineers in organizations, some accommodation of the scientist or engineer to his/her work environment is essential, if each is to maximize what the other has to offer. The perception of convergence between organization needs and personal goals no doubt eases this accommodation.

In addition, professionals, by their very interaction, create a local environment; it doesn't come prepackaged. In general, Pelz and Andrews found that scientists and engineers "were more effective when they experienced a 'creative tension' between sources of stability or security on the one hand and sources of disruption or challenge on the other." Certainly one's co-workers, perhaps more than one's supervisors, go far in challenging, providing timely criticism, and allowing one to fail without fear of reprisal.

Third, on-site studies of laboratories suggest that most time and energy is spent in "making sense" of benchwork —creating order out of an array of disordered data, and negotiating consensus on meaning and strategy for further work. If cooperation is the benchmark of laboratory research, competition is the external reality that unites research teams. It also leads to secrecy and to prudent use of the "old-boy" network— sometimes called an "invisible college" —to convey and attract information about competitors' latest findings. In the industrial sector, such informal communication to protect or disclose, as the case dictates, is commonplace. If this is repugnant to an employee of a firm embroiled in a "priority race" for patent or marketing rights, (s)he is likely to experience strain that may ultimately precipitate a change in employment. Knowledge is valuable; to share it freely can be costly to an organization even if not sharing violates the principles of one of its employees.

Fourth, because scientific-technical work is economic and political as well as intellectual, certain organizations are more or less adapted for certain kinds of tasks. Interviews with administrators of research programs of the National Cancer Institute have revealed that the civil service places undue burdens on lab personnel. Because such government employees cannot be fired, their incompetence and/or lack of cooperation compounds a highly pressurized situation. Besides the personal and professional costs it exacts, such a situation leads to waste, delay, and an overall impression that little headway on urgent problems, such as the treatment and cure of disease, is being made—at least in the government sector.

Finally, our analysis of the fit between organizations and the roles that scientists and engineers play in them has shown that the work performed by this technical labor force is part of a dynamic process. Not all are trained alike or prepared for the same job. What entry-level skills and abilities they bring to the employment market will mature and perhaps change radically over the course of their careers. We must remember that professionals age, too. As they do, their interests and capacities evolve to make them more or less attractive and/or valuable to organizations for a multitude of reasons. At any juncture in the scientist's life cycle, his or her past will be more than the total of degrees, titles, publications, patents, and roles; these are merely junctures in a rich personal history of professional experiences and accomplishments. The prospective employer, like the individual scientist or engineer, must weigh these. The respective decisions made will not only affect one career path, but alter the climate and performance of a whole organization as well.

REWARDING PERFORMANCE . . . AND OTHER THINGS

How do scientific and engineering organizations evaluate the work performance of their employees? Several answers can be offered, reflecting differences by sector. For now, we restrict the focus to one sector, the academic world. In academe, prestige is at a premium. A residual of the academic stereotype is the reward system of science. This system exchanges prestige for publication, so its chief focus is research. Research begets publications (articles, books), visibility through citation of those publications, and name recognition. The more readily one is recognized for past research achievements, the greater is the likelihood that one will be recognized in the future. Such "accumulation of advantage" gives a competitive edge to scientists with a track record, at a prestigious institution, etc. Research funds seem to flow relatively unimpeded to recognized scientists, allowing them to generate, in turn, more publications and citations.

The Stratification of Rewards

One by-product of this spiraling of advantage is the lure of positions at other institutions. In a very basic sense, one could say that a job is a reward. Scientists trained at prestigious institutions secure positions at other prestigious institutions—one manifestation of what is called "sponsored mobility." "Inbreeding" and selection of one's successors—the elite—is a prerogative of successful scientists. Such factors as one's degree-granting institution or the reputation of one's mentor are seen as affirmations of organizational wisdom. Whether wisdom is considered "bogus" or not is quite subjective. In academe, anyway, most rewards are seen as earned, most recipients as deserving. Everyone knows an "old boy" who bends the rules to favor some over others, but few admit to being one. The same goes for luck. "Discovery favors the prepared

mind," said Pasteur: who cares if some minds are more prepared than others? The system supposedly identifies the best talent, who, in turn, perpetuate themselves. Those not so identified are withheld credit due them. The "reward system" doles out punishment, it seems, as well. Any competitive system must do so; science is no exception.

If rewards derive mainly from research, what is it about research that is especially significant for careers? At the most fundamental level, we know that among those who publish, 20 percent or so produce over half the literature. In 1979, 5,400 scientific and technical journals published two million articles worldwide. The Institute for Scientific Information assures us that 2,500 journals capture 98 percent of the literature that researchers ever consult. Even so, the distribution of authors who are cited in a given year is highly skewed: 20 percent receive the bulk of citations. This too is deceptive, however, because most published papers are never cited; a few attract a lot of attention. Then again, in some specialties, if a paper is not cited within two years of its publication, it will be ignored forever; in others such as most social science specialties, a decade might pass before some enterprising researcher notices that a fruitful lead already exists *in print*. In all, the periodical literature represents a huge archive, a repository of mundane findings, redundant theories, and stillborn ideas.

Yet the act of publishing does yield some reward. It is added to one's *curriculum vitae* to signify an active research program, the ability to pass the editorial scrutiny of "peers," and, above all, execution of the research role. Since publication is so central to a research career, we should examine briefly some of the theories of what leads to more, or less, publication.

Theories of Publication Productivity

According to one theory, the social response to published research constitutes a reinforcement of the behavior. Thus, publishing scientists continue to publish. The opposite of this phenomenon would mean that repeated rejections of manuscripts submitted for publication would convince the author that research is not his/her calling. The theory predicts that research activity will subsequently wane and publications cease; for some people the behavior is "extinguished." Such a process is assumed to occur in the transition of scientists and engineers out of the research role. In short, if one can't "cut it" in research, one seeks other outlets, perhaps new fervor in the classroom and attentiveness to students outside, or heightened sensitivity to one's co-workers as the prospect of landing an administrative post looms. In both cases, reorientation in career values and goals is taking place.

A second theory views creativity as a special motivating force. Because scientists and engineers have an insatiable creative impulse, they need to satisfy it by producing more and more. This "sacred spark," though seemingly innate, is kindled long before college and graduate school. Indeed, psychological profiles of scientists have traditionally revealed them to have been highly intelligent, curious children (usually first-born) of professional families, and excited by the manipulation of things instead of human interaction. Some would be classified as geniuses on the basis of IQ (150+) alone. However, intelligence is a poor discriminator of creative talent in science, since those with the Ph.D. are all in the upper 5–10 percent of the distribution for the population at large.

This finding has led in the last fifteen years to an exploration of "cognitive styles." It is not intelligence that sparks creativity, but the motivation to approach the world in particular ways. How does one *feel* as well as *think* about a subject? A "convergent" thinker seeks the single right answer, the "divergent" thinker relishes the invention of many possible right answers. Or, to take another typology, based on a psychological (projective) test, "integrators" are able to recognize previously unrecognized problems and have the technical skills to solve them; "problem solvers" can solve already-formulated problems but lack the ability to recognize new ones; "problem recognizers" have difficulty solving problems; and "technicians" possess neither the ability of recognition nor solution (of any but the most conventional problems). Integrators might be seen as the most innovative of the cognitive styles, technicians as the least. We know science and engineering are populated by all of these types.

Nevertheless, it has been asserted that the creative professionals experience, without relent, an "essential tension," which culminates, or renews itself, in throwing off the shackles of vision that graduate training invariably brings. To challenge the orthodox way of seeing things, yet know how to apply one's tools to the solution of an old problem or creation of a new one, is rare in science. Few are open minded enough or possess the fortitude to overcome the "trained incapacity" or mental set inculcated in college and (even more so) graduate school. This incapacity is the way we are taught to view our disciplinary subject matter; what we are told *not* to look for and at are those phenomena that fall outside our "conceptual boxes." Such myopia, however, has the unfortunate consequence of stifling creativity—in the sense of generating new boxes or expanding the contents of those we already see and use.

Those whose research career reflects the essential tension usually accumulate a stock of tangible awards to prove it. On the other hand, extreme novelty is threatening to a research community. As Mitroff and Kilmann recently asked, "Are scientists great because their speculations have somehow proved fruitful or because they are willing to risk bold speculations in the face of extreme criticism from their peers?" Without knowing the distribution of cognitive styles (as opposed to the types of identity discussed above) among engineers versus scientists, or by field and sector of employment, we can't automatically conclude that the correlations among productivity, creativity, and reward are high. Indeed, we know that inequalities in rewards are very real. What, we may ask, are the sources of inequality?

Inequality in Rewards

Among the most widely regarded honors in science are election to a national academy, e.g., the National Academy of Engineering, and receipt of various prizes and medals, the best known being the Nobel Prize. While studies of rewards are legion, studies of the psychological or cognitive characteristics of NAE members and Nobel laureates are not. Hence, the reinforcement, sacred spark, and cognitive-style theories remain largely untested. Ironically, we know the most about an eminent, and extraordinarily small, fraction of the scientific population. Yet in the absence of necessary data, we are left to conjecture about unequal access to opportunity in science and the disparate allocation of rewards by such factors as gender.

Consider just a few indicators of gender disparities in rewards for scientific merit:

1. From 1946 to 1976, 50 percent of the total number of Nobel Prize winners were United States scientists; yet only 3 out of 172, or 1.7 percent (one each in physics, chemistry, and physiology or medicine), was a woman.

2. Of 1,256 members of the National Academy of Sciences (as of 1978), 33 (2.6 percent) were women. NAS President Philip Handler even contends that marriage is a greater hindrance to the scientific career of women than that of men. Although more men than women Ph.D.s marry, the divorce rate of the women is twice that of the men.

3. The highest scientific award of the United States, the Medal of Science, was given to 132 persons from 1962 to 1977. Among them was one woman (awarded it in 1970). In addition, social scientists are ineligible.

Other data relate these very prestigious awards to more conventional ones, such as positions and salaries. Perhaps the most telling findings have been reported by the Scientific Manpower Commission. Since 1970, the proportion of women in U.S. science and technology has doubled. And while the number of women on American university science faculties grew three times faster than total faculty growth during the period 1973–77, men's academic salaries exceeded women's by approximately 20 percent in 1977. The 8 percent women among the newly elected members of the NAS is still twice the proportion of full professorships in elite universities (the Ivy League, Berkeley, Chicago, Michigan, MIT, etc.) held by women. One-third of the microbiologists employed by the federal government in 1978 were women; their average salary was 20 percent less than that of their male colleagues. Finally, unemployment rates for women continue to be two to five times higher than for men in the same field with the same level of training.

Thus, inequality of rewards knows no sectoral or organizational boundary. Gender and race (blacks and ethnic minorities have fared only slightly better than women for the past decade) are supposedly irrelevant to the performance and recognition of scientific work. That such inequalities persist in *all* phases of the scientific career is a sad commentary on the effectiveness of disciplines as *professions* to restructure opportunity and reward scientists for what they do, not for who they are.

It is organizations themselves, and hence the scientists and engineers within them, that have been unwilling, impotent, or both, to balance the privileges of sponsorship, reputation, and advantage. Instead, we are left to ponder the statistics Zuckerman presents in her book on Nobel laureates in the United States between 1901 and 1972, *Scientific Elite.* During the period of her study, thirteen elite universities granted the doctoral degree to 85 percent of the Nobel laureates, 80 percent of the members of the National Academy of Sciences, and 55 percent of the other scientists who received their Ph.D.s. One conclusion is undeniable: where one's career "ends up" depends very much on where it begins. The intervening years will chronicle the maximization of early advantages or their neutralization. In guiding one's career, the scientist or engineer must safeguard his/her own self-interests, and garner appropriate benefits. The resultant heterogeneity of careers attests, in the aggregate, to the unpredictability of this labor force. What, then, is the outlook for careers in science and engineering?

FUTURE TRENDS IN SCIENTIFIC AND ENGINEERING CAREERS

In 1974 a prominent science policy analyst asked, "Are scientists obsolete?" His question, although rhetorical, served to remind the science policy community that for all its planning, forecasting,

and rational decision making, the supply and demand of technical manpower in the U.S. were out of synchronization, and perhaps out of control. The irony of this situation is that a "postindustrial" society needs the most educated, most specialized personnel to steer it through a minefield of late twentieth century dilemmas: safe and plentiful energy sources, preservation of the environment, the engineering of old and new forms of life, war or peace for the planet Earth. Certainly, the federal government has successfully stimulated the training of specialized personnel. What is present now are imbalances, by industry and employment sectors, to hire and utilize the available expertise.

One result is the "Ph.D. glut." Relief from it, according to one editorial in *Science,* can come in two ways:

> First, we can make more widely understood the utility of doctoral education, thereby creating demand where none now exists. Second, we can hope to make the expectations of students more realistic, thereby broadening the scope of acceptable employment goals. Each of these has promise for narrowing the gap between supply and demand, and each is something we can hope to affect by our own actions.

But "our own actions" have been reluctant at best. Graduate faculty do not easily part with the cheap labor of graduate assistants. Prestigious institutions do not readily bow to suggestions, sometimes punctuated by the withdrawal or infusion of federal training grants, to downgrade their doctoral programs in selected disciplines to master of science degrees that are more in keeping with market demands. What is in the national interest is frequently not in the institution's interest. As long as its faculty can be less than conscientious in training doctoral candidates for promised jobs that never materialize, reforms in training practices will lag behind projected employment estimates. And retraining institutes and continuing education programs for vintage Ph.D.s have not caught on to relieve the problems of obsolete knowledge and dead-end careers.

Outlook for the 1980s

Projections for the 1980s indicate that an underemployed doctorate-holding labor force is not about to disappear. The current number of science and engineering Ph.D.s in the United States labor force will increase nearly 50 percent by 1987. The number of traditional employment positions—those in the three sectors we have discussed—available to these Ph.D.s will increase only 35 percent. Between now and the end of the decade, perhaps as many as 100,000 people must find jobs in areas unrelated to their training. (One Indiana law enforcement agency has recruited philosophy Ph.D.s as deputy sheriffs and reports overwhelming success.) Seventy percent of the 100,000 will find work in industry. At the same time, the number of science and engineering Ph.D.s in university faculty positions is expected to grow by only 11 percent. And only continued nontenuring of young faculty and lucrative inducements for early (age 55) retirement will make such modest growth possible.

Looking a decade ahead and beyond, the soundest projections concern the gains in engineering manpower and womanpower. At all degree levels, demand for engineers is anticipated to rise by 34 percent; many of these degree recipients will be women, and overall most of the engineers will enter the job market with only a baccalaureate in hand—which will more than suffice. The irony is that the demand for engineers (and computer scientists) may

exceed the supply because too few Ph.D.s are willing to (re)enter the university to train them! The lure of the private sector is difficult to counteract.

By comparison, for those who secure a position in the life or social sciences, the outlook on earnings is bleak. Although chemists' salaries increased 83 percent in the 1970s, the cost of living rose 94 percent. In constant dollars, the chemist today is earning 6 percent less than (s)he did ten years ago. Similarly, some middle-level engineers complain that their salaries have not risen as fast as the pay given to engineers just out of college. Such "salary compression" means that five years of on-the-job experience may earn one only $3,000 more than the starting salary for another engineer recently hired as one's subordinate.

Such findings have prompted policy analysts to ask "Is the U.S. lead in R&D on the decline?" Derek Price claims that, in 1967, 33 percent of the world's scientific and technological knowledge was generated in the United States, which has 7 percent of the world population. In 1967, the United States had five times the average share of world affluence. By 1978, the U.S. share in world science and technology was 25 percent. Our affluence is now 3.5 the world's average. Unless heroic measures are taken, the lead will be reduced to double before the year 2000.

The nations that have rebounded to positions of contention, if not leadership, in world science and technology are Japan and West Germany. We'll forgo the temptation to belabor the irony, but one thing remains the same: the United States is still the training center for the world's scientific labor force. More foreign nationals receive master and doctoral degrees here, especially in physics, math, and engineering, than in any other nation. (However, if engineering degrees alone are considered, Japan's annual output exceeds ours, 75,000 to 60,000.) To absorb this labor force *and* use its expertise (many foreign nationals never return home; 1.3 million have joined the U.S. labor force since 1966) we must have a more stable economy than the kind we have had since the first Mideast oil embargo in 1974. To underestimate the impact of such economic instability on the career choices of new degree-holders is inexcusable.

The Perils of Projection

Despite the perils of projections, they continue to be made in the hope that anything is better than extrapolating current trends. (Indeed, "futurology" has become a discipline in itself.) Yet such extrapolations dominate projections. For example, the 1976 National Science, Engineering, and Technology Policy and Priorities Act, in addtion to restoring the President's science adviser (eliminated by Nixon in the early 1970s), created the Office of Science and Technology Policy and mandated that it prepare an *Annual Science and Technology Report* and a comprehensive *Five-Year Outlook on Science and Technology.* The first *Outlook* contains a National Academy of Sciences chapter called "Academic Science and Graduate Education," in which the authors conclude that the coming period will "be a time of adjustment for universities and academic science as they attempt to deal with such new circumstances as more stringent financial conditions, declining undergraduate enrollments, a sharp reduction in the number of new faculty positions, and the need to meet new regulatory and other administrative requirements." As a nonfuturologist interpreting these and the data presented above, I stake little of my reputation on a prognostication of the career future for the anxious reader. So here goes.

For the scientist, the academic sector is definitely not the place to go. Jobs will be scarce, remuneration inadequate, security short-lived. Only those resigned to soft-money salaries in special research institutes and centers need apply. Budding research managers and administrators, in contrast, have some choice. Someone must administer those institutes and centers, coordinate their personnel, and keep the soft money flowing. Success in such ventures should bring career opportunities for positions with real clout, discretionary budgets, and the freedom to exercise managerial creativity in the name of intellectual excellence.

The forecast for industrial, government, and nonprofit corporate (or nontraditional) employment is better. Only the most committed, entrepreneurial, and shrewd researchers should seek glory in a research career. Women and minorities will make noticeable gains, but the time it takes to overcome disadvantaged backgrounds may rival the duration of one's professional life expectancy—forty years. The choices one makes at age 25–30 (when the doctorate or other terminal degree is granted) are not insurmountable, but they do establish a tone, an early pattern, for later career decisions.

Somewhere between this brightness and gloom sits the engineer. For those trained in electrical, mechanical, civil, or industrial engineering, the continued growth of hardware- and software-based industries will provide more than ample employment opportunities. The private sector may prove to be more volatile for nuclear, petroleum, and chemical engineers. Clearly, the greatest challenge is to academically inclined engineers. The need to forge cross-sector ties prevails. A former member of both the Office of Science and Technology Policy and the Office of Management and Budget recently editorialized:

Some engineering faculty members already perform research in industrial laboratories, research institutes, or contract research groups outside the academic structure. These extra-academic arrangements provide salary supplements, special research challenges, and access to better equipment, while ensuring adequate protection of proprietary interests. More opportunities may exist for such arrangements, and they should be assessed as an alternative to losing or failing to recruit faculty members.

Dr. George Ansell, Dean of Engineering at Rensselaer Polytechnic Institute, observes:

> When the best data show about 5 percent cannot find jobs within a month of graduation, then people say there is a big surplus. If companies cannot find all the students they want in the top 25 percent of the class, they talk about a shortage. The fact is that engineering supply and demand have been in good balance and I believe this will continue.

In general, engineering educators foresee the following trends. First, realizing that the Japanese have surpassed us in the ability to apply new knowledge rather than discover it, engineering schools are rediscovering the field of design. Computer-aided design and its companion, computer-aided manufacturing, or CAD/CAM, have replaced the paper-and-pencil approach. Second, programs in "manufacturing science" and "manufacturing engineering" are beginning to appear. This specialty relates to the first trend as well as to the rise of robotics as keys to efficient production. Finally, programs that combine engineering and management will proliferate. This stems from the realization that an engineer can possess technical maturity, but lack the management skills to communicate, delegate responsibility, inspire, and lead.

Conclusions on and Prospects for Career Change

The reader contemplating a career in science or engineering has been duly alerted: your career destiny is not in your hands alone. The age of the "mobile professor" and the "organization man" has gone the way of the academic stereotype. In an age of "supply-side economics" and inflation, what was once considered a moral "calling" to the craft work of science and engineering is to others a paycheck, a living—nothing less, nothing more. This does not mean that scientists and engineers have become less dedicated or more crass; rather, they have become more "pluralistic" in what they put into, and seek to squeeze out of, their careers.

Post-Sputnik events have shaped the production and use patterns of the U.S. scientific and engineering labor force and created great diversity of opportunity in technical careers. The opportunities, however, are constrained by harsh realities. In some ways, U.S. science and technology have overspecialized; at the same time, the technical work force has grown so large that imbalances in the supply-demand equation persist. For some individuals, organizations, and sectors, imbalance is an advantage; for others, it is a disaster more chronic than acute.

Career choice is a cultural event. But like all cultural events, it is subject to social forces. The individual and aggregate responses of scientists and engineers are as idiosyncratic as educators and employers allow. Idiosyncrasy is a strength—if it can be harnessed to effect a fit among national needs, organizational goals, and individual preferences. A vital outcome of this process are what we call, and study as, career patterns. As the century draws to a close there will be room for many kinds of careers, but decidedly less room for certain kinds than in the recent past. Nevertheless, only when the pressing problems of industrial and postindustrial society are solved will the obsolescence of scientists and engineers be imminent. The future of this labor force is not in doubt, just the patterns of that future.

RECOMMENDED READINGS

Ben-David, Joseph. *The Scientist's Role in Society.* Englewood Cliffs, N.J.: Prentice-Hall, 1971.
The emergence of "the scientist" in European and American cultures.

Cotgrove, S., and Box, S. *Science, Industry and Society: Studies in the Sociology of Science.* London: Allen and Unwin, 1970.
British students prepare for technical careers in industry.

Fisch, Rudolf. "Psychology of Science." In *Science, Technology, and Society: A Cross-Disciplinary Perspective,* I. Spiegel-Rosing and D. de S. Price, eds. London and Beverly Hills: Sage, 1977.
A review of the major issues, research findings, and lacunae in the psychology of science.

Fiske, Edward B. "Engineering-School Shortcomings Lead to U.S. Lag." *New York Times Supplement,* 28 March 1982, p. 6.

Fowler, Elizabeth M. "Engineering Shortage? Well, That Depends." *New York Times Supplement,* 28 March 1982, pp. 5, 18.

Gendron, Bernard. *Technology and the Human Condition.* New York: St. Martin's Press, 1977.
A critical analysis of views on the social role of technology.

Goodfield, June. "Humanity in Science: A Perspective and a Plea." *Science* 198 (1977): 580–85.
An historian of biology tries, autobiographically, to bridge the "two cultures" of science and the humanities.

Hixson, Joseph. *The Patchwork Mouse.* Garden City, N.J.: Anchor Doubleday, 1976.
The true story of how a career in cancer research was destroyed by pressures to attract research funding and make a major discovery. Fraud in science is not tolerated—if it is detected.

Kuhn, T. S. *The Essential Tension: Selected Studies in Scientific Tradition and Change.* Chicago: University of Chicago Press, 1977.
Essays by the historian of science who wrote the influential *Structure of Scientific Revolutions.*

Layton, Edwin T., Jr. *The Revolt of the Engineers.* Cleveland and London: Press of Case Western Reserve University, 1971.
Traces the clash between engineering's two traditions of professionalism from 1900 to 1940—one oriented to independent action, the other to the business system.

Lynn, Walter R. "Engineering and Society Programs in Engineering Education." *Science* 195 (1977):150–55.
Argues that engineering education requires a better integration of values from "liberal" education, values that enhance decision-making capability.

Nagi, S. Z., and Corwin, R. G., eds. *The Social Contexts of Research.* London: Wiley, 1972.
Social scientists on the social organization of research, including the role of research support, and the economics and politics of research.

National Research Council. Summary Report 1978: *Doctorate Recipients from United States Universities.* Washington, D.C.: National Academy of Sciences, 1979.
Annual survey of science and engineering Ph.D. recipients summarizing predoctoral experiences and postdoctoral plans according to significant social variables (gender, ethnicity) and disciplinary categories.

National Science Board. *Science Indicators 1978.* Washington, D.C.: National Science Foundation, 1979.
A biennial report first issued in 1972 on the health of U.S. science and technology. Presents statistical data on manpower, publications, citations, and patents.

Omenn, Gilbert S. "Engineering: Lessons from Medical Schools." *Science* 215 (1982): 1461.
Ways to relieve the individual and institutional plight of engineering.

Pelz, Donald C., and Andrews, Frank M. *Scientists in Organizations: Productive Climates for Research and Development,* rev. ed. Ann Arbor: University of Michigan, 1976.

A 20-year compendium of the authors' researches on creativity, productivity, and organizational climates.

Perrucci, R., and Gerstl, J., eds. *The Engineer and the Social System.* New York: Wiley, 1969.

The social and professional context of engineering, addressed to the engineering student. Chapters on recruitment, the relationship among American science, business, and engineering, and engineering unionism.

Price, Derek de Solla. *Little Science, Big Science.* New York: Columbia University Press, 1963.

A statistical introduction to the "science of science" in all its historical and political splendor.

Teich, Albert H., ed. *Technology and Man's Future,* 2nd ed. New York: St. Martin's Press, 1981.

Vetter, Betty M. *Supply and Demand for Scientists and Engineers.* Washington, D.C.: Scientific Manpower Commission, 1982.

Ziman, John. *The Force of Knowledge.* New York: Cambridge University Press, 1976.

A theoretical physicist introduces British undergraduates to the history of science, technology, and medicine.

Zuckerman, H., and Merton, R. K. "Age, Aging, and Age Structure in Science." In *A Theory of Age Stratification,* M. W. Riley et al., eds., vol. 3. New York: Russell Sage, 1972.

Demography and stratification of the scientific community, including an inventory of scientific roles and rewards and a discussion of gerontocracy (control by the old) in science.

Zuckerman, Harriet. *Scientific Elite: Nobel Laureates in the United States.* New York: Free Press, 1977.

A comprehensive sociology of eminent scientists.

Leadership and the Professional

Morgan W. McCall, Jr.

Center for Creative Leadership

Scientists and engineers rarely spend their entire working lives in the disciplines they learned in school. More commonly, they spend a good deal of their careers in managerial or leadership roles of one sort or another. Even staying within the laboratory environment, a young graduate hired as a researcher will often move in a few years to head a branch or section, perhaps moving on to become a division or department head in early or mid-career. Many science and engineering graduates pursue managerial careers outside their specialties, with or without formal managerial training.

The individual often finds him- or herself managing other professional employees. Morgan McCall explores some of the problems and opportunities this involves. Drawing on available research as well as his own personal experience as a manager of professionals, McCall explores the following questions:

How do professionals (particularly engineers and scientists) differ from other kinds of employees, and how do these differences affect managerial action?

What changes can a professional expect if he or she opts for a managerial job?

What do we know about effective leadership of professionals in organizational settings?

The goals here are straightforward. The first is to help managers of professionals understand their situation. The second is to give professionals, who may deliberately or by fate end up managing professionals, some reasonable expectations about the nature of the managerial job.

A scientist usually conceives of managing as alien to his interests. Managers are usually looked down upon by scientists because they do not measure up to the high standards of technical competency that scientists see themselves as holding.

—A chemist reflecting on his work experience

At work, I'm a very difficult SOB, and that's not a character recommendation I'm particularly proud of. I feel guilty very often, but I'm so difficult that no one works for me unless they're good enough and tough enough. I explode all the time. I'm like the office plague; I snoop into everything and everyone wishes I'd stay out so I don't screw it up. But that lab is my baby.

—L. Janos, 1980

The explosion of technology has caused a dramatic increase in the number of professionals in the work force (1.7 million in 1970—about one in every fifty workers), and all indications are that knowledge industries will continue to grow (Kaufman, 1974). This is sufficient reason for interest in how to manage professionals, but their critical role in the invention and development of technology (often held out as the answer to society's many problems) creates a sense of urgency to use this talent effectively. Are professionals so different from other workers that leading them is a special challenge? Certainly the quotations above suggest some eccentricity in professionals, as workers and as managers, as do the new organizational structures emerging to accommodate professionals at work, including matrix designs and innovation-focused adhocracy.

We will address four topics here. The first order of business is to look at who is being led. Who are these "professionals"? What are they like and how are they different from the rest of us? Where is this "leading" taking place and how important is the setting?

The second topic is supervision, or the leadership of small groups of professionals. What can the "chief" or supervisor do that might make some difference in the productivity of his or her professional subordinates?

Third, what are the broader aspects of leadership? How do groups of professionals come to affect the organization and what does leadership at the interface look like?

Finally, we examine the tough choice faced by many professionals: to accept an opportunity to become a manager or to stay in a specialty area. Is it true that managerial work is the antithesis of scientific work?

WHO IS BEING LED?

They are about like other people, as assorted as cobblers, labor leaders, Javanese dancers, throat specialists, whalers, minor canons, or asparagus growers.

—Sinclair Lewis, quoted by S. James, 1980

The term "professional" is ambiguous. Doctors, lawyers, CPAs, engineers, scientists, and many others are called professionals, and battles for legitimacy occur as excluded groups, such as managers, seek recognition as professionals. Given the diversity of occupations typically considered professional, there is no reason to believe that professionals constitute a homogeneous class. As will be shown, scientists and engineers differ from each other in many ways, in spite of their professional status. Recognizing this ambiguity does not prevent a discussion of leadership and professionals, but it does dictate certain limitations. This chapter is based on research findings, and most of the research on professionals has been done with scientists and/or engineers. Furthermore, there are different kinds of scientists and engineers who vary dramatically in terms of education and training—in short, some are more "professional" than others. To accommodate these differences, we will define professionals by the degree to which they fit characteristics identified by Kerr, Von Glinow, and Schriesheim (1977):

1. **Expertise.** They have prolonged, specialized training.
2. **Autonomy.** They have the right to decide on the means and ends in their work.
3. **Commitment.** They are devoted to their work and to their profession.
4. **Identification.** Their lot is cast with their profession and their fellow professionals.
5. **Ethics.** They aspire to be unemotional and unselfish in the conduct of their professional activities.
6. **Collegial maintenance of standards.** They take responsibility for setting and enforcing standards for their profession.

For our purposes, then, leaders of professionals are managers of people who value expertise, autonomy, etc. (primarily scientists and engineers). These people can be found in all kinds of organizations, from small private firms to universities, the space agency, and high technology industries. For the most part, the research reported here was done in large, complex organizations.

As noted earlier, most of the research on this type of leadership deals with scientists and/or engineers. In general, scientists are more "professional" against the stereotype because they are generally more committed to professional goals than engineers (who tend to

identify more with business goals) (Rotondi, 1975; Barth and Vertinsky, 1975). Furthermore, over 90 percent of engineers do not have doctoral degrees and fully one-third do not belong to a professional society (Kerr et al., 1977). In fact, scientists and engineers typically have an uneasy peace with one another, and getting them to work together can be a key managerial challenge (Sayles and Chandler, 1971). Scientists and engineers also differ in vocational interest patterns (see Table 1) (Holland, 1973).

These differences have two important implications. First, all professionals, even scientists and engineers, are not alike. There are immense differences among occupations and among individuals within occupations (see, for example, Gough and Woodworth, 1960). To speak of leadership of professionals is to speak in simplified terms about complex realities.

Second, the available research does not always distinguish among the types of professionals studied. Generalizations drawn from that research can be misleading to the extent that the variation among occupations comprising professional samples is as great as the variation between professionals and nonprofessionals.

With these reservations, we can proceed to describe professionals in general, relative to nonprofessionals. A summary of the research (Filley, House, and Kerr, 1976) suggests that professional workers are more likely than their nonprofessional counterparts to

- Be seen by the organization as esoteric and more interested in their narrow specialties than in solving organizational problems
- See the organization as too pragmatic, solving problems by the seat-of-the-pants approach
- Be less loyal to the employing organization and more critical of it

Table 1. Differences in Vocational Interests

Scientists: Investigative Type	Engineers: Realistic Type
• Prefer symbolic, creative investigation • Value science, scholarship in problem solving • Adverse to persuasive, social, repetitive activities • Deficient in persuasive competence • Avoid enterprising occupations • See themselves lacking in leadership ability	• Prefer to manipulate objects • Solve problems with realistic competence • Avoid activities of social occupations • Deficient in social competencies • Recognize their own low human relations skills

Source: Adapted from Holland, 1973, and Campbell, 1974.

• Place less importance on money and more importance on the freedom to pursue projects of interest to them and on the quality of facilities and support services

• Accept authority based on expertise rather than hierarchy

• Emphasize professional values over organizational goals.

Obviously, the potential for conflict between professionals and the bureaucratic organizations employing them is high (Schriesheim, Von Glinow, and Kerr, 1977), but conflict is not inevitable. Professionals' commitment to the organization will be stronger when job opportunities outside the firm are absent or inferior to those within, when the organization bestows high prestige on its professional groups, as the professionals grow older, and as they move into management (Filley, House, and Kerr, 1976). The challenge of leading a less organizationally committed professional group is clearly different from, if not greater than, leading a committed one.

We have defined professionalism as a function of expertise, autonomy, commitment, identification, ethics, and collegial maintenance of standards. Although professionals differ among themselves in many ways, professionally oriented people differ even more from the less professionally oriented on many dimensions, including commitment to the organization, problem-solving approach, feelings about authority, and value of organizational rewards. These differences can amount to what has been called a "cosmopolitan" value system (see, e.g., Goldberg, 1976), which is, essentially, devotion to the profession and its standards that supersedes commitment to the organization and its goals.

Understanding these general differences about professionals is part of the foundation for looking at the leadership of professionals. Unfortunately the other parts are not well researched, and so can only be mentioned.

First, professionals often have some choice about the type of organization they will work in. Universities may be more consonant with the general professional value system described by Kerr, Von Glinow, and Schriesheim (1977) than are commercial enterprises. It is likely, therefore, that professionals who choose careers in industry are to some degree sympathetic to the exigencies of private enterprise.

Second, the structure of the organization is likely to affect at least some of the leadership problems faced. We know, for example, that the problems in project management differ from those in functional management (Reeser, 1969). Project organization generates more job insecurity because projects end and people must be reassigned; and leaders may have to create "makework" to keep people occupied between projects. Other structural factors are obviously important, such as the differences between an R&D lab isolated from ongoing operations and an organization with a high percentage of professionals on-line.

A third factor is the mission of the professionals. Leadership of a mission to produce new ideas or technological innovation would seem fundamentally different from leadership to use, develop, or improve that which already exists, even though both activities involve professional workers.

This is not to say that general conclusions about the leadership of professionals cannot be drawn. Rather, it emphasizes that generalities are not a substitute for thoughtful consideration of the situation at hand. Among the considerations are the degree of conflict between professional and organizational values; the structural relationships between professionals and the rest of the organization, and the structure of the professional groups themselves; and the kind of mission or goal they are pursuing.

SUPERVISION: LEADERSHIP OF PROFESSIONAL GROUPS

> Leadership, then, is the ability to tie men and women to one's person and cause. But how is that done? Leadership is obviously a combination of many things. . . . When pressures increase, we turn to those we trust to act in the general interest. . . . Some people simply seem to have an aura around them that inspires trust and confidence. We have faith in them and in their ability to deal with matters in a way that will be satisfactory to us. They inspire our

> confidence and we grant them our loyalty. These are the qualities that unite followers and that leaders, somehow, in some mysterious way, are able to call forth. Quite simply, we know leadership when we experience it.
> —L. P. Williams, 1980

For our purposes, leadership is defined as a relationship between a formal leader and a follower group consisting of professionals. For the most part, the research has not considered the context in which the group is embedded, thereby assuming that groups of professionals (generally in R&D settings) are similar. The "test" of leadership is some measure of group output, such as peer performance ratings, or the number of patents or papers.

We have already shown that professionals seek autonomy and have high levels of expertise. This suggests that leadership might not have as much impact on group performance for professionals as it does for nonprofessionals. Our first question, then, is how much difference does leadership make?

Kerr (1977) has argued that certain individual, task, and organizational characteristics can "neutralize or substitute for the formal leader's ability to influence work group satisfaction and performance for either better or worse." These "substitutes for leadership," Kerr argues, are particularly prevalent in professional settings:

> There are several reasons why the working environment of professionals employed in organizations presents special opportunities for leadership substitutes to flourish and hierarchical leadership to be consequently less important. The professional's expertise, normally acquired as a result of specialized training in a body of abstract knowledge, often serves to reduce the need for structuring information; furthermore, a belief in peer

review and collegial maintenance of standards often causes the professional to look to fellow professionals rather than to the hierarchical leader for what informational needs remain.

In an empirical study of leadership effects on eighty-one subunits of a research organization, Barnowe (1975) concluded that "clearly, the better part of variation in research outcomes was attributable to factors other than leadership." He went on to suggest that the behavior of leaders was more important when scientists were disadvantaged in some way, as when they are inexperienced or when they cannot easily consult with colleagues.

In another study of twenty-one research teams at NASA, Andrews and Farris (1967) tried to determine how much scientific performance varied from team to team. In short, if there is no variation in performance, differences in supervisory practices couldn't be having much effect. Looking at innovation (generation of *new* knowledge), productiveness (extending knowledge from previous lines of research), contribution (general contribution of knowledge to the field), and usefulness (degree to which the work was valuable to the organization), Andrews and Farris found that only innovation was significantly related to the particular team a scientist belonged to.

A lot of professional performance, then, seems to be independent of supervisory behavior. This does not mean that leadership is irrelevant (although it may be at times), but it does suggest clear limits on how much impact an individual leader can hope to have on a professional group. Even limited impact, if in the right place, can be enough to make a big difference, and leader behavior may have additional subtle or indirect effects on professionals.

If leadership does not fully explain professional performance, what does seem to matter? If we knew that, we might gain insight into how leaders can affect performance. Pelz and Andrews (1976) looked at 1,311 scientists and engineers in industrial, university, and government settings. They found that technical achievement flourished when antithetical forces existed, for instance when there were *both* environmental demands (conditions of challenge) and protection from the environment (conditions of security), creating a tension between security and challenge. Pelz and Andrews suggest that the more productive groups:

- Did not focus exclusively on either basic or applied science, but rather did some of each
- Had individuals who pursued their own ideas independently but who also interacted vigorously with their colleagues
- Managed to pursue one main project while avoiding overspecialization in one area
- Were neither loosely nor rigidly structured
- Gave members strong influence on decision makers, although that influence was shared with supervisor, colleagues, and clients
- Consisted of scientists who argued about ideas while supporting each other personally.

If these characteristics do in fact differentiate productive from less productive groups, effective supervisory leadership is more orchestration than direct application of authority. It seems a matter of creating and/or maintaining (or at least not destroying) conditions that foster scientific productivity. Clearly, the supervisor is not the only factor determining those conditions, but what does it take for the leader to make some difference? The research suggests many possibilities, which can be clustered into four general areas: technical competence, controlled freedom, acting as a metronome, and work challenge.

Technical Competence

The supervisor's technical competence is related both to scientific productivity and to the scientists' willingness to comply with management directives (Kaufman, 1974; Andrews and Farris, 1967; Thamhain and Gemmill, 1974; Schriesheim et al., 1977). We saw earlier that professionals accept expertise based rather than hierarchically based authority, but far more is involved. Leaders of productive groups serve many roles that depend on technical expertise, including:

- Recognizing good ideas emerging inside and outside the group (Clagett, 1966; Farris, 1972; Andrews and Farris, 1967)
- Defining the significant problems (Clagett, 1966)
- Influencing work goals on the basis of expertise (rather than authority) (Baker and Wilemon, 1977)
- Providing technical stimulation (Clagett, 1966).

This constellation of activities shows that leaders arbitrate among points of view by suggesting, pushing, prodding, and choosing alternatives on the basis of technical knowledge. A leader without technical competence must find ways to do this through others, while establishing his or her expertise in another area (e.g., management control and cost systems) and while providing freedom to the professionals without creating chaos (Kaufman, 1974; Andrews and Farris, 1967).

Controlled Freedom

How the supervisor makes decisions, both technical and administrative, is related to productivity. Unfortunately, the relationships are complex, so there are no simple rules of thumb available (Clagett, 1966). In general, leaders of productive groups create controlled freedom, a condition under which decision making is shared but not given away, and autonomy is partially preserved. A critical element of this seems to be collegial give-and-take in decision making, a kind of consultation with group members that produces a high level of discourse and intellectual stimulation (Clagett, 1966), especially around critical decisions on goals and resources. Apparently scientists will accept a decision if they understand the logic behind it and have had the chance to critically evaluate various alternatives.

Controlled freedom does not imply that decisions are totally in the hands of the group; in fact, laissez faire management is negatively related to productivity (Andrews and Farris, 1972; Cummings, Hinton, and Gobdel, 1975). Leaders of effective groups emphasize explicit goals but not the means of reaching them. They know the technical details of their people's work without overemphasizing control and monitoring (Cummings, Hinton, and Gobdel, 1975). Furthermore, effective leaders apply, and high-performing scientists want, relatively high pressure (Andrews and Farris, 1972). Scientists and engineers simply do not perform best in a completely relaxed environment.

It is often suggested that effective leaders of professionals buffer their people completely from administrative matters. Apparently this is not entirely true. Members of higher performing groups were involved to some extent in the solution of day-to-day operating problems, ranging from mundane matters to budgetary and policy issues (Clagett, 1966).

Controlled freedom, then, might be seen as a tough-minded form of participative decision making. Decisions must be made and the leaders must see to it that they are. When there is no consensus, the leader can (and should) decide, but only after give-and-take on the alternatives. Failure to take such responsibility—essentially, giving total freedom to subordinates—can result in professionals continually arguing about what they should work on (Kaufman, 1974). One of the most difficult leadership challenges may be staying loose while getting on with it.

Leader as Metronome

This image comes from Sayles and Chandler's (1971) intensive study of NASA, and is perhaps the best statement of the subtlety of leadership in professional groups. Looking at how project managers attempted to control the technical activities of others (including, incidentally, people outside their own groups), Sayles and Chandler described the project manager's job as one that "widens or narrows limits, adds or subtracts weights where trade-offs are to be made, speeds up or slows down actions, increases emphasis on some activities and decreases emphasis on others." These activities reflect leadership as rearranging priorities, changing sequences, responding to the ebb and flow of events: letting self-directed people do what they are good at while influencing them through the pace, the timing, the order.

Work Challenge

One of the most important things to a professional, if not *the* most, is to do challenging work (Kaufman, 1974). In a study at Bell, for example, 55 percent of professionals leaving the company early in their careers did so because of unchallenging work (cited in Kaufman, 1974). Supervisors seen as emphasizing work challenge are rated higher on overall performance, and tend to create a climate of involvement and willingness to disagree (Thamhain and Gemmill, 1974).

The importance of challenging work is not, of course, unique to professionals. Most people would like to use their skills to make a contribution and accomplish something challenging. With professionals, who are independent and inclined to define "important" in relation to the profession rather than the organization, the leader again has a problem. The individual professional's definition of what is challenging must be reconciled with organizational goals and with needs for teamwork and coordination. What is the leadership skill required? Weick (1980) might describe it as the management of eloquence, that is, using language to influence how people think about themselves:

> Leaders who manage eloquence worry less about getting their subordinates to do something and more about supplying their subordinates with interesting versions of what they are doing.

In short, the leader must not only find interesting things to do, he or she must also help others stay interested and see the point. In at least one study (cited in Hellriegel and Slocum, 1974), high performing labs were seen as dominant, active, competitive, a clear reflection that something was challenging in them.

In summary, leaders of productive professional groups use their technical competence to evaluate and select among ideas, walk a tightrope between overcontrol and too much autonomy, make subtle changes in priorities and sequences, and ensure and channel professional challenge in the work. Human

"A masters degree from M.I.T., a Ph.D. from Cal Tech, and my greatest achievement has been inventing a low-cholesterol cat food!"

relations skills, which figure so prominently in most leadership theories, do not seem related to the productivity of scientific groups. As Kaufman (1974) put it:

> It is the recognized competence of the manager, rather than his human relations skills, that is most important in encouraging professionals to keep up to date. Respect for their superior's competence and judgment is the most important reason professionals comply with his directives.

One study measured leaders' effectiveness at motivating others, letting people know where they stand, and sensitivity to differences among people (all human relations skills). The researchers found no relationships between these skills and the rated innovation of the groups. They concluded that, compared to nonprofessionals, scientists are more interested in the work itself than in the social conditions surrounding it (Andrews and Farris, 1967). Other research has indicated that professionals tend to draw support from colleagues rather than from superiors (Clagett,

1966), a finding compatible with Kerr's notions, mentioned earlier, of substitutes for leadership.

Andrews and Farris also found that the highest innovation occurred when the supervisor was seen as a poor administrator (administrative skills were defined as carrying out scheduling and planning, and handling intergroup relations). The lowest innovation occurred when supervisors were seen as effective at both administrative and human relations functions.

In spite of these findings, it is premature to conclude that human relations and administrative skills are irrelevant or undesirable for supervisors of professionals. First, the long-term effects of sloppy administration and insensitivity to people may be severe, even though short-term consequences are not as apparent. Second, a supervisor's preoccupation with administrative and human relations activities may be at the expense of other activities more directly related to performance of the group. Thus, what is not done may be the key element.

All this may mean that the primary skill for leaders of professionals is knowing how to use their technical competence. People apparently will follow and accept (at least in the short run) the decisions of a supervisor who is technically competent, in spite of deficiencies in human relations or administrative skills. Other eccentricities may also be accepted, as Janos's description of a lab director shows:

> Wasserburg neither appears nor acts like a casting office concept of someone who is director of the world's most prestigious rock-dating laboratory. "He looks like he's coming apart," says his friend William Fowler. "Here's this rumpled, prickly cactus, wearing a western string tie, smoking with an FDR cigarette holder, cussing like a drill sergeant, ogling pretty women, exploding like a string of Chinese firecrackers, who also happens to be the most precise measurement-maker in the world." All who know him well acknowledge the depth of Wasserburg's warm and emotional nature.

In conclusion, the effectiveness of professional groups is determined by many things other than the supervisor. The supervisor, however, is not irrelevant and has a part to play in orchestrating the work of others. One aspect of this is direct and based on competence: the leader must take an active role in stimulating the group, in calling attention to ideas and sorting them out, in evaluating proposals and ideas, in seeing to it that necessary decisions get made, and in keeping the objectives reasonably clear.

The second aspect is indirect, subtle: the leader needs to nurture, protect, and preserve the creative tensions that seem to spawn high levels of professional productivity. These include controlled freedom, metronomic changes in pace and emphasis, and work challenge balanced between personal and organizational values, as well as the tensions suggested by Pelz and Andrews (1976).

Breakpoint Leadership: Action at the Interface

> [Erasmus] apparently felt that reform should be left to men of action, the princes and cardinals who could bring power to bear if they could be persuaded of the need to act . . . So when the storm of the Reformation broke, he retired to his scholarly nook, and tried his best to avoid taking sides. . . .
>
> Luther was not a cool, rational scholar. He was, instead, a volcano of emotions. . . .
>
> Luther was a totally committed religious zealot; Erasmus was a pious scholar. Therein lay the difference.
> —L. P. Williams, 1980

> The leaders of superb performers tend to live by the dicta, "Try something. Fix it. Don't analyze it to death."
> —T. J. Peters, 1980

To this point we have looked at leadership in terms of a supervisor and a small group of professional subordinates. Much of that job revolves around the effective use of technical competence. As Sayles and Chandler (1971) have described it, the leader is raising questions, confronting, challenging, playing devil's advocate, and making decisions in the face of conflicting technical judgments. For many managers of professionals, especially at lower levels, this is the primary challenge. But at some point on the way up the managerial ladder, a different kind of leadership demand emerges. When influencing other parts of the organization is as important, or more important, than influencing a subordinate group, leadership is at a breakpoint. Effectiveness is no longer measured simply as group productivity, but involves such things as impact on organizational direction, influence across organizational and even hierarchical boundaries, and securing and protecting organizational (and external) resources

"Insurance forms! Government grant forms! Requisition forms! It was a lot easier being a mad-scientist in the old days!"

and support. If supervision's call for action through others puts a modest strain on professional values, breakpoint leadership represents an earnest move into management.

For many professionals the first breakpoint leadership role is that of project manager. In any case, project managers have received research attention while other breakpoint jobs have not, so by necessity we will deal primarily with them. There is no obvious reason to assume that the skills required of project managers are irrelevant at higher levels, although project management has unique characteristics.

The project manager has been described as a hybrid of a scientist, an engineer, and an administrator; he or she can seldom use formal authority to get things done and must reconcile the conflicting goals of professionals, clients, and functional managers (Organ and Greene, 1972). In addition to the vicissitudes of a group of subordinate professionals (or perhaps several groups), the project manager must cope with all manner of other groups and people in and out of the organization, over whom he or she has little formal control. The manager must be an adroit bargainer, able to negotiate, sell, cajole, and convince in a "ceaseless round of 'political' give-and-take" (Sayles and Chandler, 1971). He or she must be able to bypass the formal hierarchy when necessary and engage in improvised, off-the-record discussions. To maintain linkages among groups, the project manager may have to form (or fracture) coalitions, generate rapport among warlords, and serve as translator for the various technical languages involved. As Sayles and Chandler put it:

> The heart of project management is the influencing of outside organizational units to conduct their necessary (for you) activities in such a way that they integrate technically, financially, and timewise with other components of the project. It is particularly difficult to control at a distance the coordination of scientific experiments which are under the control of scientific investigators. Such men tend to consider independence from external authorities one of the canons of professionalism and modern scientific method.

Ironically, leaders of professionals may have their greatest problem leading professionals not directly subordinate to them.

Organizations that contain significant project structure (matrix or frequent ad hoc project teams, for example) have been described by Mintzberg (1979) as the most political of all structures, "un panier de crabes." In such an environment, the most intense conflict occurs between project teams and the supporting functional departments; the least intense between the project manager and his or her subordinates (Baker and Wilemon, 1977).

In many organizations, of course, professionals (particularly scientists) may be separated from the rest of the organization in an R&D location. There, organizational rules may be relaxed (for example, dress codes or nine-to-five hours) to accommodate professional "eccentricities" without affecting other parts of the organization. In such a structure, breakpoint leadership occurs where the lab interfaces with the line organization. The manager must keep the rest of the organization excited about the scientists' work (Pelz and Andrews, 1976) to ensure continued support and to have impact on organizational direction.

It is also at the breakpoint that the manager of professionals is less likely to have a professional boss. This adds a new level of complexity, because professionals and nonprofessionals tend to have different orientations. Unfortunately, how to manage a nonprofessional boss has not received much research attention. Research on the relationships between project managers and their bosses suggests that project managers may not want to be too visible to their bosses: the boss is only one of several clients to be served (Organ and Greene, 1972). Too much time with the boss, and thus overexposure to one viewpoint, may reduce the dynamic tension that multiple clients create.

In summary, leadership at the breakpoint is dramatically different from

supervision. Where supervision of a group of professionals draws heavily on technical competence and its constructive use, breakpoint leadership requires political and diplomatic skills. Supervision requires knowing how professionals think and how to stimulate them to use their talents; breakpoint leadership requires knowing how the organization works and how to use power and influence to get things done. One type of leadership produces technical innovation; the other makes that innovation an organizational reality. Although technical competence may (it doesn't always) herald success at lower levels of management, it will not by itself sustain leadership at a breakpoint.

THE CHOICE TO LEAD

Thus managerial work is hectic and fragmented, requiring the ability to shift continually from person to person and from one problem to the next. It is almost the opposite of the studied, analytical, persisting work pattern of the professional, who expects and demands closure: the time to do a careful and complete job that will provide pride of authorship.

—L. R. Sayles, 1980

The professional faces a fundamental dilemma. Frequently, he abhors administration, desiring only to be left alone to practice his profession. But that freedom is gained only at the price of administrative effort—raising funds, resolving conflicts, buffering the demands of outsiders. That leaves the professional two choices: to do the administrative work himself, in which case he has less time to practice his profession, or to leave it to administrators, in which case he must surrender some of his power over decision making. And that power must be surrendered, it should further be noted, to administrators who, by virtue of the fact that they no longer wish to prac-

tice the profession, probably favor a different set of goals.
—H. Mintzberg, 1979

At some point many professionals will have to decide whether or not to embark on the managerial ladder. Although some may naturally gravitate toward either the technical or the supervisory path, many young professionals may not be sure which path to take when the opportunity is presented (Klimoski, 1973). The choice is important, for two reasons. First, managerial jobs are quite different from technical jobs. The differences increase as one moves up the hierarchy, and the longer one stays in management the less likely one is to return to research (Kaufman, 1974). Second, there will be strong pressures to accept management responsibility, even in organizations that offer a dual ladder for professionals.

Managers Are Different

Researchers describe research as primarily an individual activity requiring long stretches of uninterrupted time. The important thing about it is the influence a discovery has on one's colleagues (Roe, 1965). Managerial work is almost the exact opposite: it requires extensive contact with other people, and is highly fragmented with little reflective time (Mintzberg, 1973). One's contributions are weighed in organizational terms. These work differences are reflected in vocational interest patterns, which show managers to be oriented toward enterprising activities and political and economic achievement, averse to scientific activities, and inclined to work with people rather than with symbols or objects; they see themselves as being aggressive and sociable (Holland, 1973; Campbell, 1974). The contrast with both scientists and engineers (see Table 1) is stark.

Furthermore, studies of how managers and professionals spend their time

show dramatic differences; managers spend much more time talking and attending meetings, and the differences increase as one moves up the hierarchy (Hinrichs, 1964).

Many professionals enter the managerial world expecting to continue their research. But in her interviews with scientists, Roe found that any managerial job takes significant time away from research and that higher level jobs stop it altogether. Comments from scientists who accepted managerial roles are most telling:

> "I tried for a while to carry on with my research program, but this didn't work out very well, and I presently gave it up. . . ."

> "It soon became obvious that I couldn't do personal research and be a chairman. . . . I can't do research by delegation."

In summary, the move to management is a change of careers for most professionals, especially if they stay in management beyond the first level.

Pressures to Go into Management

There are many reasons for professionals to choose the managerial track, even in dual-ladder organizations. A prominent reason, as Mintzberg (1979) has observed, is that power in professional bureaucracies flows to administrators, not professionals. Because managers make the important decisions about organizational direction and resources, to climb the professional ladder is to move away from power (Kaufman, 1974). A quote from Lebell (1980) illustrates that, for many professionals, management is the way to get things done:

> My managers are mostly engineers or scientists who accept management roles as the only way to get the job

done.... Their subordinates know
they'd rather be doing honest work
than managing.

So a major reason for professionals to
enter management is to control resources
and direction (Goldberg, 1976).

A second reason for choosing management is the belief of many professionals that success, as defined by the
organization, lies in management, even
where a professional ladder is offered
(Klimoski, 1973; Goldberg, 1976). To be
passed up for a management position, or
to pass one up, might be seen as a sign of
inability, rather than unwillingness, to
fill a managerial role (Schriesheim, Von
Glinow, and Kerr, 1977).

A third factor leading to a career in
management is professional obsolescence. Chemists, for example, can read
only about .5 percent of the articles in
chemistry (Kaufman, 1974). Management
can become an escape from the pressure
to keep up, although, ironically, "the
immediate supervisors of specialists
have been found to be somewhat more
knowledgeable about newly emerging
fields than their subordinates" (Kaufman, 1974).

Different factors seem to determine
whether one is promoted than determine
which path one will take. One large
study found the best predictor of promotion into either the professional or managerial ladder was technical competence (Rosen, Billings, and Turney,
1976). This finding is consistent with
our earlier discussion of supervision
and with other research, for example,
Gantz, Erickson, and Stephenson (1972),
who found perceived creativity to be
highly related to promotion rate.

Those professionals choosing the
managerial ladder tend to be more like
managers to begin with than their fellow
professionals are (Klimoski, 1973;
Rosen, Billings, and Turney, 1976).

They are more likely to see themselves
as being aggressive, gregarious, and
self-confident. They are likely to feel
more comfortable in a leadership role,
and to see challenges and rewards in
the job. In her 1965 study of eminent
scientists, Roe concluded that, whether
they ended up in research or administration, none of them regretted their
choice and all were happy in their work.
Perhaps the most telling evidence of this
comes from the statements of two scientists, the first from one who opted out of
management, the second from one who
stayed in:

I did that for about a year and a half
and I found out I didn't want to be
chairman of anything. The thing that
really made me stop and realize how
horrible it was is that I found myself
liking it. It was all this trivia. It's so
wonderful being an administrator because you're busy all the time, and you
don't have to think. One day I was
going around the laboratory deciding
where to put new stuff.... I found
myself liking it, so I quit.

If you go into administration you must
believe that this is a creative activity
in itself and that your purpose is something more than keeping your desk
clean. You are a moderator and an
arbiter and you try to deal equitably
with a lot of different people, but
you've also got to have ideas and
you've got to persuade people that
your ideas are important, and see
them into reality. The problems in a
position like mine are almost unbeliev-
able in their diversity and importance.
This is part of the excitement of it. In
both research and administration the
excitement and the elation is in the
creative power. It's bringing things to
pass.

A career as a manager and a career
as a professional are quite different.

Each can be challenging and immensely rewarding. The failure to recognize the differences is a major reason some professionals are unsuccessful or unhappy as managers.

CONCLUSION

Professionals, scientists and engineers in particular, are not alike. The more they hold in common such values as autonomy in doing work and commitment to the profession and professional colleagues, the more they represent a special leadership situation. This is because the professional values described by Kerr, Von Glinow, and Schriesheim (1977) are likely to run counter to organizational values: pay, seniority, and benefits; authority based on hierarchical influence; allegiance to organizational goals; a proprietary view of science; and others. These conflicts not only reduce the leader's potential influence (especially as it flows from formal authority and control over rewards), but also limit the organization's hold over successful professionals, who are likely to have other opportunities.

Given the special characteristics of this leadership situation, it is not surprising that effective supervision of professional groups seems to be rooted in technical competence rather than in organizationally endowed authority. It is clear, however, that competence is not enough. It must be used wisely to stimulate the professionals to recognize and define interesting problems and to provide critical evaluation of ideas. Effective supervision also requires more subtle skills in making decisions (staying loose while getting on with it), in orchestrating work flow (through timing, pace, ordering, and nudges) and in creating and defining work challenge.

Supervision of professional groups requires one set of skills, but leadership at a breakpoint demands quite another. Where professional units interface with the larger organization, effective leadership takes on a decidedly managerial tone. It becomes, essentially, knowing how to use power and influence to get things done in the organization. It also requires considerable ability to translate technicalities into exciting and comprehensible language for the rest of the organization. To other professionals, effective breakpoint leaders are likely to appear to have sold out their professional values.

It is not an easy choice for a good professional to leave a technical specialty to enter management. And it is leaving the specialty, since few people can do effective managerial and technical work at the same time. The key is to recognize that managerial work and professional work are both challenging, but in different ways. Managers typically work in a fragmented way and at a nonreflective pace, talk with many different kinds of people, and specialize in getting others to accomplish organizationally relevant goals. Professionals tend to work at a less hectic pace with longer periods of time to concentrate on a single or a few projects. They tend to work alone or in small teams and take pride in ownership of an idea or innovation. For some professionals, the lure of added clout—increased opportunity to get things done—leads to a managerial career. To create conditions that help other professionals get important things done is no small accomplishment and carries with it substantial gratification. To see the work that professionals have done through to reality is equally demanding and rewarding. These are the acts of leadership on which both individual professionals and organizations—and ultimately society itself—depend.

REFERENCES

Andrews, F. M., and Farris, G. F. "Supervisory Practices and Innovation in Scientific Teams." *Personnel Psychology* 20 (1967): 497–515.

———. "Time Pressure and Performance of Scientists and Engineers: A Five-year Panel Study." *Organizational Behavior and Human Performance* 8 (1972):185–200.

Baker, B. N., and Wilemon, D. L. "Managing Complex Programs: A Review of Major Research Findings." *R&D Management* 8 (1977):23–28.

Barnowe, J. T. "Leadership and Performance Outcomes in Research Organizations: The Supervisor of Scientists as a Source of Assistance." *Organizational Behavior and Human Performance* 14 (1975):264–80.

Barth, R. T., and Vertinsky, I. "The Effect of Goal Orientation and Information Environment on Research Performance: A Field Study." *Organizational Behavior and Human Performance* 13 (1975):110–32.

Campbell, D. P. *Strong Vocational Interest Blank: Manual for the Strong-Campbell Interest Inventory.* Palo Alto, Calif.: Stanford University Press, 1974.

Clagett, G. S. *Organizational Factors in Scientific Performance in an Industrial Research Laboratory.* Final Technical Report. Milwaukee: University of Wisconsin, 1966.

Cummings, L. L.; Hinton, B. L.; and Gobdel, B. C. "Creative Behavior as a Function of Task Environment: Impact of Objectives, Procedures, and Controls." *Academy of Management Journal* 18 (1975):489–99.

Farris, G. F. "The Effect of Individual Roles on Performance in Innovative Groups." *Research and Development Management* 3 (1972):23–28.

Filley, A. C.; House, R. J.; and Kerr, S. *Managerial Process and Organizational Behavior,* 2nd ed. Glenview, Ill.: Scott, Foresman, 1976.

Gantz, B. S.; Erickson, C. O.; and Stephenson, R. W. "Some Determinants of Promotion in a Research and Development Population." *Proceedings of the 80th Annual Convention of the American Psychological Association,* 1972.

Goldberg, A. I. "The Relevance of Cosmopolitan/Local Orientations to Professional Values and Behavior." *Sociology of Work and Occupations,* 3 (1976):331–356.

Gough, H. G., and Woodworth, D. G. "Stylistic Variations Among Professional Research Scientists." *Journal of Psychology* 49 (1960): 87–98.

Hellriegel, D., and Slocum, J. W., Jr. "Organizational Climate: Measures, Research and Contingencies." *Academy of Management Journal* 17 (1974):255–77.

Hinrichs, J. R. "Communications Activity of Industrial Research Personnel." *Personnel Psychology* 17 (1964):193–204.

Holland, J. L. *Making Vocational Choices.* Englewood Cliffs, N.J.: Prentice-Hall, 1973.

James, S. "Just Plain Folk." *Executive* 6 (1980):40–44.

Janos, L. "Timekeepers of the Solar System." *Science 80,* May/June 1980, pp. 44–55.

Kaufman, H. G. *Obsolescence and Professional Career Development.* New York: AMACOM, 1974.

Kerr, S. "Substitutes for Leadership: Some Implications for Organizational Design." *Organizational and Administrative Sciences* 2 (1977):135–46.

Kerr, S.; Von Glinow, M. A.; and Schriesheim, J. "Issues in the Study of 'Professionals' in Organizations: The Case of Scientists and Engineers." *Organizational Behavior and Human Performance* 18 (1977):329–45.

Klimoski, R. J. "A Biographical Data Analysis of Career Patterns in Engineering." *Journal of Vocational Behavior* 3 (1973):103–113.

Lebell, D. "Managing Professionals: The Quiet Conflict." *Personnel Journal* 59 (1980): 566–72.

Mintzberg, H. *The Nature of Managerial Work.* New York: Harper and Row, 1973.

———. *The Structuring of Organizations.* Englewood Cliffs, N.J.: Prentice-Hall, 1979.

Organ, D. W., and Greene, C. N. "The Boundary Relevance of the Project Manager's Job: Findings and Implications for R&D Management." *R&D Management* 3 (1972):7–11.

Pelz, D. C., and Andrews, F. M. *Scientists in Organizations.* Ann Arbor: University of Michigan, 1976.

Peters, T. J. "A Style for All Seasons." *Executive* 6 (1980):12–16.

Reeser, C. "Some Potential Human Problems of the Project Form of Organization." *Academy of Management Journal* (1969):459–67.

Roe, A. "Changes in Scientific Activities with Age." *Science* 150 (1965):313–18.

Rosen, N.; Billings, R.; and Turney, J. "The Emergence and Allocation of Leadership Resources Over Time in a Technical Organization." *Academy of Management Journal* 19 (1976):165–83.

Rotondi, T., Jr. "Organizational Identification: Issues and Implications." *Organizational Behavior and Human Performance* 13 (1975): 95–109.

Sayles, L. R. "Managing on the Run." *Executive* 6 (1980):25–26.

———, and Chandler, M. K. *Managing Large Systems.* New York: Harper and Row, 1971.

Schriesheim, J.; Von Glinow, M. A.; and Kerr, S. "Professionals in Bureaucracies: A Structural Alternative." *North-Holland/TIMS Studies in the Management Sciences* 5 (1977): 55–69.

Thamhain, H. J., and Gemmill, G. R. "Influence Styles of Project Managers: Some Project Performance Correlates." *Academy of Management Journal* 17 (1974):216–24.

Weick, K. "The Management of Eloquence." *Executive* 6 (1980):18–21.

Williams, L. P. "Parallel Lives." *Executive* 6 (1980):8–12.

Assessing the Social Impacts of New Technologies

Alan Porter
Georgia Institute of Technology

A recurring theme in this book has been "interconnectedness"—the fact that changes in one part of the organization affect other parts of the organization, and the environment around it. If we redesign one person's job, other related jobs get changed, too. Perhaps the new jobs attract different sorts of employees. New employees may have different needs, values, and ways of looking at the world, so that the community where they live starts to change—and so on. The ripples spread out from the original change to affect remote areas of the organization and its environment, both physical and social.

In the past few years there has been a rapid growth in interest in attempts to predict and control these "ripple effects" of the way organizations do business. For example, manufacturers have been forced by legal action to consider possible injury to people using (and even abusing) their products. Similarly, the environmental movement has generated enormous pressures on organizations that pollute the air and water around their plants. Permission to build large plants now often requires that an "environmental impact statement" be prepared, a detailed document spelling out all the likely significant impacts the project will have on the physical environment, and how they will be controlled.

Growing numbers of scientists and engineers are becoming involved in these "technology assessment" activities, and a growing body of techniques for these purposes are being developed. Alan Porter provides a brief overview of the main current approaches, and outlines the primary uses and limitations of each. Drawing on one example in some detail, he shows how the techniques are used and what roles engineers and scientists typically play in the process. He also considers the difficult practical and ethical questions that are involved in doing studies of this sort.

The engineer or scientist can no longer aspire to be merely a technician. He or she must mesh effectively with the organizational context. Changes in one part of the organization may bring about changes in other parts of the organization, and in the outside environment as well. The activities of one individual affect other individuals and their work activities, who in turn affect others, so that the effects of the original actions ripple outward, much as a wave spreads from a stone thrown into a calm pond.

The ripple effect does not stop at the organizational boundaries. Individuals affect processes and products that may alter the environment in which the organization operates. Unless the interactions between the organization and the environment go smoothly, severe problems may result. Recent product liability cases, such as that involving the safety of the Ford Pinto in rear-end collisions, bring home the economic threats to industry from inadvertent and delayed impacts of products. Chemical industry dumping of dangerous by-products into the environment have made Love Canal a shorthand term for industrial irresponsibility that cries for government regulation. The federal government and a number of state governments require that an environmental impact statement (EIS) be prepared when there is reason to suspect that proposed developments in which they are involved will significantly affect the environment. As technological development continues, the extent of interactions with the natural and social environment mushrooms. It behooves any organization to "look before it leaps" to gauge the effects its actions will likely have.

Increasingly, engineers and scientists are becoming involved in such activities, which we call "technology assessment" (TA). A general approach and a number of specific useful techniques can be described. We first offer a conceptual framework to use in considering how an organization's activities can impinge on its environment. Building on one example, we will illustrate the TA approach and how certain techniques could be used, and also address the difficult practical and ethical questions that are involved in doing studies of this sort.

THE TECHNOLOGICAL DELIVERY SYSTEM

The notion of a technological delivery system (TDS) is sketched in Figure 1. The idea of a TDS was originated by Edward Wenk, Jr., a designer of submarines who became involved in national engineering policy. He devised the TDS schematic to emphasize that "the organization" does not operate as a closed system. Rather, it must address its relationships with the elements in its context. Let us work through the parts and relationships of the TDS by using an example.

Whirlpool Corporation devised a trash masher compactor in the early 1970s. Despite the fact that Whirlpool had been in the forefront of firms committed to technological forecasting (the anticipation of new developments) and technological assessment (the anticipation of the effects such new developments will have), they elected to market the trash masher without conducting a detailed TA. After a relatively brief time they met with an onslaught of criticism in terms of the environmental hazards resulting from the nondecomposition of compacted trash in landfills, possible damage to municipal incinerators from the characteristics of compacted garbage, and scare stores about the possibility of mashing pets or even children. At that point Whirlpool undertook a year-long TA, carefully documenting the

Figure 1.   Technological Delivery System

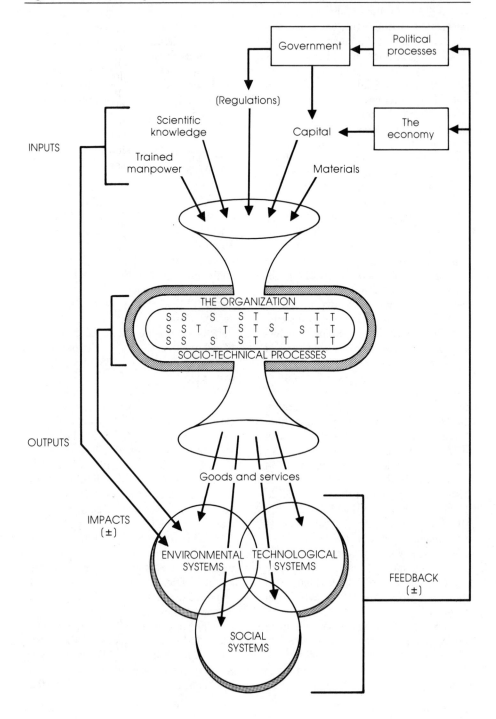

effects of compacted trash through a paper study and experimental testing of the behavior of the product, as described by Richard C. Davis, former manager of the technological forecasting unit of Whirlpool. We will take liberty with this basic example to illustrate the potentials for organizational interaction with the environment, and anticipation of the effects of such interactions through TA.

If we focus on Figure 1 with the development of a trash masher in mind, we can begin by noting input requirements: trained manpower (mechanical engineers, foremen), scientific knowledge (strength of materials), applicable regulations (electrical standards, restrictions on compacted materials), capital, and natural materials. As a side note, the organization might just as soon not receive certain of those impacts, namely imposed regulations, but sometimes it welcomes them (e.g., the trucking industry's opposition to deregulation).

Moving down to the organization itself, it should be noted that a variety of forms are possible—a goods producer like Whirlpool or a service provider, whether industrial, governmental, or academic. Within the organization some complex of technical and social processes operates on the inputs to produce certain goods and/or services (i.e., outputs). Many functions could be differentiated: for example, research and development, planning, management, production, marketing, and public relations/lobbying. Several of these functions require explicit consideration of the external environment—planning, management, marketing, and public relations/lobbying. Technology assessment would be of particular interest to such units. In the case of the trash masher, the planning department needs to provide information on the likely impact in terms of market potential, profitability, and possible negative consequences and their reper-

cussions. Management needs to balance out such information to decide whether or not to produce a trash masher, and what technical features need to be designed to maximize the beneficial effects and minimize the negative ones. Public relations could be involved in reassuring a leery public as to the safety of the compactor; and lobbying can provide lawmakers with the organization's point of view in terms of regulations or special considerations.

The goods and services produced affect various contextual systems. For instance, compacted trash posed potential environmental system problems by being nonbiodegradable; it also posed problems for technological systems, namely incinerators. Social system representatives, perceiving undue expenses to local government and concerned about the environment, generated a variety of responses. TV talk show interviews heightened the level of concern, and some communities went so far as to ban sales of trash compactors.

In addition, the organization's inputs and processes may affect environmental, technological, and/or social systems. For instance, were Whirlpool to develop a large-scale compactor business, it would likely provide additional jobs for the community in which production took place, and require production and transportation of increased quantities of raw materials, such as steel. The production facility itself might affect its environment: construction of a new plant could cause population increases for a community, in turn requiring construction of schools and other facilities; it could increase the level of air pollution, worsening health problems for certain local residents. A full-blown TA of the implications of a trash masher would do well to address the full range of possible impacts so that management would be well informed as it reaches critical decisions.

The organization is likely to get feedback when its products impact (affect) the external system. The negative vibrations over the trash masher were reflected in political processes, which led to banning the device in certain governmental jurisdictions. Sales suffered. However, on (belated) completion of the TA, the negative impacts were largely ameliorated and the feedback became more favorable. In particular, this meant the removal of the bans on sales and an increase in sales of trash compactors in general. Obviously, the organization depends on positive feedback on its performance.

Examination of the technological delivery system suggests another strategy. Rather than pump out goods and services and assess the reactions that take place, one would do better to try to anticipate the impacts. Several distinct planning functions can be identified in this regard. First, the organization must determine that its products are technically feasible. Whirlpool could not tool up and produce trash compactors until it was convinced that they would work. Second, marketing must determine whether someone is likely to buy the product. Third, one should ask the broader "impact analysis" questions. Following the "EPISTLE," one may be concerned with

>   Economic
>
>   Psychological
>
>   Institutional/political
>
>   Social
>
>   Technological
>
>   Legal, and
>
>   Ecological (environmental) impacts.

During the 1970s, impact analysis boomed under such labels as technology assessment, environmental impact assessment, social impact assessment, and risk assessment. We now turn our attention to this activity and its relationship to the engineer in the organization.

TECHNOLOGY ASSESSMENT— WHAT IT IS

Technology assessment is the study of the prospective impacts on society resulting from the introduction or modification of a given technology. Technology assessment became an identifiable activity largely through the efforts of the United States government in the early 1970s. The Congress created its own Office of Technology Assessment in 1972 to provide staff assistance on technological issues. Various agencies in the federal executive branch picked up on the theme and developed their own technology assessment and environmental impact assessment capabilities. In particular, the National Environmental Policy Act of 1969 mandated that environmental impact statements be filed for many projects. Technology assessment can be distinguished from other activities because it has the following essential features:

- It focuses on the *effects* of innovations, emphasizing the indirect impacts as well as the direct ones.

- It is *future oriented;* it tries to predict future effects. (Had Whirlpool performed its TA before commercial introduction of the trash masher, this would have been more in line with the basic concept as we present it.)

- In principle, it is *systematic, comprehensive,* and *interdisciplinary* in nature.

- It is *policy oriented;* information is produced to assist in decision making.

Organizations, both public and private, need to perform technology assessment. Wise management of technology requires the best information possible on which to base decisions—before, not after, the fact. Sound social ethics require that our technological society carefully attend to its effects on its own people and habitat. More immediately, the firm must engage in TA as a matter of self-defense. When technological developments require huge investments in time and resources, mistakes are too costly. Whether one is deciding to construct a supersonic transport (e.g., the Concorde), invest in a nuclear power plant, or go into production with a trash compactor, one needs the fullest information possible on the effects of the investment. Corporate officers need to beware of potential regulations constricting the innovation, potential economic changes making it no longer viable, and court actions—from product liability to criminal charges. Moreover, technology assessment is not all negative (it is not "technology harassment"). It is good business to look ahead to uncover new opportunities, to make designs more economical and effective, and to enhance public support.

But how, one might ask, is this relevant to the working engineer who has not yet reached the level of top management? The answer is, it depends. In the most remote case, one may be concentrating purely on the technical aspects of a product or a process; that person's work will have to be related to impact assessment considerations by others. Relating may take the form of prescribed standards, or even necessary modifications in designs to take account of their potential consequences. This process leads to a second level of involvement in which a technical specialist is required to interact with assessment personnel in working out designs, compromises, pilot tests, and so on. In the Whirlpool case, one might imagine that after the

results of the incinerator testing, modifications in the design of the trash compactor might have required careful interaction of just this sort. At the third level, engineers become involved in doing TA. In fact, most of the TAs performed involve engineers and physical scientists as project leaders and as key project personnel in these interdisciplinary efforts. (See Frederick Rossini, Reading #4.) At the fourth level, the engineer moving inexorably into management must integrate technical and impact considerations in making critical corporate decisions on whether to adopt new processes and products, and whether modifications are required.

Having described what TA is and why one ought to do it, we now present a general framework for technology assessment, then consider specific techniques that are used in its performance.

TECHNOLOGY ASSESSMENT— HOW TO DO IT

Technology assessments can take a variety of forms. Typically, they are one-shot studies ranging in effort from less than the equivalent of one professional working for one year (a person-year) to more than twenty person-years. Sometimes organizational policy-making processes fit this one-shot model well. This would be the case when there is a "go–no go" decision to be made about a given technology (e.g., whether to go into the trash compactor business). However, other policies are ongoing and incremental in nature, as when one makes marginal improvements in a product, such as a compactor, from year to year. In such situations it is appropriate to consider an assessment *program* made up of a combination of study efforts. These might include:

- Macro assessments (comprehensive, large-scale), which consider the full range of possible impacts and policies, considered in significant depth (on the order of magnitude of five to ten person-years of work)
- Mini assessments, which focus on a few areas of concern in depth or on all areas for breadth, without so much detail (these might be considered to be about an order of magnitude smaller in effort than the macro assessment)
- Micro assessments, modest research efforts to identify the key issues or to establish the broad dimensions of a problem (possibly an order of magnitude smaller still than the mini assessment, e.g., about one person-month of effort)
- Testing, active experimentation on a pilot scale to find out specific effects of the technology in question (as exemplified in Whirlpool's considerations of the trash masher's burning and decomposition characteristics)
- Monitoring, the continuing collection of focused information concerning the effects of the technology in operation (one might imagine surveying incinerator operators concerning compacted trash)
- Evaluations, to determine the positive and negative effects of ongoing functioning of the technology in projects or programs to determine whether alterations are needed.

For example, were a firm to consider introduction of a "trash eater" to take over the market from the trash compactors, there might be value in a program such as the following:

- Evaluation of the competitive technology (various brands of trash compactors) to determine the size of the market potential, the features that seem most attractive, the problems that could be overcome by a new product, and possible indications of associated problems (e.g., differential regulations by federal and local officials)
- A micro assessment by a brainstorming group composed of corporate planners, R&D personnel, and marketing people to identify the critical issues that will determine whether the company should undertake development of a trash eater
- A mini assessment focused on the economics and environmental acceptability of the two primary technological options—a biological mechanism and a physical grinding mechanism—that have been proposed
- A full-blown macro assessment encompassing all possible implications of development, both internal to the organization and external, considering the whole "EPISTLE" gamut for the biological option that appears to be the first choice
- Testing of the biological trash eater with respect to the key uncertainties uncovered in the assessment efforts (e.g., best procedures for disposal of the final waste product).

Such a composite assessment program illustrates the flexibility and continuity possible in developing organizational policy information.

Another distinction worth noting is the focus of a given assessment. A given organization may have reason to use any or all of the following three possibilities.

- Project assessments address a particular localized development (e.g., a new power plant facility). Such a study is usually constrained in the range of technical features considered and the geographical extent of the impacts addressed, as in the case of a local environmental impact statement.

- Technology-focused assessments address innovative technologies (e.g., the trash eater). Uncertainties in the technology itself and in the extended time frame of the innovation process are critical features.

- Problem-oriented assessments focus on possible solutions to a specific problem. Whirlpool again provides a handy illustration of such a possibility in their analysis of what an oil shortage would mean for the firm, conducted prior to the 1973 Arab oil boycott. That study identified all the uses of petroleum products by Whirlpool in their fuels, processes, and products, leading to identification of alternative sources (i.e., they purchased gas wells), and alternatives to petroleum-based products (e.g., silicone lubricants). While they could not predict the exact occurrence of the oil boycott and subsequent petroleum price increases, they were better prepared as a consequence of their technology forecasting and assessment.

Having discussed these global aspects of technology assessment, let us now turn to a specific approach to the conduct of such studies. Figure 2 notes ten components that should be accomplished in almost any assessment. Naturally, emphases will vary according to the type of study, scale of effort, and major information needs.

Problem definition/bounding. The first activity of an assessment is to decide what specific question it is addressing. This entails specification of the technology, the critical issues of concern, the breadth and depth of coverage based on available resources, and the intended users of the study. The

Figure 2. Ten Components of a TA

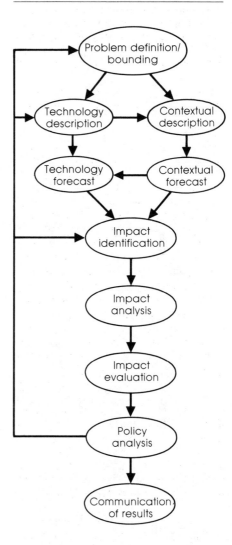

last is critical so that one can determine the information needs and devise a study targeted to those needs. A proper first question to be raised is whether the assessment should be done at all in the form proposed. If this is resolved in the affirmative, six areas deserve consideration: the time horizon to be considered, the spatial extent of impacts to be addressed, institutional bodies to be directly considered, the range of applications of the technology to be considered, the impact sectors of greatest interest (of the EPISTLE range of possibilities), and any explicit policy options to be weighed.

Technology description. The nature and feasibility of the technology in question must be described accurately. If one gets the subject wrong, the rest of the assessment will be an exercise in futility. This component activity demands involvement of subject matter experts in addition to any other sources of sound information. Joe Armstrong and Willis Harman of Stanford University have suggested that about 20 percent of an assessment's resources be devoted to technology description on a first pass. Technology description should not be limited merely to functional description. Rather, it must enrich the perspective to consider alternative implementations and configurations, closely related technological factors (i.e., reliance on other developing technologies or competition with other developments), and potential uses.

Technology forecast. This is the effort to anticipate the character, intensity, and timing of changes in the relevant technologies. One will want to forecast developments in the focal technology and also in competing technologies, as well as possible innovations that could directly affect the focal technology (e.g., fiber optic cables would affect the implementation of a picture phone system). Forecasting rests heavily on the technology description, but it also depends on the contextual description and forecast. Forecasts are likely to rely on a blend of documented data and expert opinion. Three general principles of forecasting, elucidated by William

Ascher, pertain: (1) methodological sophistication contributes little to this sort of forecasting; (2) the core assumptions are critical (i.e., biological trash eaters are feasible; the nation's economy will remain robust); and (3) a short-time horizon correlates strongly with forecasting accuracy. Taken together, these imply the forecast should be current, even if it is simple. Thus, the assessment team will probably wish to generate its own forecasts rather than rely on more elaborate ones prepared some years before.

Contextual description. Contextual factors in the development and outcomes of any given technology are important. An accurate forecast depends on accurate assessment of the influences on development. For instance, as suggested by Figure 1, the assessors should identify the governmental units that are likely to be interested in the technology in question. Beyond this, it is important to note the political forces that could come into play. Who will be the supporters and who the opponents of the development in question? To answer that, one must backtrack down the feedback path (see Figure 1) to consider the impacted systems—environmental, technological, and social. For example, a study conducted some years ago for the National Aeronautics and Space Administration attempted to ascertain the implications for V/STOL (vertical and short take-off and landing) aircraft. The assessors rightly perceived that such a technology would have to compete with other technologies, namely conventional jet aircraft and helicopters. In one aspect they attempted to determine the economic viability of V/STOL craft operating in California. They identified the competition to be the dominant intrastate airline, PSA. They concluded that the new aircraft would be economically competitive.

However, they missed an essential element of the social systems associated with the conventional technology. PSA had built its market through fierce price competition. The assessors had made the unrealistic assumption that they could beat the current PSA fare and succeed. However, it would surely have been more realistic to assume that PSA would lower its fare still further to meet this new competition, leaving V/STOLs uneconomic. In general, contextual description requires a careful mixing of quantitative and qualitative descriptors to gauge correctly the implications vis-à-vis the focal technology.

Contextual forecast.   Contextual forecasting should generate the most plausible future configurations of those dimensions of the society that come to bear through and on the technological delivery system. This implies a need to address probable social changes (e.g., shifts in popular values), political changes, economic directions, and institutional and legal changes (e.g., the effect of deregulation on the airline industry). This component requires something like an inverse of the "EPISTLE" relationships considered in the impact identification, analysis, and evaluation components. Here we are concerned with how those broad-ranging factors affect the technology; there we were concerned with how the technology affects them. Not surprisingly, contextual forecasting is probably the least developed and least credible assessment component. Provision of a range of qualitative alternative futures in the form of scenarios (comprehensive portraits of future situations) is the typical approach.

Impact identification.   "Impacts" are the products of the interaction between a technology and its societal context. Direct impacts are those effects directly attributable to the technology itself; higher order impacts are the products of the direct effects. Identification of impacts may follow disciplinary lines, as in the use of "EPISTLE," or an alternative classification may be used to identify impacts according to the parties affected by them. For instance, one could use a checklist to identify possible impacts of the trash eater on the consumer, the municipal refuse collector, and so on. Alternatively, one might try to devise a tree that would track direct impacts to indirect ones, as in the analogy of a cue ball striking a pool ball, which strikes another ball, and so on. Impact identification can use more or less extensive literature search and expert opinion survey techniques. Selection of the more important impacts for further study is essential, for one often identifies a seemingly endless list of possibilities. The intended study users can help at this juncture by indicating what they think the more critical impacts will be. At this same time, they may also be able to relate possible policy alternatives to the impact identification, in turn helping to focus the remainder of the assessment work.

Impact analysis.   Refines the impact identification component. In this step the assessors attempt to determine the likelihood and importance of possible impacts. Disciplinary expertise may play an important role in such areas as environmental modeling (e.g., air pollution dispersal models) and cost-benefit analysis. Certain future-oriented techniques, to be discussed shortly, may also contribute to impact analysis.

Impact evaluation.   This necessary component integrates the information provided through the impact analyses to enable comparison of alternatives. It is not of much use to decision makers simply to catalog an array of possible impacts. One must go further, to specify evaluation criteria and apply them. Criteria need not be limited to economic utility. Issues of equity and nonmaterial (e.g., religious, aesthetic) values also deserve consideration. These may be applied by the assessment team alone or with representation of the parties-at-interest. In any event, the evaluation process should be made clear to the study users. This highly judgmental component can be performed qualitatively and/or by using quantitative techniques.

Policy analysis. Policy analysis compares alternatives for implementing technologies and for dealing with their undesirable and desirable consequences. Early in the assessment process, the relevant policy makers and their options must be identified. Their participation in the assessment is usually an asset. Unless they are inappropriate, explicit policy recommendations are desirable if the assessors can convince the users of their credibility and balanced treatment of the issues. Policy analysis may well be the most important component of the assessment. Unfortunately, practice to date in this regard has often been lacking, as time and resources often run thin by this stage of the assessment process.

Communication of results. For communication to be effective, significant efforts must be made to facilitate information flow to and from study users. The assessment results are most likely to be used by the people who mandated the study, those who regard the subject as important, and those who face decisions pertinent to the issues addressed. Study utility can be enhanced by early identification of the intended audience, well-thought-out interaction with the audience over the course of the study, and use of a variety of means to disseminate credible information.

At this point, the reader may think that an assessment is an orderly process, unfolding step-by-step as shown in Figure 2. Wrong! *Iteration*, redoing of component parts of the assessment based on findings uncovered in other components, is absolutely essential. As indicated by the feedback arrows in Figure 2, an effective assessment must take into account information generated in the later component stages to refine the earlier ones. To describe the "technology," one must know the alternative formulations of the technology accurately —but that information is dependent on the policy analysis. Likewise, impact identification depends not only on the forecasted technological developments and context, but also on the policies followed in guiding the technology to development. In a participatory sense, it is only after the potential impacts are identified that the social context can relate to the technology, to influence its development. This is illustrated by the reactions to the early introduction of the trash masher. The need to perform iterations of the study components means that the assessors must plan time and resources for this. No neat and clean "PERT" chart based on a linear step-by-step approach will work well. In fact, the whole process can become quite disorderly if one realizes that the actual problem definition/bounding may be significantly affected by information developed through the assessment process, as one learns more about the technology, options, and potential impacts.

Assessment Techniques

We might now ask about the actual activities that take place in completing the ten component steps of an assessment. There exists a great range of analytical techniques, but detailed treatment of these and their usage is beyond our purpose here. Rather, we shall briefly consider a selected list of techniques (Table 1) and illustrate how one might select among them (and among many others) in the conduct of a particular assessment study.

Returning to our hypothetical micro-assessment of a biological trash eater, for the problem definition/bounding task, we would probably use no technique more elaborate than brainstorming. However, we might wish to use something like interpretive structural modeling, wherein we try to capture the essential elements in the technological delivery system and their relationships to help us formulate the appropriate study. Description of the technology would probably rely heavily on informal opinion measurement (e.g., asking experts within the organization) along with an appropriate literature review (particularly emphasizing "monitoring" of recent developments). Contextual description is apt to be informal. It may involve brainstorming, gathering of selected opinions, identifying the parties relevant to the trash-eater technological delivery system (e.g., the concerned governmental agencies, environmental groups, industrial competition), as well as factual statistical information on the market in terms of sales of competitive trash compactors, and other pertinent information.

Technology forecast could well make use of trend extrapolation to project time series data concerning trash handling innovations, and the substitution profiles as one innovation takes over the market from another. Expert opinion on the prospects for trash-eater development might be assessed by means of a Delphi. That entails a repeated survey of an identified group of knowledgeable persons in which the group is polled on a number of likely development issues on the first round of the survey. That information is summarized and fed back (anonymously) for them to revise their individual judgments in a second round.

The process is repeated (limited by the patience of the participants and the marginal gain in information) until results converge (typically in about three rounds). The contextual forecast might include several elements. Trend extrapolation might be employed on a number of relevant data series, such as cost and availability of selected materials (e.g., steel and electricity), sales of trash compactors, and the demographic makeup of the society (e.g., an aging American population may be somewhat less inclined to try novel technologies). In addition, because of the great uncertainties in projecting societal contexts, we are likely to want to use scenarios. We might postulate, say, three alternative development scenarios for the trash eater. An optimistic one might take into account good economic conditions, ready public acceptance of the new device, and a variety of factors thought to influence the reception of the trash eater. A pessimistic scenario might consider these same factors, but with each at unfavorable levels (for instance, an economic recession of some depth during the time period of concern). The third scenario might be projected as a most probable sequence of developments. The intent of providing a range of alternatives is to allow the study users to develop sensitivity to what factors might fit together to give a realistic portrayal.

Identification of the possible impacts of a biological trash eater might make use of checklists and relevance trees. Lists might be checked for possible health effects, economic implications, environmental effects, and so on. Trees could be used to try to figure out the potential secondary impacts of the direct effects. Impact analysis would probably not involve sophisticated quantitative modeling, but a technique such as cross-impact matrices could well be used to ascertain the possible interactions among the effects identified. Cross-

Table 1.   Assessment Techniques

Technique	Description	Uses
Brainstorming	A group or individuals generate ideas with no criticism allowed	Problem defintion Generating lists of potential impacts, affected parties, policy sectors, etc. Performing microassessments
Interpretive structural modeling	Directed graph representation of a particular relationship among all pairs of elements in a set to aid in structuring a complex issue area	Developing preliminary models of issue areas Impact evaluation
Trend extrapolation	A family of techniques to project time-series data using specified rules	Technology forecasting, both parameter changes and rates of substitution Social forecasting
Opinion measurement	A variety of techniques (including survey, panel, and Delphi) to accumulate inputs from a number of persons, often experts in an area of interest	Technology forecasting and description Social forecasting and description Impact identification Impact analysis, especially social
Scenarios	Composite descriptions of possible future states incorporating a number of characteristics	Social forecasting Technology forecasting Impact analysis Policy analysis Communication of results
Checklists	Lists of factors to consider in a particular area of inquiry	Impact identification Policy-sector identification
Relevance trees	Network displays that sequentially identify chains of cause-effect (or other) relationships	Impact identification and analysis
Cross-impact matrices	Two-dimensional matrix representation to indicate interactions between two sets of elements	Impact identification and analysis Analyzing the consequences of policy options
Simulation models	Simplified representation of a real system used to explain dynamic relationships of the system	Technology forecasting Impact analysis
Sensitivity analysis	A general means to ascertain the sensitivity of system (model) parameters by making changes in important variables and observing their effects	Impact analysis Policy analysis
Probabilistic techniques	Stochastic properties are emphasized in understanding and predicting system behaviors	Technology forecasting Impact analysis Impact evaluation
Cost-benefit analysis	A set of techniques employed to determine the assets and liabilities accrued over the lifetime of a development	Economic impact analysis Environmental impact analysis
Export base models	Estimates regional changes through a multiplier applied to the development in question	Economic impact analysis
Decision analysis	Formal aid to compare alternatives by weighing the probabilities of occurrences and the magnitudes of their impacts	Impact evaluation Policy analysis
Policy capture	A technique for uncovering the decision rules by which individuals operate	Impact evaluation Policy analysis

impact analyses can be performed quantitatively (with computer manipulation of sizeable matrices if a number of impacts are included) or qualitatively, for the purpose of flagging possibly interesting interactions. Cost-benefit analysis would also be a candidate for balancing out the relative gains and losses involved in introduction of this new technology. Impact evaluation probably would not call on such techniques as formal decision analysis or policy capture; it is usually preferable to involve the policy makers in qualitative judgment of the value of the summed impacts. Accordingly, policy analysis would also likely be a judgmental endeavor in this case.

Some of the techniques are particularly conducive to sensitivity analysis (the varying of parameter values and/or relationships to ascertain effects). Like scenarios, trends can be extrapolated to show high and low ranges of possible developments. Cross-impact matrices and simulation models are designed, in general, so that values may be varied to see their implications. Likewise, probabilistic and decision analysis techniques can compare alternatives under different conditions, and cost-benefit analysis can tally up the implications of underlying changes.

The last point to note concerns the communication of results as a function of the techniques used. For instance, in an extensive survey/review of the uses made of technology assessments, Mark Berg and his colleagues at the University of Michigan found dramatic differences in the credibility of different techniques. For instance, statistical analysis and cost-benefit analysis are highly credible; Delphi techniques, cross-impact analysis, and brainstorming are notably less credible among public sector users. Some techniques lead nicely to visual presentation of findings that jump out at the audience; others may intimidate the audience by the appearance of "black magic" manipulations of the data in ways too difficult to understand. The assessors must gauge the sophistication of their audience and know the techniques that they find credible; engineers may appreciate techniques that others do not, and vice versa.

SOME UNDERLYING ISSUES

We have mentioned the potential ways in which engineers could become involved with technology assessments. Let us now take a deeper look at the implications of becoming actively involved in the preparation of a TA.

The best way to conduct a TA appears to be to appoint a *core team* of about three to five members who remain with the project and guide it through to completion. Such a team would typically involve an appropriate breadth of expertise to fit the assessment topic. For instance, in studying a biological trash eater, one might want to involve a biological scientist, a mechanical engineer, an economist, a corporate planner, and a sociologist in the core team. What is most interesting about such a group is the dynamic of their interaction.

The interaction of interdisciplinary teams is likely to depend on personalities, training, and problem-solving orientation. Some people are more comfortable than others in working in team situations; some are more able to deal with diffuse, ill-defined problems than others. It is important to watch for the biases that training imparts. For instance, observations of TA teams indicate that the performance of the social impact assessment sometimes generates bitter hostilities between data-oriented social scientists and "hard" scientist or engineer project leaders. In an interesting reversal of image, the "hard" types were sometimes skeptical of the possibility of assessing social impacts and thus felt that "seat-of-the-pants" speculation was desirable, leaving the social scientists frustrated at not being able to do what they perceived as the best possible job. Some professionals are unwilling to go beyond the data in hand to attempt prediction of any sort. In one instance, agricultural scientists doing some research for an assessment refused to make any extrapolations about the development of higher yield plants and their insect resistance, leaving the project leaders with the nasty job of having to do that extrapolation without solid expertise behind it. Or, one may find that fellow core team members have drastically different perceptions of how much quantification is really useful. This is particularly the case in a TA where one must blend qualitative and quantitative information sensibly. An unsettling observation, based on TAs performed, is that one disciplinary group has been singled out as difficult to interact with. Economists, whom one might anticipate would be the bridge between the engineers/scientists and the softer social scientists, appear to be hardest to get along with. Their jargon, reliance on complex models whether or not they are applicable, unrealistic data demands, and inability to deal with anything, no matter how important, that could not be expressed in monetary terms were some of the most telling objections raised. In fact, one veteran TA project leader indicated that his preference was to use MBAs or other personnel with economic expertise rather than disciplinary economists.

The engineer in a TA often finds it difficult to achieve a balance between fact and value. Obviously, many of the aspects of an assessment involve valuations, as when one evaluates impacts,

compares alternative policies, and makes final recommendations. Perhaps less obvious are the *implicit* value choices. Beginning with the way one defines the scope of the assessment, and carrying through with decisions as to what techniques shall be used and who shall participate in the assessment process, the values of the assessors will affect the outcome. If any scientists and engineers remain who believe that such a topic can be treated in a "neutral" way, participation in one TA will dissuade them. An assessment need not press any points, but the assessment participants must make explicit the values they hold so that the study users can gauge the information presented. As little as possible of the information processing in the TA should be covert, so that one can make all the choices perfectly clear to the study users.

Value issues extend beyond the boundaries of the assessment itself. The reason for conducting the study is likely to involve value choices. For instance, in assessing the biological trash eater one may encounter a clash between the "laissez faire, economic growth" corporate position and a "go slow, why do we need it?" opposition concerned with environmental protection. Should a single study try to reflect both sets of values? Of course, it depends. For instance, a study intended to help corporate officials decide on policy with respect to a proposed innovation had best provide sufficient balance to portray accurately the likely effects of introduction, including possible active resistance. A "yes-man" assessment would be worse than none at all because it would share the tunnel visions of the study users while leading them to believe they were protecting themselves against their own biases.

A major factor in assuring a balanced

TA is extensive outsider participation in the study. Outsiders may contribute valuable new information, important opinions, preliminary evaluation of the adequacy of the study, and increased interest in making use of the final study products. There are many ways in which they can be involved in the study. A range of possibilities has been identified by Mark Berg. Outsiders can:

- Serve as active participants in the study team
- Act as members of advisory committees
- Review drafts of the TA
- Interact with the assessors in conferences and briefings
- Provide inputs such as technical data, beliefs, and attitudes about impacts.

In general, we believe that participation is an asset. However, participation may involve people with extremely different notions of what constitutes knowledge and how one attains it. For instance, public interest group representatives working with technical members of a contract research organization on a solar energy TA clashed sharply, yet provided some interesting insights. However, a proprietary corporate study might want to restrict access to the information involved. An interesting middle position was achieved in a study of automotive engines sponsored by Ford Motor Company, prepared by Caltech's Jet Propulsion Lab with a "hands-off" posture by Ford. This boosted public credibility of the study.

To sum up, value issues cannot be swept under the technical rug. Explicit attention needs to be paid to values both in terms of the internal conduct of the study and its interaction with the outside. The desirable result, in general, is a balanced treatment that reflects differences in values clearly delineated by the parties-at-interest.

CONCLUDING OBSERVATIONS

This book addresses the issues that confront an engineer who works in an organizational context. We have tried here to broaden those concerns to consider the involvement of the engineer in his/her organization in its environmental context. The idea of a technological delivery system is one way to think about that context, to enable appropriate consideration and action. One example of action is technology assessment, in which the organization specifically considers the probable effects of its processes and products on the outside environment—natural, technical, and social. The reason for a TA is that it enables the organization to anticipate accurately and to take proper action. Correct action can reduce negative impacts before they occur and rebound badly on the organization. Actions based on TA can also accentuate the potential positive impacts to profit the organization. Without doubt, the individual engineer will be touched by impact assessment activities. Indeed, (s)he may well become directly involved in one form or another. From his own experience, the author hopes that engineers and scientists will find their own involvement to be an enjoyable and profitable learning experience.

REFERENCES
Journals

Environmental Impact Assessment Review. A quarterly journal edited by Lawrence E. Susskind, Massachusetts Institute of Technology, published by Plenum Publishing Corporation, New York, NY 10011.

Social Impact Assessment. A monthly newsletter available from C. P. Wolf, Box 587, Canal St. Station, New York, NY 10013.

Technological Forecasting and Social Change. A quarterly journal covering forecasting and assessment methodology and practice, edited by Harold A. Linstone, Portland State University, published by North Holland Publishing Co., New York, NY 10017.

Textbooks

Jain, R. K.; Urban, L. V.; and Stacey, G. S. *Environmental Impact Analysis: A New Dimension in Decision Making.* New York: Reinhold, 1977.

Porter, A. L.; Rossini, F. A.; Carpenter, S. R.; and Roper, A. T. *A Guidebook for Technology Assessment and Impact Analysis.* New York: North Holland, 1980.

Managing Organizational Change

Edward J. Conlon

University of Iowa

The old proverb "There's nothing so constant as change" applies with particular strength to the world of scientific and technical work. On the one hand, the organization of a laboratory section, a project group, or a production department is liable to change at any time in response to advances in the "state of the art," the introduction of new products, or the completion of a project phase. In this sense, the scientist or engineer finds him or herself a target of change, required to adjust a way of working to a new set of colleagues, a new supervisor, or new equipment. On the other hand, scientists and engineers are themselves the originators of change. A scientific advance in the laboratory may lead to a new product or a new way of making a product, profoundly changing the work lives of many people. An industrial engineer often operates directly on changing the way people work, from redesigning a piece of equipment to introducing a new computer system. Both as originators and as targets of change, scientists and engineers are deeply involved in a wide range of change processes.

Ed Conlon provides an introduction to the management of change in organizational contexts. In the first part he outlines a model of the change process, how change is initiated, how the process unfolds, and what is required before new ways of working can become established. In the second part he reviews the wide range of techniques now available for managing organizational change, and suggests the strengths and weaknesses of each. The final part of the paper illustrates the application of these techniques to several specific situations, and indicates when change processes can be expected to reach successful or unsuccessful outcomes.

Scientists and engineers, because of their unique role in the design and development of new technologies, products, or processes, are frequently at the forefront of change and innovation. The last stage of almost any framework that formally describes the innovation process is called "implementation." My guess is that most scientists and some engineers think that implementation is mainly "someone else's problem." However, at any stage of the design or innovation process implementation should be a consideration. After all, to be useful, those better mousetraps must be adopted by the community of mousetrappers. This chapter is designed to provide a perspective on organizational change that will be useful to the scientist or engineer as developers and implementers of innovations as well as to those working as managers. All stages in the innovation process should include some planning for implementation.

A PERSPECTIVE ON CHANGE

Organizations change for a variety of reasons. Earlier in this book firms were described as continuously acting in response to their environments; their effectiveness depends on their ability to adapt (i.e., change) in response to dynamic environments. Organizational change typically involves changes in the products or procedures that are part of the input-process-output system. These changes are triggered by either (1) changes in the environments that force the firm to adapt or (2) attempts to adjust the organization to cope better with an existing situation. An example of the externally triggered change is described in the Tavistock studies (Trist, Higgen, Murray, and Pollock, 1951), in which a fairly mechanized, continuous process technology called the longwall

method was introduced into British coal mines. This technology was expected to increase production over the existing small-group method of mining. An example of internally triggered change is the Rushton experiment, in which a sociotechnical intervention was attempted in an American coal mine (Goodman, 1979). The Rushton experiment was not triggered by an environmental or technological change. It was an attempt to manage more effectively within the existing technology and environment. This distinction is important. The former is *adaptive* change, which is necessary for the firm to maintain an economically competitive position. The latter is a *remedial* change, which may or may not be demanded on economic grounds and perhaps is not as obviously "necessary."

We need to distinguish between implementation and organizational development. Implementation is treated here as the general process of introducing a new behavior or pattern of behaviors into an organization. In contrast, organizational development (OD) is "a method for facilitating change and development in people (e.g., styles, values, skills), in technology (e.g., greater simplicity, complexity), and in organizational processes and structures (e.g., relationships, roles)" (Friedlander and Brown, 1974). Implementation refers only to *how* a new pattern may be brought about, not *why* it should be brought about. OD consists of a set of values and/or theories about people, groups, organizations, and society in general that generate *rationales* for behavioral changes. For example, suppose the management of a department store chain wishes to introduce a computerized management information system that would continually update inventory, price, and labor use data. The behavioral part of the implementation problem would focus on how to overcome resistance to change and create conditions that provide the smoothest possible transition from the old way of doing things to the new way. The rationale for the change is never addressed in the implementation process. OD, however, would deal with why the information system was chosen and how it would be expected to affect individual, group, and organizational performance. Stated differently, OD is oriented toward the general problems of improving the effectiveness of organizations, whereas implementation deals only with how to get new behaviors to be adopted and to persist in organizations.

One way to view organizational change is as the converse of stability. Most managers desire and value stability because it implies certainty and fits the pervasive classical perspective on organizations as "well-oiled machines" programmed to cope with most plausible situations. From that perspective, if change must occur, managers prefer that it should be planned change; that is, a predictable movement from a less desirable stable state to a known, more desirable stable state. Not surprisingly, the field of planned change is replete with technologies for achieving, in a fairly programmed way, particular desired states (e.g., more productive, safer, or with less conflict). With this perspective, we could write about organizational change as consisting of a cataloging and description of change technologies organized according to their goals and objectives.

As we have seen, however, individuals and organizations are at best only intendedly rational. Many, perhaps most, organizational problems force managers to behave in an experimenting or trial-and-error mode where alternatives are tried and later revised based on feedback (Lindblom, 1965). Realistically, organizational change cannot be approached as a programmable sequence. Complexity is inherent to most change situations. We first attempt to conceptualize the process of change and to prepare the reader to deal with change by thinking analytically about the change process. This should provide the scientist, engineer, or manager with sufficient information to experiment or solve problems in situations requiring behavior change.

We then outline the basic implementation process in five stages. Accompanying the discussion is a perspective on how organizations control behavior. Subsequently, we discuss several approaches to OD in terms of their rationales (i.e., values or notions about organizational effectiveness) and particular approaches to implementation. Finally, the general concept of process (i.e., the means through which change is controlled, communicated, and diffused) is discussed.

IMPLEMENTATION

Targets of Planned Change

Past reviews of the field of planned change (Leavitt, 1964; Friedlander and Brown, 1974; Alderfer, 1976) indicate that the various approaches to changing organizations are often categorized or distinguished according to the target of change: that is, what is changed to produce the desired effect. For example, Friedlander and Brown categorize the approaches to change as being either *techno-structural* or *human processual*. Techno-structural approaches are those that produce the desired effects through alterations of the technology and/or structure of the firm (see Chapter 10). Such programs may require changes in the reward system, supply system, decision-making procedures, norms, and other elements of the formal structure. In contrast, the human processual approach centers on the people and human processes (e.g., communication, decision making) employed in a firm. These approaches are often used when interpersonal relationships seem to be a problem in an organization. Typically, the focus is directly on the behavior of managers or other incumbents in the firm. For example, sensitivity training (i.e., T-grouping) attempts to modify the interpersonal style of managers through a controlled process of behavioral experimentation, feedback, and self-discovery by the managers. This approach attempts to create an effect by changing the individual rather than his/her environment.

The manager should ask, "For my goals, what type of approach should I use?" However, the answer to this question cannot be obtained without a detailed examination of the situation. The implementation framework presented here begins by assuming that *organizational change always involves some desired change in work behavior.* The techno-structural versus human relations distinction emphasizes the primary means through which the behavior will be altered and held in place. In particular, in techno-structural change, behavioral change is presumed to follow from changes in the structure and/or task employed by the firm, and the permanent change in structure causes the new behavior to persist. In human-relations approaches, some change in the individual (knowledge, attitude, skill, etc.) causes change and persistence in a new behavior. When we assume that all planned change ultimately involves behavior, answering the question of which approach to use to change behavior becomes a series of questions about the nature of the new behavior, the existing behaviors that may compete with it, what factors influence or control the new behavior, and how best to get the

new behavior to be adopted and to persist over time. The answers to these questions suggest which approaches may be used to generate planned change, solutions that may often involve both techno-structural and human relations approaches.

A Process Model of Implementation

A process model of behavior change, derived from Lewin's (1951) three-stage perspective, suggests that a sequence of processes is required to successfully produce change.

Step one: Determining beginning and end states. First, the planner of change should specify what behaviors she or he wishes to change. For example, in the Rushton coal mine study (Goodman, 1979), a sociotechnical intervention/experiment, a general objective was to involve the entire work group (about nine men) at the coal face in decision making. The existing behavior (state A) was that the supervisor (the first level foreman) was responsible for making all decisions about where to mine, the assignment of miners to activities, the ordering of supplies, and other decisions that could affect productivity. Because of the nature of coal mining, these decisions were not programmable. The desired state (state B) was for the work group to make these decisions and to take responsibility for them. The role of the foreman would be changed from line manager to safety monitor and adviser. Because of the very general nature of the desired behavior in this case, the research team prescribed specific procedures, including a daily planning session at the beginning of each shift for each group at the coal face. It was expected that the planning session would institutionalize group decision making. The planning session, then, was a specific behavioral goal that could be prescribed succinctly and monitored by the research team.

The importance of understanding planned change in terms of old and new behavior cannot be underestimated. It is difficult to design a successful strategy for change without specifying what new activities one wants to initiate and what existing behaviors those activities compete with.

Step two: Unfreezing the old behavior(s). Lewin referred to the elimination of the forces that motivated an existing behavior as "unfreezing." In the context of organizational change, a new desired behavior either replaces or competes with an existing, less desired behavior. In the Rushton case, group decision making was intended to replace autocratic decision making by the supervisor. In state A, the equilibrium of motivational forces supported a continued deference by the group to the supervisor for certain classes of decisions. Unfreezing involved changing those forces, hence eliminating that deference.

Unfreezing can be conceptualized through the motivational model described in Chapter 4. According to that model, one wants the new behavior to be preferred over the old behavior in terms of its likely costs and benefits. This might involve (1) devaluing the old behavior by disassociating it from valued outcomes or (2) introducing alternative behaviors that are valued over the existing one. Conceptually, this may seem simple when, in fact, unfreezing is operationally very complex.

Behaviors in organizations are sustained by various influencing agents. The key to unfreezing (and refreezing) behaviors is understanding the motivational bases for behavior, that is, the factors that influence behavior. Several authors have provided classifications of such factors that tend to converge on three modes of influence: externally

based compliance, social identification, and internalization. Essentially, the influencing agents are created by the organization, by the work group or by the individual.

Unfreezing formal organizational influences. Organizations generally influence behavior through formal structures such as rules, procedures, reward systems, and job designs. Informally, some organizations have "climates" that affect the behavior of employees. From the perspective of managing change, organizational influences have the advantage of being relatively controllable by management. For example, a rule that governs a given behavior may be changed so that it no longer sanctions its performance. Similarly, reward or performance appraisal systems can be altered to demotivate old behaviors and motivate new ones. Unfortunately, manipulations of formal structures are often not as discretionary as they may initially appear and may require a considerable amount of negotiation. For example, company policy may constrain an individual manager from modifying the reward system to fit his or her particular sphere of responsibility. Hence, unfreezing may involve policy changes that require considerable upward influence.

Unfreezing social influences. Social influences generally originate when work groups attempt to regulate behavior through applying their own rewards and punishments. Rothlisberger and Dickson (1939) documented the use of "binging"—a hard rap on the upper arm —by a group of workers opposing performance above the usual group standard. Similarly, group norms or standards are levels of behavior that maximize positive returns (i.e., reinforcements) to an individual from the group. Any deviations result in fewer positive returns. Many behaviors that appear to be irrational from the perspective of obtaining organizational rewards are sustained by countervailing group norms.

Unfortunately, behaviors that are strongly influenced by social sanctions are very difficult for managers to unfreeze. Since it is often unclear how and why norms originate, they generally cannot be removed by eliminating their origins. Theoretically, a norm may be directly attacked by making it irrational for individuals to adhere to it or by introducing a competing norm that will provide greater returns. Operationally, however, norms are notoriously resistant to change and often require radical intervention, for example, breaking up the group or coopting powerful members of the group to reject the norm.

Unfreezing intrinsic influences. A third motivational basis is at the individual level. Behavior may result from characteristics of the person, including skills, abilities, beliefs, attitudes, and values. It is important to understand that these attributes can cause the person to behave independently of forces in the external environment. For example, the individual with strong goal identifications performs well because of the implications of that performance for the organization's achieving its goal, a goal the individual values. The individual who is strong in task involvement performs because of his or her attraction to factors intrinsic to the task itself (challenge, interest, etc.) or because of identification with the task, as might occur in a craft or professional environment.

Unfreezing behavior that is primarily intrinsically motivated typically involves replacement of the behavior with an equally attractive alternative. Disconfirming an individual's beliefs about intrinsically valued tasks is difficult—if not impossible. Therefore, the key to change is to provide an acceptable alternative. Generally, individuals high in goal involvement must be convinced that the alternative to the existing behavior

is more likely to maximize goal attainment (i.e., it is better for the organization). The person higher in task identification must be shown that the alternative has the same characteristics as the existing task, or better (e.g., more challenge, more variety, more significance). If the alternative fails to dominate the existing behavior in either the sense of goal identification or task involvement, unfreezing will be very difficult.

Unfreezing and resistance to change. "Resistance to change" refers to unwillingness of the worker to adapt to or accept an organizational change. Lawrence (1970) suggests that resistance occurs more for "social" than technical reasons. In particular, change is typically not resisted because workers do not believe in the technical superiority of a new method or technology, but rather because of nontechnical attachments (i.e., sentiments) to old procedures or concerns about the process or methodology of change. Lawrence gives the example of a production worker who is accustomed to jointly evaluating and implementing new work procedures with a certain industrial engineer. When a different engineer approached her to impose a new procedure, she resisted. This difference in response may be attributed to the contrast between the collaborative manner in which the worker was accustomed to working with the first engineer and the impositional style of the second engineer. The second engineer deprived her of the esteem she usually felt when attempting new procedures. This example serves to illustrate the importance of the process used to implement change. *Unfreezing occurs most readily when the act of change itself is made as rewarding as possible.*

Step three: Moving the behavior. Generally, individuals need to be trained in the desired new behavior. Stated differently, the moving stage establishes a capability for the new behavior by assuring that incumbents know what is expected of them and have the skills to perform. The desired behavior may be as simple as having workers in a carpet mill pick up cuttings and ends and place them in containers for recycling or other uses. In this case, the behavior can be performed at an adequate level without extensive training or experience and can easily be explained verbally or pictorially. Often, however, the moving stage requires a considerable effort to establish a capability for the behavior. For example, in the Rushton coal mining example of group decision making, the work teams required a great deal of training in mine safety, ventilation, roof support, etc. This was necessary because many of the new decisions would involve technical considerations, and effective participation of all members of the work teams in the decision-making process required a baseline level of knowledge in all areas of mining.

It is not our purpose here to present an extensive discussion of training methodology. It is important, however, to consider two aspects of the behavior to be introduced. First, what are the necessary skills and experience levels required for adequate performance of the behavior? To the extent that individuals do not possess the necessary ability, training or other assistance should be provided. Second, how can the new behavior most effectively be communicated? This step requires consideration of the complexity of the behavior to be introduced and a decision about the appropriate mode of training.

Step four: Refreezing the behavior. Refreezing is the process by which a new behavior becomes an ongoing part of the work routine. In a way, refreezing is unfreezing in reverse: that is, the same types of motivational influences that were eliminated for the undesired behaviors in the unfreezing stage are established for the new behavior. This process is essential if the new behavior is to persist reliably over time.

The key question in managing refreezing is how best to establish a motivational basis for the new behavior. Several subissues are involved. First, what is the preferred motivational basis for the behavior? This is really a question of feasibility. For example, would it be feasible to rely on goal identification or task involvement to sustain the group planning sessions prescribed in the Rushton study? Goal identification would work only if the planning sessions were viewed as important for goal attainment and if the members of the work force had strong organizational goal identifications. Task involvement would work only if the planning sessions were viewed as significantly improving the amount of identity, variety, or significance of the task, and if individuals in the work force valued these task attributes. At Rushton, workers were oriented toward production goals because of competition among and pride within work groups. Workers also believed that the economic gains resulting from productivity increases would eventually be shared. If there is a basis for personal goal attainment, what remains is to demonstrate a link between the planning session and productivity gains, a relationship that was not obvious to the work force at Rushton. Because the desired behavior was a group activity, it was reasonable to expect group norms and socially dispensed rewards to have considerable influence. In fact, it is likely that planning could not have been institutionalized unless it was established as a group-sanctioned activity or tradition. In this case, refreezing might involve establishing a consensus in the group about the value of the planning sessions to individual members and the group as a whole. In addition, the supervisor would have to relinquish control by allowing the group to make decisions and refusing to make them her- or himself. A variety of techniques, called "team building" (Dyer, 1977), are available to assist managers in generating positive norms and attitudes toward a new activity. In general, the group should be permitted some involvement in the decision to implement planning so that commitment to and understanding of the new procedure are maximized. Finally, one may consider establishing organizational controls on the behavior. For example, workers could be paid for holding planning sessions, or punished for not holding them. The planning sessions would become bound by rules and would require monitoring by the organization. In essence, controlling new behavior through organizational sanctions would place on the organization the burden of assuring that the group makes decisions. There are some obvious problems with such control in this case. Aside from the costs of surveillance, it is inconsistent for a firm first to delegate decision making to the rank and file and then force the execution of decisions through extrinsic means.

The choice of control mechanisms for the new behavior requires an analysis of those individual, group, and organizational influences that are likely to affect the performance of the new behavior over time. By analysis, we mean an assessment of the likelihood that the behaviors could or would be affected by each type of influence and the costs implicit in creating and maintaining each influence link. In some cases, there may be little doubt that a certain type of influence will have an impact on behavior. In other cases, the costs and benefits of control may require a careful analysis.

Step five: Evaluating state B.   We suggested earlier that a large part of the management process involved trial-and-error experimentation with means to achieve the desired ends. The first of our five steps emphasized the need for specifying the desired ends (behaviors) that would result from the planned change. This, the fifth and last step in the model, is an evaluation of the ends.

Were the desired behaviors obtained and are they persisting? If not, the manager should examine the reasons why. Was all resistance to change overcome? Were competing behaviors eliminated? Was sufficient training supplied for the employees to perform the new behavior? Is the new behavior sufficiently motivated (i.e., influenced)? In short, steps two through four should be reviewed for their adequacy or shortcomings.

Another issue is the choice of the behavioral goals. Were the correct behaviors implemented, given the overall objectives of the change? For example, in the Rushton case, one might ask if the planning session was an adequate and appropriate vehicle for establishing group decision making (at another level, one might ask if group decision making was appropriate). If the behavioral goals are found to be inadequate, step one must again be performed; that is, new behaviors should be developed and prescribed.

Summary of Implementation Issues

Innovations are rarely implemented in the orderly manner suggested above; the sequence is considerably more interdependent than is implied by the stages described. For example, in changes that require job redesign, the actual introduction of new technology contributes simultaneously to the dissolution of old behavior and to the institutionalization of new behavior. The value of the stages framework is to identify necessary subprocesses that must be dealt with in the overall task of implementation. The framework can be used to develop a checklist of subgoals and/or related processes to be accomplished during implementation.

ORGANIZATIONAL DEVELOPMENT

Organizational development is used to diagnose organizational problems as well as to implement change. Thus far, we have discussed implementation without stating what should be implemented or why. The "whats" and "whys" are the domain of OD.

A "problem," as defined by OD, is a state that exists in an organization that is not what could or should be, given the available resources. A diagnosis is an evaluation of an organization against some standards or norms. Standards may be developed from perspectives on organizational effectiveness that range from empirically based models of organizational effectiveness to value-laden views of how organizations ought to be. An example of the former would be the information-processing views of organizations espoused by Simon (1973), which see organizational effectiveness as the direct result of how well the organization is able to adapt to its environment by acting as effectively as possible on the information it has available. In contrast, a more humanistic perspective, such as that espoused in the earlier work of Argyris (1973), suggests that people are essentially self-actualizing and that the effective organization will use human potential best by acting

as a vehicle for self-actualization. Based on such perspectives, OD consultants prescribe changes. Simon, for example, might look for instances where decisions were being made with inappropriate information or with inadequate rewards and punishments. Argyris might evaluate organizations in terms of their impact on human potential and productivity.

A different kind of diagnosis is the client-centered approach, in which the diagnosis of a problem is made by members of the organization (e.g., top managers) with the assistance of a consultant. Rather than imposing models or values on the client, the consultant gets the client organization to explore its own values (what it would like to be) and to determine how these values would be reflected in organizational activities. The consultant provides input and direction on how the organization may adopt or adapt those activities. The organization is asked to act on its own articulations of effectiveness.

Friedlander and Brown (1974), in a review of OD, categorize approaches to diagnosis and change. We shall use these categories, along with several additions, to illustrate and compare the variety of OD perspectives. The major details of the discussion are outlined in Table 1.

Socio-technical Systems Theory

Lynne Markus has provided a detailed discussion of socio-technical systems theory (see page 232). Our concern here is with the goals and procedures that socio-technical systems theorists use to implement change.

Generally stated, the objective of the socio-technical systems approach is to find an optimal matching between the

Table 1.   Various Approaches to the Change Process

Class of OD effort	Approach to unfreezing	Approach to moving	Approach to refreezing
Sociotechnical systems theory	Rational argument that present system is suboptimal "Shaping" process in which incumbents discover and evaluate new alternatives	Work patterns evolve through expert guidance Training is offered as necessary New technology may be implemented	New patterns develop, social norms form, and results reinforce the new patterns
Job redesign	Appeal to human needs, motives, and satisfaction Suggest changes in the way work is done that better serve worker preferences	Enrich task by improving task variety, significance, identity, autonomy, and feedback	Task experience leads to natural payoffs that sustain it
Survey feedback	Provide data to disconfirm old patterns	Data lead to incumbent problem solving, aided or unaided by consultants	Data hold behavior in place, or may lead to further shaping
Group development	Difficult to categorize Focus on group consensus about the need for change	Use of group discussion, problem solving, and joint goal setting Exercises for conflict resolution	Establishment of new group norms, goals, demands, etc.
Individual development	Disconfirmation of old patterns through interpersonally generated feedback	Experimentation with new behavior in a situation providing interpersonal feedback	Continued individual feedback about the impact of the new behavior

technological demands of the task and the social system that develops to perform that task. The behavioral goals center on developing practices and procedures that facilitate matching. For example, if a task required intensive coordination among members of a work group, a consultant might suggest planning sessions to facilitate coordination and periodic job rotation to enhance members' understanding of each other's jobs. Socio-technical interventions generally consist of an assortment of such behavioral prescriptions.

Unfreezing in socio-technical systems theory is accomplished primarily through the persuasion of individuals that specific new practices are needed and should be beneficial, and actual experience of individuals with those practices. Persuasion may be based on rational arguments that derive from systems theory. Unfreezing through experience is accomplished by getting individuals or groups to "experiment" with the new practices. The ability of such experimentation to unfreeze behaviors depends on the perceived costs and benefits of the new behavior relative to the alternatives.

The moving stage is the adoption of the desired behavioral or technological changes. Often, moving requires training at new skills or new technologies.

For example, for the coal miners to trade jobs successfully, they had to be trained to operate machinery and become familiar with the safety regulations and work patterns of the new jobs.

Refreezing occurs when the new work patterns, better matched to the technology, occur regularly. Several factors mitigate the ease with which refreezing can occur. One important issue is the degree to which the new behaviors or technology interferes with prior social structures that had some utility to the workers. For example, if job rotation disturbs a status hierarchy, complete refreezing would require less reliance on such structures. In effect, the new state would have to provide payoffs sufficient to compensate employees for discarding previously valued states or traditions such as status. The second factor is the difficulty of adjusting to the new state. Because socio-technical change often involves significant changes in how work is done, extensive risks (e.g., failures during the learning period) may act as temporary barriers to refreezing. The more unpleasant the adjustment period, the greater the force necessary to extinguish the old behavior and hold the new behavior in place. Often, this requires frequent restatement and refocusing on the rationale for change and the development of group norms favoring the new state.

Job Redesign

The essential differences between job redesign and socio-technical change are that (1) the former has an explicit focus on the task rather than the task *and* the social setting, and (2) the approaches have different theoretical rationales. Socio-technical change deals with interacting systems; job design is theoretically nested in a model of individual human needs (see Dan Brass, Reading #3).

The decision to engage in job redesign should result from evidence that individuals are dissatisfied with tasks. An analysis should be performed that examines both needs and tasks and assesses, based on theory, what kind of design changes, if any, are warranted (Frank and Hackman, 1975). In theory, unfreezing should be simple if individuals perceive that the intended changes will significantly improve their task satisfaction. However, as is true for socio-technical change, a short-term effect of redesign may be the disturbance of valued social structures or interpersonal relationships.

In job redesign, moving typically involves restructuring tasks either through enlargement or enrichment. In job enlargement, the way in which work is done (the objective technology) is not changed, but the allocation of tasks to personnel is changed. For example, the production of legs for a particular table may require four different, sequential lathing operations. An initial job design could conceivably have four different work positions and four different jobs, one for each of the operations. An example of enlargement is grouping two or more of the operations together. In job enrichment significant changes may be made in the way products are manufactured or services are delivered. For example, some automotive manufacturers, such as Volvo, have experimented with alternatives to the traditional assembly-line technology in an attempt to better fit tasks to human needs.

Refreezing involves successful adjustment of workers to the new enlarged or enriched task. Because these models of change involve alterations of organizational technologies, job descriptions, and other structures, employees may have little choice about adoption. They may, however, have influence through variations in work quality, work quantity, absenteeism, job actions (e.g., strikes), and other means of asserting power. Hence, refreezing means that participants must experience the benefits of change, which should overcome the short-term costs of changing.

Survey Feedback

In survey feedback, change is fostered by providing individuals with information about various aspects of work and the work environment. Generally, this involves the institutionalization of a formal information-gathering, summarizing, and reporting system (Nadler, 1977). Survey feedback techniques may vary in the type of information provided, the frequency with which it is provided, and to whom it is reported. For example, workers may be provided with productivity data at monthly meetings. In other instances, questionnaires may be used to assess such factors as job satisfaction, morale, organizational climate, task perceptions, and other elements of the work situation. Information may be provided only to group leaders, or to the entire group. The frequency may vary from daily to weekly, monthly, or longer. The exact format of the feedback system depends on the goals of the users and the context in which it is implemented.

The major assumption in survey feedback is that individuals are capable of using the information provided to (1) identify behaviors that should be changed and (2) to change them. For example, if a supervisor is provided with feedback that she or he is perceived as cold and distant, it is assumed that behaviors can be changed to eliminate those perceptions. The role of feedback is to cue and provide directions for change. The main idea is that individuals will learn from the data, and such learning will lead to beneficial changes.

Unlike the socio-technical and job redesign techniques, survey feedback does not necessarily alter the structure of the work place. There is not a major source of external influence on behavior, thus control of change resides predominantly in the work force. Unfreezing occurs mainly as a result of individuals or groups discovering the inadequacy of their present mode(s) of behavior. Moving is a response to the perceived need for change. A major concern is the ability of job incumbents to successfully alter their existing behavior to bring about desired results. Refreezing is accomplished through continuous feedback. For example, if a manager changes his or her behavior in response to feedback about being cold and distant, the next wave of feedback should indicate if the behavior change yielded the intended result. If so, it is presumed that the new behavior will persist; if not, the actor is free to experiment further in order to achieve the desired result. It should be obvious that the timing and accuracy of feedback are crucial issues.

Group Development

Group development programs may have a variety of objectives, including setting group goals, improving interpersonal relations, and analyzing roles. For example, team building (Dyer, 1977) is a technique used in a group to clarify individual expectations and set group objectives, reducing the potential for interpersonal conflict. Other techniques in this category, such as third party interventions (Walton, 1967), deal with the productive resolution of conflict among groups. (See also Chapter 8.)

The objective of most group development programs is to change group behavior by generating a consensus among the members about the goals of the group, the means that will be used to attain those goals, and the relative contribution of the various group members to goal attainment. Such techniques focus on relationships among members of a group, including norms, sentiments, and communications.

A unique characteristic of group development approaches to change is the intensive use of the group as a control mechanism. New behaviors are held in place through the operation of interpersonal influence. Group development exercises are intended to generate a consensus about the expectations held by individual members on the range of appropriate behaviors for each member. This consensus serves to legitimate the application of sanctions against members who fail to conform with these expectations.

The process of unfreezing is complicated when existing group norms are to be changed. When there are no such norms, the behaviors to be unfrozen are typically under individual influence. The group development process reduces the incidence of these behaviors by bringing group influence to bear against them. Existing norms, however, imply that group influences already control behaviors. Unfreezing requires elimination of these norms either by demonstrating their costs or by altering the composition of the group, for example, by removing opinion leaders and/or adding new members.

Moving, in group development, generally involves group discussions of expectations, goals, and problem areas, facilitated by a consultant from outside the group. These discussions serve to clarify the individual orientations of members toward the group and to generate a consensus about how the group should operate and perform. As stated earlier, this process legitimates the application of reinforcements for compliance or noncompliance with shared expectations.

Refreezing is greatly facilitated by

the operation of social influence processes. Behaviors are held in place by the reinforcement contingencies implicit in group norms. It is possible, however, for new patterns of behavior to evolve as a result of the group development procedure. Specifically, groups may feel free to experiment with new behavior, and the "moved" behaviors may move even further. For example, in the Rushton case, the newly introduced behavior of each jobholder communicating job-relevant information to his counterpart on the next shift evolved, after its introduction, into a "communication by representation" strategy wherein each group had an informal communicator who would gather information for the group and pass it on to the next group's communicator. The important aspect of this is that the objectives of communication were still being met, but in a form more acceptable to the workers.

Individual Development

Individual development techniques focus on individual workers and their behavior, the basic control or influencing agent being the actor him- or herself. Such techniques are used when the source of a problem is thought to be the behavior of an individual. For example, transactional analysis is used to improve the ability of individuals to engage in productive interpersonal relationships, showing how existing behavior is non-optimal and then either prescribing and training new styles of behavior, or facilitating the discovery of new styles by the actor. The rationales for such changes come from a variety of theoretical perspectives on organizational and/or human performance.

Unfreezing is generally accomplished through a facilitated feedback process. In laboratory training, the individual is placed in a setting where she or he can obtain feedback from others about the impact of her or his interpersonal style. In this way, the existing style may be critically evaluated by the subject in terms of its impact on others.

Moving may occur purely as a process of feedback and discovery (learning by experimentation) or may be specifically prescribed by a facilitator. The former is typical of T-group training. The latter is more common in skills training programs, such as those prescribing participative management styles.

Refreezing is the major problem for individual development techniques. Sensitivity training has been severely criticized for its inability to create behaviors that transfer back to the work setting or that tend to persist (Campbell and Dunnette, 1968). The reason for this is the reliance on the individual as a control mechanism. Organizations and work groups, as social influence networks, often tightly control the behaviors of employees. The graduate of sensitivity training, with newly found behavioral insights, returns to the work setting but faces interpersonal expectations of others that negatively reinforce the new behaviors. Successful refreezing requires attention to the context in which the behavior will occur; that is, either the actor must be "inoculated" against social influences on returning to the work setting, or the context must be adequately prepared for the impact of the new behavior.

Summary

A central theme in all approaches to OD is a change in behaviors or procedures that reflect a theoretical perspective on organizational effectiveness. Each approach must deal with the problem of implementation, but the tools and procedures available for implementation vary across the OD approaches.

Another concept that cuts across all approaches to change is the intervention *process*, that is, the style in which change is communicated and implemented.

PROCESS CONSIDERATIONS

It is sometimes said that, in organizational change, process supersedes content. Research has shown that the manner in which change is introduced is important. Most theorists recommend that participants be involved in the planning and implementation of change because empirical results suggest that participatively introduced changes are more durable than imposed changes. Below, we shall briefly examine the adoption of change as a personal decision, to explain the reasons behind the research findings.

Adoption as a Choice

The adoption of new behavior by actors may be seen as a *decision*. The context of change provides a situation in which the actor is faced with a decision about his or her behavior. This decision involves (1) an existing behavior and (2) a set of expectations about the outcomes of behavior to be adopted. The preferred alternative should be made more desirable than the other alternatives. This is done, according to rational choice models (see Chapter 2), by developing a set of expectations in the actors that cause the desired behavior to be preferred.

Mitchell (1973) discusses the impact of participation on motivation in a way that is consistent with the decision framework suggested here. First, participation tends to clarify organizational contingencies for employees. In terms of expectancy theory, participation should improve an individual's concept of the outcomes associated with a behavior and lead to a set of accurate beliefs about performance outcome relationships. Second, participation should increase the likelihood that employees will work for outcomes they value. Through participation, "employees should be able to help set work standards, negotiate on working conditions, and influence reward structure" (Mitchell, 1973). Third, participation increases the impact of social influences through the legitimizing effect of group discussion on behavior. If a new behavior emerges through a process of group consensus, group members should perceive an expectation on the part of others that they will perform the new behavior. The consensus can lead to the development of group sanctions and norms to support the behavior. Participation also increases the degree to which an individual can control her or his own behavior. We would predict stronger motivation for individuals to adopt behaviors when they have had an opportunity to participate in the development of new behaviors, policies, or process, and the decisions to implement them.

This perspective, that the adoption of change is a choice process, may prove useful in designing and evaluating approaches to implementing change. In particular, the change agent can conceptualize the behaviors that are available to the actors and evaluate the likelihood of adoption of each in terms of their perceived costs and benefits. The process of implementation may be designed to overcome resistance to adoption by increasing the perceived net benefit of the desired behavior and devaluing the competing alternatives.

Politics and Multiple Constituencies

Another payoff-related problem is how outcomes are distributed to powerful interest groups. In many change settings, third parties (e.g., unions) formally represent a set of goals that may be different from those of the organization. Successful process involves obtaining the support of powerful constituencies. Generally, this may be accomplished either through a cooperative venture or an exchange. A cooperative venture is feasible if both parties benefit from the change. In the Rushton project, the union had a highly publicized interest in safety, and improved safety, happily, was a goal of the intervention. When goals are not congruent, the organization may be forced to offer some commodity in exchange (e.g., pay, decision-making discretion, etc.). In either case, a failure to deal with third parties can undermine the change effort (Kochan and Dyer, 1976).

REFERENCES

Alderfer, C. "Change Processes in Organizations." *Handbook of Industrial and Social Psychology,* M. Dunnette, ed. Chicago: Rand McNally, 1976.

Argyris, C. "Some Limits of Rational Man Organizational Theory." *Public Administration Review* 33 (1973):253–67.

Campbell, J. P., and Dunnette, M. D. "Effectiveness of T-Group Experiences in Managerial Training and Development." *Psychological Bulletin* 70 (1968):73–104.

Dyer, W. G. *Team Building: Issues and Alternatives.* Reading, Mass.: Addison-Wesley, 1977.

Frank, L. L., and Hackman, J. R. "A Failure of Job Enrichment: The Case of the Change That Wasn't." *Journal of Applied Behavioral Science* 11 (1975):413–36.

Friedlander, F., and Brown, L. "Organization Development." *Annual Review of Psychology* (1974):25.

Goodman, P. *Assessing Organization Change.* New York: Wiley, 1979.

Kochan, T. A., and Dyer, L. "A Model of Organizational Change in the Context of Union-Management Relations." *Journal of Applied Behavioral Science* 12 (1976):59–78.

Lawrence, P. R. "How to Deal with Resistance to Change." In *Organizational Change and Development*, G. Dalton, P. R. Lawrence, and L. Greiner, eds. Homewood, Ill.: Irwin-Dorsey, 1970.

Leavitt, H. "Applied Organizational Change in Industry: Structural, Technological and Humanistic Approaches." In *Handbook of Organizations*, J. March, ed. Chicago: Rand McNally, 1965.

Lewin, K. *Field Theory in Social Science*, D. Cartwright, ed. New York: Harper, 1951.

Lindblom, C. *The Intelligence of Democracy.* New York: MacMillan, 1965.

Luthans, F., and Kreitner, R. *Organizational Behavior Modification.* Glenview, Ill.: Scott, Foresman, 1975.

Mitchell, T. "Motivation and Participation: An Integration." *Academy of Management Journal* 16 (1973):670–79.

Nadler, D. *Feedback and Organization Development: Using Data-based Methods.* Reading, Mass.: Addison-Wesley, 1977.

Rothlisberger, F. J., and Dickson, W. J. *Management and the Worker.* Cambridge, Mass.: Harvard University Press, 1939.

Simon, Herbert A. "Applying Information Technology to Organization Design." *Public Administration Review* 33 (1973):268–78.

Trist, E., Higgen, G., Murray, H., and Pollack, A. *Organizational Choice.* London: Tavistock, 1963.

Walton, R. E. *Interpersonal Peacemaking: Confrontation and Third Party Consultation.* Reading, Mass.: Addison-Wesley, 1969.

Author Index

379

Subject Index